Organizational Architecture:

A Managerial Economics Approach

THE IRWIN SERIES IN ECONOMICS

Organizational Architecture:

A Managerial Economics Approach

James A. Brickley

Clifford W. Smith, Jr.

Jerold L. Zimmerman

William E. Simon Graduate School of Business Administration University of Rochester

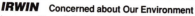
© Richard D. Irwin, a Times Mirror Higher Education Group, Inc. company, 1996

Irwin Book Team

Publisher:
Senior sponsoring editor: *Gary Nelson*
Developing editor: *Ellen Cleary*
Senior marketing manager: *Ron Bloecher*
Project editor: *Denise Santor-Mitzit*
Production supervisor: *Laurie Kersch*
Assistant manager, desktop services: *Jon Christopher*
Designer: *Crispin Prebys*
Compositor: *Wm. C. Brown Publishers*
Typeface: *10/12 Times Roman*
Printer: *Wm. C. Brown Publishers*

◤◥ **Times Mirror**
◣ **Higher Education Group**

Library of Congress Cataloging-in-Publication Data

Brickley, James A.
   Organizational architecture : a managerial economics approach /
James Brickley, Cliff W. Smith, Jerold L. Zimmerman.
      p.   cm.
   Includes bibliographical references and index.
   ISBN 0-256-20224-9
   1. Managerial economics.   2. Organization.   I. Smith, Clifford W.
II. Zimmerman, Jerold L., 1947–   .   III. Title.
HD30.22.B73   1996
338.5'024658—dc20   95–36326

Printed in the United States of America
1 2 3 4 5 6 7 8 9 0 WCB 2 1 0 9 8 7 6 5

To our wives—Cindy, Bernie, and Dodie

Preface

Microeconomics provides an important set of tools for managerial problem solving and decision making. After presenting these tools, most textbooks focus on applications such as pricing, decision making under uncertainty, capital budgeting, and understanding the effects of government policy and regulation. Until now, however, the existing textbooks rarely emphasize how managers might use economic principles to manage their organizations. There is little comprehensive coverage of such important topics as developing effective performance-evaluation systems and compensation plans, allocating decision rights among employees, or managing transfer-pricing disputes among divisions. This omission is both significant and problematic, given the increased pressure on managers to structure more efficient, smoothly-operating organizations. Increasing global competition and technological change ultimately are pressuring major organizational restructurings and industry realignments.

Business and economic students want to develop skills that will better prepare them to manage this process and make them more effective managers.

While the popular press and existing literature on organizations are replete with jargon—TQM, reengineering, outsourcing, teaming, venturing, empowerment, and corporate culture—they fail to provide managers with a systematic, comprehensive framework for solving organizational problems. This book, *Organizational Architecture: A Managerial Economics Approach,* uses economic analysis to develop such a framework. The book presents this important material in an organized, integrated, and accessible manner.

Through this text, students gain an understanding of the basic tools of microeconomics and use them to solve managerial problems. While the book covers the standard economic problems of pricing and production, it pays special attention to organizational issues. In particular, the book helps students to better understand how the firm's business environment and strategy are important determinants of organizational design and how changes in the environment and strategy affect efficient design. They will also obtain a solid conceptual framework for structuring more effective organizations. In particular, students will understand how focusing on the three key features of *organizational architecture*—the assignment of decision rights, the performance-evaluation system, and the reward system allows them to structure organizations to achieve their desired results. Finally, students will better understand the interrelations and co-determination of many corporate policies such as strategy, financing, accounting, marketing, operations, compensation, and human resources. This understanding, in turn, provides a more integrated and comprehensive view of material presented elsewhere in the curriculum.

There are many topics that could be covered in an economics textbook. This book focuses on those topics that are most relevant to managers. For instance, the text spends little time on public policy topics, such as minimum wage legislation, antitrust policy, and income redistribution. However, the book provides an in-depth treatment of compensation policy, the make-versus-buy decision, and business process reengineering.

Over the last two years, we have learned much from writing this text. Instructors request a modern book based on sound theory and solid applications. The response from our reviewers of earlier drafts has been quite positive. We have seen growing interest in this subject, as more and more journal articles, academic meetings, and courses appear

all around the world. In response to the demands of an unusually vocal marketplace, we decided to publish this paperback forerunner edition. Our main text will be published in time for classes in Fall 1996. Although the forerunner edition is low on pedagogy, it is high in content. The main text will have both. Over the next year we will add the end-of-chapter problems to offer students more opportunities to apply the material learned in the chapters and refine the book's exposition.

Our book, in its current and future forms, will be an effective tool in a variety of classes including managerial economics and organizational economics at the MBA, executive MBA, or undergraduate level. We suggest that all students read chapters 1–3 that provide the basic tools and framework for the text. Chapters 4–6 cover the basic managerial economics material of demand, costs and production, and competition and monopoly. Instructors focusing on the economics of organizations can skip these chapters without loss of continuity if the students have had a basic microeconomics course. Chapters 8–14 provide a comprehensive framework to understand organizational architecture and should be covered in sequence. Finally, chapters 15–18 cover a variety of topics (leadership, outsourcing, quality and reengineering, and ethics) that can be assigned based on available time and specific interests. We believe that instructors and students will enjoy the structure and presentation of this text. They will also appreciate the real-world emphasis in the book.

This project has benefited from an extensive development effort. Seventeen colleagues both in the US and overseas have reviewed the manuscript and given us detailed feedback for which we are very grateful. And to date far too many people to name have responded to our market surveys about the changing environment of the MBA economics curriculum; their thoughts have shaped in large part the direction of this text and we'd like to take this opportunity to thank them for their help. In addition, meeting with more than sixty of our colleagues at the Conference on Market-Based Management at the University of Kansas in May 1995 provided additional feedback and encouragement about this project.

We owe a significant debt to our colleagues at Rochester, in particular to Michael C. Jensen and William H. Meckling. Mike and Bill first began teaching MBA courses on the economics of organizations at Rochester in the 1970s. Their work has profoundly affected our thinking on these issues. No amount of citations nor acknowledgments can adequately reflect the encouragement and stimulation they provided both in person and through their writings.

Lastly, this book represents work in progress. Development is on-going as we continue to learn and as the research develops. The economics of organizations is a very exciting area of inquiry. We hope that a small portion of that excitement is communicated through this text. We welcome any feedback. If you would like to share your thoughts on this work or your classroom experiences, please feel free to write or e-mail to us at the University of Rochester. Thank you in advance for your help.

Jim Brickley
(Brickley@ssb-facstaff.ssb.rochester.edu)
Cliff Smith
(Smith@ssb-facstaff.ssb.rochester.edu)
Jerry Zimmerman
(Zimmerman@ssb-facstaff.ssb.rochester.edu)

Contents

Organizational Architecture:

A Managerial Economics Approach

CHAPTER 1 Introduction

Francis Baring, along with his brother John, established Barings Bank in London in 1762. Their bank prospered by facilitating international trade. Barings helped finance the British effort in the American Revolutionary War and, thereafter, Barings' credit reopened trade with the United States. In 1803, the bank helped both the United States finance the Louisiana Purchase, and Britain its wars against Napoleon. So great was the bank's influence that in 1818 Duc de Richelieu observed, ''There are six great powers in Europe: England, France, Prussia, Austria, Russia, and Barings Brothers.''

In 1890 the bank was shaken when loans that it had made in Argentina defaulted, but it survived with a bailout engineered by the Bank of England. The family rebuilt the bank and, although it never regained its prior preeminence, it remained a gilt-edged institution run largely by members of the family and owned primarily by a charitable foundation. In recent years, its influence has grown significantly, in part due to its substantial Far East securities business.

On February 22, 1995, Barings' board of directors met to review the 1994 results. The bank had a small rise in profits—a quite reasonable result in what had been a dreadful year for most of its competitors. One large contributor to those results had been a very profitable securities operation in Singapore. But that afternoon, matters changed dramatically. The Singapore office's star trader, Nick Leeson, unexpectedly walked out of the office and disappeared.

As senior management examined the bank's records, it became clear that something was very wrong. In principle, Leeson engaged in a simple operation—arbitraging security prices between the Osaka Stock Exchange and the Singapore International Monetary Exchange (SIMEX).[1] Leeson should have been able to lock

---

[1] The specific securities Leeson traded were futures contracts on the Nikkei 225—the main Japanese stock market index.

1

in a virtually riskless profit by simultaneously selling the security on the exchange with the higher price while buying it on the exchange with the lower price. Although price differences are typically small, arbitraging in enough volume can produce a substantial profit.

In this arbitrage business, although Barings would accumulate large positions in the securities on both exchanges, those it bought and those it sold should balance: There was supposed to be no net exposure. Yet what management found as they reviewed the bank's records was that Leeson had bought securities in both markets—in effect, he had made an enormous bet that the security price would rise. But the price had fallen, and now the solvency of the bank was threatened.

How could this have happened? It appears that Leeson circumvented the bank's internal controls. The Singapore branch was small, and Leeson effectively controlled both trading and the firm's back office systems; he used that control to conceal losses and disguise the true nature of his activities—he was able to "cook the books." In one instance, he apparently told senior management that a number of his trades were on behalf of clients and not the bank. And the bank's internal control systems did not uncover the deceit.

By March 6, the bank's aggregate losses totaled $1.4 billion. Leeson, who had been arrested by German police at the Frankfurt airport, was fighting extradition back to Singapore. And Barings, Britain's oldest merchant bank, had been sold to ING (the large Dutch financial institution) for £1. Thus, Barings' owners had lost their entire investment.

The Barings collapse was ultimately caused by a poorly designed organization. As *The Wall Street Journal* noted:

> "What is emerging from the documents and from interviews with current and former Barings executives is a fatally flawed organization: one that ignored at least several warning signs going back not just weeks and months, but years; one that so wanted to ensure the continuation of profits from Singapore—which boosted bonuses—that it was reluctant to impose tight controls; one that had a deeply split staff, which ultimately may have contributed to its downfall."[2]

Three general aspects of the bank's organization contributed to the failure: the broad range of authority and responsibilities granted to Leeson; gaps in the bank's systems to evaluate, monitor, and control its employees; and aspects of the firm's compensation system. Let's examine each in more detail.

First, Leeson had responsibility for both proprietary and customer trading as well as effective control of the settlement of trades in his unit. This broad assignment of decision rights created the opportunity for him to circumvent the bank's internal controls. As the *Financial Times* noted:

> "The cause of the trouble in the Barings case was not simply that records were being falsified on the spot. In Singapore, Mr. Leeson was in the process of settling transactions

---

[2]M. Branchli, N. Bray, M. Sesit, "Barings PLC officials may have been aware of trading position," *WSJ*, March 6, 1995, p. 1.

as well as initiating them. A watertight line between dealing and operational responsibility, crucial to internal control, was missing."[3]

In reaction to the Barings collapse, SIMEX changed its rules to require that member firms ensure that proprietary traders not handle customer business and that the head of the dealing section not take charge of the settlement process.

Second, Leeson compromised the firm's performance evaluation system. He misrepresented trades for the bank as customer trades and hid losses. A better designed and executed monitoring system would have identified these problems before the solvency of the institution was threatened.

Third, the bank's compensation system encouraged Leeson to speculate while discouraging senior managers from exercising tighter control over their trading star. Barings traditionally had paid out approximately 50 percent of gross earnings as annual bonuses. But a system where managers participate in annual profits—but not in losses—can encourage excessive risk-taking. This dysfunctional incentive can be most pronounced when a small bet loses, and the employee tries to make it up by doubling the bet. If this second bet also loses, there can be a strong incentive to double up again and "go for broke."

Organizational Architecture

The example of Barings illustrates a critical idea: The design of the organization matters. A bad organizational design can result in lost profits and even in the failure of the institution. With the benefit of hindsight, we certainly can examine Barings and identify elements of its organization that if changed might have forestalled this debacle. But the critical managerial question is whether one could have reasonably identified the potential problems before the fact and designed a more productive organization. After all, Barings management did not. We believe the answer to this managerial question is a resounding *yes*. What is required is a rich framework that can be consistently applied to examine organizational issues. That is the primary objective of this book—to offer a systematic framework for analyzing organizational problems and designing more effective organizations.

We are not the first to recognize the importance of organizational structure or to offer advice on how to improve it. The business section of any good bookstore displays an array of prescriptions: *Benchmarking, Empowerment, Total Quality Management, Re-engineering, Outsourcing, Teaming, Corporate Culture, Venturing, Matrix Organizations, Just-In-Time Production, Downsizing.* The list seems virtually endless. All agree that the design of the firm and the associated policies chosen by management can have a profound effect on performance and firm value. All buttress their recommendations with anecdotes of firms that followed the author's recommendations and were fabulously successful. But the proffered advice tends to focus on particular facets of the organization such as the compensation

---

[3]"The box that can never be shut," *FT*, February 28, 1995, p. 17.

system or how decision rights are assigned. Comparing various books, the advice is frequently inconsistent and offers little guidance as to which tools are most appropriate in which circumstances. Ultimately, the literature fails to provide managers with a systematic framework for solving organizational problems.

In this book we seek to provide an integrative approach to the structure of organizations. We identify three fundamental facets of what we call organizational architecture: (1) the allocation of decision rights, (2) the structure of systems to evaluate the performance of individuals and business units, and (3) the methods of rewarding individuals. (Not coincidentally, these are the same three aspects of the organization we highlighted in the Barings case.)

The Economics of Organizational Architecture

In our analysis of organizations we build on a number of disciplines: accounting, finance, marketing, management, political science—but especially economics. We apply the tools of economic analysis that have been employed successfully to explain a broad range of problems in finance, pricing, and accounting to provide a coherent analysis of organizational architecture. At its essence, economics provides a theory of how individuals make choices. We use economics to examine how managers can design organizations to motivate individuals to make choices that enhance firm value.

Economics has long been applied to questions of pricing policy—for example, "What is the impact of alternate strategies for pricing products on customer decisions and their implications for firm value?" In our analysis, we apply the same tools to examine questions of organizational design. For example, "What is the impact of alternate strategies for structuring jobs on employee decisions and their implications for firm value?"

It is surprising how little attention economists have historically directed to questions of organizational structure. In traditional economic analysis, the firm is generally characterized simply as a "black box" which transforms inputs (labor, capital, and raw materials) into outputs. Little consideration is given to the internal structure of the organization. Although more attention has been paid recently, there still has been little effort devoted to synthesizing the material in an accessible form that emphasizes the managerial implications of the analysis. We apply the basic tools of economics to examine the implications of decisions such as centralization versus decentralization, the bundling of tasks into specific jobs within the organization, the use of objective versus subjective performance measures, the compensation of employees through fixed versus incentive compensation, and retaining activities within the firm versus outsourcing.

In our analysis, two fundamental ideas from standard economic analysis are used repeatedly: optimization and equilibrium. With regard to optimization, it is crucial to understand that individuals face powerful incentives and can be incredibly resourceful in devising methods to exploit the opportunities they face. In choosing corporate policies managers must anticipate potential responses by customers, suppliers, or employees that might produce undesirable outcomes. Failure to do so invites individuals to ''game'' the system and can result in the total failure of well-intentioned policies.

Moreover, ideas of equilibrium—the interplay of supply and demand in product, labor, and capital markets—represent important challenges to managerial decisions. Understanding how prices and quantities change in response to changes in costs, product characteristics, or the terms of sale is a critical managerial skill. For example, increases in petroleum prices accompanying the Gulf War prompted oil companies to increase production, encouraged petrochemical companies to alter their input mix to economize on a now more expensive input, made salespeople reevaluate their decisions about contacting potential customers by phone rather than in person, and encouraged auto producers to focus more on gas economy in the design of new models. Yet these incentives to change depend on the structure of the organization. A salesperson is less likely to switch to greater reliance on telephone and mail if the firm reimburses sales expenses than if the salesperson is responsible for the costs of contacting potential customers.

Economic Darwinism: GM and Chrysler

At the beginning of 1994, two competing organizational architectures exist in the U.S. auto industry for new model development. General Motors places strong emphasis on functional specialties, establishing small teams that consist of experts from the same functional field. Each team is charged with a particular assignment that relates to their area of specialization. One team might have the primary responsibility for the design of the body of the vehicle while another might be charged with developing the drive train. The teams work simultaneously on their specific tasks. Some of the individuals on the teams also serve on cross-functional teams that are charged with coordinating the development process across functional areas.

In contrast to GM, Chrysler Corporation places nearly all decisions about the development of a new vehicle in the hands of a single cross-functional product team. Chrysler's platform teams include engineers, designers, financial analysts, marketing experts, and manufacturing people who all report to a single project leader. This leader has authority over all team members and their work.

General Motors CEO Jack Smith attributed important operational differences at Chrysler and GM to these differences in organization. Chrysler took three years to bring the new Viper to market; GM regularly takes more than five. And a look at the bottom line reveals that Chrysler earned about $7 for every $100 in sales for 1994; GM earned just 70 cents.

Suggested by Bradley A. Stertz, ''Detroit's New Strategy to Beat Back Japanese Is to Copy Their Ideas,'' *The Wall Street Journal*, October 1, 1992, p. 1.

---

[4]See Alchain (1950), Stigler (1951), Fama and Jensen (1983).

Economic Darwinism

Competition in the marketplace provides strong pressures for efficient production decisions—including organizational decisions. Competition among firms dictates that only those firms with low costs will survive. If firms adopt inefficient, high cost policies—including high cost compensation plans and organizational structures—competition will place strong pressures on these firms to either adapt or close.

GM and Chrysler offer only two illustrations of how firms differ when they make fundamental decisions about the organization of their activities. Fortunately, for firms like GM, the decision-making process is an ongoing one. In fact, by 1995, GM had reorganized its production lines in a manner that more closely resembled the Chrysler model, reflecting a major force at work in industries around the globe—"survival of the fittest" or what we will call "Economic Darwinism."[4] The collapse of Barings, Charles Darwin might have noted, is an example of how competition tends to weed out the less fit.

In the biological systems that Darwin analyzed, the major forces at work were random mutations in organisms and shocks to the external environment (changes in weather, for example). But in the economic system on which we focus, purposeful voluntary changes—like GM copying Chrysler—occur. If the cover article in this week's *Fortune* reports an innovative inventory control system at Toyota, managers across the country, indeed around the globe, will ask, "Would that work in my company, too?" Undoubtedly the managers with the strongest interest in trying it will work in firms with current inventory problems.[5] Some will change to the new system with success, others with disastrous results. However, before any change is made, it is important to analyze its likely consequences and forecast its impact on the firm. Therefore, while competition in markets tends to produce surviving firms with efficient organizational architectures, uncritical experimentation with the organizational innovation *du jour* can expose the firm to an uncomfortably high risk of failure.

Purpose of the Book

The primary purpose of this book is to provide a solid conceptual framework for analyzing organizational problems and designing more effective organizational architectures. The book also provides basic material on microeconomics and discusses how it can be used to make operational decisions, such as input, output, and pricing

---

[5]This raises the question of why any firm with an innovative idea would voluntarily disclose it. Perhaps the free publicity outweighs the lost competitive advantage.

decisions. In addition, this material supplies a set of tools and an understanding of markets that is important in making good organizational decisions.

Our approach to organizations begins with two basic notions: People act in their own self-interest, and information is often asymmetric—individuals do not all share the same information. As we have indicated, this framework suggests that three critical elements of organizational architecture are the assignment of decision rights, the performance-evaluation system, and the reward system. Successful organizations assign decision rights in a manner that effectively links decision-making authority with the relevant information to make good decisions. Correspondingly, successful organizations develop performance-evaluation and reward systems that provide self-interested decision-makers with appropriate incentives to make value-increasing decisions.

A powerful feature of this economic framework is that it can be readily extended to incorporate many other managerial policies such as finance, accounting, information systems, operations, and marketing policies. In this sense, it can play an important integrating role, which is becoming increasingly important with cross-functional teams.

The book is organized as follows:

Part 1: Basic Concepts lays the groundwork for the book. Chapter 2 summarizes the economic view of behavior, stressing management implications. Chapter 3 presents an overview of markets, provides a rationale for the existence of organizations, and stresses the importance of knowledge. Chapters 4 through 6 cover the traditional microeconomics topics of demand, production and cost, and market structure. These three chapters provide the reader with a basic set of microeconomic tools and use these tools to analyze basic operational policies such as input, output, and product-pricing decisions. These chapters also provide important background material for the subsequent chapters on organizations—a good understanding of the market environment is important for making sound organizational decisions.[6]

Part 2: Organizational Architecture develops the core framework of the book. Chapters 7 and 8 provide a basic overview of the organizational design problem. Chapters 9 and 10 focus on two aspects of the assignment of decision rights within the firm—the level of decentralization chosen for various decisions, and the bundling of various tasks into jobs and then jobs into subunits. Chapters 11 and 12 examine compensation policy. First we focus on the level of compensation necessary to attract and retain an appropriate group of employees. Then we discuss the composition of the compensation package, focusing on the mix of salary, fringe benefits,

---

[6]Chapters 2 and 3 should be read by all. A reader familiar with microeconomics can proceed directly to chapter 7 to focus on organizational issues. (Such a reader, however, might find the material in Chapters 4–6 as helpful review.) Others should read Chapters 4–6 before moving on to the material on organizations.

and incentive compensation that maximizes the value of the firm. In Chapters 13 and 14, we analyze individual and divisional performance evaluation.

Part 3: Applying the Economic Framework to Managerial Decisions uses the framework that we have developed to provide insights into contemporary management issues. We examine leadership, outsourcing, total quality management/reengineering, and ethics.

The Economist's View of Behavior

In June 1992, the State of California filed charges alleging that Sears Auto Centers were overcharging customers an average of $230 for unneeded or undone repairs. These charges were followed by similar allegations by the State of New Jersey. Ultimately, Sears admitted that ''some mistakes did occur'' and agreed to a settlement for an amount up to $20 million. Sears, however, maintained that its management was not previously aware of the problem and did not condone or encourage the defrauding of customers. This auto-repair scandal imposed significant costs on Sears. As the complaints became public, the stock price of Sears declined by about 6 percent, while sales at the auto centers declined significantly.

To limit these costs, it was important for Sears' management to act quickly to address the problem. As a first step, the management had to make assumptions about what initially motivated employees to recommend unneeded repairs. Only then could management choose a policy to address the situation. For example, if management thought the problem was caused by a ''few bad apples'' the likely response would have been to fire the dishonest employees. If instead, management thought the problem was caused by disgruntled workers taking out their frustrations on customers, a likely response would have been to adopt a job-enrichment program to increase worker satisfaction and, it would be hoped, customer service. Many alternative assumptions and responses are possible.

The example of Sears illustrates a general point—managers' responses to a problem are likely to depend on their underlying model of behavior. Most managerial actions involve trying to affect the behavior of individuals, such as employees, customers, union officials, and subcontractors. Managers employing different assumptions or models about what motivates behavior are likely to take different actions and make different decisions.

We begin this chapter by briefly summarizing the framework economists use to examine behavior. Some graphical tools are introduced to aid in the analysis. We then use this economic framework to analyze the problem at Sears Auto Centers. The managerial implications of this analysis are discussed. Finally, we contrast the economic view of behavior with alternative views, and discuss why the economic framework is particularly useful in managerial decision making.

Throughout this chapter, we focus on how this economic view can be used by management to understand and manage the behavior of employees. In subsequent chapters, we use the economic framework to study other topics of managerial interest, such as consumer demand.

Rational Choice: A General Overview

Unlimited Wants and Limited Resources

Individuals have unlimited wants. For example, people generally want more money, better houses, cars, and clothing. Many people also want to improve the plight of the less fortunate—starving children in foreign countries and the homeless. People are concerned about religion, immortality, and gaining the respect and love of others.

In contrast to wants, resources are limited. Households face limited incomes that preclude all the purchases and expenditures that individuals in the households would like to make. There are a finite number of trees and fixed amounts of land and other natural resources. There are only 24 hours in the day. People do not live forever.

Rational Choice

Economists assume that individuals make rational choices. By rational choice, economists mean that individuals can assign priorities to their wants and choose the most preferred option available. For example, a person confronted with a choice between vanilla and chocolate ice cream can tell you whether she prefers one to the other or is indifferent between the two. The person correspondingly chooses the preferred alternative. Similarly, an individual with a $1,000 per month budget considers the many ways to spend the money and then chooses the package of goods and services that maximizes personal happiness. The individual cannot make all desired purchases on a limited budget. However, the choice is personally optimal given the limited resources.

Rational choice does not mean that people are necessarily selfish and interested in only their own well-being. For example, people can care about charity, family, religion, and society and still make rational choices. The individual on the $1,000 budget might decide to donate $100 to a church. In this case, the donation brings the person greater happiness than alternative uses of the money.

Rational choice also does not imply that individuals are supercomputers that make infallible decisions. Individuals are not endowed with perfect knowledge and foresight nor is additional information costless to acquire and process. For example, investors do not have enough information to always pick winners in the stock market. Rational individuals, however, do the best they can in the face of imperfect knowledge; they learn from their experience and do not make the same mistakes in judgment time after time.

Opportunity Costs

Since resources are constrained, individuals face costs in making choices. Using limited resources for one purpose precludes their use for something else. For example, if you use four hours to play golf, you cannot use the same four hours to paint your house. The *opportunity cost* of using a resource for a given purpose is its value in the best alternative use. For example, the opportunity cost of using four hours of time to play golf is the value of using the four hours in the next best alternative use.

Economic analysis frequently involves a careful consideration of the relevant opportunity costs. For example, if you start a new pizza parlor and hire a manager at $30,000/year, the $30,000 is an explicit cost. Are you better off managing the restaurant yourself? The answer depends (at least in part) on the opportunity cost of your time. If you can earn a maximum of $30,000 in your next best alternative, the cost of managing the pizza parlor yourself is the same as hiring an outside manager. The cost of self-management is an implicit cost that should be considered in deciding whether to manage the unit yourself.

Marginal Analysis

Marginal costs and benefits are the incremental costs and benefits that are associated with making a decision. It is the marginal costs and benefits that are important in economic decision making. An action should be taken when the marginal benefits of the action exceed the marginal costs. For example, in deciding whether or not to spend a $1 on an ice cream cone, a consumer considers the marginal benefit associated with the cone. If this marginal benefit is greater than the marginal cost of $1, the consumer purchases the cone. The consumer purchases additional cones as long as the marginal benefits exceed $1. The consumer quits buying cones at the point where the marginal benefits equal the marginal cost. Beyond this point, the marginal benefits of an additional cone are less than the marginal costs (at some point the consumer will value an additional cone at less than its price of $1).

Marginal analysis is a cornerstone of modern economic analysis. In economic decision making, "bygones are forever bygones." Costs and benefits that do not vary with the decision are *sunk* and hence are irrelevant. For example, you may have purchased your home 20 years ago for $20,000. However, this cost is irrelevant when considering whether or not to sell the house today (ignoring tax considerations that can affect the marginal costs and benefits).

Marginal Analysis: An Example

You are offered a contract to install a wood floor for $20,000. The opportunity cost of your labor and other operating expenses (excluding the wood) is $15,000. You have the wood for the job in inventory. It originally cost you $6,000. However, price declines have reduced the market value of the wood to $2,000, and this value is not expected to change in the near future. Should you accept the contract?

You should compare the marginal costs and benefits from the project. The marginal benefit is $20,000. The marginal cost is $17,000—$15,000 for labor and operating expenses and $2,000 for the wood. The historic cost for the wood of $6,000 is not relevant to the decision. You can replace the wood used for the job for $2,000. The $4,000 drop in the value of the inventory is a sunk cost that is irrelevant to the decision (ignoring the tax considerations). Since the marginal benefits exceed the marginal costs, you would be better off to accept the contract than to reject it.

Creative Nature of Individuals

In the rational-choice model, individuals maximize their *utility* (personal happiness) given resource constraints. It is important to note that people are quite creative and resourceful in minimizing the effects of constraints.[1] For example, consider the government's imposition of the 55 mile-per-hour speed limit. This regulation constrains drivers by increasing the fines for fast driving. Individuals responded by developing radar detectors and other technology that have allowed drivers to reduce the likelihood of getting caught and thus the expected fines. This technology reduces the effect of the legal constraint and increases the utility of the drivers using the technology. Similarly, when the government increases tax rates, almost immediately, accountants and financial planners begin developing clever ways to reduce the impact of the new tax laws. The creative nature of individuals has important managerial implications which we discuss later in this chapter.

Graphical Tools

Economists use a set of graphical tools to illustrate how individuals make choices. We begin by introducing these tools. We then use them to analyze the problems at Sears Auto Centers.

---

[1]See M. C. Jensen and W. H. Meckling, "The Nature of Man," Harvard University, September 1992.

Are Criminals Rational?

Criminals are often considered to be irrational and psychologically disturbed. Evidence, however, suggests that criminal behavior can be explained, at least in part, by the rational-choice model. Rational choice predicts that a criminal will consider the marginal costs and benefits of a crime and will commit the crime only when the benefits exceed the costs. Under this view, increasing the costs of crime (length of prison terms) will reduce crimes. Ehrlich (1973) studied whether the incidence of major felonies varied across states with the expected punishment. He found that the incidence of robberies decreased about 1.3 percent in response to each 1 percent increase in the proportionate likelihood of punishment. The incidence of crime also decreased with the severity of the punishment. Criminals have certainly shown creativity and ingenuity in developing methods to reduce the likelihood of getting caught.

Suggested by I. Ehrlich, 1973, "Participation in Illegitimate Activities: A Theoretical and Empirical Investigation," *Journal of Political Economy*, v.81.

Preferences and Utility Functions

Goods are things that people value. Goods can include standard economic goods like food and clothing and less tangible goods such as love of family and charity. The economic model of behavior makes four basic assumptions about individual preference:

> *Comparability.* An individual can always rank two bundles of goods in terms of preference. Ties in preference are permitted. For example, given a choice between chocolate and vanilla ice cream an individual either prefers one to the other or is indifferent between the two.

> *Transitivity.* If a person likes chocolate ice cream better than vanilla and prefers vanilla to strawberry, that individual necessarily prefers chocolate to strawberry.

> *Nonsatiation.* More of each good is preferred to less (in the relevant range).

> *Substitution.* For a given increase in the quantity of any one good, the individual is willing to give up at least a small portion of any other good. This statement implies that there are no absolute needs—substitutions are always possible.

These four assumptions are sufficient to allow us to represent an individual's preferences by a *utility function*. A utility function is a mathematical function that relates total utility to the level of goods consumed. The concept can be illustrated most conveniently under the assumption that the individual cares about only two goods. The insights from the two-good analysis, however, readily extend to the case of additional goods (food, housing, clothing, respect, charity, etc.).

FIGURE 2.1   Indifference curves.

These indifference curves picture all combinations of food and clothing that yield the same amount of utility. Northeast movements are utility increasing. Indifference curve B pictures higher utility than indifference curve A.

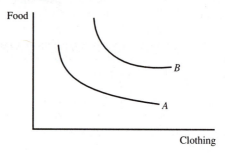

Assume that an individual only values food and clothing. In general form, the individual's utility function can be written as follows:

$$\text{Utility} = f(\text{food, clothing}). \tag{2.1}$$

The individual prefers more of each good—thus utility is increasing in both food and clothing. An example of a specific utility function is:

$$\text{Utility} = \text{Food}^{.5} * \text{Clothing}^{.5} \tag{2.2}$$

With this utility function, if the individual has 16 units of food and 25 units of clothing, total utility is 20 ($16^{.5} * 25^{.5} = 4 * 5$).

The utility function ranks alternative market baskets in the *order* of most preferred to least preferred, but does not indicate how much one market basket is preferred to another (the ranking is ordinal not cardinal). For example, if the utility index is 100 for one combination of food and clothing and 200 for another, the individual prefers the second combination. However, the second bundle does not make the person twice as well off as the first bundle. This formulation also does not allow one person's utility of a bundle to be compared to another person's utility.

Indifference Curves

Preferences implied by the utility function can be illustrated graphically through *indifference curves*. An indifference curve pictures all the combinations of goods that yield the same utility. For example, given the utility function in equation 2.2, holding utility constant at 20, either 16 units of food and 25 units of clothing or 25 units of food and 16 units of clothing keeps the individual indifferent. Figure 2.1 pictures two indifference curves. The individual is completely indifferent between the combinations of food and clothing along a given curve. For example, if given a choice between any two points on curve *A*, the individual would say that he does not care which one is selected.

Indifference curves have negative slopes. If the person obtains a smaller amount of food, the only way the individual can be equally as well off is to obtain more clothes. North and east movements in graphs like Figure 2.1 are utility increasing. Holding the amount of food constant, utility increases by increasing clothing (an eastward movement). Holding the amount of clothing constant, utility increases by increasing the amount of food (a northward movement). Thus the individual in Figure 2.1 would rather be on indifference curve *B* than *A*.

Economists typically assume that indifference curves are convex to the origin (bow in as in Figure 2.1). Convexity is a behavioral assumption about how individuals value goods. If a person has a lot of one good (for example, food), that individual will give up a relatively large amount of the good to obtain a small portion of the other good (for example, clothing). Thus the indifference curves in Figure 2.1 are relatively steep at high levels of food. In contrast, if the person has a small amount of a good, she will only substitute a small amount of the good for a large amount of the other good. Correspondingly, the indifference curves in Figure 2.1 flatten as the person has less food and more clothing.

Constraints

The individual in our example would like to have infinite amounts of food and clothing. Unfortunately, the individual faces a budget constraint that precludes this choice. For illustration, assume that the individual has an income of *I*, and the prices per unit of food and clothing are P_f and P_c respectively. Since the individual cannot spend more than *I*, he faces the following constraint:

$$I \geq P_f F + P_c C, \text{ where} \tag{2.3}$$

F and *C* represent the units of food and clothing purchased. The constraint indicates that only market baskets that cost less than *I* are feasible. Rearranging terms, the constraint can be written as:

$$F \leq I/P_f - (P_c/P_f)C. \tag{2.4}$$

Figure 2.2 pictures the constraint. All combinations of food and clothing on or to the left of the line are possible. Combinations to the right of the line are not possible. The *F*-intercept (on the vertical axis) of the line, I/P_f, indicates how much food can be purchased by the individual if the entire income is spent on food and no clothing is purchased. The *C*-intercept is correspondingly I/P_c. The slope of the line is minus one times the ratio of the two prices $-P_c/P_f$. We refer to the ratio, P_c/P_f, as the *relative price* of clothing. It represents how many units of food must be given up to acquire a unit of clothing (the opportunity cost of clothing). For example, if the price of clothing is $2 and the price of food is $1, the relative price of clothing is 2. In this case, clothing is twice as expensive as food. To keep total expenditures constant, two units of food must be given up for every unit of clothing purchased. The relative price of food is P_f/P_c.

FIGURE 2.2   **Constraint.**

The constraint reflects the feasible combinations of food and clothing that are available to the individual given her income (I). The vertical and horizontal intercepts respectively show the amounts of food and clothing that can be purchased if no income is spent on the other good. Shifts in I cause parallel shifts in the constraint. The slope of the constraint is equal to minus one times the ratio of the prices of the two goods. The slope of the constraint changes with changes in the ratio of the two prices.

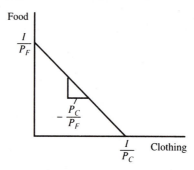

The constraint changes with changes in the individual's income and the relative prices of the two goods. Changes in income result in parallel shifts of the constraint—the slope is not affected. An increase in income shifts the constraint outward (to the right), while a decrease in income shifts the constraint inward. The slope of the constraint changes with the relative prices of the two goods. If the price of clothing increases relative to the price of food, the constraint becomes steeper. If the price of clothing falls relative to the price of food, the constraint becomes flatter.

Individual Choice

Within this economic framework, the goal of the individual is to maximize utility given the constraint. Utility is maximized at the point of tangency between the constraint and an indifference curve.[2] Figure 2.3 portrays the optimal choice. The individual could choose points like 1 and 2 on indifference curve *A*. However, point 3 on curve *B* is preferred. The individual would prefer to be at any point on curve *C*. However, points on curve *C* are not possible given the constraint.

---

[2]For simplicity, we ignore the possibility of corner solutions: the points where the budget constraint intersects the axes. With corner solutions the individual spends all income on only one good.

FIGURE 2.3   Optimal Choice.

The individual is best off by choosing point 3 where the constraint is tangent to indifference curve B. This combination of food and clothing yields higher utility than feasible alternatives (for example, points 1 and 2). The individual would prefer points on indifference curve C. These points are not feasible given the constraint.

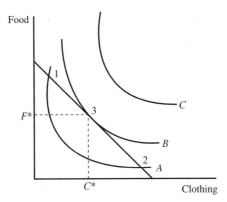

Motivating Honesty at Sears

To analyze the problem at Sears Auto Centers, assume that employees value two goods, money and integrity. Thus, a typical employee's utility function is:

$$\text{Utility} = f(\text{money, integrity}). \tag{2.5}$$

Money is meant to symbolize general purchasing power; it allows the purchase of goods such as food, clothing, and housing. Integrity is something the employee values for its own sake—being honest in the dealings with other people makes the person feel good and is valued for that reason. (The analysis in this chapter is framed in a simple one-period context and does not consider future monetary returns from developing a good reputation. In Chapter 7, we extend the analysis and consider these multi-period effects.)

We assume that integrity can be measured on a numerical scale with the individual preferring higher values. For example, 5 units of integrity provide more utility than 4 units of integrity. In actuality, measuring a good like integrity on a numerical scale may be very difficult. This complication, however, does not limit the qualitative insights that are gained from the analysis.

Salespeople at Sears Auto Centers were paid a commission based on total sales. In addition, they had sales quotas for particular products and services. Missing these quotas could result in job loss as well as lower pay. Individual sales apparently could be increased and sales quotas met by being dishonest (for example, telling customers that they needed new shock absorbers when they did not).

FIGURE 2.4   Hypothetical Constraint Facing a Worker at Sears Auto Center.

The constraint pictures the maximum amounts of money and integrity that are possible for the worker given the compensation scheme and conditions at the store. If the employee sacrifices all integrity and recommends many unnecessary repairs he can earn a maximum of $' a month. Fewer sales are made if the employee recommends fewer unnecessary repairs (selects a higher level of integrity) and income is lower since the worker is paid a commission on sales. I_c represents complete honesty.

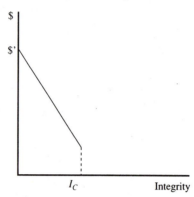

Given the customer volume at the store and the commission rate, there is some maximum amount that a salesperson can earn even if he recommends repairs to all customers. If the salesperson recommends fewer repairs, income will decline. If the employee is completely honest and recommends no unnecessary repairs, sales quotas would be difficult to meet resulting in potential job loss and less income. Figure 2.4 pictures a hypothetical constraint facing a typical salesperson at Sears. This constraint depicts the maximum amounts of money and integrity that are possible given the compensation plan and conditions at the store.[3] If the employee sacrifices all integrity he can earn $' a month. If the employee is perfectly honest the employee earns much less (there is some floor on income that depends on the traffic from customers with legitimate problems). Intermediate options along the constraint are possible. Of course, the employee would like to earn more than $'. However, given the constraint higher earnings are not possible.

The employee chooses a combination of integrity and compensation that places the individual on the highest indifference curve. This choice occurs at the point of tangency between the employee's indifference curve and the constraint. Management can alter the constraint facing salespeople by changing the compensation scheme. In the Sears case, lowering the sales commission (in favor of a fixed hourly wage) reduces the monetary gains from selling more products through dishonest

---

[3]For simplicity, we assume the constraint is linear. This assumption is not necessary for our analysis.

FIGURE 2.5   **Optimal Choices of a Worker at Sears Auto Center under Two Different Compensation Plans.**

Case 1 reflects the original compensation plan. In this case, compensation consists of a high sales commission and the constraint is relatively steep. In Case 2, the firm pays a higher portion of the wage as a fixed salary and a lower commission rate. The slope of the constraint is flatter. The result is that the individual chooses a higher level of integrity in Case 2 than Case 1.

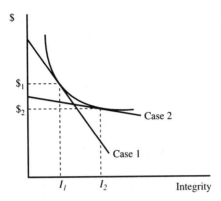

behavior and thus flattens the constraint. Changing the slope of the constraint results in a different tangency point and thus a different choice. Figure 2.5 shows how the optimal choice of the employee changes when the sales commission is decreased. The result is more honest behavior. Consistent with this analysis, Sears actually responded to the problem by changing the compensation scheme from commission to straight salary. It also eliminated sales quotas and introduced a program to reward personnel for high levels of customer satisfaction.

Managerial Implications

The analysis illustrates how economic analysis can be used to analyze and address management problems. Management is interested in affecting the behavior of individuals, such as workers, customers, union leaders, and subcontractors. Understanding what motivates individuals is critical. The economic approach views individual actions as the outcomes of maximizing personal utility. Managers can understand and affect these outcomes by analyzing and manipulating the constraints faced by the individuals. For example, management can motivate workers through compensation plans and customers through pricing decisions.

The outcome of individuals making rational choices is a function of both constraints and preferences. Individuals try to get on the highest indifference curve given the constraints they face. Our discussion of management implications, however, has intentionally focused on altering constraints. As a management tool, the value of focusing on personal preferences is often limited. Preferences are not generally observable and virtually anything can be explained as simply a matter of personal tastes. Also it is difficult to change what a person likes and does not like. For example, a preference-based explanation for why employees were dishonest at Sears is that these workers liked to be dishonest. This explanation, however, is unhelpful in giving management guidance on how to address the problem. It suggests that Sears might try to fire dishonest workers and replace them with workers that care more about personal integrity. However, the inability to observe personal preferences limits the viability of this approach.

The fact that individuals are clever and creative in minimizing the effects of constraints greatly complicates the management problem. Changing incentives will affect employee behavior; however, it is often in a perverse and unintended manner. For example, consider the Soviet Union's early attempts to adopt incentive compensation to motivate workers. Taxi drivers started driving at high speeds around Moscow streets without passengers, while lamp manufacturers started producing light fixtures that would fall out of ceilings. Both actions can be traced to the incentives provided by the compensation plan. Taxi drivers were rewarded for total miles traveled (with or without passengers), while the lamp manufacturers were rewarded on the weight of production (inducing the manufacturer to use lead rather than lighter inputs!). Presumably Sears initially adopted a commission plan to motivate salespeople to work harder. The dishonest behavior was undoubtedly a side effect that was not anticipated at the time of plan adoption.

In summary, the economic approach to human behavior has important managerial implications. In particular, the "principle of substitution" suggests that a manager can motivate desired actions by setting appropriate incentives. However, the other major conclusion is that the manager should be very careful because improper incentives can motivate perverse behavior.

Perverse Incentives at Lincoln Electric

Lincoln Electric is a successful company that manufactures arc welding equipment. It is famous for a strong emphasis on incentive compensation. This incentive program appears to be a primary source of the high productivity of Lincoln's production workers. At one point, Lincoln Electric decided to extend its incentive compensation program to clerical workers. Counters were installed on typewriters and secretaries were paid on the number of characters typed. This policy resulted in an increase in the amount of typing. The program, however, was discontinued when it was discovered that a secretary spent her lunch hour with her finger on the keyboard typing worthless pages in order to increase her compensation.

Suggested by N. Fast and N. Berg, 1975, "The Lincoln Electric Company," Harvard Business School Case #376–028.

Finally it is worth noting that the economic view is less useful for forecasting exactly what each person will do (individual preferences are largely unobservable). Rather the focus is on aggregate behavior and what the typical person will tend to do. For example, an economist might not be very good at predicting which of several people will jump into a body of water to save a child. However, the economist will be successful in predicting that rescue attempts are more likely in a still pond than a raging river (the costs are higher in the latter case). Managers are typically interested in establishing an organizational structure that will work well independent of the specific people filling particular jobs. Individuals come and go, and the manager wants an organization that will work well with these changes. In this context, the economic framework is likely to be very useful.

Alternative Models of Behavior

We have shown how the economic view of behavior can be used by managers decision making. We now discuss three other models that are commonly used by managers (either explicitly or implicitly) to explain behavior.[4] We introduce these models in the context of motivating employees and discuss the implications as they relate to Sears Auto Centers.

Happy-is-Productive Model

Managers sometimes assert that happy workers are more productive than unhappy workers. Managers following this happy-is-productive model see as their goal to design work environments that satisfy workers. Psychological theories, such as Maslow's and Herzberg's, are frequently used as guides for increasing job satisfaction.[5]

Maslow's theory is based on a hierarchy of five needs (see figure 2.6). According to Maslow, individuals focus initially on filling lower-level needs (for example, food, water, and air). As these needs are filled, individuals move to filling higher level needs, culminating in the need for self-actualization. Herzberg's theory is similar to Maslow's. He argues that job dissatisfaction and satisfaction should be considered separately, and that two types of factors are present across organizations: hygienes and motivators. Hygiene factors include company policy, supervision, compensation, and working conditions. Insufficient hygiene factors lead to job dissatisfaction. However, hygiene factors do not contribute to job satisfaction. Motivators include factors such as responsibility, recognition, and opportunities for

---

[4]See M. C. Jensen and W. H. Meckling, "The Nature of Man," Harvard University, September 1992.

[5]See F. Herzberg, B. Mausner, and B. Snyderman, *The Motivation to Work,* John Wiley, New York, 1959, and A. H. Maslow, *Motivation and Personality,* 2nd ed., Harper and Row, New York, 1970.

FIGURE 2.6   Maslow's Hierarchy of Needs.

According to Maslow's theory, individuals focus initially on lower level needs (for example, physiological needs). As these needs are filled, individuals move to filling higher level needs. According to the happy-is-productive model, job satisfaction and work effort can be enhanced by designing work environments that help employees fill their needs.

Maslow's Pyramid

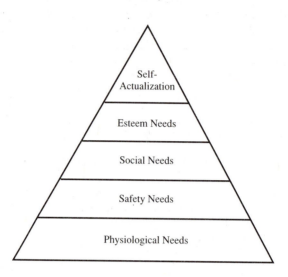

1. Physiological Needs   Need for food, water, and air

2. Safety Needs   Need for security, stability, and the absence
                              from pain, threat, and illness

3. Social Needs   Need for love, affection, and belonging

4. Esteem Needs   Need for feelings of achievement and self-
                              esteem, also for the recognition and respect
                              of others

5. Self-Actualization Needs   Need to realize one's potential and
                              self-fulfillment

advancement. According to Herzberg, job satisfaction increases with motivating factors.

A manager adhering to this happy-is-productive model might suggest that the problem at Sears was motivated by disgruntled employees who took out their frustrations on customers. This view implies that Sears could reduce the problem by focusing on filling the appropriate needs of workers to promote increased job satisfaction and better customer service. For example, Sears might undertake job-enrichment programs to help workers fill their needs for esteem and self-actualization.

Note that the economic and happy-is-productive models do not differ based on what people care about. The economic model allows individuals to value love, esteem, and self-actualization, as well as the standard economic goods such as food, clothing, and shelter. However, in the economic model these are goods that individuals value and not *needs*. Maximizing individuals make substitutions as opportunity costs change, and thus no good is viewed as an absolute necessity. The primary difference of the models, however, is what motivates individual actions. In the happy-is-productive model, workers exert high effort when they are happy. In contrast, in the economic model workers exert effort because of the rewards.

As an example to contrast the models, consider offering an employee tenure plus a large salary that is paid to a worker independent of performance. The happy-is-productive model suggests the worker will be more productive if the additional job security and high salary increases job satisfaction. The economic model suggests the worker would exert less effort (since the worker gains no additional compensation for working harder and is less likely to be fired).

Good-Citizen Model

Some managers subscribe to the good-citizen model. The basic assumption is that employees want to do a good job. They take pride in their work and want to excel. Under this view, managers have three primary roles. First, they need to communicate the goals and objectives of the organization to workers. Second, they need to help workers discover how to achieve these goals and objectives. Finally, managers should provide feedback on performance so that workers can continue to enhance their efforts. There is no reason to have incentive pay since individuals are intrinsically interested in doing a good job.

This view suggests that the problems at Sears were motivated by a misunderstanding by employees about what was good for the company. Employees presumably thought that increasing sales was in the company's interests, even if it required a certain amount of dishonesty. The management of Sears could motivate employee honesty by clearly communicating to the employees that honesty is important to the company. For example, managers of each automotive center might be instructed to hold a series of employee meetings to stress the value of employee honesty and customer service.

Product-of-the-Environment Model

The product-of-the-environment model argues that the behaviors of individuals are largely determined by their upbringings. Some cultures and households promote positive values in individuals, such as industry and honesty, while others promote negative traits, such as laziness and dishonesty. This model suggests that Sears has dishonest individuals in their automotive centers. A response is to fire these workers and replace them with honest workers from better backgrounds.

Which Model Should Managers Use?

Individuals' behavior is a complex topic. Any behavioral model is unlikely to be useful in all contexts. For example, the economic model is unlikely to be helpful in predicting whether a given individual might prefer red shirts to blue shirts (selling at the same price). Our focus, however, is on managerial decision making. In this context, there are reasons to believe that the economic model is particularly useful.

Managers are frequently interested in fostering *changes* in behavior. For example, managers want consumers to buy more products, employees to exert more effort, and labor unions to weaken their demands for wage increases. In contrast to other models, the economic framework provides managers with concrete guidance on how to alter behavior. Desired behavior can be encouraged by changing the relevant costs and benefits facing the decision maker. For example, incentive compensation can be used to motivate employees, while price changes can be used to affect consumer behavior.

There is ample evidence to support the hypothesis that the economic framework is useful in explaining changes in behavior. The most common example of rational behavior is that consumers tend to buy fewer products at higher prices. The evidence, however, suggests that the model is also useful in explaining behavior in many other contexts, including voting, the formation, dissolution, and structure of families, drug addiction, and the incidence of crime.[6]

Rational Choice and Voting Behavior

The rational-choice model has proven useful in explaining behavior in many contexts including corporate voting. For example, the model implies that shareholders who own large blocks of stock have a stronger incentive to invest in voting on corporate issues than nonblockholders (since blockholders gain more from an appreciation in share value and are also more likely to affect the outcome of the election). Consistent with this prediction, Brickley, Lease, and Smith (1988) find that blockholders are more likely to vote in elections on antitakeover amendments than nonblockholders. Interestingly, they also find that financial institutions such as banks and insurance companies, which frequently derive benefits from lines of business under management control, are less likely to oppose management on management-sponsored proposals than other shareholders without potential business relationships. This outcome is also predicted by the rational-choice model.

Suggested by J. A. Brickley, R. C. Lease, and C. W. Smith, "Ownership Structure and Voting on Antitakeover Amendments," *Journal of Financial Economics* 20, January/March 1988, pp. 267–291.

---

[6]See G. S. Becker, 1993, "Nobel Lecture: The Economic Way of Looking at Behavior," *Journal of Political Economy* 101, 385–409.

The good-citizen model, in contrast, does not appear to be very useful in predicting behavior in business settings. Management would be an easy task if employees would work harder and produce higher quality simply upon request. The happy-is-productive model also has significant limitations. First, it has been speculated that psychologists have enumerated several hundred needs that are thought to motivate people.[7] Thus, which of the many alternative needs should managers focus on to make people happy? Second, and perhaps more importantly, the evidence suggests that there is little relation between job satisfaction and performance. Sometimes, managers might want to follow the implications of the product-of-the-environment model and fire employees with undesirable traits. However, this approach is unlikely to be useful in solving most managerial problems. Also it can be illegal.

Happy-is-Productive vs. Economic Explanations of the Hawthorne Experiments

Seven productivity studies were conducted at Western Electric's Hawthorne plant over the period 1924–1932. All seven studies focused on the response of assembly workers' productivity when different independent variables were manipulated (for example, length of break times and workday). Surprisingly, productivity rose almost regardless of the particular manipulation. For example, it is claimed that productivity increased whenever illumination of the work area changed regardless of the direction of the change. This result, known as the Hawthorne Effect, is among the most discussed findings in psychology, and is often taken as support for the happy-is-productive model. In particular, the workers in the experiment were given special attention and nonauthoritarian supervision relative to other workers at the plant. Also, the affected workers' views on the experiments were solicited by management, and the workers were given more responsibility. These actions allegedly met employee needs and correspondingly increased job satisfaction and performance.

Parsons (1974) presents evidence that the findings of the Hawthorne experiments can be explained by accompanying changes in the compensation plan. Prior to the experiment all workers were paid based on the output of a group with about 100 workers. During the experiment, the compensation plan was changed to base pay on the output of only five workers. In this case, a given worker's output more directly affects her own pay, and economic theory predicts increased output. Interestingly, the last of the original Hawthorne experiments observed workers where the compensation plan was not changed. In that experiment, there was no change in output.

Suggested by H. M. Parsons, "What Happened at Hawthorne?" *Science* 183, March 8, 1974, pp. 922–932.

---

[7] See E. Lawler III, *Pay and Organizational Effectiveness: A Psychological View*, McGraw-Hill, New York, 1971.

CASE STUDY—
INTERWEST HEALTHCARE CORP

Interwest Healthcare is a nonprofit organization that owns 10 hospitals located in three western states. Cynthia Manzoni is Interwest's chief executive officer. Robert Harris, Interwest's chief financial officer, and the administrators of the ten hospitals report to Manzoni.

Harris is deeply concerned because the hospital staffs are not being careful in data entry for the firm's management information system. This data involves information on patient intake, treatment, and release. The information system is used to compile management reports, such as those relating to the costs of various treatments. Also the system is used to compile reports that are required by the federal government under various grant programs. Harris reasons that without good information the management and government reports are less useful and potentially misleading. Harris is worried about the managerial implications and the potential loss of federal grants. The federal government periodically audits Interwest and might discontinue aid if the reports are deemed inaccurate.

Harris has convinced Manzoni that a problem exists. She also realizes the importance of an accurate system both for management planning and maintaining federal aid. Six months ago she invited the hospital administrators and staff members from the corporate financial office to a retreat at a resort location. The purpose was to communicate to the hospital administrators the problems with the data entry and to stress the importance of doing a better job. The meeting was acrimonious. The hospital people accused Harris of being a bureaucrat who did not care about patient services. Harris accused the hospital staffs of not understanding the importance of accurate reporting. By the end of the meeting, Manzoni thought that she had a commitment by the hospital administrators to increase the accuracy of data entry at their hospitals. However, six months later Harris claims that the problem is as bad as ever.

Manzoni has hired you as a consultant to analyze the problem and to make recommendations that might improve the situation. Answer the following questions:

1. What are potential sources of the problem?
2. What information would you want to analyze?
3. What actions might you recommend to increase the accuracy of the data entry?
4. How does your view of behavior affect how you might address this consulting assignment?

Summary

This chapter summarizes the way economists view behavior. In the economic model, individuals are seen as having unlimited wants and limited resources. They rank alternative uses of limited resources in terms of preference, and they correspondingly choose the preferred alternative. Individuals are clever in figuring out ways of maximizing their utility (happiness) in the face of resource constraints. Individuals are not necessarily selfish. They can care about charity, family, religion, and society. They are also not infallible supercomputers.

The *opportunity cost* of using a resource is the value of the resource in the best alternative use. For example, the cost of using five hours to work on this textbook is the value of the authors' time in working on the next best alternative (for example, consulting). Economic decision making requires careful consideration of the relevant opportunity costs.

Marginal costs and benefits are the incremental costs and benefits that are associated with the decision. For example, in deciding whether to purchase an ice cream cone, the marginal cost is the price and the marginal benefit is the extra value of eating one more ice cream cone. It is the marginal costs and benefits that are important in economic decision making. Action should be taken when the marginal benefits are greater than the marginal costs. *Sunk costs* that are not affected by the decision (e.g., past money spent on ice cream) are not relevant.

We use the economic model to analyze a problem at Sears Auto Centers where state regulators discovered that workers were lying to customers about needing repairs. A *utility function* is a mathematical function. It relates total utility to the amounts that an individual has of the items that the individual cares about (*goods*). Preferences implied by a utility function are pictured graphically by *indifference curves*. Indifference curves picture all combinations of goods that yield the same amount of utility. Economic decision making involves maximizing utility given resource *constraints*. Graphically, the constraint shows all combinations of goods that are feasible to acquire. The optimal choice is where the indifference curve is tangent to the constraint. At this point, the individual is at the highest level of utility possible given the constraint.

Changes in the constraint result in changes in the optimal choice. An important implication is that managers can affect behavior by changing constraints to promote desired behavior. For example, Sears' management responded to the dishonesty problem by reducing incentive compensation for sales and increasing incentive compensation for customer satisfaction. Managers, however, have to be careful in manipulating incentives. Individuals are clever at maximizing their utility and setting the wrong incentives can have perverse consequences. For example, the Soviets tried to motivate taxi drivers based on miles driven. Miles driven went way up, but trips were often taken without passengers.

We contrast the economic model with three other models of behavior that managers often use. The implications of these views are considered in the context of Sears Auto Centers. We argue that the economic model is likely to be particularly useful in managerial decision making.

Throughout this chapter, we focus primarily on how managers might use the economic view to analyze and control the behavior of employees. As we will see, however, the economic view is very powerful and is useful in explaining behavior in a variety of different contexts.

CHAPTER 3

Markets, Organizations, and the Role of Knowledge

During the greater part of the twentieth century, the Soviet Union and the United States were involved in an acrimonious debate over the merits of free-market versus centrally-planned economies. The Soviet belief in the superiority of central planning was summed up in Premier Nikita Khruschev's famous prophecy, "We will bury you." During the 1990s, however, the world witnessed the rapid collapse of many of the centrally-planned economies in the world. The Soviet Union broke apart. The Berlin Wall was dismantled, and East and West Germany were reunited. Communist governments throughout Eastern Europe were replaced.

These events appear to support the contention that central economic planning does not work. However, upon closer inspection it is evident that a substantial amount of central economic planning is conducted in free-market economies. Indeed most of the production in modern economies occurs within firms, where resource-allocation decisions are made by managers in a manner that is often akin to central planning. For example, management through administrative actions dictate the output mix of the firm, as well as the methods of production. These decisions can involve billions of dollars of resources and thousands of employees. Indeed, the size of the largest firms, such as IBM and General Motors, actually exceeds that of many national economies. If central planning is so bad, why do firms rely so heavily on it in free-market economies?

In this chapter, we examine three questions: How do free-market systems work? What are the relative advantages of free-market systems compared to centrally-planned economies? Why do we observe so much economic activity conducted within firms in market economies?

FIGURE 3.1   **Efficient Production**

This graph assumes that the economy can produce only two goods: guns and butter. The graph shows all efficient combinations of production. We call this graph the boundary of the opportunity set. The society cannot produce outside the boundary because of limited resources. It can produce at any point on or inside the boundary. Points inside the boundary involve inefficient production. Productive efficiency *means that the economy is producing at a point on the boundary.* Economic efficiency *means that the economy is producing at a point on the boundary that is preferred by society.*

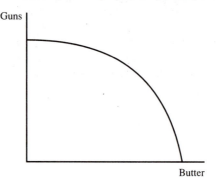

Answers to these questions are particularly important for managers for two reasons. First, management must have an understanding of how markets work to make good input, output, and pricing decisions. Second, national economies are like firms in that they are human creations to direct economic activity. Understanding the relative advantages and disadvantages of markets, central planning, and firms is directly relevant to understanding firm-level issues, such as whether or not to decentralize decision rights to workers and whether to make or buy the firm's inputs.

Goals of an Economic System

Primary goals of any economic system are to produce efficiently (not to waste resources) and to produce the combination of outputs that is most preferred by its citizens. For illustration, assume that only two goods are produced in the economy: guns and butter. Figure 3.1 graphs the amounts of guns and butter that can be produced by the society if efficient production techniques are used. We will refer to this graph as the *boundary* of the *opportunity set*. The society cannot produce outside the boundary (to the northeast) because it has limited resources. It can produce any combination of goods on or below the boundary. However, points inside the boundary involve inefficient production. The economy achieves *productive efficiency* when it produces at a point on the boundary.

Not all points that are productively efficient are equally preferred by its citizens. For example, a country at war is unlikely to want to devote all resources to the production of butter even if butter is produced efficiently. *Economic efficiency* means that the economy is at a point on the boundary that is preferred by its citizens.

The concept of economic efficiency requires defining some appropriate criterion for what is best for society. People, however, are likely to disagree on this issue. For example, one person might want the society to produce only butter and give it all to him, while another person might want the society to produce nothing but guns and give them all to her. Economics is silent on how a society should weigh these differences in individual preferences to form economic goals. Economists, therefore, generally focus on a more limited definition of efficiency, *Pareto efficiency*. An allocation of resources is said to be Pareto efficient if there is no alternative that keeps all individuals at least as well off but makes at least one person better off.

As an example, assume that the economy produces 1,000 tons of butter and no guns and each individual has an equal share. The allocation is not Pareto efficient if there is a subset of individuals who want to convert their butter to guns and can do so without reducing the utility of other individuals in the society. Based on the concept of Pareto efficiency, its citizens are better off if the economy produces more guns and less butter. This action increases the utility of some individuals without reducing the utility of others. If this action adversely affects even one person, the move is not Pareto improving and an economist cannot say whether the move is good or bad from a societal viewpoint.

In centrally-planned economies, the government decides what to produce and how to produce it. In free-market economies, these decisions are decentralized to individuals in the economy. In theory, any allocation of resources that can be achieved by a free-market economy can also be achieved by a centrally-planned economy—at least in concept, the central planner can order any feasible production and distribution of goods. We now examine how free-market systems work and how such systems can produce a Pareto-efficient allocation of resources. We then discuss why free-market economies are more likely to result in efficient resource allocations than centrally-planned economies.

Property Rights and Exchange in a Free-Market Economy

Property Rights

A *property right* is a socially enforced right to select the uses of an economic good. A property right is *private* when it is assigned to a specific person. Private property rights are *alienable* in that they can be transferred (sold or given) to other individuals. For example, the owner of an automobile can use the automobile as he sees fit (within some limits), and can restrict others from using the vehicle. The owner also can sell the automobile. The government provides police and a court system to help enforce these property rights.

An important feature of a *free-market economy* is the use of private property rights. Owners of land and other resources have the legal rights to decide how to use these resources and frequently trade these rights to other individuals. They are free to start new businesses and to close existing businesses. In contrast, in centrally-planned economies property tends to be owned by the state.

Gains From Trade

To understand how a market economy works, it is necessary to understand the motives for trading property rights. Why do people buy and sell? The answer is to make themselves better off.

The economic model assumes that people are rational. They order their preferences and take actions that maximize their utility. Given this assumption, voluntary trade must be *mutually advantageous*. The ability to say no prevents consenting adults from being exploited in a trade. Trade takes place because the buyer places a higher value on the item than the seller. The corresponding *gains from trade* make both parties better off. For example, if one individual is willing to pay up to $16,000 for an automobile and another person is willing to sell the automobile for as little as $10,000 the potential gains from trade are $6,000 ($16,000 − $10,000). If the automobile trades at $13,000 both individuals are $3,000 better off. The buyer gives up $13,000 to buy something that she values at $16,000, while the seller obtains $13,000 for something he values at only $10,000. At other prices between $10,000 and $16,000, the total gains are still $6,000, but they are not split evenly. For example, at a price of $15,000, the buyer gains $1,000 in value, while the seller gains $5,000.

Where do the gains from trade come from? One source is differences in preferences. The buyer and seller may simply place different values on the item of trade. For example, some people value new automobiles more than others. Another important source of gains is that the seller may be able to produce the item more cheaply than the buyer and thus has a *comparative advantage* in its production. In advanced economies, individuals specialize in producing products where they have a comparative advantage and make trades to acquire other goods and services. Specialization greatly enhances the standard of living of a society. Imagine, for example, if you had to be completely self-sufficient (making your own clothing, growing your own food, building your own house, producing your own vehicles for transportation, etc.). Your overall standard of living would be much lower than it is living in a modern, specialized economy.

In most transactions, the buyer and seller do not have all the information they would like to know. For example when purchasing an automobile, the buyer is unlikely to know as much about the car as the seller. After buying the car, the buyer may discover problems with the vehicle that cause the individual to regret the purchase. Nevertheless, the trade was mutually advantageous at the time of the trade, given the preferences of the buyer and seller and the information they had at the time of the trade. If either party had not expected that the gains from the transaction would be positive they would not have made the trade. The economic model posits that people learn from their mistakes and do not consistently lose in transactions. On average, individuals must be satisfied with their trades after the fact, or they will refuse to trade.

A common misconception is that trade takes place because people have too much of some goods—people sell to others what they cannot use themselves. This view, however, does not explain why individuals sell houses, cars, jewelry, land, and other resources that they highly value and have in short supply. The economic explanation for trade argues that trade does not take place because people have too little or too much of a good. Rather trade takes place whenever a person is willing to pay a higher price for a good than it is worth to the owner. For example, you might love your new sports car. However, you would sell it if someone offered you a high enough price.

Strategic-Business Planning Ignoring the Economics of Trade

During the 1970s many firms adopted a particular form of strategic business planning. All projects of the firm were ranked based on growth potential and market share. Projects with high growth potential and high market share were called stars,while projects with low growth potential and market share were referred to as dogs. Dogs were sold, while stars were kept. Funding for the stars came from cash cows, projects with high market share and low growth potential.

The idea behind this process is to treat the projects of a firm like stocks in a portfolio. Through systematic analysis, winners are to be kept and losers sold. Money is invested in the winners to enhance the firm's competitive advantage. While the idea sounds intriguing, its underpinnings are inconsistent with the basic economics of trade—sell if, and only if, you can get a price that exceeds the value of keeping the item yourself. This principle implies that, contrary to the process, dogs should be kept unless they can be sold at sufficiently high prices. Similarly, stars should be sold if the price is sufficiently high.

By the 1980s, many firms found that violating the basic principles of trade had led them to accumulate suboptimal collections of projects. Large increases in stock prices were observed as these firms reshuffled plants, divisions, and subsidiaries through sell-offs, spin-offs, and divestitures.

Suggested by "The New Breed of Strategic Planner," *Business Week*, September 17, 1984, 62–68.

It is important to recognize that trade is an important form of creation. The act of trading produces value that makes individuals better off. Gains from trade also provide important incentives to move resources to more productive uses. An individual who can make the most productive use of a resource will be willing to pay a higher price for the resource than other potential users. The owner has the incentive to trade with this individual since the owner gets to keep the proceeds from the sale.

FIGURE 3.2   **Supply and Demand in the PC Industry.**

The demand curve shows the number of PCs that consumers want to purchase at each price. The supply curve shows the number of PCs that producers want to sell at each price. Equilibrium is where the two curves cross. Here the quantity supplied equals the quantity demanded. If the price is above the market-clearing price of P$_c$ there is a surplus of PCs. Producers supply more PCs than consumers want to purchase. If the price is below the market-clearing price there is a shortage. Producers supply fewer PCs than consumers want to purchase. Surpluses and shortages put pressure on prices and quantities to move to equilibrium levels.

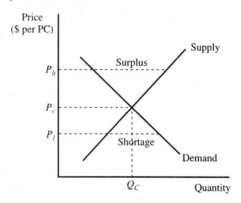

Basics of Supply and Demand

Gains from trade explain why individuals buy and sell. But what coordinates the separate decisions of millions of individuals in a free-market economy to prevent chaos? Why aren't there massive surpluses produced of some goods and huge shortages of other goods? What restricts the amounts demanded by the public to the amounts supplied? The answers to these questions lie in the price system.

The Market Mechanism

The basic economics of a price system can be illustrated through standard supply/ demand diagrams. As an example, Figure 3.2 displays a supply/demand diagram for a particular model of personal computer (PC)—for example, a 486 machine with standard quality and features. The vertical axis on the graph shows the price for a PC, while the horizontal axis shows the total quantity of PCs demanded and supplied in the market for the period (for example, a month).

The market includes all potential buyers and sellers of this type of PC. We assume that there are many buyers and sellers. Individual transactions are so small in relation to the overall market that the price is unaffected by any single sale or purchase. No buyer or seller has market power—all trades are made at the going market price. We label this type of market as *competitive*. (In Chapter 6 we analyze *noncompetitive* market structures.)

The *demand curve* (D) tells how many total PCs consumers are willing to buy at each price. The demand curve slopes downward because consumers typically buy more if the price is lower. For example, consumers are more likely to buy PCs if the price is $500 than if the price is $5,000.

The *supply curve* (S) shows how many PCs producers are willing to sell at each price. The curve slopes upward—at higher prices producers are able and willing to produce and sell more units. For example, at a price of $500 most potential producers cannot cover their costs and will refrain from production. In contrast, at $5,000 more units will be manufactured and brought to market.

The two curves cross at the *market-clearing* price, P_c, and quantity, Q_c. At the market-clearing price, the quantity of PCs demanded is exactly equal to the quantity supplied. Here the market is said to be in *equilibrium.*

There are strong pressures in markets that push prices and quantities toward their equilibrium levels. To see why, assume the market price is above the equilibrium price, such as P_h in figure 3.2. At this higher price, there is a *surplus* of PCs—suppliers produce more PCs than consumers are willing to purchase. This surplus places downward pressure on prices as suppliers compete to try to sell their products. As prices fall, fewer PCs will be produced and more will be demanded, thus reducing the surplus. In contrast if the price is below the market-clearing price, such as P_l in figure 3.2, there is a *shortage* of computers. Here consumers will bid up the price of PCs as they compete for the limited supply. As prices rise, producers will increase their output and consumers will demand fewer PCs, thus reducing the shortage. When the market is in equilibrium there is no pressure on prices and quantities— the quantity demanded exactly equals the quantity supplied. The market is stable at this point.

Supply/demand diagrams like Figure 3.2 are snapshots at a point in time. As time passes, both supply and demand curves are likely to change. Figure 3.3 shows the effects of a shift in demand in the PC market. The first graph pictures a shift in demand to the right. Here there is an increase in demand since at each price consumers demand more PCs. Demand for PCs might increase for a variety of reasons including an increase in the purchasing power of consumers and a decline in the prices of supporting software. These types of changes motivate consumers to purchase more PCs at any given price. At the old equilibrium price there is a shortage of PCs after the demand shift. This shortage motivates an upward pressure on prices which in turn stimulates more production. The end result is a higher equilibrium price and quantity. The second graph shows that the opposite effect occurs when demand shifts to the left. This decrease in demand can also be motivated by a variety of factors (for example, a recession that causes businesses to reduce their purchases of PCs or an increase in personal tax rates that reduces consumers' purchasing power).

Figure 3.4 shows the effects of a shift in supply in the PC market. The first graph displays a shift in supply to the right. A rightward shift implies an increase

FIGURE 3.3   The Effects of a Shift in Demand on the Equilibrium Price and Quantity of PCs.

The initial equilibrium is where the demand curve, labeled D_1, intersects the supply curve, labeled S_1. The first graph shows the effects of an increase in demand. The result is a higher equilibrium price and quantity. The second graph shows the effects of a decrease in demand. The result is a lower equilibrium price and quantity.

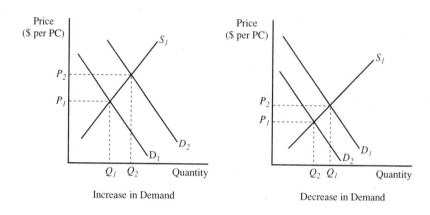

Increase in Demand   Decrease in Demand

FIGURE 3.4   The Effects of a Shift in Supply on the Equilibrium Price and Quantity of PCs.

The initial equilibrium is where the demand curve, labeled D_1, intersects the supply curve, S_1. The first graph shows the effects of an increase in supply. The result is a lower equilibrium price and an increase in equilibrium quantity. The second graph shows the effects of a decrease in supply. The result is a higher equilibrium price and lower equilibrium quantity.

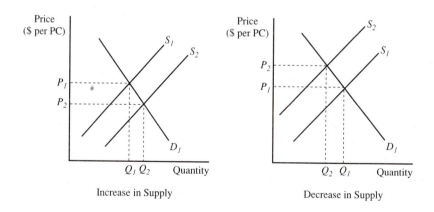

Increase in Supply   Decrease in Supply

in supply since at each price producers supply more PCs. Many factors might motivate an increase in supply. For example, a decline in the prices of labor and other inputs used for manufacturing PCs will make PC production more profitable and increase supply. At the old equilibrium price there is a surplus of PCs after the supply shift. This surplus places downward pressure on prices which in turn stimulates more demand. The end result is a lower equilibrium price and higher equilibrium quantity. The second graph shows the opposite effect occurs when supply shifts to the left.

Shifts in Demand and the Price of Office Space in Texas

During the 1980s there was a dramatic slowdown in energy-related industries. This slowdown reduced business activity in Texas substantially and reduced the demand for office space in major cities such as Houston and Dallas.

Economic theory predicts that a decrease in demand will result in lower prices and quantities. Indeed, this is exactly what happened in Texas. During this period, rental rates for commercial property in Texas cities declined dramatically.

Prices as Social Coordinators

The equilibrium of supply and demand highlights the crucial role that prices play in coordinating the consumption and production decisions of individuals. For example, if too few PCs are being produced prices will be high. High prices signal to would-be producers to shift from producing lower-valued products to producing computers. Because property rights are private, individuals reap the reward from redirecting their efforts and therefore have strong incentives to shift production.

High Prices and Criminal Activity: Computer Chips Become a Big Black-Market Item

The strong incentives that high prices provide to suppliers to bring products to markets can unfortunately be seen in the activities of criminals. Intel 486 chips sold for about $450 to $500 in 1993. These prices motivated increased theft of computer chips. For example, six masked men in September 1993 overwhelmed employees at one of Intel's eight distributors, making off with $739,000 of microprocessors. Many similar robberies have been reported. According to *The Wall Street Journal*, ''Forget drugs. Forget arms. If you want to make a black-market killing these days, steal computer chips. Chips are the dope of the '90's.'' Fortunately, the high prices of computer chips have also motivated legal activity to increase chip supply—other computer companies have developed products to compete with Intel.

Suggested by E. J. Gonzales, ''Chips Become Big Black-Market Item,'' *The Wall Street Journal*, September 16, 1993, p. B1.

If everyone trades in the market place, and all mutually advantageous trades are completed, the price system results in a Pareto-efficient resource allocation—no one can be made better off by changing the allocation without making someone else worse off.[1] No government intervention or central planning is required. Rather consumers and producers, acting in their own self-interest, react to price signals in a manner that produces an efficient resource allocation. Prices act to control and coordinate the many individual decisions made in the economy.

Nobel Prize Winner Ronald Coase and the Power of Free Markets

Externalities exist when the actions of one party affect the utility or production possibilities of another party. Externalities can potentially prevent a free market from being efficient. For example, if the owner of a night club plays loud music at 3:00 A.M. it can adversely affect the welfare of the surrounding neighbors. Since the owner does not directly bear the costs of reducing the neighbors' welfare, he appears to have no incentive to consider these costs, and thus from a societal viewpoint is likely to play the music too loud.

Prior to 1960, most economists thought that externalities would surely prevent a free-market system from producing an efficient allocation of resources. Government intervention seemed to be needed to enhance efficiency. For example, the traditional recommendation would have been to tax the owner of the club for playing loud music at a rate that reflects the costs to the neighbors. Given this tax, the owner takes into account the costs he imposes on his neighbors when he decides whether or not to play loud music.

In 1960, Nobel Prize winner Ronald Coase presented a convincing argument that free-market exchange is much more powerful in producing efficient results than many economists thought. As long as property rights can be traded there will be a tendency to rearrange these rights to enhance economic efficiency. The often recommended government intervention might be unnecessary and in many cases undesirable. For example, assume that the owner of the club has the legal right to play loud music. The neighbors can always offer to pay him not to play the music. Thus, the owner faces a cost for playing music (that is, if he plays the music there is an opportunity cost of not getting compensation from his neighbors). In this case, the owner will play the music only if it is more valuable to him than the costs to his neighbors. This efficient solution is obtained without a music tax.

Coase's argument convinced most economists that externalities were less of a problem than previously thought. Nevertheless, as Coase points out, free-market exchange will not always solve the problem of externalities. The costs of negotiating and enforcing contracts can preclude efficient solutions. For instance, the owner of the club might stop playing music for a payment that is far less than the collective damage imposed on the neighbors from the loud music. Nevertheless, the costs of bargaining with the owner and the costs of reaching agreement on how the neighbors should split the payment can prevent this mutually beneficial agreement from being reached.

---

[1] These conditions will be met in a competitive market when trading costs are sufficiently low. Later, we will discuss factors that can motivate inefficiency in free-market economies.

Free Markets versus Central Planning: The Role of Knowledge

History suggests that the price-system is more efficient at controlling and coordinating production and consumption decisions in large economies than central planning. Without the aid of government planners, free-market economies have produced products that are highly valued by consumers and have avoided large shortages and surpluses. In contrast, in planned economies, such as the former Soviet Union, shortages, surpluses, and other production mistakes are common.

Why has central planning been less successful as an economic system? A primary reason is the price system motivates better use of knowledge and information in economic decisions. The next two sections elaborate on this point.

Spontaneous Creation of Markets: Evidence from Prisoner-of-War Camps

One interesting feature of markets is how they often arise without any conscious thought or human direction. As an example, economist R. A. Radford studied economic activity inside prisoner-of-war camps during World War II. In these camps, prisoners obtained rations from the Red Cross consisting of food, cigarettes, and other items. Of course, not all prisoners valued individual items the same. The English preferred drinking tea to coffee, while French prisoners preferred coffee to tea. Some prisoners smoked heavily, while others did not. Potential gains from trade quickly motivated trading among prisoners. Before long, an organized market developed. Cigarettes became the common currency. Prisoners quoted prices for goods in terms of the number of cigarettes. The price of individual items depended on supply and demand. For example, the price of chocolate would drop dramatically if a new shipment from the Red Cross substantially increased the supply. The markets at the prisoner-of-war camps were very active and emerged without any central planner saying "Let's create a market." The welfare of the prisoners was significantly enhanced by the presence of markets (although they benefitted a lot more when they were set free!).

Suggested by R. A. Radford, 1945, The Economic Organization of a P.O.W. Camp,*"Economica* v. 12.

General and Specific Knowledge

Knowledge can be divided into two broad categories: *general knowledge* and *specific knowledge*.[2] General knowledge is inexpensive to transfer. Examples include prices and quantities—a storekeeper can easily tell you that the price of sugar is $1

---

[2]See M. C. Jensen and W. H. Meckling, "Specific and General Knowledge, and Organizational Structure," *Contract Economics*, L. Werin and H. Wijkander, eds. Basil Blackwell, Oxford, U.K., 1992.

per pound. Specific knowledge is expensive to transfer. The following types of knowledge are often specific in nature:

1. *Idiosyncratic knowledge of particular circumstances.* The employee on the spot is most likely to know if a particular truck has room for additional cargo or if a certain customer wants to purchase a particular product.

2. *Scientific knowledge.* The knowledge of how recombinant DNA works is not easily transferred to others.

3. *Assembled knowledge.* An accountant who has completed a client's tax returns for several years is likely to have assembled important knowledge about the relevant parts of the tax code and the idiosyncrasies of the individual's income and deductions. Another example is learning to operate a complex machine.

Specific knowledge is critical in properly allocating resources. Many economic opportunities are short-lived and must be acted on quickly by the person on the spot (with the specific information of the opportunity) or lost. Not incorporating the proper scientific or assembled knowledge into economic decisions can have costly implications. For an economic system to be successful, it must promote the use of the relevant specific knowledge in economic decisions.

Use of Specific Knowledge at Apple Computer

Apple's PowerBook was the first portable Mac. It had so many bells and whistles that it weighed 17 pounds. It did not do well in the market. In 1990, Apple began completely reworking the design of the computer from the consumer's viewpoint. The entire product-development team of software designers, industrial engineers, marketing people, and industrial designers were sent into the field to observe potential customers using other products. The team discovered that people used laptops on airplanes, in cars, and at home in bed. People did not want just small computers but mobile computers. In response, Apple designed two distinctive features for the PowerBook, the TrackBall pointer and the palm rest in the front of the keyboard. The new product was easy to use and distinctive. Sales improved.

The knowledge of what customers really wanted in a laptop computer was acquired by a team of workers who interacted closely with customers. The team members also had important scientific and assembled knowledge that allowed them to take this new information and use it to design a marketable product. Finally, they had the authority to modify the product based on their findings. It is less likely that this specific knowledge would be incorporated in product design in a large centrally-planned economy— where a central office is in charge of making decisions on literally millions of products.

Suggested by "Hot Products, Smart Design Is the Common Thread," *Business Week*, June 7, 1993, pp. 54–57.

Specific Knowledge and the Economic System

Nobel Prize winner Friedrich Hayek made a convincing argument that free-market economies are more likely to incorporate the relevant specific knowledge in economic decision making than centrally-planned economies.[3] Specific knowledge by definition does not lend itself to statistical aggregation and is costly to transfer. In addition, a central planner does not generally have the mental or computing ability to process large amounts of this type of information. Thus Hayek concluded that central planning will often ignore important specific knowledge in economic decisions.

Nobel Prize Winner F. A. Hayek
on the "Miracle" of the Price System

"It is worth contemplating for a moment a very simple and commonplace instance of the action of the price system to see what precisely it accomplishes. Assume that somewhere in the world a new opportunity for the use of some raw material, say, tin, has arisen, or that one of the sources of supply of tin has been eliminated. It does not matter for our purpose—and it is significant that it does not matter—which of these two causes had made tin more scarce. All that the users of tin need to know is that some of the tin they used to consume is now more profitably employed elsewhere and that, in consequence, they must economize tin. There is no need for the great majority of them even to know where the more urgent need has arisen, or in favor of what other needs they ought to husband the supply. If only some of them know directly of the new demand and switch resources over to it, and if the people who are aware of the new gap thus created in turn fill it from still other sources, the effect will rapidly spread throughout the entire economic system. This influences not only all the uses of tin but also those of its substitutes and the substitutes of these substitutes, the supply of all things made of tin, and their substitutes, and so on. All this takes place without the great majority of those instrumental in bringing about these substitutions knowing anything at all about the original cause of these changes. The whole acts as one market, not because any of its members surveys the whole field, but because their limited individual fields of vision sufficiently overlap so that through many intermediaries the relevant information is communicated to all. The mere fact that there is one price for any commodity—or rather that local prices are connected in a manner determined by the cost of transport, etc.—brings about the solution which (if conceptually possible) might have been arrived at by one single mind possessing all the information which is in fact dispersed among all the people involved in the process."

From F. A. Hayek, 1945, "The Use of Knowledge in Society," *American Economic Review* v. 35.

---

[3]F. A. Hayek, 1945, "The Use of Knowledge in Society," *American Economic Review* v. 35.

In contrast, in a market system economic decisions are decentralized to individuals who are likely to have the relevant specific knowledge. For example, technical and marketing geniuses, like William Gates at Microsoft and Michael Dell at Dell Computer, are free to start new businesses and to market products of their choosing. The information that motivates these decisions does not have to be transferred to some central office in Washington, where centralized production decisions are made.

Private property rights are critical to making a free-market economy work because they provide strong incentives for decentralized decision makers to act on their specific information—the wealth effects of economic decisions are borne directly by the resource owners. For example, if you own a piece of property you have incentives to use the land productively because you get to keep the profits. If another person can make more productive use of the land than you can, the land can be sold. In this manner, property rights will tend to be rearranged so that decision rights over resources are linked with the relevant specific knowledge.

The critical importance of private property rights helps to explain why centrally-planned economies have had difficulty in converting to free-market systems. Allocating property rights to individuals for resources previously controlled by the state is a political nightmare. Any process for partitioning these property rights has big winners and losers and thus will cause huge controversy. Also these economies do not have established legal systems for handling property-right disputes and generally do not have stable governments that give individuals confidence that their property rights will be protected.

Transaction Costs and the Existence of Firms

Hayek's argument pushed to the extreme suggests that all resources should be allocated through market transactions and that firms should not exist. Indeed, at least in theory, firms do not have to exist. All production and exchange could be carried out by market transactions. For example, in the case of the PC, each consumer could buy all the parts that make up the PC in separate market transactions and then pay someone to assemble them. In reality, of course, most computers are made by firms and only the final products are sold to the consumer.

Ronald Coase in his paper, "The Nature of the Firm" (*Economica, 1937*), provides the answer to the question of why resources are allocated both by markets and firms. His basic argument is that economic transactions involve costs. For example, searches have to be made for potential trading partners, prices and contract terms have to be negotiated, etc. The optimal method of organizing a given economic transaction is the one that minimizes these *transaction costs*.[4] In some cases, the method will be market exchange. In other cases, the method will involve firms.

A primary set of costs of using markets for exchange involve the discovery and negotiating of prices. For example, firms have the following potential two advantages:

1. *Fewer transactions.* If there are N customers and M factors of production, a firm can hire the M factors and sell to the N customers. The total transactions are $N + M$. In contrast, if each customer contracts separately with each factor of production there are $N \times M$ transactions. For example, a computer might require ten workers for assembly. If there are 1,000 customers and each customer negotiates with each worker, there are a total of 10,000 transactions. If a firm hires the ten workers and sells computers to the 1,000 customers, there are 1,010 transactions.

2. *Informational specialization.* Think of buying a PC. How much do you know about buying each part separately? PC producers on the other hand are specialized in this knowledge. The consumer buying from a firm only has to be concerned with the quality of the end product.

Government regulation also can have an effect. For example, sometimes firms can produce more cheaply because they avoid taxes at various stages of production compared to market transactions. Later in the book, we discuss other costs of using markets for economic transactions.

The economy, however, is not one big firm. We observe markets playing a major part in resource allocation. The reason is that resource allocation by firms also involve transaction costs. For example, as firms become larger, it becomes increasingly difficult for managers to make efficient and timely decisions. Also, as we will discuss in Chapter 7, as a firm grows decisions must be delegated to nonowners of the firm, and there are costs of motivating these nonowners to work in the interests of the owner.

Individuals involved in trade and production have incentives to implement cost-reducing methods of organization because there are more profits and gains to be shared. For example, at a given price, more profits can be generated if costs are reduced. In competitive markets, individuals will constantly search for new and better ways to reduce these costs to improve their competitive advantage and profits. The end result is that economic activities will be organized within firms when the cost is lower than using markets and vice versa. Also, as we will see, this same process has important implications for the internal design of organizations.

---

[4]It is not always possible to separate transactions costs from the basic costs of production. For example, the optimal method of production can depend on the way the transaction is organized. Therefore it is more precise to say that the optimal method of organization is the one that minimizes total costs (production and transaction costs). The basic arguments, however, are easier to explain if we focus on transaction costs.

Firms vs. Markets When Markets Ruled

Economic theory argues that economic activities are organized in firms when the cost is lower than using markets and vice versa. Today much of the economic activity in the world is conducted within firms. In fact, it is hard to envision a world where large firms do not play an important role in the production and distribution of products. The importance of firms, however, is a relatively recent phenomenon. Indeed, prior to the middle of the 19th century there were almost no large firms. Most production was conducted by small owner-managed operations. The activities of these operations was coordinated almost entirely through market transactions and prices. To quote Alfred Chandler in describing business organization before 1850:

> "The traditional American business was a single-unit business enterprise. In such an enterprise an individual or a small number of owners operated a shop, factory, bank or transportation line out of a single office. Normally this type of firm handled only a single economic function, dealt in a single product line, and operated in one geographic area. Before the rise of the modern firm, the activities of one of these small, personally owned and managed enterprises were coordinated and monitored by market and price mechanisms."

The large firm became feasible only with the development of improved energy sources, transportation, and communications. In particular, coal provided a source of energy that made it possible for the factory to replace artisans and small mill owners, while railroads enabled firms to ship production in large quantities to newly emerging urban centers. The telegraph allowed firms to coordinate activities of workers over larger geographic areas. These developments tended to make it less expensive to coordinate production and distribution using administrative controls, rather than to rely on numerous market transactions among all the intermediaries in the system.

Suggested by A. D. Chandler, *The Visible Hand: The Managerial Revolution in American Business,* Harvard University Press, Cambridge, Massachusetts, 1977.

Managerial Implications

We began this chapter with an overview of how free-market economies operate. An understanding of this topic is critical if managers are to make productive economic decisions. For example, it is important to understand how a shift in either supply or demand affects product prices. In the next three chapters, we extend this analysis and examine in more detail how managers might optimally make input, output, and pricing decisions.

We also discussed the role of knowledge in determining the effectiveness of alternative economic systems and the importance of transaction costs in determining whether or not economic transactions are conducted within markets or organizations. While we have focused our discussion at the economic-system level, these issues are directly relevant to understanding firm-level decisions on organizational architecture. In particular, if firms are to be productive they must be structured in ways that promote the use of the relevant specific knowledge and economize on the costs of organization. Starting in Chapter 7, we extend the concepts introduced in this chapter to questions of organizational design.

Summary

A primary goal of any economic system is to produce efficiently and to produce the combination of outputs that is most preferred by society. The optimal output combination requires value judgments about how to weigh individual preferences. Economists, therefore, focus on a more limited definition of efficiency, *Pareto efficiency*. An allocation is Pareto efficient if there is no alternative that keeps all individuals at least as well off but makes at least one person better off.

An important feature of a free-market economy is the use of *private property rights*. A property right is a socially enforced right to select the uses of an economic good. A property right is private when it is assigned to a specific person. Private property rights are *alienable* in that they can be transferred (sold or gifted) to other individuals.

In free markets, property rights are frequently exchanged. Trade occurs because it is *mutually advantageous*. The buyer values the good more than the seller, and there are *gains from trade*. Trade is an important form of creation. Trading produces value that makes individuals better off. Gains from trade also motivate the movement of resources to more productive users.

Prices coordinate the individual actions in a free-market economy. If too little of a good is being produced, prices will be high and producers have incentives to increase output to exploit the profit opportunity. If too much of a good is being produced, prices will be low and producers will have incentives to cut production. The market is in *equilibrium* when the quantity supplied of a product equals the quantity demanded. There are strong pressures in competitive economies that move the market towards equilibrium. In equilibrium, there are no *shortages* or *surpluses*. Equilibrium prices and quantities change with changes in the supply and demand for products.

Competitive markets will produce a Pareto-efficient allocation of resources if the costs of making mutually advantageous trades are sufficiently low. In theory, any allocation of resources that a free-market economy can produce could also be produced by a centrally-planned economy. Free-market economies, however, have been more successful than centrally-planned economies. One important reason for the relative superiority of free markets is that the price system motivates more effective use of knowledge and information in economic decisions.

General knowledge is inexpensive to transfer, while *specific knowledge* is expensive to transfer. Specific knowledge is very important in economic decisions. Central planning often fails because important specific knowledge is not incorporated in the planning process. In market systems economic decisions are decentralized to individuals with the relevant specific knowledge. Prices convey general knowledge that coordinates the decisions of individuals. Private property rights provide important incentives to individuals to act productively, since they bear the wealth effects of their decisions.

Conceptually, all economic activity could be conducted through market transactions. However, even in free-market economies, much economic activity occurs within firms, where administrative decisions rather than market prices are used to allocate resources. Firms exist because of the *transaction costs* of using markets. The primary costs of using markets involve the discovery and negotiating of prices. Organizing transactions within firms also involve costs. Individuals have incentives to organize transactions in the most efficient manner—to increase the gains from trade. Economic activities will tend to be organized within firms when the cost is lower than using markets and vice versa.

This chapter provides important background information on both markets and organizations. In Chapters 4–6, we extend the analysis of markets and study important managerial decisions such as outputs, inputs, and pricing. In the remainder of the book, we extend the analysis of organizations and cover a variety of important topics about organizational design. A reader interested primarily in organizational design can move directly to Chapter 7 without loss of continuity.

CHAPTER 4 Demand

The Players Theater Company (PTC) is a regional repertory theater in the Midwest. Each year, it produces six plays, ranging from Shakespeare to contemporary musicals. PTC had priced its tickets at $30. On a typical night, about 200 of the theater's 500 seats were filled. The PTC board met on December 20, to discuss a possible price decrease to $25. Advocates of the proposal argued that the decrease in ticket prices would increase the number of tickets sold and the revenue for the theater company.

At the meeting the PTC board engaged in a heated debate over the proposal. It soon became evident that the board did not have enough information to make a sound decision. For instance, nearby restaurants, which serve PTC customers, had indicated that they were planning to make substantial price increases at the first of the year. Would this increase affect the demand for PTC tickets and thus PTC's optimal pricing policy? While customers might buy more tickets at lower prices, would total revenue necessarily increase? Would it be better to attract additional customers by improving the quality of PTC plays or by lowering price? After much discussion, the proposed decrease in price was tabled for further study.

The discussion at the PTC board meeting highlights the fact that managers require a good understanding of product demand to make sound pricing decisions. An understanding of product demand is also important for managerial decisions on advertising, new product developments, and capital investment projects.

In Chapter 3, we presented a brief introduction to supply and demand analysis. In that chapter, we introduced the notion of a demand curve and briefly discussed some of the factors that might cause the demand curve to shift. The purpose of this chapter is to provide a more detailed analysis of demand. The chapter is organized as follows. First, we discuss the concept of demand functions. Second, we examine three important factors that affect the demands for most products: the price of the product, prices of other products, and income. Third, we consider the difference between firm-level and industry-level demand curves. Fourth, we examine the relations among total revenue, marginal revenue, and price elasticities for linear

47

demand curves. Fifth, we consider the demand for specific product attributes. Sixth, we provide a brief discussion of the estimation of demand functions. The technical appendix shows how to calculate point elasticities and derives the equation for marginal revenue for a linear demand curve.

Demand Functions

Managers want to know what factors affect the demands for their products. Only by understanding these factors can managers make sound decisions on pricing, capital expenditures, and other strategic issues. A *demand function* is a mathematical representation of the relations between the quantity demanded of a product and the various factors that influence this quantity. In its most general form, a demand function can be written as:

$$Q = f(X_1, X_2, \ldots X_n), \tag{1}$$

where the X_i's are the factors that affect the demand for the product.

In this chapter, we focus on three factors that are particularly important in determining the demand for most products. These factors include the price of the product, the prices of other products, and the income of individuals. The analysis, however, can easily be extended to include other variables, such as advertising expenditures.

For concreteness, we continue to focus on PTC as an example. We assume that PTC's demand function for tickets on any given night can be expressed by the following linear function:

$$Q = 117.5 - 6.6P + 1.66P_S - 3.3P_R + 6.6I, \tag{2}$$

where P is the price of PTC tickets, P_S is the price of tickets at a nearby symphony hall, P_R is the average price of meals at nearby restaurants, and I is the average per capita income of area residents (in \$000's).[1]

As our initial starting point, we assume PTC tickets are currently priced at \$30, while symphony tickets and meals are priced at \$50 and \$40, respectively. Income is \$50. At these values, PTC is selling 200 tickets per night. We now provide a more in-depth examination of how each of the various factors affect the demand for PTC tickets.

---

[1]Note that this function assumes that PTC can sell fractional tickets. This assumption does not have a material effect on our analysis. However, it allows us to draw continuous demand curves. One way to think of quantity in this example is as the *average* number of tickets sold in an evening. In this case, fractional tickets are possible.

FIGURE 4.1   Demand Curves.

Panel A shows the demand curve for the Players Theater Company (PTC) tickets. By convention, price is placed on the vertical axis, while quantity is placed on the horizontal axis. The equation for PTC's demand curve is P = 60 − .15Q. The curve indicates that, for example, 200 tickets are purchased at $30 and 133 tickets are purchased at $40. Panel B indicates that the demand curve shifts to the right as income increases from $50 to $51—at each price consumers buy more tickets. Movements along a demand curve are motivated by changes in price and are called changes in the quantity demanded. *Movements of the entire demand curve are motivated by other factors, such as changes in income, and are referred to as* changes in demand.

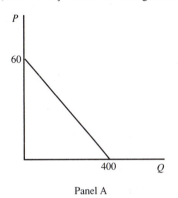

Panel A

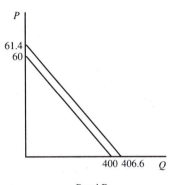

Panel B

Determinants of Demand

Price of the Product

Demand Curves.   A *demand curve* for a product displays how many units will be purchased at each price, over some particular length of time, holding all other factors fixed.[2] For instance, Panel A of Figure 4.1 shows the demand curve for PTC tickets. By convention, price is placed on the vertical axis, while quantity is placed on the horizontal axis. The equation for PTC's demand curve is:

$$P = 60 - .15Q. \tag{3}$$

This equation is obtained by substituting the current values of the other variables into equation (2) and solving for P. The equation indicates that, for example, 200 tickets are purchased at $30 and 133 tickets are purchased at $40.

---

[2]Note for the technically inclined: It is possible to derive an individual's demand curve from the indifference curve/budget line analysis presented in Chapter 2. The price of one good, say food, is varied, holding the price of other goods and money income-fixed. The person's optimal choices are recorded. The individual's demand curve simply plots the optimal choices of the good (in this case food) against the associated prices. Firm-level demand curve, in turn, is the sum of the demands of all individuals at each price.

The demand curve holds other factors fixed. Changes in income and the prices of symphony tickets and restaurant meals will cause shifts in the position of the demand curve (the intercept changes). For instance, Panel B of Figure 4.1 indicates that the demand curve shifts to the right as income increases from $50 to $51—at each price consumers buy 6.6 more tickets. Movements along a demand curve are motivated by changes in price and are called *changes in the quantity demanded.* Movements of the entire demand curve are motivated by other factors, such as changes in income, and are referred to as *changes in demand.*

First Law of Demand.   As we discussed in Chapter 3, as a general rule demand curves slope downward—individuals purchase less (or certainly no more) of a product as the price increases. For instance, PTC's demand curve has a slope of $-.15$. It is conceptually possible that individuals might purchase more of a product as the price rises; however, researchers have been able to identify almost no cases where this behavior is observed (holding other factors constant).[3] The negative slope of demand curves has become known as the *First Law of Demand.* This "law" suggests that managers are safe to assume that the quantity demanded for their products varies inversely with price. For example, PTC board members would be foolish to think that they would sell more tickets if they raised the price.

Learning the First Law of Demand the Hard Way

Mercury One-2-One is a British mobile-phone company. As a promotion to attract new customers, the company offered *free* telephone calls on Christmas to customers who signed on between November 8 and Christmas Eve.

The company "never dreamed its customers would be so generous in spreading the holiday cheer." The promotion generated more than 33,000 hours of calls, jamming the network and prompting hundreds of complaints from people who couldn't get through to place their calls. The volume on Christmas was about 10 times the daily average. Many people placed overseas calls and simply left the phone line open, logging free international calls of up to 12 hours. The average call was about 1 1/2 hours long and the typical caller rang up about $60 in charges—equal to the average *monthly bill* of a cellular company in the United States. The promotion ended up costing the firm millions of dollars. In addition, one member of Parliament has vowed to file a complaint with Britain's Board of Trade. To quote one executive of the company, "There's certainly been insatiable demand."

Suggested by Kyle Pope, "Phone Company's Gift of Gab Jams Its Lines," *The Wall Street Journal,* December 28, 1994, B–1.

---

[3]Products with demand curves with upward slopes are called *Giffen goods.* Try as they might, economists have failed to provide convincing evidence that any Giffen good actually exists. For a review of one prominent attempt, see George J. Stigler, 1947, "Notes on the History of the Giffen Paradox," *Journal of Political Economy* 55, 152–56.

Elasticity of Demand.   Demand curves vary in their sensitivity of quantity demanded to price. In some cases, a small change in price leads to a big change in quantity demanded, while in other cases a big change in price leads to a small change in quantity demanded. Information on this sensitivity is critically important for managerial decision making. For instance, PTC would not want to lower its ticket prices to $25 if it could fill the theater by reducing the price to only $28.

One measure of the responsiveness of quantity demanded to price is the slope of the demand curve. This measure is not very useful, however, because it depends on the particular dimensions in which the economic quantities are quoted. For instance, if the slope of a demand curve is −2 when the quantity is expressed in tons, it can be increased to 4,000 by simply stating the quantity in pounds. Thus, the magnitude of the slope coefficient provides limited insights into the sensitivity of quantity demanded to price. Economists, therefore, have devised a dimensionless measure of this sensitivity known as the *price elasticity* of demand, η. Generally this elasticity is simply referred to as the *elasticity of demand.*

Price elasticity measures the *percentage change in quantity demanded from a one percent change in price*. The elasticity can be approximated between any two points using the concept of *arc elasticity*.[4] The formula for arc elasticity is:

$$\eta = - \,[\Delta Q/(Q_1 + Q_2)/2] \div [\Delta P/(P_1 + P_2)/2], \qquad (4)$$

where Δ represents the change between the two points. Note that the first law of demand indicates that all price elasticities are negative. Convention, however, dictates that we state the elasticity as a positive number. This convention is achieved by placing the negative sign on the first term in equation (4).

Figure 4.2 displays two points on PTC's demand curve for theater tickets. As shown in the figure, the arc elasticity between these two points is 1.4. Thus, a one percent change in price will motivate consumers to change the quantity of tickets purchased by approximately 1.4 percent.

The elasticity of demand tends to be high when there are good substitutes for the product. For instance, the elasticity of demand for PTC tickets is likely to increase with the number of competing events in the city. With many entertainment options, a small increase in the price of PTC tickets might motivate consumers to attend other events. In contrast, when the alternatives are limited, more customers will decide to pay the higher price for PTC tickets, rather than stay at home.

Price elasticities lie between zero and infinity. If the price elasticity is zero, quantity demanded is unaffected by price. In this case, as shown in Figure 4.3, the demand curve is vertical. If the price elasticity is infinite, a small increase in price

---

[4]Price elasticity can be measured at a point on the demand curve. The concept of *point elasticity*, however, requires elementary knowledge of calculus and, more importantly, a smooth mathematical demand curve. While our example assumes such a curve, data on demand is often available for only a few price/quantity combinations. We show how to calculate point elasticities in the Appendix.

FIGURE 4.2   Arc Elasticity.

This figure displays two points on PTC's demand curve for theater tickets. As shown in the figure, the arc elasticity between these two points is 1.4. Thus, a one percent change in price will motivate consumers to change the quantity of tickets purchased by approximately 1.4 percent.

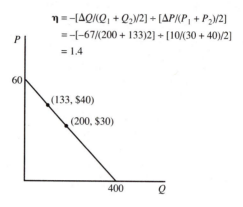

$$\eta = -[\Delta Q/(Q_1 + Q_2)/2] \div [\Delta P/(P_1 + P_2)/2]$$
$$= -[-67/(200 + 133)2] \div [10/(30 + 40)/2]$$
$$= 1.4$$

FIGURE 4.3   Range of Price Elasticities.

Price elasticities lie between zero and infinity. If the price elasticity is zero, quantity demanded is unaffected by price. In this case, as shown in the figure, the demand curve is vertical. If the price elasticity is infinite, a small increase in price will cause the person to purchase none of the product, and the demand curve is a horizontal line.

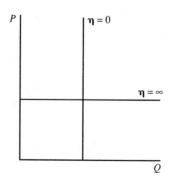

will cause the person to purchase none of the product, and the demand curve is a horizontal line.

Increased Foreign Competition and Demand Elasticities

Price elasticities for products usually increase with available substitutes. In recent years, there has been a dramatic increase in the amount of foreign competition facing many American companies. The result has been an increase in the demand elasticities for many American products. One example is film produced by Eastman Kodak. For years, Kodak had a virtual world-wide monopoly in the production of film. Correspondingly, consumers were relatively insensitive to the price of Kodak film—they had no alternative sources. Currently, Kodak faces intense pressure from the Fuji Corporation from Japan. Competition also comes from producers of ''store-brand'' film, such as the 3-M Corporation in the United States (store-brand film is sold under the store names at large discount drug and grocery stores). As a result, the demand for Kodak film is much more price-elastic. This change in price elasticities has motivated Kodak to change its pricing and product development strategies (it can no longer focus exclusively on selling high-quality film at high prices).

Elasticity often varies along a demand curve. For instance, with a linear demand curve elasticity will be extremely high when the quantities are very low and will approach zero as the quantities become large (try calculating some arc elasticities along PTC's demand curve). We discuss this topic in greater detail below.

Short-Run versus Long-Run Effects of Increases in Gasoline Prices

In the 1960s, gasoline sold for about 25 cents per gallon in the United States. At this price, Americans tended to purchase large automobiles with poor gas mileage. In the early 1970s, Americans experienced a significant gasoline crisis. Not only did the price rise, but for a time there was a shortage of gasoline and people had to wait in line literally for hours to receive gasoline. The increase in gasoline prices and waiting times resulted in a near-term decline in the quantity demanded of gasoline (people carpooled, drove less frequently, etc.). The longer term effect was much greater as companies in response to consumer demand began designing smaller, more fuel-efficient automobiles. Currently, many cars travel at least 20 miles per gallon (and often much more). In the 1960s, many cars travelled fewer than 10 miles per gallon.

Second Law of Demand.   Demand tends to be more elastic or responsive to price changes over the long run than the short run. This tendency is referred to as the

FIGURE 4.4   Price Elasticities and Total Revenue.

How total expenditures on a product change with price depends directly on the price elasticity. This figure shows the relation between price changes, total revenue, and price elasticities.

PRICE CHANGES, TOTAL REVENUE, AND PRICE ELASTICITIES

INELASTIC DEMAND ($\eta < 1$)

⇑P ⇒ ⇑TOTAL REVENUE

⇓P ⇒ ⇓TOTAL REVENUE

UNITARY ELASTICITY ($\eta = 1$)

ΔP ⇒ NO CHANGE IN TOTAL REVENUE

ELASTIC DEMAND ($\eta > 1$)

⇑P ⇒ ⇓TOTAL REVENUE

⇓P ⇒ ⇑TOTAL REVENUE

second law of demand. For instance, an increase in PTC ticket prices is likely to result in an immediate decline in tickets sold. However, the long-run effect will be even larger, as consumers identify other entertainment options or fail to renew season tickets (these effects will cause the demand curve to shift to the left). Similarly, a large increase in the price of heating oil will result in a near-term decline in quantity demanded. Over time, the effect will be larger as consumers better insulate their homes and shift to gas furnaces.

Price Changes and Total Revenue.   How total expenditures on a product change with price depends directly on the price elasticity. In particular, total revenue is calculated by multiplying the quantity purchased times the price (that is, $P*Q$). If price elasticity is one (*unitary elastic*), a one percent change in price results in an offsetting one percent change in quantity and the total revenue stays the same. In contrast, if demand is *inelastic* (value less than one) a one percent increase in price results in less than a one percent decrease in quantity and total revenue increases. A price decrease, on the other hand, results in a decrease in revenue. Finally, if demand is *elastic* (value greater than one) an increase in price results in a decline in revenue, while a decrease in price results in an increase in revenue. These relations are summarized in Figure 4.4. We discuss these relations in greater detail below.

Prices of Other Products

Complements versus Substitutes.   A second factor that affects the demand for a product is the prices of related products. For instance, if the local symphony raises its ticket prices, consumers will be more likely to attend the PTC than the symphony. Thus, there is a positive relation in equation (2) between the demand for PTC tickets and the price of symphony tickets. Goods that compete with each other in this manner are referred to as *substitutes*. In contrast, if the local restaurants raise their prices, the demand for PTC tickets falls (note the negative sign in the demand function). For instance, some potential PTC customers will choose to stay home because the price for an "evening on the town" has increased. Products like theater tickets and meals at restaurants which tend to be consumed together are *complements*. Classic complements are bread and butter. If the price of bread rises, the demand for butter falls.

Cross Elasticities.   One frequently used measure of substitution between two products is the *cross elasticity of demand*. Cross elasticity is defined as the *percentage change in the demand of a good, given a one percent change in the price of some other good*. Cross elasticities between any two goods, X and Y, can be calculated using a formula that is analogous to equation (4):

$$\eta_{xy} = [\Delta Q_x/(Q_{x1}+Q_{x2})/2] \div [\Delta P_y/(P_{y1}+P_{y2})/2]. \tag{5}$$

Unlike price elasticities, which are always positive (when you multiply them by minus one), cross elasticities can be either positive or negative. Substitutes have positive cross elasticities, while complements have negative cross elasticities.

Complementarity between Computer Hardware and Software

Over the past decade there has been a dramatic decrease in the price of personal computing. Not only has the price of PCs decreased, but their quality and computing power have improved significantly as well. This decrease in the price of personal computing has significantly increased the quantity demanded of PCs. In addition, however, it also increased the demand for software products. Today, some of the largest companies in the world (for example, the Microsoft Corporation) specialize in the production of software for PCs. Computer hardware and software are complements and thus have negative cross elasticities.

Whether or not a commodity has strong substitutes or complements depends, in part, on how finely the commodity is defined. For instance, Pepsi and Coke might have relatively large cross elasticities. The cross elasticities between colas, more broadly defined, and other soft drinks are likely to be much smaller.

Cross-elasticities are of fundamental importance because managers frequently want to forecast what will happen to their own sales as other companies change their prices. For example, the PTC board is concerned about the effects that a forthcoming increase in restaurant prices would have on their ticket demand. If meals in local restaurants and theater tickets are strong complements, the increase in restaurant prices will cause a significant decline in the demand for PTC tickets. In this case, the PTC board might want to offset this shift in demand by lowering ticket prices, advertising more heavily, etc. In contrast, if meals and tickets are weak complements, the increase in meal prices will have little effect on ticket demand. In this example, a $10 increase in meal prices will result in 33 fewer ticket sales per night. Using the formula in equation (5), the corresponding cross elasticity between these two points [(200, $40);(167, $50)] is −.81—a one percent increase in meal prices is associated with a .81 percent decline in ticket sales.

Income

Normal versus Inferior Goods. A third factor than can affect the demand for a product is the income of potential buyers. As a person's income increases more products are purchased. Thus, the combined expenditures for all products rise with income. The demand for specific products, however, can either rise or fall as income increases. For example, while the demand for *luxury goods,* such as gourmet foods and jewels, would be expected to increase with income, the demand for other goods, such as processed meat and cabbage, might decline. Goods for which demand increases with income are called *normal goods.* PTC tickets, in our example, are a normal good. Goods for which demand declines with income are called *inferior goods.*

Income Elasticities. The sensitivity of demand to income is measured by the *income elasticity.* The income elasticity is defined as the *percentage change in the demand of a good, given a one percent change in income (I).* Income elasticities can be calculated using the following formula:

$$\eta_I = [\Delta Q/(Q_1+Q_2)/2] \div [\Delta I/(I_1+I_2)/2]. \tag{6}$$

The income elasticity is positive for normal goods and negative for inferior goods.

The income elasticities of a firm's products have important implications. Firms producing products with high income elasticities are subject to cyclical fluctuations. They tend to grow rapidly in expanding economies and contract sharply in depressed economies. Managers must anticipate these fluctuations in managing cash flows and making hiring decisions. In contrast, the demand for products with low income elasticities are more stable over economic cycles. Studies indicate that goods like domestic servants, medical care, education for children, and restaurant meals tend to have relatively large income elasticities, while goods such as most food products, gasoline, oil, and liquor have relatively small (in absolute value) income elasticities.

Other Factors

We have concentrated on three of the most important factors that can affect the demand for a product—the product's own price, prices of other products, and money income. Other factors, such as advertising expenditures, also can be important. In all cases, the analysis is similar. Demand might go up or go down given a movement in some other variable. Sensitivity can be measured by the appropriate elasticity factor—for instance, an advertising elasticity. Obviously, managers do not have the time to consider all conceivable variables that might have small impacts on the demand for their products. Good managerial decision making, however, generally requires managers to understand the effects of the most important factors.

Industry Versus Firm Demand

We have concentrated our analysis on firm-level demand. Demand functions and demand curves, however, can be defined for entire industries. For instance, a demand function could be specified for the entertainment industry in PTC's market area. Such a function would relate the total ticket sales for all entertainment events to factors that affect this demand. Managers are often interested in total industry demand because it provides important information on the size of their potential markets and trends that will affect them. Moreover, estimates of industry demand sometimes can be obtained very inexpensively from outside analysts and business publications.

Firms within an industry compete directly, and their products are likely to be relatively strong substitutes. The overall industry, on the other hand, is less likely to have strong substitutes. For instance, a person wanting to go to an entertainment event might choose among several options based on price. Entertainment events, as a whole, have fewer alternatives. Thus, the demands for individual firms within an industry tend to be more price-elastic than for the entire industry.

Demand Elasticity for Gasoline

The industry-level demand for gasoline is relatively inelastic—the price of gasoline can change substantially and have little effect on the overall quantity demanded. The demand elasticities facing individual gas stations, however, are much larger. For instance, if several gas stations are located at the same intersection, an individual station can lose substantial business to its local competitors by raising its price.

Properties of Linear Demand Curves

The PTC decision on whether or not to lower prices depends on the relation between price and total revenue. We indicated that this relation depends on the price elasticity of demand. We now provide a more in-depth analysis of this relation and discuss PTC's optimal pricing policy. Through this analysis, we illustrate the properties of linear demand curves. Knowing these properties is useful for subsequent analysis in this book.

PTC's total revenue (*TR*) on any given night is equal to the quantity of tickets sold times the price. Price is given by the demand curve in equation (3). Thus, total revenue can be expressed as:

$$TR = P \times Q \tag{7}$$
$$= (60 - .15Q)Q$$
$$= 60Q - .15Q^2.$$

Figure 4.5 graphs PTC's demand and total revenue curves. Note that total revenue increases as price decreases up to the midpoint of the demand curve. Thus, over this range the demand curve is elastic—the percentage decline in price is smaller than the percentage increase in quantity demanded. Past the midpoint, price declines result in reduced total revenue and thus the demand curve is inelastic over this range. The elasticity is unitary at the midpoint.

An important concept in economics is *marginal revenue,* which is defined as *the change in total revenue given a unitary change in quantity.* Intuitively, the marginal revenue for the first unit is price. Thus, the intercepts of the demand and marginal revenue curves are the same. As quantity continues to expand, marginal revenue is below price—to sell an extra unit the price charged for all units must decrease. Marginal revenue is positive up to the midpoint of the demand curve (total revenue is increasing over this interval). At the midpoint, marginal revenue is zero and the demand elasticity is one. Beyond the midpoint, marginal revenue is negative—the increase in revenue from selling another unit is less than the decline in revenue from lowering price. In the appendix, we show that marginal revenue (*MR*) for a linear demand curve is a line with the same intercept as the demand curve, but with twice the negative slope. The equation for PTC's marginal revenue (see Figure 4.5) is:

$$MR = 60 - .3Q. \tag{8}$$

All of PTC's costs are fixed and do not depend on the quantity of tickets sold on a given evening—the actors and utilities have to be paid regardless of how many people are in the audience. Thus, PTC's objective is to maximize its total revenue (for PTC, with costs fixed, maximizing total revenue is the same as maximizing total profit). Figure 4.5 indicates that revenues are maximized at a price of $30. Therefore, under current conditions PTC should not lower its price to $25. The upcoming increase in restaurant prices, however, will change the optimal pricing policy.[5]

---

[5]As a practice exercise, solve for the optimal pricing policy, given the change in meal prices. Assume that the price of a meal increases from $40 to $50. (Hint: the optimal price of PTC tickets declines.)

**FIGURE 4.5   Demand, Total Revenue, and Marginal Revenue for Linear
Demand Curves.**

*This figure graphs PTC's demand and total revenue curves. Total revenue increases as
price decreases up to the midpoint of the demand curve. Thus, over this range the demand
curve is elastic—the percentage decline in price is smaller than the percentage increase in
quantity demanded. Past the midpoint, price declines result in reduced total revenue and
thus the demand curve is inelastic over this range. The elasticity is unitary at the
midpoint. An important concept in economics is* marginal revenue, *which is defined as* the
change in total revenue given a unitary change in quantity. *In the appendix, we show that
marginal revenue (MR) for a linear demand curve is a line with the same intercept as the
demand curve, but with twice the negative slope. The marginal revenue curve for PTC is
pictured in the figure.*

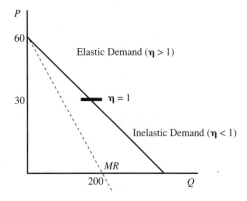

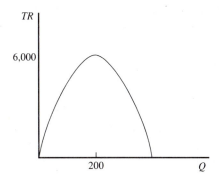

Note that, in contrast to this example, most firms do not want to maximize total
revenue. PTC is a special case in that all its costs are fixed. In most firms, both costs
and revenues increase with output. A profit-maximizing firm must consider both
effects. We discuss this issue in greater detail in Chapters 5 and 6.

Product Attributes

Thus far we have taken the *attributes* of the product as given. For instance, our analysis of the demand for PTC tickets is based on the existing quality and selection of plays, the starting times, the quality of seating, and so on. Given these characteristics, we examined how price and other factors affect the demand for PTC tickets.

Consumer demand, however, also plays an important role in the design of the initial product. For instance, do local consumers prefer Shakespeare or contemporary plays? Do they value comfortable seating or seating that is close to the stage? Can the anticipated decrease in demand from increased restaurant prices be offset by changing the starting time of the plays? For instance, delaying the starting time by one hour might give people more time to eat at home before they go to the play.

Answers to these types of questions play an important role in managerial decision making. Indeed, when managers speak of the importance of understanding consumer demand, they are often referring to understanding the specific product attributes that are important to customers. Marketing managers are responsible for understanding the broad range of product attributes that affect demand. These include price, product design, packaging, promotion and advertising, and distribution channels. This broad focus on demand has played an especially important role in Total Quality Management (TQM) programs that have been adopted by firms throughout the world (see Chapter 17).

An important problem facing most firms is how to incorporate information about such matters as consumer demand, which may be held by many people throughout the firm, into the decision-making process for product design. We defer discussions of this problem until Parts 3 and 4 of the book. These sections provide important insights into how to design the firm's organizational architecture to help assure that the relevant information is incorporated in the decision-making process.

Understanding Consumer Demands at The GAP

Companies spend considerable resources trying to determine the specific preferences of their customers. One industry where the knowledge of consumer preferences is particularly important is the apparel industry. Popular fashions frequently change, and successful firms must be "close to the customer." The importance of knowing customer demands is highlighted by the following statement of the president of The GAP:

"We just keep trying to figure out what people wear on a regular basis. Our business is reading signals from the customer day in and day out."

The GAP's prominence in apparel retailing suggests that this activity can pay off.

Susan Caminti, "The GAP Reading the Customer Right," *Fortune*, December 2, 1991, p. 106.

Demand Estimation

In the PTC example, we specified the demand function. Managers of companies are not so lucky—they must estimate their own demand functions. Sometimes it is easy to estimate demand, at least for the very near term. Other times it is very difficult. Some companies use data and statistical techniques to provide numerical estimates of demand functions. Other companies use a more qualitative approach.

Demand estimation is a complex topic that is largely beyond the scope of this book. Here we simply provide a brief discussion of the three major techniques used in estimating demand: the *interview, direct-market,* and *statistical* approaches. The intent is to provide insights into some of the costs and benefits of each approach. These insights make managers more informed consumers of demand estimates and provide guidance into what type of demand analysis to conduct in a given situation.

Interview Approach

The interview approach attempts to estimate demand through customer surveys and questionnaires. Perhaps the most naive version of this approach is simply to ask consumers what they will purchase under different prices. The answers to this question can be very unreliable. First, people have incentives to lie since they want the firm to have low prices. Second, even if they try to tell the truth, they can have difficulty forecasting what they would actually purchase in the marketplace.

More sophisticated approaches to consumer interviewing are possible. For example, a consumer might be asked about the difference in price between two substitute products. If the consumer has purchased one of the products and does not know the price of the other, the consumer is likely to be relatively insensitive to price.

Sometimes companies use a *simulated market* where people are given play money and asked to simulate purchase decisions. These experiments can yield useful insights. Again, however, the decisions a person makes with play money need not resemble the decisions the person would make with real money.

Consumer surveys play a particularly important role in providing information about what attributes are valued by customers. For example, many businesses ask customers to fill out customer service and complaint forms. Also, businesses often follow up sales or service with telephone calls to customers to ask about product quality and customer satisfaction. Among the most important sources of information about customer preferences are the direct contacts that salespeople and other company representatives have with their customers. All of the interview approaches, however, can produce wildly inaccurate information if the sample is not representative of the population of customers (for instance, if the sample has a disproportionally high number of wealthy individuals.).

Direct-Market Approach

A second approach is to use direct-market tests. For instance, PTC might decrease its price to $25 and see how much demand changes. An advantage of this approach is that the observed reactions are actual purchasing decisions. Companies frequently test market new products in a few ''representative'' cities.

There are at least two limitations to the direct-market approach. First, direct-market experiments can be risky. For instance, customers lost from a price increase might never be regained, even if the price were lowered. Alternatively, it might be difficult to raise prices once a firm had lowered them (customers might be angry and purchase from other companies). Second, direct-market tests are not controlled experiments, and several changes might be occurring at the same time. For instance, PTC might lower its price at the same time as the symphony. The corresponding change in demand would reflect both effects. Many firms, however, are not like PTC in that they operate at multiple locations. For instance, if a firm has the flexibility to vary prices across multiple locations, it has the potential to gain more information than if it is limited to experimenting at one location.

Statistical Approach

Often companies use standard statistical techniques, such as regression analysis, to estimate demand functions. Developments in computers and large data bases (on sales, prices, and other relevant factors) have significantly increased the viability of this approach. By using statistical techniques, the effects of specific factors can often be isolated. Also, it is possible to analyze large samples of actual market data to obtain more reliable results.

While the statistical approach has the potential to provide managers with important information on demand, managers should realize that there are potential problems with this approach. Just because a researcher can produce many pages of computer output with corresponding graphs does not mean that the analysis is well done or not subject to question. Below, we briefly discuss three types of problems that statistical researchers encounter in estimating demand.

Omission of Important Variables. The problem of *omitted variables* can be illustrated by an example.[6] Assume that the true demand function of a company is:

$$\text{Sales} = 120 - 2P + 8A + .04I, \tag{9}$$

where P is the price of the product, A is advertising expenditures, and I is income. Figure 4.6 presents a table with actual data for 1992, 1993, and 1994. While this data is potentially available to the statistician who wants to estimate demand, the statistician does not necessarily know that both advertising and income are important

---

[6]This example is based on an example from William J. Baumol, *Economic Theory and Operations Analysis,* Prentice Hall, Englewood Cliffs, New Jersey, 1977, 234–236.

FIGURE 4.6   An Example of the Omitted Variables Problem.

The true demand curve of the company in this example is: Sales = 120 − P + 8A + .04I. The data for 1992–1994 are presented in the table. While this data is potentially available to the statistician who wants to estimate demand, the statistician does not necessarily know that both advertising and income are important determinants of demand. (The statistician can ignore price since it is constant over the period.) If the statistician omits income and uses statistical techniques to estimate a relation between advertising and sales, she will obtain the following equation: Sales = 140 + 48A. The model seems to predict sales perfectly (based on the data in the table). The equation, however, significantly overstates the true influence of advertising and can lead to serious mistakes in decision making. The omitted-variables problem is present whenever important variables are left out of the analysis that are correlated with the explanatory variables that are included in the analysis.

	Omitted Variables Problem		
	1992	*1993*	*1994*
Income (*I*)	3,000	4,000	3,500
Advertising (*A*)	2	3	2.5
Price (*P*)	10	10	10
Sales (*S*)	236	284	260

True Demand: $S = 120 - 2P + 8A + .04I$
Estimated Demand: $S = 140 + 48A$

determinants of demand. Suppose that the statistician ignores income and uses statistical techniques to estimate a relation between sales and A.[7] The standard technique of regression analysis would yield the following equation:

$$\text{Sales} = 140 + 48A. \tag{10}$$

The model seems to predict sales perfectly (based on the data in the table). The equation, however, significantly overstates the true influence of advertising and can lead to serious mistakes in decision making. For instance, based on this analysis, the company might budget far too much for advertising. The omitted-variables problem is present whenever important variables are left out of the analysis that are correlated with the explanatory variables that are included in the analysis.[8]

Multicollinearity.   If the factors that affect demand are highly correlated (tend to move together), it may be impossible to estimate the individual effects with much precision. For instance, two important variables in the demand function might be

---

[7]Note that the statistician does not have to worry about controlling for price since it was constant over the period ($10).

[8]Note that the problem does not always result in overstated coefficients on the explanatory variables. Depending on the nature of the correlation among the explanatory variables, the coefficients can either be overstated or understated.

FIGURE 4.7   An Example of the Identification Problem.

A firm has collected data on past prices and sales for three years. The demand curve curve has shifted over the three years (due to shifts in income, prices of other goods, etc.). The company has also charged different prices in all three years. Connecting the three price/ quantity points provides a very poor estimate of the current demand curve (labeled D_3 in the graph). The three points are equilibrium *points, given all conditions that affect the demand and price of the product at each point in time. They are not three points along the same demand curve.*

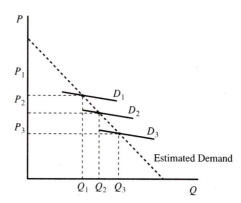

income and education. If high income is almost always associated with high education it can be impossible to separate out the two effects.

Identification Problem.   Another potentially important problem that can confront the statistical researcher is the so-called *identification problem.* This problem can also be illustrated by example. Suppose a firm has collected data on past prices and sales. For instance, in the most recent three years, the following sales and price combinations have been observed: (10, $10), (12, $8), and (14, $6). Is it valid for the researcher to connect these three points as an estimate of the demand curve? Due to the identification problem, the answer is generally no.

The important point is that these data combinations reflect the demand curve and pricing decision of the firm at each point in time. If the demand curve has shifted over the three years, due to changes in factors such as income or advertising, the points come from three different demand curves. Thus, connecting the points does not provide an estimate of the current demand curve. For illustration, assume in our analysis that the demand curve has shifted in each year and that the firm has also changed its prices. As shown in Figure 4.7, the resulting combinations of price and quantity are observed *equilibrium* points, given the conditions during the relevant time period. Connecting these points provides a poor estimate of the current demand curve, $D_3.$

Sometimes the analyst does not have enough information to solve the identification problem and is better off using consumer surveys or market experiments to estimate demand. Other times, the statistician has enough information to identify the demand function (for example, by using specialized statistical methods). One special case, in which the researcher does not have to worry about the identification problem is when the *demand curve is stable*. For instance, suppose the demand curve did not shift over the three years and all the sales/price combinations were motivated by changes in the pricing policy of the firm. In this case, a reasonable estimate of the demand curve can be obtained from the observed sales/price combinations.

Implications

We have discussed some of the difficulties that companies face in trying to estimate the demand for their products. These problems can be difficult to solve. Nevertheless, estimates of demand play a critical role in decision making, especially the pricing decision. Successful managers address these problems the best that they can, given imperfect knowledge and limited resources.

Difficulties in Estimating the Demand Curves for Common Stock

There has been a long-running debate over the demand elasticities of common stocks of individual firms. Many economists argue that these demand curves are perfectly elastic, since there are numerous stocks with similar risk-return characteristics available in the market. In this case, the demand curves for individual stocks are horizontal. Other people argue, however, that each stock is unique and has very few substitutes. Here, the individual demand curves would be downward sloping.

Managers care about the slopes of the demand curves for their common stock, since these slopes affect the price at which they can sell new securities. If demand curves slope downward, price must be decreased below the current market price to sell new securities. If demand curves are horizontal, new securities can be issued at the current market price. Managers, of course, want to sell new stock at the highest possible price.

The existing empirical evidence suggests that stock prices decline by about three percent when firms announce new issues of common stock. This finding seems to suggest that the demand curves for common stocks are downward sloping. This finding, however, is subject to alternative interpretations. In particular, if the stock-market thinks that firms tend to issue new stock when they are in financial trouble, an announcement of a new issue will cause the entire demand curve to shift to the left and price will decline (since the market infers new information that the firm is in distress). Hence, the observation that prices decline when new stock is issued is not sufficient to allow us to identify the price elasticity of a firm's common stock—the price decrease might be due to either a shift in demand or a shift in quantity demanded.

This example illustrates that it is not always easy to estimate demand curves, even when prices and quantities are readily available. Indeed, the data on prices and volumes for publicly-traded securities are among the best available in the world.

Summary

An understanding of product demand is critical for many managerial decisions, such as pricing, capital investment, and advertising. This chapter provides a basic economic analysis of demand.

A *demand function* is a mathematical representation of the relations between the quantity demanded of a product and the various factors that influence this quantity. We focus on three factors that are particularly important in determining the demand for most products. These factors include the price of the product, the prices of other products, and the money income of individuals.

A *demand curve* for a product displays how many units will be purchased at each price, over some particular length of time, holding all other factors fixed. Movements along a demand curve are motivated by changes in price and are called *changes in the quantity demanded*. Movements of the entire demand curve are motivated by other factors, such as changes in income, and are referred to as *changes in demand*.

Normally, demand curves slope down—quantity demanded varies inversely with price. This relation is often referred to as the *First Law of Demand*. Demand curves vary in their sensitivity of quantity demanded to price. *Price elasticity* is defined as the percentage change in quantity demanded from a one percent change in price. The price elasticity tends to be high when there are good substitutes for the product. Demand tends to be more elastic over the long run than the short run. This tendency is referred to as the *second law of demand*. How total revenue from a product changes with price depends directly on the price elasticity. A price increase results in an increase in expenditures when demand is *inelastic* and a decrease in expenditures when demand is *elastic*. Total expenditures remain unchanged when demand is *unitary*.

A second factor that affects the demand for a product is the price of related products. Goods that compete with each other are referred to as *substitutes*. Products which tend to be consumed together are *complements*. One frequently used measure of substitution between two products is the *cross elasticity of demand*. The cross elasticity is positive for substitutes and negative for complements.

A third factor that can affect the demand for a product is the money income of potential buyers. The sensitivity of demand to income is measured by the *income elasticity*. The income elasticity is positive for *normal goods,* and negative for *inferior goods.*

Demand curves can be defined for individual firms or entire industries. The price elasticities for individual firms within an industry are generally higher than for the industry as a whole.

An important concept in economics is *marginal revenue,* which is defined as *the change in total revenue given a unitary change in quantity.* Marginal revenue for a linear demand curve is given by the line with the same intercept as the demand curve, but with twice the negative slope. Total revenue increases with quantity when marginal revenue is positive, and decreases with quantity when marginal revenue is negative.

The standard economic analysis of demand takes the *attributes* of the product as given. Information about consumer demand, however, is also important in the initial design of products. Parts 3 and 4 of this book provide important insights into how to design the firm's organizational architecture to help assure that this type of information is incorporated in the decision making process.

There are three basic approaches that managers use to estimate demand: the *interview approach,* the *direct-market approach,* and the *statistical approach.* All three approaches can suffer from significant problems. Nevertheless, managers have to do the best that they can given imperfect information and limited resources. Knowledge of the potential pitfalls makes managers more intelligent users of demand estimates.

TECHNICAL APPENDIX[1]

In the chapter, we presented formulas for arc elasticities (that estimate elasticities between two points on the demand curve). This appendix shows how to calculate elasticities at single points on the demand curve. It also derives the equation for marginal revenue for a linear demand curve.

Point Elasticities

Elasticities measure the percentage change in quantity demanded for a percentage change in some other variable. There are several ways to express the formula for an elasticity. One way, using price elasticity as an example, is:

$$\eta = -(\Delta Q/Q)/(\Delta P/P) = -(\Delta Q/\Delta P) \times (P/Q). \qquad (A1)$$

By definition, as the change in P goes to zero, the limit of the first term, $(\Delta Q/\Delta P)$, is the partial derivative of Q with respect to P. Thus, at a particular point on the demand curve the elasticity of demand for small changes in P is given by:

$$\eta = -(dQ/dP) \times (P/Q). \qquad (A2)$$

As an example consider the demand function for PTC theater tickets:

$$Q = 117.5 - 6.6P + 1.66P_S - 3.3P_R + 6.6I. \qquad (A3)$$

The point elasticity at the current price/quantity combination of $30 and 200 tickets is:

$$\eta = -(-6.6) \times (\$30/200) = 1. \qquad (A4)$$

Recall that this is the value that we derived graphically in the text.

Other point elasticities, for example point cross elasticities, can be calculated in a similar fashion—simply substitute the appropriate variable (for example, the price of another product) for P in equation A2.

---

[1]This appendix requires elementary knowledge of calculus.

Marginal Revenue for Linear Demand Curves

Marginal revenue (*MR*) is the change in total revenue for an additional unit of quantity. As the change in quantity becomes very small the limit of this definition is the partial derivative of total revenue with respect to Q.

Linear demand curves take the following form:

$$P = a - bQ. \tag{A5}$$

Thus, total revenue, $P \times Q$ can be written:

$$TR = (a - bQ) \times Q \tag{A6}$$
$$= aQ - bQ^2.$$

Marginal revenue is:

$$MR = dTR/dQ = a - 2bQ. \tag{A7}$$

This formula is a line that has the same intercept as the demand curve, but with twice the negative slope.

CHAPTER 5 Production and Cost

In 1994, domestic steel prices increased as the U. S. economy recovered from a recession.[1] Indeed, the steel market was the strongest it had been in 20 years. After significant price increases earlier in the year, domestic steel companies were planning to increase sheet-steel prices by another 10 percent at year end. In the tight electro-galvanized markets, price increases as high as 20 percent were expected. United States automobile manufacturers were among the companies most affected by these price increases, since they are major users of domestic steel.

To counter the effects of the increase in domestic steel prices, U. S. auto companies began seeking new overseas suppliers. For instance, in July of 1994 General Motors invited foreign bids for sheet steel from foreign companies, such as Sidmar, Solldac, Thyssen, and Klockner. The increases in steel prices also placed pressure on U. S. automakers to use other raw materials in the production process. For example, auto companies were expected to increase their use of aluminum in engines, transmissions, body components, heating and cooling systems, and suspension systems in 1995.[2] Some of these applications were expected to replace cast iron or steel with aluminum. In addition, auto companies increased their research on new ways to use plastics, magnesium, and recyclable materials in the production process. The increases in steel prices were also expected to affect the companies' pricing and output decisions.

This example raises a number of questions that are of interest to managers. First, how do firms choose among substitutable inputs in the production process? How does the optimal input mix change with changes in the input prices? How do changes in input prices affect the ultimate cost of production and the output choices

---

[1]See "General Motors Eyes Imports to Counter Price Increases," *Metal Bulletin,* July 11, 1994, p. 21.
[2]See Al Wrigley, "Automotive Aluminum Use Climbing in 1995's Models: Automotive Applications Will Use Some 120 Million lbs. in 1995," *American Metal Market,* August 9, 1994, p. 1.

of firms? This chapter addresses these and related questions. We begin by a brief discussion of what managers attempt to accomplish (their underlying objective function). Other major topics in sequence include production functions, optimal input choice, costs, profit maximization, cost estimation, and factor demand curves. A technical appendix derives the factor-balance equation.

Managerial Objectives

A firm's profit (II) is the difference between its total revenues (*TR*) and total costs (*TC*):

$$\text{II} = TR - TC. \tag{1}$$

For instance, if a company has sales of $1,000,000 and costs of $750,000 it earns a profit of $250,000.

In this chapter, we assume that managers strive to maximize single-period firm profits. Thus, managers make input, output, and pricing decisions with profit maximization as their sole objective. This perspective is a reasonable starting point because if firms fail to make profits over time they will cease to exist.[3] Thus, most managers are under constant pressure to make profits. As we discuss in subsequent chapters, however, conflicts can arise between managerial self-interest and profit maximization. These chapters also discuss how these conflicts are reduced through mechanisms such as incentive compensation. These mechanisms help to make profit maximization a reasonable first approximation of the managers' objective function.

CEO Turnover and Firm Profits

A standard assumption in microeconomics is that managers strive to maximize profits. One reason why managers are likely to be concerned about profits is that poor profits and stock-price performance increase the likelihood that they will be fired. For instance, studies have found that firms in the worst decile of performers were about 1.5 times as likely to have a management change as firms in the best decile of performers.

Suggested by Jerold B. Warner, Ross L. Watts, and Karen H. Wruck, 1988, "Stock Prices and Top Management Changes," *Journal of Financial Economics* 20, 461–492 and Michael S. Weisbach, 1988, "Outside Directors and CEO Turnover," *Journal of Financial Economics* 20, 431–460.

Chapter 4 examined the revenue component of the profit equation. This chapter analyzes costs. Costs depend on the production technology available to the firm and the prices charged for inputs into the production process. We begin by discussing production technology.

---

[3]Finance courses extend the single-period analysis to multiple periods, where the objective is to maximize the *present value* of all expected future profits.

Production Functions

Definition

A *production function* is a descriptive statement that relates inputs to outputs. It specifies the *maximum* possible output that can be produced for a given amount of inputs. Production functions are determined by the available technology. Production functions can be expressed mathematically. For instance, given existing technology an automobile supplier is able to transform inputs like steel, aluminum, plastics, and labor into finished auto parts. In its most general form, the production function is expressed as:

$$Q = f(x_1, x_2, \ldots .x_n), \qquad (2)$$

where Q is the quantity produced and $x_1, x_2, \ldots .x_n$ are the various inputs used in the production process.

To simplify the exposition, suppose that the auto part in this example is produced from just two inputs, steel and aluminum. A specific example of a production function in this context is:

$$Q = S^{1/2} A^{1/2}, \qquad (3)$$

where S is pounds of steel, A is pounds of aluminum, and Q is the number of auto parts produced. With this production function, 100 pounds of steel and 100 pounds of aluminum will produce 100 auto parts over the relevant time period; 400 pounds of steel and 100 pounds of aluminum will produce 200 auto parts, etc.[4]

Returns to Scale

Returns to scale refers to the relation between output and the variation of *all inputs* taken together. With *constant returns to scale* a one percent change in all inputs results in a one percent change in output. For example, equation (3) presents a production function with constant returns to scale. If the firm uses 100 pounds of each input it produces 100 auto parts. If the firm increases both inputs by one percent to 101 pounds it produces 101 auto parts.[5] With *increasing returns to scale* a one percent change in all inputs results in a greater than one percent change in output. An example of such a production function is:

$$Q = SA. \qquad (4)$$

Here, 100 pounds of steel and 100 pounds of aluminum produce 10,000 auto parts, while 101 pounds of steel and aluminum produce 10,201 auto parts (a two percent

---

[4]Note: $100^{1/2} \times 100^{1/2} = 10 \times 10 = 100$, and $400^{1/2} \times 100^{1/2} = 20 \times 10 = 200$.
[5]Note: $101 = [(100 \times 1.01)^{1/2}] \times [(100 \times 1.01)^{1/2}]$.

FIGURE 5.1   Returns to a Factor.

This table shows the total, marginal, and average products of S for the production function, Q = $S^{1/2} A^{1/2}$. Input A is held fixed at 9 units. The total product of S is the total output for each level of S; the marginal product of S is the incremental output from one additional unit of S; the average product of S is total output divided by the total units of S.

Units of S	Total Product of S	Marginal Product of S	Average Product of S
1	3.00	3.00	3.00
2	4.24	1.24	2.12
3	5.20	.96	1.73
4	6.00	.80	1.50
5	6.70	.70	1.34

increase in output). With *decreasing returns to scale,* a one percent change in all inputs results in a less than one percent change in output. An example is:

$$Q = S^{1/3} A^{1/3}. \tag{5}$$

In all our examples, the returns to scale are the same over all ranges of output. For instance, equation (3) always displays constant returns to scale, while equation (5) always displays decreasing returns. It is possible to have production functions that vary in returns to scale over the range of output. For instance, such a production function might have increasing returns to scale when output is relatively small, followed by constant returns to scale as output continues to increase, and finally decreasing returns to scale when output is high. Other combinations are possible.

Returns to a Factor

Returns to a factor refers to the relation between output and the variation in only one input, *holding other inputs fixed.* Returns to a factor can be expressed as total, marginal, or average quantities. The *total product* of an input is the schedule of output obtained as that input increases, holding other inputs fixed. The *marginal product* of an input is the change in total output associated with a one-unit change in the input, holding other inputs fixed. Finally, the *average product* is the total product divided by the number of units of the input employed.

To illustrate these concepts, consider the production function: $Q = S^{1/2} A^{1/2}$. Figure 5.1 presents the total, marginal, and average product of S, holding A fixed at 9.[6] For this particular production function, total product increases as S increases. Marginal product, however, is declining. This means that while total product increases with S, it does so at a decreasing rate. Average product is also decreasing over the entire range.

---

[6]Note that this production function assumes that production does not have to take place in discrete units. For instance, output might be expressed in tons, where production in fractions of a ton is possible.

More generally, marginal and average products do not have to decline over the entire range of output. Indeed, many production functions display increasing marginal and average products over some ranges. In actuality, however, most production functions reach a point after which the marginal product of an input declines. This observation is often called the *law of diminishing returns,* which states that the marginal product of a variable factor will eventually decline as the input is increased. To illustrate this principle, consider the classic example of farming a piece of land. Land is fixed at one acre and no output can be produced without any workers. If 10 units of output can be obtained by hiring one worker the marginal product of the first unit of labor is 10. The change in output might be even greater as the firm moves from one to two workers. For instance, two workers might be able to produce 25 units of output by working together and specializing in various tasks. The marginal product of labor is 15 and thus, over this range, marginal product is increasing. Eventually, as the firm continues to add more workers (holding the amount of land fixed) output will grow at a slower rate. Indeed, at some point total output might actually decline with additional workers because of coordination or congestion problems. In this case, marginal product is negative.

Food Intake and Productivity: An Example of Diminishing Returns

Economist John Strauss analyzed data from a survey of farmers from a small West African country, Sierra Leone. Through this analysis, he was able to estimate the relation between an individual's agricultural output and daily caloric intake. Between zero and 5,200 calories per day, he found a positive association between output and caloric intake. The relation, however, was subject to diminishing marginal returns. For instance, for workers consuming about 1,500 calories per day, a one percent increase in caloric consumption increased agricultural output by about .5 percent. This impact of caloric consumption on output, however, declined steadily with increases in caloric consumption. For instance, for workers consuming 4,500 calories per day, a one percent increase in calories increased output by only .12 percent. Beyond 5,200 calories per day, the estimated relation was negative—additional caloric intake *reduced output.* Apparently, beyond that point the marginal product of food intake was negative.

Suggested by John Strauss, 1986, "Does Better Nutrition Raise Productivity?" *Journal of Political Economy* 94, 297–320.

Optimal Input Choice

Production Isoquants

Most production functions allow some substitution of inputs. For example, suppose that a firm with the production function $Q = S^{1/2} A^{1/2}$ wants to produce 100 auto parts.

FIGURE 5.2   Isoquants.

An isoquant shows all possible ways to produce the same quantity. There is a different isoquant for each possible level of production. This figure shows the isoquants for 100, 200, and 300 auto parts for the production function: $Q = S^{1/2} A^{1/2}$.

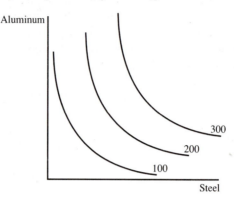

In this case, there are many different combinations of S and A that will produce the 100 auto parts. For instance, 100 auto parts can be produced using 100 pounds of steel and 100 pounds of aluminum, 25 pounds of steel and 400 pounds of aluminum, or 400 pounds of steel and 25 pounds of aluminum. Figure 5.2 graphs all the possible combinations of inputs that can be used to produce exactly 100 auto parts (assuming efficient production). This curve is called an *isoquant* (the term is derived from the term *iso,* meaning the same, and *quant* from quantity). An isoquant shows all possible ways to produce the same quantity. There is a different isoquant for each possible level of production. Figure 5.2 shows the isoquants for 100, 200, and 300 auto parts.

Production functions vary in terms of how easily inputs can be substituted for one another. In some cases, no substitution is possible. For instance, suppose that in order to produce 100 auto parts you must have 100 pounds of aluminum and 100 pounds of steel, to produce 200 auto parts you must have 200 pounds of aluminum and 200 pounds of steel, etc. Having extra steel or aluminum without the other metal does not increase output—steel and aluminum are *perfect complements.* As shown in Figure 5.3, isoquants in the case of perfect complementarity take the shape of right angles. At the other extreme are *perfect substitutes,* where the inputs can be freely substituted for one another. For instance, suppose that one auto part can always be produced using either a pound of steel or a pound of aluminum. In this case, the firm can produce 100 auto parts by using 100 pounds of aluminum, or 100 pounds of steel, or any combination in between. As shown in Figure 5.3, the corresponding isoquant is a straight line. Most production systems have isoquants that are between the two extremes. As depicted in Figure 5.3, these isoquants have curvature, but are not right angles. The degree of substitutability of the inputs is

FIGURE 5.3   Isoquants for Perfect Complements, Perfect Substitutes, and the "Normal Case."

Production functions vary in terms of how easily inputs can be substituted for one another. In some cases, inputs are perfect complements and no substitution is possible. Here, isoquants take the shape of right angles. At the other extreme are perfect substitutes, where the inputs can be freely substituted for one another. Here, isoquants are straight lines. Most production functions have isoquants that are between the two extremes. These isoquants have curvature, but are not right angles.

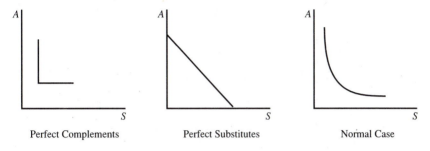

Perfect Complements   Perfect Substitutes   Normal Case

determined by the curvature—the closer the isoquant is to a right angle (the more convex) the lower the substitutability.

Generally, it is assumed that isoquants are convex to the origin (as pictured in the last example in Figure 5.3). Convexity implies that the substitutability of inputs depends on the relative amounts of the two inputs being used. In our example, if the firm is using a large quantity of steel and little aluminum, it must substitute a relatively large quantity of steel for a small quantity of aluminum in order to keep output the same (see Figure 5.2). For instance, aluminum might be much better suited than steel to construct some components of the auto part. As the firm uses more aluminum relative to steel, the ability to substitute aluminum for steel declines. Most "real-world" production functions display this property.

Substitution of Inputs in Home Building

House builders in the Pacific Northwest use large quantities of wood in the construction of residential houses. For instance, wood is used for frames, siding, floors, roofs, etc. Homebuilders in the Southwest (for example, Arizona) use much more stucco and tile in home construction. An important reason for this difference is that, in contrast to the Pacific Northwest, the Southwest does not have large nearby forests. This example suggests that homebuilders are able to substitute among inputs in building a home. Homebuilders in the Southwest, however, still use wood to frame the house—the substitution of wood for other inputs is not complete.

FIGURE 5.4   Isocost Curves.

Isocost lines *depict all combinations of inputs that cost the same amount. In this example,*
$P_S = \$.50/lb.$ *and* $P_A = \$1/lb.$ *The figure shows isocost lines for $100 and $200 of*
expenditures. The slope of an isocost line is minus one times the ratio of the input prices—
in this example, $-.5.$ *Isocost lines for different expenditure levels are parallel.*

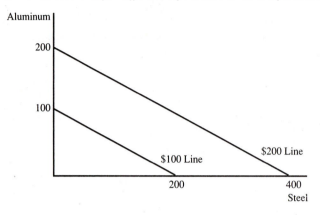

Isocost Lines

Given that there are many ways to produce a given level of output, how does a firm
choose its input mix? The answer depends on the costs of the inputs. Suppose that
the firm faces competitive input markets and can buy as much of any input as it
wants at the going market price. The price of steel is denoted P_S, while the price of
aluminum is denoted P_A. Total expenditures (E) are equal to the sum of the quantities
of each input used in the production process times their respective prices. Thus,

$$E = P_S S + P_A A. \tag{6}$$

Isocost lines depict all combinations of S and A that cost the same amount. For
instance, assume $P_S = \$.50/lb.$ and $P_A = \$1/lb.$ and the constant expenditure level
is $100. In this case,

$$\$100 = \$.5S + \$A, \tag{7}$$

or equivalently,

$$A = 100 - .5S. \tag{8}$$

Figure 5.4 graphs this isocost line. Note that the intercept, 100, indicates how many
pounds of A could be purchased if the entire $100 is spent on A. The slope of $-.5$
is minus one times the ratio of the two prices (P_S/P_A)—since aluminum is twice as
expensive as steel, .5 units of A can be given up for one unit of S and the expenditures
remain the same.

Holding the prices of the inputs constant, isocost lines for different expenditure levels are parallel. Figure 5.4 illustrates this property for the isocost lines for $100 and $200. Note that the further away the line is from the origin the higher is the total expenditure. Holding output constant, the firm would like to be on the lowest possible isocost line. The slope of an isocost line changes with changes in the ratio of the input prices. As depicted in Figure 5.5, if the price of steel increases to $1, the line becomes steeper (slope of −1). Here, the firm must give up one pound of *A* to obtain one pound of *S*. Alternatively, if the price of steel falls to $.25, the line becomes flatter (slope of −.25). In this case, the firm only has to give up one-quarter pound of aluminum for every pound of steel. Similarly, the slope of the line changes with changes in the price of aluminum. What determines the slope of the line are the *relative prices* (recall, the slope is $-P_S/P_A$).

Cost Minimization

For any given level of output, Q^*, managers will want to choose the input mix that minimizes the costs. As shown in Figure 5.6, the optimal mix (S^*, A^*), occurs at the point of tangency between the isoquant for Q^* and an isocost line. The managers would like to produce the output less expensively (on an isocost curve closer to the origin). However, lower-cost production is not possible. The firm could select other input mixes to produce Q^*. As shown in Figure 5.6, however, any other input mix (such as S', A') would place the firm on a higher isocost line.

In the appendix, we show that at the optimal input mix the following condition holds:

$$MP_S/P_S = MP_A/P_A, \qquad (9)$$

where MP_i = the marginal product of input i. (Recall that the marginal product of an input is described in Figure 5.1.) Condition (9) has a straight-forward interpretation. The marginal-product-to-price ratio indicates how much additional output can be obtained by spending an extra dollar on the input. At the optimal output mix this quantity must be the same for all inputs. Otherwise, it would be possible to increase output without increasing expenditures by reducing the use of inputs with low ratios and increasing the use of inputs with high ratios. For instance, if the ratio is 10 units per dollar for aluminum and 20 units per dollar for steel, the firm could increase output by 10 units by spending one less dollar on aluminum and one more dollar on steel. Expenditures would remain constant. The firm is not at an optimal input mix when this type of substitution is possible.

Changes in Input Prices

An increase in the relative price of an input will motivate the firm to use less of that input and more of other inputs. Figure 5.7 shows how the optimal input mix for producing Q^* changes in our example as the price of steel increases—the firm uses less steel and more aluminum to produce the output. This effect is called the *substitution effect*. The strength of the substitution effect depends on the curvature of

FIGURE 5.5   Isocost Lines and Changes in Input Prices.

This figure shows the effect of changes in input prices on the slopes of isocost lines. The solid line shows the isocost line when the price of aluminum is $1 and the price of steel is $.50. The dotted line shows the isocost line when the prices of both inputs are $1. Total expenditures in each case are $100.

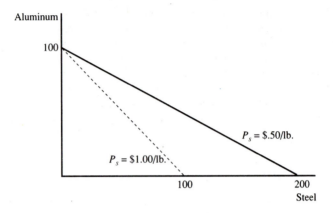

FIGURE 5.6   Cost Minimization.

The input mix that minimizes the costs of producing any given output, Q*, occurs where an isocost line is tangent to the relevant isoquant. In this example, the tangency occurs at (S*, A*). The firm would prefer to be on an isocost line closer to the origin. However, the firm would not have sufficient resources to produce Q*. The firm could produce Q* using other input mixes, such as (S', A'). However, the costs of production would increase.

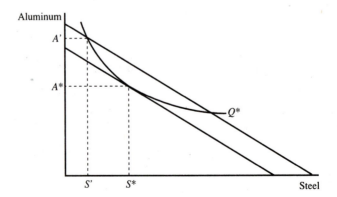

FIGURE 5.7   Optimal Input Mix and Changes in Input Prices.

This figure shows how the optimal input mix for producing a given output, Q*, changes as the price of an input increases. In this example, the price of steel increases and the firm uses less steel and more aluminum to produce the output. This effect is called the substitution effect. *The strength of the substitution effect depends on the curvature of the isoquant. The greater the curvature, the higher the complementarity between the inputs and the less the firm will substitute between the two inputs.*

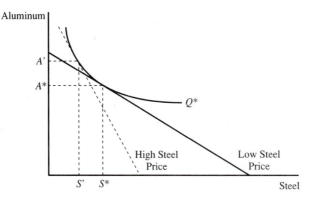

the isoquant. The greater the curvature, the higher the complementarity between the inputs and the less the firm will substitute between the two inputs for any given change in prices. The substitution effect helps to explain the reactions of automobile companies to increases in domestic steel prices during 1994. These companies increased their use of foreign steel. They also searched for new ways to replace steel with other inputs such as aluminum.

Minimum Wage Laws

In 1994, the minimum wage that an employer could pay a worker in the United States was $4.25/hour. Since he first took office in 1992, President Clinton advocated an increase in this minimum wage. He argued that $4.25/hour was too low and that the poor would be substantially better off by increasing the wage. The analysis in this chapter indicates why many economists and politicians were skeptical about this claim. While it is true that the increase in minimum wage would make some workers better off by increasing their wages, other workers would be made worse off. In particular, the increase in the wage rate is likely to motivate firms to move away from low-skilled workers toward more automation. Thus, the number of workers hired at the minimum wage is likely to decline with an increase in the wage. Those obtaining jobs are better off; workers who want a job but can't find one are worse off.

Cost

We have analyzed how firms should choose their input mix to minimize the costs of production. We now extend this analysis to focus more specifically on the costs of producing different levels of output. Analysis of these costs plays an important role in output and pricing decisions. Topics of discussion include cost curves, opportunity costs, fixed versus variable costs, the short run versus the long run, short-run cost curves, long-run cost curves, and the minimum efficient scale.

Cost Curves

The *total cost curve* depicts the relation between total costs and output. Conceptually, the total cost curve can be derived from the isoquant/isocost analysis discussed above. For each possible level of output, there is a lowest cost method of production, as depicted by the tangency between the isoquant and the isocost line. The total cost curve simply graphs the cost of production associated with the isocost line and the corresponding output. For instance, if the lowest cost method of producing 100 auto parts is $1,000, one point on the total cost curve is (100, $1000). If the lowest cost method of producing 200 parts is $1,500, another point is (200, $1,500), etc. *Marginal cost* is the change in total costs associated with a one unit change in output. *Average cost* is total cost divided by total output.

Figure 5.8 illustrates the total, marginal, and average cost curves for a hypothetical firm.[7] Total costs increase with output. Between zero and Q_1, total costs increase but at a decreasing rate (the curve is concave). Over this range, marginal costs are decreasing.[8] Past Q_1, total costs are increasing at an increasing rate (the curve is convex) and marginal costs are increasing. Average costs are declining when marginal cost is below average cost and are rising when marginal cost is above average cost. This relation is a general rule. To see why, suppose that the average cost is $10 and marginal cost is $9. Since the cost of producing one more unit is below $10, the average cost must fall as the extra unit is produced. Alternatively, if average costs are $10 and marginal costs are $11, average costs must rise with additional production. Marginal costs and average costs are equal at the minimum point of the average cost curve.

Opportunity Costs

Managers must be careful to use the correct set of input prices in constructing cost curves. In Chapter 2, we defined *opportunity cost* as the value of a resource in its

---

[7]This figure illustrates a common pattern for cost curves. All firms do not have cost curves with the same shapes.

[8]Note for the technically inclined: The marginal cost at a point is equal to the slope of the total cost curve at that point ($MC = \partial TC/\partial Q$). Thus, marginal costs are decreasing when the total cost curve is concave and increasing when it is convex.

FIGURE 5.8   Cost Curves.

This figure illustrates the total, marginal, and average cost curves of a hypothetical firm. Total costs increase with output. Between zero and Q_1, total costs increase but at a decreasing rate (the curve is concave). Over this range, marginal costs are decreasing. Past Q_1, total costs are increasing at an increasing rate (the curve is convex) and marginal costs are increasing. Note that average costs are declining when marginal cost is below average cost and are rising when marginal cost is above average cost. This relation is a general rule.

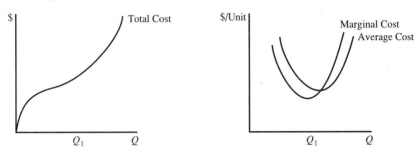

next best alternative use. Current market prices for inputs more closely reflect opportunity costs than *historical costs*. For instance, if an auto supplier purchases 1,000 pounds of aluminum for $1,000 and subsequently the market price increases to $2,000, the opportunity cost of using the aluminum is $2,000. If the company uses the aluminum it must pay $2,000 to replace it. Alternatively, the current inventory could be sold to another firm for $2,000. Thus, the firm forgoes $2,000 if it uses the aluminum in its production process.

Baseball Averages

We have discussed how marginal cost is below average cost when average cost is falling and above average cost when average cost is rising. This relation is a general property of averages and marginals. A useful illustration is a baseball player's batting average. The batting average is defined as the number of hits divided by the number of times at bat. Suppose a player starts a game with an average of .300. If the player gets one hit out of four at bats the marginal batting average for the day is .250 and the overall average must drop. If the player gets two hits out of four at bats the marginal is .500 and the player's batting average must rise.

The *relevant costs* for managerial decision making are the opportunity costs. It is important to include the opportunity costs of all inputs whether or not they have actually been purchased in the market place. For instance, if an owner spends time working in his firm the opportunity cost is the value of the owner's time in its next best alternative use.

Short Run Versus Long Run

Cost curves can be depicted for both the *short run* and the *long run*. The short run is the operating period during which at least one input (typically capital) is fixed in supply. For instance, in the short run it might be impossible to change the plant size or change the number of machines. In the *long run* the firm has complete flexibility—no inputs are fixed.

The definitions of short run and long run are not based on calendar time. Rather, the length of each period depends on how long it takes the firm to vary all inputs. For consulting firms, operating out of rented office space, the short run is a relatively brief period. On the other hand, for large manufacturing firms with heavy investments in plant and equipment, the short run might be a relatively long time period.

Short-run cost curves are sometimes called *operating curves* because they are used in making near-term production and pricing decisions. For these decisions, it is often correct to take the plant size and certain other factors as given (since these factors are beyond the control of the managers in the short term). Long-run cost curves are referred to as *planning curves,* since they play a key role in longer-run planning decisions relating to plant size and equipment acquisitions.

Fixed and Variable Costs

In the short run, some costs are fixed and do not vary with output. These *fixed costs* are incurred even if the firm produces no output. For instance, the firm has to pay the managers' salaries, interest on borrowed capital, lease payments, and property taxes whether or not it produces any output. *Variable costs,* in contrast, increase with the level of output. These costs include items like raw material, fuel, and certain labor costs. In the long run all costs are variable.

Short-Run Cost Curves

Figure 5.9 displays the short-run cost curves for a hypothetical firm. For this firm, suppose that the basic plant size is fixed and that all other inputs are variable. The left panel pictures total costs. Total costs are the sum of the fixed costs (FC) and total variable costs (TVC). The shape of the total cost curve is completely determined by the shape of the total variable cost curve. Fixed costs simply shift the position of the curve. Between Q and Q_1 the total cost curve is concave. Over this range, the marginal productivity of the variable factors is increasing (assuming fixed input prices). Past Q_1, the total cost curve is convex and the marginal productivity of the variable factors is decreasing. This type of pattern is expected given the law of diminishing returns. At low output levels, the fixed inputs are not efficiently utilized. Increasing the variable inputs increases output significantly. Over this range, costs

FIGURE 5.9   Short-Run Cost Curves.

This figure displays the short-run cost curves of a hypothetical firm. The left panel pictures total costs (TC). Total costs are the sum of the fixed costs (FC) plus the total variable costs (TVC). The shape of the total cost curve is determined by the shape of the total variable cost curve. Fixed costs simply shift the position of the curve. The right panel pictures marginal and average costs. Average fixed costs (AFC) are total fixed costs divided by output. Average fixed costs decline with output since the fixed costs are being spread over more units. Marginal costs (MC) decline up to Q_1 and then increase beyond that point due to diminishing returns. Marginal costs depend only on the variable input factors and are completely independent of the fixed costs. *Average variable costs (AVC) are total variable costs divided by output. Average total cost (ATC) and AVC decline as long as marginal cost is lower than the average cost and increase beyond that point. Marginal cost is equal to both ATC and AVC at their respective minimum points. Average total cost is always larger than AVC, since ATC = AFC + AVC. However, this difference becomes smaller as output increases and AFC become less important.*

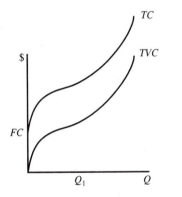
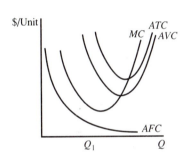

increase but do so at a decreasing rate. Eventually, the marginal productivity of the variable inputs declines, and it becomes increasingly expensive to produce extra units of output.

The right panel pictures marginal and average costs. Average fixed costs (AFC) are total fixed costs divided by output. Average fixed costs decline with output since the fixed costs are being spread over more units. Marginal costs (MC) decline up to Q_1 and then increase beyond that point due to diminishing returns. Note that marginal costs depend only on the variable input factors and are *completely independent of the fixed costs.* Average variable costs (AVC) are total variable costs divided by output. Average total cost (ATC) and AVC decline as long as marginal cost is lower than the average cost and increase beyond that point. Marginal cost is equal to both ATC and AVC at their respective minimum points. Average total cost is always larger than *average variable cost,* since ATC = AFC + AVC. However, this difference becomes smaller as AFC become less important with increased output.

FIGURE 5.10   Long-Run Average Costs as an Envelope of Short-Run Average Cost Curves.

In the long run, the average cost of production (LRAC) is less than or equal to the short-run average cost (SRAC) of production. Indeed, the LRAC curve can be thought of as an envelope of the short-run average cost curves. This figure illustrates this concept. The figure shows four potential plant sizes. Each of the four plants provides the low-cost method of production over some range of output. For instance, the smallest plant provides the lowest cost method of producing any output from zero to Q_1, while the next largest plant provides the low-cost method of producing outputs from Q_1 to Q_2, etc. The solid portion of each curve indicates the minimum long-run average cost for producing each level of output, assuming that there are only these four possible plant sizes.

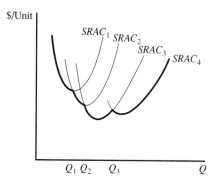

Long-Run Cost Curves

In the short run, firms are unable to adjust their plant sizes. In the long run, however, if a firm wants to produce more output it can build a larger, more efficient plant. Thus, in the long run, the average cost of production (*LRAC*) is less than or equal to the short-run average cost of production. Indeed, the *LRAC* curve can be thought of as an *envelope* of the short-run average cost curves. Figure 5.10 illustrates this concept. The figure shows four potential plant sizes. Each of the four plants provides the low-cost method of production over some range of output. For instance, the smallest plant provides the lowest cost method of producing any output from zero to Q_1, while the next largest plant provides the low-cost method of producing outputs from Q_1 to Q_2, etc. The solid portion of each curve indicates the minimum long-run average cost for producing each level of output, assuming that there are only these four possible plant sizes.

If we extend this analysis, by assuming that there are many different plant sizes that vary only slightly in size, the resulting *LRAC* curve will be relatively smooth as pictured in Figure 5.11. This figure also pictures the long-run marginal cost curve (*LRMC*). As we have discussed, the marginal cost is below average cost when average cost is falling and above average cost when it is rising. The two are equal at the minimum average cost.

FIGURE 5.11   Long-Run Average and Marginal Cost Curves.

If there are many different plant sizes that vary only slightly in size, the resulting long-run average cost curve (LRAC) is relatively smooth, as pictured in this figure. The long-run marginal cost (LRMC) is below average cost when average cost is falling and above average cost when it is rising. The two are equal at the minimum average cost. The minimum efficient scale is defined as the plant size at which LRACs are first minimized (Q* in this example).

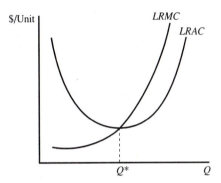

With constant input prices, the shapes of cost curves are determined entirely by the underlying production function. For instance, if long-run average costs are falling, the corresponding production function must display increasing returns to scale. With increasing returns to scale, a one percent increase on input expenditures results in a greater than one percent increase in output and average costs must fall. In contrast, when average costs are increasing, the production function displays decreasing returns to scale. With decreasing returns to scale, a one percent increase in input expenditures results in a less than one percent increase in output and average costs must rise. Finally, constant average costs imply constant returns to scale. A common justification for U-shaped curves (as pictured in figure 5.11) is that in practice it is often difficult to vary all factors of production even in the long run. For instance, a firm might be able to vary plant size and other inputs; however, duplicating managerial talent can be more difficult. If some inputs can't be varied, the law of diminishing returns suggests that the marginal and average cost curves will eventually turn upward, forming a U-shape. Long-run average cost curves, however, can take different shapes.

Input prices also can affect the shapes of the cost curves. For instance, declining average costs can be motivated by discounts on large volume purchases. Alternatively, if the firm bids up the price of inputs with large purchases, average costs can rise with increased output.

Minimum Efficient Scale

The *minimum efficient scale* is defined as that plant size at which long-run average costs reach their minimum point. In figure 5.11, this minimization occurs at Q^*. The minimum efficient scale affects both the optimal plant size and the level of potential competition.

Average production costs are minimized at the minimum efficient scale. As we discuss in the next chapter, competition tends to motivate firms to adopt this plant size. If firms build plants that depart significantly from minimum efficient scale, they will be at a competitive disadvantage and typically will either have to change the plant size or be forced out of business. One complicating factor, however, is transportation costs. If transportation costs are high, the inefficiencies of smaller regional plants can be overcome by the cost savings for transporting the product to customers. In this case, when total production and distribution costs are considered, firms with plants that are smaller than the minimum efficient scale can survive in a competitive market place. Also, some firms with plants below the minimum efficient scale are profitable because they specialize in particular niches of the market that are not well served by larger, less specialized firms. For instance, auto companies often purchase parts from smaller companies that specialize in making the parts to meet the companies' particular specifications.

DeLorean Automobiles

The difficulties of competing with plant sizes significantly below the minimum efficient scale is highlighted by the experience of the DeLorean Motor Company. John Z. DeLorean was a high-ranking executive at General Motors. He left GM in 1979 to form his own automobile company, the DeLorean Motor Company. The strategy of the new company was to specialize in high-priced luxury sports cars. The company's first (and only) car was the stainless-steel DMC12 with a list price of $29,000 (a very high price in the early 1980s). Although the minimum efficient scale is relatively large in auto production, DeLorean felt he could compete by designing higher quality sports cars than the large auto companies. Planned production for 1980 was 3,000 cars. The company soon ran into financial difficulties. In 1982, DeLorean was arrested for conspiring to buy and distribute 220 pounds of cocaine, valued at $24 million. Federal officials asserted that DeLorean was entering the drug business to help save his ailing automobile company. Although DeLorean was later acquitted on these charges, the company still faced insurmountable financial difficulties and soon went out of business.

Generally, the number of competitors will be large and the competition more vigorous when the minimum efficient scale is small relative to total industry demand. For instance, suppose that a potential entrant to an industry sees established firms making a substantial profit. If the firm would have to produce 10 percent of the market's output to be cost efficient, it is likely to drive the price down upon entry and is less likely to enter the market than if it would only need to produce one percent of the market's output for efficient production. Industries where the average costs decline over a broad range of output are characterized as having *economies of scale*. Significant economies of scale limit the number of firms in the industry. The level of competition among the existing firms can vary significantly. However, threat of entry is less important than in industries where economies of scale are low. The threat of potential new competitors is often an important consideration in a firm's strategic planning. In Chapter 7, we provide a more detailed analysis of how a firm's market structure affects managerial decision making.

Public Utilities

The production of electric power is typically associated with large economies of scale—the average cost of producing electricity decreases with the quantity produced. This production characteristic implies that it is generally more efficient to have one large plant that produces power for an area than several smaller plants. A problem with having one producer of electrical power in an area, however, is that the firm has the potential to "overcharge" consumers for electricity since there are limited alternative sources of supply. Concerns about this problem provide one motivation for the formation of public utility commissions that regulate the prices that utility companies can charge consumers.

Profit Maximization

Thus far, we have focused on the costs of producing alternative levels of output. However, what output level should managers choose to maximize firm profits? To answer this question, we use the concept of *marginal analysis* that we initially introduced in Chapter 2.

Marginal costs and benefits are the incremental costs and benefits that are associated with making a decision. It is the marginal costs and benefits that are important in economic decision making. An action should be taken when the marginal benefits of the action exceed the marginal costs. In deciding whether or not to produce one more unit of a product, the marginal benefit is the marginal revenue, while the marginal cost is equal to the marginal production cost (including any distribution costs). Fixed costs do not affect the decision. The firm should produce extra units as long as the *MR* is greater than the *MC*. The firm should not produce extra units when *MR* is less than *MC*. At the *profit-maximizing level of production* the following condition holds:[9]

$$MR = MC. \tag{10}$$

---

[9]Note for the technically inclined: Since profits equal total revenues minus total costs, equation 10 is the first-order condition for profit maximization. This condition holds at both minimum and maximum profits. At the maximum, the marginal cost curve cuts the marginal revenue curve from below (the second-order condition).

FIGURE 5.12   Optimal Output and Changes in Marginal Cost.

This figure illustrates that an increase in marginal cost (from MC to MC') lowers the optimal output of the firm.

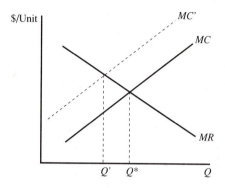

As we saw in Chapter 4, marginal revenue depends on the demand curve for the product. This demand curve will be affected by the degree of competition in the product market. The next chapter presents a detailed analysis of the output decisions of firms in different market settings.

The increase in steel prices in 1994 increased the total costs for automobile manufacturing. Typically, such an increase is accompanied by an increase in the *marginal costs* of production. In this case, the increase in steel prices would not only mean a substitution away from steel to other inputs, but also a decline in output. Figure 5.12 shows this effect. Note that this analysis holds other factors constant. If the demand for automobiles is increasing at the same time (thus shifting marginal revenue upward) the net effect can be an increase in output. However, the increase in output will be less than if there were no increase in steel prices.

Cost Estimation

Our discussion indicates that a detailed knowledge of costs is important for managerial decision making. Short-run costs play a very important role in operating decisions. For instance, when the marginal revenue from increased output is above the short-run marginal cost of production, profits can be increased by producing more output. Alternatively if marginal revenue is below the short-run marginal cost, output should be reduced. Long-run costs, in turn, provide important information for decisions on optimal plant sizes and location. For instance, if economies of scale are important, it is more likely to be optimal to build one large plant and transport the product to regional markets. Alternatively, if economies of scale are small it is more likely to be optimal to build smaller regional plants to reduce transportation costs.

If managers are to incorporate costs in their analyses in this manner they must have good estimates of how short-run and long-run costs are related to various factors, both within and beyond the control of the firm. Among the most commonly used statistical techniques for estimating cost curves is regression analysis. This technique estimates the relation between costs and output, controlling for other factors that affect costs such as input prices. The data for this analysis can either be time-series data on costs, output, and other variables, or cross-sectional data, which includes observations on variables across firms or plants at a point in time.

A detailed discussion of cost estimation is beyond the scope of this book. Suffice it to say that some of the same types of problems arise in cost estimation as arise in the case of demand estimation (for example, omitted variables problems). Among the most common problems in cost estimation are difficulties in obtaining data on the relevant costs. Cost estimates are often based on accounting reports, which record historical costs. As we have discussed, these historical costs do not always reflect the real opportunity costs of using a resource.

One of the most serious problems complicating cost estimation is the fact that most plants produce multiple products. Multiple products are produced in the same plant because there are synergies. Instead of producing two different types of cereals in two plants, it is usually cheaper to produce them in one plant. The fixed resources can be used more efficiently. Once a plant is producing multiple products, the total and average cost of a product can only be calculated by allocating the fixed costs to the products. However, this allocation if often arbitrary and complicated by the existence of joint costs. Cost accountants use the accounting records to track the costs of individual products. Fixed and variable resources used by each product are recorded. These product costs, calculated by the cost accountants, are typically used to estimate short-run and long-run average and marginal costs.

Despite these estimation problems, cost curves play an important role in managerial decision making. It is important, however, that managers maintain a healthy cynicism when using these estimates. For instance, in making major decisions it is generally important for managers to examine whether a tentative decision is still attractive with reasonable variations in the estimated parameters of the cost function (that is, to conduct *sensitivity analysis*).

Factor Demand Curves

In discussing the optimal input mix, we showed that the following condition must hold for efficient production:

$$MP_i/P_i = MP_j/P_j, \tag{11}$$

for all i and j. The marginal-product-to-price ratios reflect the incremental output from an input associated with an additional dollar expenditure on that input. Thus, the reciprocals of these ratios reflect the dollar cost for incremental output or the marginal cost:

$$P_i/MP_i = P_j/MP_j = MC. \tag{12}$$

FIGURE 5.13   **Factor Demand Curve.**

The demand curve for a factor of production is the marginal revenue product curve *(MRP)*
for the input. The marginal product is defined as the marginal product of the input times
the marginal revenue. It represents the additional revenue that comes from using one more
unit of the input. The firm maximizes profits when it purchases inputs up to the point
where the price of the input equals the value of the marginal product.

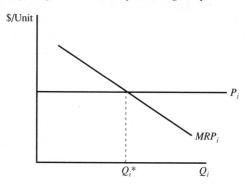

At the profit maximizing output level, $MR = MC$. Therefore, at the optimal output
level the following condition must hold:

$$P_i/MP_i = MR, \qquad (13)$$

or equivalently:

$$P_i = MR \times MP_i. \qquad (14)$$

Equation (14) is the firm's demand curve for input i.[10] It has a straight-forward
interpretation. The right-hand side of the equation represents the incremental revenue that the firm obtains from employing one more unit of the input (the incremental output times the incremental revenue). We call this incremental revenue the
marginal revenue product (MRP_i) of input i. Thus, the firm optimally employs additional units of the input up to the point where the marginal cost of the input (its
price with constant input prices) is equal to the marginal revenue product of the
input. Intuitively, if the marginal revenue product is greater than the input price,
the firm increases its profitability by using more of the input. If the marginal revenue
product is less than the price of the input, the firm increases profitability by reducing
the use of the input. Profits are maximized when the two are equal. Figure 5.13

---

[10]Note for the technically inclined: The marginal product of input i can depend on the levels of
other inputs used in the production process. Thus, the demand curve for an input must allow other
inputs to adjust to their optimal levels as the price of input i changes. This adjustment is not
important if the marginal product of input i is not affected by the levels of the other inputs.

illustrates the demand curve for an input.[11] At the current input price of P_i, the firm uses Q_i* units of the input.

Our discussion of the profit-maximizing output level and the optimal use of an input might appear to suggest that these decisions are two distinct choices. The two decisions, however, are directly connected. Once the firm chooses the quantities of inputs, output is determined by the production function. Thus, profit-maximizing firms choose the output where marginal revenue equals marginal cost *and* produce that output in a manner where the price of each input is equal to its marginal revenue product. For instance, in our initial example, the increase in steel prices would be expected to motivate a *simultaneous* adjustment in the number of automobiles produced and the method used to produce them.

Summary

In this chapter, we assume that managers strive to *maximize profits*. Given this objective, it is important for managers to understand both revenues and costs. The last chapter analyzes revenues. This chapter focuses on costs.

A *production function* is a descriptive statement that relates inputs to outputs. It specifies the *maximum* possible output that can be produced for a given amount of inputs. *Returns to scale* refers to the relation between output and the variation of *all inputs* taken together. A production function displays *constant returns to scale* when a one percent change in all inputs results in a one percent change in output. With *increasing returns to scale,* a one percent change in all inputs results in a greater than one percent change in output. Finally, with *decreasing returns to scale,* a one percent change in all inputs results in a less than one percent change in output. *Returns to a factor* refers to the relation between output and the variation in only one input, *holding other inputs fixed.* Returns to a factor can be expressed as total, marginal, or average quantities. The *law of diminishing returns* states that the marginal product of a variable factor will eventually decline as the input is increased.

Most production functions allow some substitution of inputs. An *isoquant* pictures all combinations of inputs that produce exactly the same quantity of output. The optimal input mix to produce any given output depends on the costs of the inputs. An *isocost line* pictures all combinations of inputs that cost the same amount. *Cost minimization* for a given output occurs where the isoquant is tangent to the isocost line. Changes in input prices change the slope of the isocost line and the point of tangency. When the price of an input increases, the firm will partially substitute this input for other inputs (*substitution effect*).

Cost curves can be derived from the isoquant/isocost analysis. The *total cost curve* depicts the relation between total costs and output. *Marginal cost* is the change in total costs associated with a one unit change in output. *Average cost* is total cost

---

[11]Note for the technically inclined: The second-order condition for maximum profits assures that the demand curve for the input is the *downward sloping* portion of the marginal revenue product curve. Thus, Figure 5.13 displays only the downward-sloping portion of the curve.

divided by total output. Average costs are falling when marginal costs are below average costs, while average costs are rising when marginal cost is above average costs. Average and marginal costs are equal when average costs are at a minimum.

Opportunity cost is the value of a resource in its next best alternative use. Current market prices more closely reflect the opportunity costs of inputs than *historical costs.* The *relevant costs* for managerial decision making are the opportunity costs.

Cost curves can be depicted for both the *short run* and the *long run.* The short-run is the operating period during which at least one input (typically capital) is fixed in supply. During this period, *fixed costs* can be incurred even if the firm produces no output. In the long run, there are no fixed costs—all inputs and costs are *variable.* Short-run cost curves are sometimes called *operating curves* because they are used in making near-term production and pricing decisions. Fixed costs are irrelevant for these decisions. Long-run cost curves are referred to as *planning curves,* since they play a key role in longer-run planning decisions relating to plant size and equipment acquisitions.

The *minimum efficient scale* is defined as that plant size at which long-run average costs are minimized. The minimum efficient scale affects both the optimal plant size and the level of potential competition. Industries where the average costs decline over a broad range of output are characterized as having *economies of scale.*

The profit maximizing output level occurs at the point where *marginal revenue equals marginal cost.* At this point, the marginal benefits of increasing output are exactly offset by the marginal costs.

Managers often use estimates of cost curves in decision making. A common statistical tool for estimating these curves is regression analysis. One common problem in statistical estimation is the difficulty of obtaining good information on the opportunity costs of resources. Another problem with estimating cost curves involves allocating fixed costs in a multi-product plant. Cost accountants track the costs and estimate product costs.

The *marginal revenue product (MRP_i)* of input i is equal to the marginal product of the input times marginal revenue. Profit-maximizing firms use an input up to the point where the *MRP* of the input equals the price of the input. At this point, the marginal benefits of employing more of the input are exactly offset by the marginal costs.

TECHNICAL APPENDIX[12]

This appendix derives the "factor-balance equation"—equation (9) in the text:

$$MP_i/P_i = MP_j/P_j. \tag{A1}$$

---

[12]This appendix requires elementary knowledge of calculus.

This condition must hold if the firm is producing the output in a manner that minimizes costs (assuming an interior solution).

Recall that at the cost-minimizing method of production the isoquant and isocost line are tangent. Thus, they must have equal slopes. The factor-balance equation is found by setting the slope of the isoquant equal to the slope of the isocost line and rearranging the expression. In the text, we showed that the slope of the isocost line is $-P_j/P_i$. We now derive the slope of an isoquant.

Slope of an Isoquant

The production function in the two input case takes the following general form:

$$Q = f(x_i, x_j). \tag{A3}$$

To find the slope of an isoquant we totally differentiate equation (A3). We set this differential equal to zero since quantity does not change along an isoquant:

$$dQ = [\partial Q/\partial x_i \, dx_i] + [\partial Q/\partial x_j \, dx_j] = 0. \tag{A4}$$

The slope of the isoquant is defined by dx_i/dx_j. Thus,

$$\text{Slope of an isoquant} = -(\partial Q/\partial x_j)/(\partial Q/\partial x_i) \tag{A5}$$
$$= -MP_j/MP_i. \tag{A6}$$

This expression has a straight-forward interpretation. For illustration, assume that at some fixed combination of x_i and x_j the marginal product of i is one and the marginal product of j is two. At this point, the slope of the isoquant is two. It says that two units of i can be given up for one unit of j and output will stay the same. This is true by definition since j has twice the marginal product of i.

Factor-Balance Equation

At the cost-minimizing production method, the slope of the isoquant is the same as the slope of the isocost line:

$$-MP_j/MP_i = -P_j/P_i. \tag{A7}$$

Rearranging this expression gives us the factor balance equation:

$$MP_i/P_i = MP_j/P_j. \tag{A8}$$

This expression generalizes to production functions with more than two inputs.

Market Structure

Sealed Air Corporation manufactures a wide variety of protective packaging materials and systems.[1] Among its most famous products are the packing bubbles that "everyone loves to pop." Other products include padded mailing envelopes, pads for absorbing moisture in supermarket meat packages, and equipment and supplies for creating customized foam for packaging fragile or unusually shaped items.

Founded in 1960, Sealed Air initially had strong patent protection on its major products. This protection shielded the company from competition and allowed it to make 45 to 50 percent profit margins. Given the market environment, the company did not face competitive pressures to contain costs or invest wisely. Rather the company concentrated on developing a sales force and selling products. The company grew and prospered. By the late 1980s, however, Sealed Air faced a much different market environment. Most of its major patents had expired, and the top management anticipated a substantial increase in competition. The management knew that it would have to lower the prices for its products, as new firms entered the industry. It also expected the firm to be at a competitive disadvantage, given its inefficient operations and high costs. Historically, the company had faced more competition in Europe, where it did not have strong patent protection, and had fared poorly.

In response to increased competition, the management of Sealed Air initiated several major policy changes to increase the company's efficiency. It launched a manufacturing improvement program to increase the quality of production and reduce costs. It instituted stringent capital budgeting procedures to limit unproductive investment. It substantially increased the leverage of the firm to place pressure on employees to generate enough cash flow to service the debt (and avoid bank-

---

[1]See, Karen Hopper Wruck, "Sealed Air Corporation's Leveraged Recapitalization," Harvard Business School, Case number 9–391–067, 3/30/91.

ruptcy). It also increased financial incentives throughout the firm to focus on efficiency and cash flow. For the most part, these changes appear to have had the desired effect—earnings performance and stock price increased substantially following the policy changes.

The example of Sealed Air illustrates how the policy choices of a firm, such as pricing, leverage, and production techniques, are significantly influenced by the market environment. Policies that work in a protected market environment often have to be changed radically in more competitive environments. It is important that managers understand the firm's market environment and how this environment affects optimal decision making. The purpose of this chapter is to increase that understanding by exploring the implications of alternative market structures. Our primary focus is on the output and pricing decisions of firms in alternative market structures. Subsequent chapters examine in more detail how other policies, such as aspects of the firm's organizational architecture, depend on the market environment.

The chapter is organized as follows. We begin by discussing markets and market structure in more detail. We then provide an analysis of competitive industries. Perfect competition is at one end of a continuum based on the level of competition within the industry. Perfect competition is an important benchmark and provides important managerial implications for firms operating in most market settings. Next, we discuss barriers to entry that can limit competition within an industry. This section is followed by an analysis of the market structure at the other end of the continuum: monopoly. In a monopolistic industry there is only one firm. In contrast to firms in competitive industries, a monopolist has substantial power in setting prices. After a brief discussion of a hybrid structure, monopolistic competition, we examine the pricing policies of monopolistic firms in more detail. Finally, we consider the case of oligopoly, where a small number of firms constitute the industry.

Markets

A *market* consists of all firms and individuals who are willing and able to buy or sell a particular product. These parties include those currently engaged in buying and selling the product, as well as potential entrants. *Potential entrants* are all individuals and firms that pose a sufficiently credible threat of market entry to affect the pricing and output decisions of incumbent firms.

Market Structure refers to the basic characteristics of the market environment, including: (1) the number and size of buyers, sellers, and potential entrants, (2) the degree of product differentiation, (3) the amount and cost of information about product price and quality, and (4) the conditions for entry and exit. We begin our discussion of alternative market structures with perfect competition.

FIGURE 6.1   Firm Demand Curve in Perfect Competition.

In competitive markets, firms take the market price of the product as given. The demand curve is horizontal. The marginal revenue and average revenue are both equal to the market price.

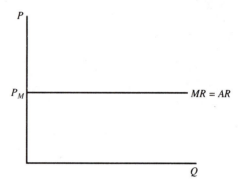

Perfect Competition

Market Structure

Competitive markets are characterized by four basic conditions:

1. A large number of buyers and sellers.
2. Product homogeneity.
3. Rapid dissemination of accurate information at low cost.
4. Free entry and exit into the market.

An example of a market that approximates these conditions is the market for wheat. In this market, there is a relatively large number of farmers that grow wheat, as well as a large number of firms and individuals who buy wheat. Wheat is a relatively homogeneous commodity (the product varies little across producers). There are limited informational disparities, and there is relatively free entry and exit.

In competitive markets, individual buyers and sellers take the market price for the product as given—they have no control over price. If a seller charges more than the market price buyers will purchase the product from other suppliers. Correspondingly, firms can always sell the product at the market price and have no reason to offer discounts to buyers. In this setting, firms view their demand curves as horizontal—a firm can sell any feasible output at the market price, P_M—but sells no output at a price above P_M. Figure 6.1 illustrates a horizontal demand curve. With a horizontal demand curve, the marginal revenue (*MR*) and average revenue (*AR*) are both equal to price.

Firm Supply

Short-Run Supply Decision.   In the last chapter, we saw that a firm's profit is maximized at the output where marginal revenue equals marginal cost. The intuition of this result is straight-forward—it makes sense to expand output as long as the incremental revenue is greater than the incremental cost. In a competitive market, marginal revenue is equal to price (P). In the short run, the firm takes the plant size (and possibly other inputs) as given. Thus, the relevant cost is the short-run marginal cost ($SRMC$). The condition for short-run profit maximization in a competitive industry is:

$$P = SRMC. \tag{6.1}$$

This condition indicates that at any price, the firm should choose the output where price equals $SRMC$. The firm, however, has the additional option of producing no output at all. When the price of the product is not sufficient to cover the average variable cost (AVC), the firm is better off producing no output. With no output the firm loses money since it generates no revenue to cover its fixed costs. However, this loss is less than it would be if the firm produced any other level of output (since the revenue from production would be less than the variable costs of production). The *no shut-down condition for the short-run* is:

$$P \geq AVC. \tag{6.2}$$

A firm's supply curve depicts the quantity that the firm will produce at each price. The preceding discussion indicates that the firm's short-run supply curve is the portion of the short-run marginal cost curve that is above average variable cost. Figure 6.2 pictures this supply curve.

Long-Run Supply Decision.   Firms can lose money in the short-run and still find it optimal to stay in business. In the long run, however, the firm must be profitable—price must be above long-run average cost ($LRAC$)—or it is better to go out of business. Thus, the *no shut-down condition for the long-run* is:

$$P \geq LRAC. \tag{6.3}$$

In the long run, the firm can adjust its plant size. Thus, the long-run supply decision of a firm is based on long-run marginal costs ($LRMC$). The long-run supply curve of a firm is the portion of the long-run marginal cost curve that is above long-run average cost. This supply curve is pictured in Figure 6.3.[2]

---

[2]Note that there is no inconsistency between short-run and the long-run profit maximization. The $LRMC$ at any given output is equal to the $SRMC$ given the firm has the optimal plant size for the output. Hence, the firm can simultaneously choose an output where $P = SRMC = LRMC$.

FIGURE 6.2   The Firm's Short Run Supply Curve.

*The firm's short-run supply curve is the portion of the short-run marginal cost curve
(SRMC) that is above average variable cost (AVC). At prices below average variable cost,
the firm is better off not producing any output.*

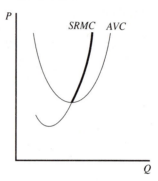

FIGURE 6.3   The Firm's Long-Run Supply Curve.

*The long-run supply curve for a firm is the portion of the long-run marginal cost curve
(LRMC) that is above long-run average cost (LRAC). If price is below LRAC the firm
should go out of business.*

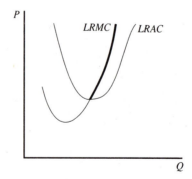

Competitive Equilibrium

In Chapter 2, we discussed how the market price in a competitive market is determined by the intersection of the industry demand and supply curves. The industry
demand curve depicts the total quantities demanded by all buyers in the market
place at each price. Similarly, the industry supply curve is comprised of the sum of
all the individual supply decisions (discussed above).

FIGURE 6.4   Competitive Equilibrium.

The left-hand side illustrates the long-run supply decision of a representative firm in the
industry. At the price, P', the firm produces Q_i'. Cost curves are defined to include a
normal rate of profit. Thus, at the price P' the firm is earning an abnormal profit. *This*
abnormal profit is the profit per unit (P − LRAC) times the total output, Q_i' and is
depicted by the rectangle abcd. The existence of abnormal profits will motivate other firms
to enter the industry. This entry will shift the supply curve to the right and lower price.
Additional entry will occur up to the point where there are no abnormal profits. This
condition occurs at a price of P*. Here, there is no incentive for firms to enter or leave the
industry (incumbents are earning a normal rate of profit), and the market is in
equilibrium. In a competitive equilibrium, firms produce output at the low point on their
average cost curves (P = LRMC = LRAC). Thus, the equilibrium is associated with
efficient production.

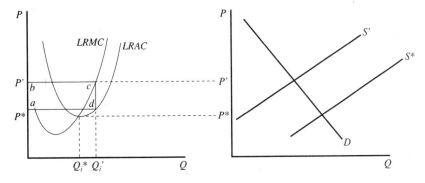

Consider as an example, the supply and demand curves, labeled *S'* and *D'*, on
the right-hand side of Figure 6.4. Here the market price is *P'*. The left-hand side
illustrates the long-run supply decision of a representative firm in the industry. At
the price, *P'*, the firm produces Q_i'. Cost curves are defined to include a normal rate
of profit (a normal return on capital is included in *LRAC*). Thus, at the price *P'* the
firm is earning an *abnormal profit*. This abnormal profit is the profit per unit
(P'−LRAC) times the total output, Q_i' and is depicted by the *abcd* rectangle. The
existence of abnormal profits will motivate other firms to enter the industry. This
entry will shift the supply curve to the right and lower price. Additional entry will
occur up to the point where there are no abnormal profits. This condition is pictured
in Figure 6.4 at a price of *P**. Here, there are no incentives for firms to enter or
leave the industry (incumbents are earning a normal rate of profit), and the market
is in *equilibrium*. In a competitive equilibrium, firms produce output at the low point
on their average cost curves *(P=LRMC=LRAC)*. Thus, the equilibrium is associated
with efficient production.

Strategic Considerations

While few markets are perfectly competitive, many markets approximate this structure. In most industries, there are strong competitive forces that tend to reduce abnormal profits over time. These forces imply that many strategic advantages (for example, being the first in a new market) are likely to be short-lived. If the conditions in the market resemble the competitive model, it is important to "move fast" to take advantage of transitory opportunities. In addition, potential entrants should realize that observed abnormal profits in an industry are likely to be "bid away" as time passes. This consideration can affect long-range capital spending and entry decisions. For instance, given the threat of increased competition, Sealed Air increased their scrutiny of internal investment proposals. In a competitive market, firms must also strive for efficiency and cost control. Inefficient firms lose money and are forced out of business. Sealed Air's management understood this implication when it undertook significant efforts to enhance efficiency.

Superior Firms

Even in relatively competitive industries there are firms that do exceptionally well over long time periods, for example by being a low-cost producer or having some particular advantage relative to competitors, such as location. However, the excess returns often do not go to the owner of the enterprise, but rather to the factor that produces the particular advantage. For example, land close to a highway interchange (and thus close to customers) often sells for a higher price than land further from the interchange and the salary of an exceptionally talented manager will be bid up by other firms. In many cases, the firms employing these factors of production earn only a normal rate of return ($P = LRAC$).

Barriers to Entry[3]

While the competitive model is a reasonable approximation in many markets, there are other industries where firms have significant market power—prices are affected substantially by the output decisions of individual firms. A necessary condition for market power to exist is that there are *barriers to entry* into the industry.

To understand what constitutes a barrier to entry, it is useful to consider the decisions of individual firms to enter an industry. Firms consider entry into new industries when they observe existing firms making large profits. For instance, if a firm such as Sealed Air is observed making large profits producing packaging materials, other firms are likely to consider entering the industry. The entry decision will depend on at least three important factors. First, a prospective entrant will be

---

[3]This section provides a brief summary of the literature in economics on barriers to entry. For a more detailed review of this literature, see Sharon M. Oster, 1994, *Modern Competitive Analysis,* Oxford Press.

concerned about whether its entry will affect the price of the product. This, in turn, depends at least in part on how the existing firms are likely to respond to a new entrant (for example, are they likely to price cut?). Second, the potential entrant will be concerned about incumbent advantages—do the existing firms have advantages that make it unlikely that a new firm will enjoy similar profits? Third, the firm will be concerned about the costs of exit. How much will it cost to leave the industry if this incursion fails? We discuss each of these factors in turn.

Phantom Freight

Most of the plywood in the United States comes from the Pacific Northwest. Due to this dominance, plywood prices throughout the country are essentially the Northwest price plus shipping. If this condition did not hold, Northwest suppliers would curtail shipping plywood to cities with low prices and increase shipping to cities with high prices. The changes in supply would affect the prices in the cities until, in equilibrium, the prices across cities would differ only in transportation costs.

In a U.S. court case, Southeast timber producers were sued for charging customers the Northwest price plus shipping and then delivering locally produced plywood. It was ruled that these companies were making unjust profits because they did not actually incur the shipping costs. The jury awarded billions of dollars to the customers. Were these companies really making abnormal profits? The answer is probably not. The local production in the Southeast had a shipping advantage. However, the factor that made this advantage possible was scarce timber land in the Southeast. Presumably, the price of this scarce timber land was bid up to the point where plywood producers were only making a normal profit given the prevailing price for plywood in the Southeast (which was the Northwest price plus shipping).

Suggested by Armen Alchian and William Allen, *Exchange & Production: Competition, Coordination and Control*, 3rd edition, Wadsworth Publishing Company, Belmont, CA, 1983, pp. 228–231.

Incumbent Reactions

Specific Assets.   Specific assets are assets which have more value in their current use than in the next best alternative use. Consider the case of the Alaskan Pipeline. It has a high value in its current use. However, what else can it be used for? It can be moved only at great expense, and its alternative uses in its present location are nil. If the existing firms in an industry have invested heavily in specific assets, they are likely to fight harder to maintain position than if the assets are more general and can be shifted at low cost to alternative activities.

Economies of Scale.   Industries with large economies of scale have minimum efficient scales that are relatively large (see Chapter 5). In this case, an entrant must capture a large market share to be competitive in terms of production costs. The absolute size of the minimum efficient scale is not as important as is this scale relative to the size of the total market. For example, if the minimum efficient scale means producing output equal to 30 percent of the total market demand, price will almost certainly decline if a new entrant tries to capture this share of the market. (There is likely to be substantial price competition from incumbents.) Minimum efficient scale varies dramatically across industries. In one study, estimates of minimum efficient scale, as a percentage of industry capacity, ranged from .5 percent (fruit/vegetable canning) to over 30 percent (typewriters).[4] Globalization of markets increases the effective market size and makes entry more feasible. Consider for example the global versus American automobile industries.

Excess Capacity.   Firms with excess capacity often do not want to cut production because they can experience much higher average costs at lower output levels (depending on the slopes of their average cost curves). Potential entrants, therefore, may be less likely to enter when there is excess capacity in the industry because they fear aggressive actions on the part of incumbents. Excess capacity can exist for "innocent reasons." For example, a firm facing cyclical production or growth may have excess capacity over some time intervals. In other cases, the excess capacity may be chosen deliberately to deter entry.

Excess Capacity at Alcoa

In 1940, Alcoa lost an important antitrust case for its production strategy of holding excess capacity. The judge ruled that he could think of no better "effective" deterrent to entry.

Reputation Effects.   Potential entrants can also be influenced by the reputation of the existing firms in the industry in terms of how they react to new entry. At times it can pay for an existing firm to act against its own short-term interests, for example, by price cutting, to establish a reputation as a tough competitor. Threats by firms to cut prices if new entry occurs, however, are not always credible. If new firms actually enter, the existing firms might not follow through on their threats because they would be harmed by their own price cuts. In this case, it can be reasonable for potential entrants to ignore the threats—the potential entrants know that the incumbents are "bluffing."

Incumbent Advantages

Precommitment Contracts.   Existing firms often have long-term contracts for raw materials, distribution outlets, shelf-space, and delivery of the final product.

---

[4]K. Lancaster and R. Dulaney, 1979, *Modern Economics: Principles and Policy*, Rand McNally, p. 211.

These contracts can serve as a deterrent to entry, since the parties are precommitted to dealing with the incumbent firms rather than new entrants.

Licenses and Patents.   Sometimes entry is limited by government actions, such as licensing requirements and the awarding of patents. For instance, the number of doctors is significantly limited by state licensing requirements. This restriction allows doctors to charge higher prices than if entry were unrestricted. Regulators justify licensing with arguments based on consumer protection. Whether or not consumers benefit from stringent licensing, however, is debatable (given they pay higher prices). The standard patent life is 17 years. For this period of time, other firms are not allowed to copy the innovation, and the firm with the patent is granted some potential monopoly power. The purpose of patents is to give increased incentives to innovate. From a practicable standpoint the effectiveness of a patent in blocking entry can vary dramatically (patents can be circumvented by clever design, for example). Historically, Sealed Air had derived its market power from strong patent protection. However, this protection had expired by the late 1980s, leaving the firm vulnerable to increased competition.

Learning-Curve Effects.   In some industries, average costs are driven down through production experience. As firms produce more units, they learn how to lower unit costs. Learning-curve effects can result in new firms having a cost disadvantage relative to existing firms. Whether these effects are important, depends on whether the new firms can simply copy the techniques learned by the existing firms through their experience. In the case of Sealed Air, costs had not been driven down by learning effects. Indeed, entry was invited by Sealed Air's inefficient production.

Pioneering Brand Advantages.   Sometimes a firm will benefit from being the first in an industry. For instance, in some industries (prescription drugs as an example) a satisfied customer might be reluctant to switch brands even if the price is substantially lower. This tendency is likely to be strongest in *experience goods* which have to be tried by the customer to ascertain quality; customers might not try a new pain reliever because they are afraid that it might not be as effective as existing brands. Where quality can be judged by inspection, prior to purchase, the advantage of the incumbent is likely to be lower. Sometimes the incumbent's advantage with an experience good can be overcome by newcomers through (1) free samples, (2) endorsements, or (3) government certification. However, each of these methods is likely to entail additional costs and deter entry.

Costs of Exit

Another important entry consideration is the cost of exiting an industry. In some industries, it is possible to "hit and run." For instance, forming a new company to replace asphalt on driveways requires little investment in specialized equipment or training. A new firm can enter quickly when the profit potential is high and exit at low cost, if profits decline. In other industries, especially those with specific assets, the costs of exit can be high. Here, firms can bear significant costs, such as moving employees to new locations and liquidating plants and other assets, when they decide to exit. High exit costs deter initial entry.

Government Restrictions on Exit

Some regulators want to restrict companies from closing plants. These regulators appear motivated by concerns over people who lose their jobs when a company closes a plant. Restrictions on plant closings, however, are likely to reduce the desirability of entry into an industry—firms will be reluctant to enter an industry if they can't exit easily if they are losing money. Thus, the potential effects of government restrictions on exit are less vigorous competition in the affected industries, higher consumer prices, and lower levels of employment.

Monopoly

Market Structure

Barriers to entry can limit the threat of competition and give incumbent firms market power. While perfect competition is at one end of the spectrum, at the other end is *monopoly,* where there is only one firm in the industry. Here, the industry and firm demand curves are one in the same.

Profit Maximization

Suppose that a monopolist charges the same price to all customers (below, we relax this assumption). As we discuss below, such a pricing policy might be motivated by government regulation or the inability to prevent resale among customers. The firm's objective is to choose the price/quantity combination along its demand curve that maximizes profits. As we have discussed, this combination occurs where $MR = MC$.

For illustration, consider the following linear demand curve:

$$P = 200 - Q. \tag{6.4}$$

Assume that marginal cost is constant at $10. Recall from Chapter 4, that the MR curve for a linear demand curve is a line with the same intercept and twice the negative slope. Figure 6.5 pictures the demand curve, MR curve and MC curve in this example. Optimal output occurs at 95 units, where $MR = MC$. To sell this output, the firm charges a price of $105. The firm makes $95/unit profit ($105 − $10) for a total profit of $9,025 ($95 × 95), as indicated by the rectangle *abcd*.

FIGURE 6.5   Monopoly.

This figure illustrates the price and output decisions of a monopolist. In the example, demand is P = 200 − Q. Marginal costs are $10. Optimal output occurs at 95 units, where MR = MC. To sell this output, the firm charges a price of $105. The firm makes $95/unit profit ($105 − $10) for a total profit of $9,025 ($95 × 95), as indicated by the rectangle abcd. There are consumers who are willing to pay more than the marginal cost of production who do not receive the product. Thus, not all the gains from trade are exhausted—the outcome is inefficient. The associated loss in potential gains from trade is pictured by the triangle cde. Consumers along the corresponding segment of the demand curve value the product for more than $10, but less than $105 dollars. The firm does not lower the price to sell to these consumers because it does not want to lower the price for other customers. From the firm's standpoint the gain from selling to additional customers is more than offset by the loss from having to charge a lower price to all customers.

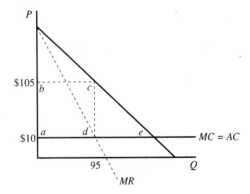

In contrast to pure competition, consumers facing monopolistic suppliers pay more than the marginal cost of production and the firm earns abnormal profits. For instance, up until the time its patents expired Sealed Air had near monopoly power in some product markets and correspondingly made substantial profits. Monopolies produce lower output than competitive industries. In our example, if the industry were competitive the market price would be $10 (the marginal cost) and total quantity sold would be 190 units.

Government Regulation

Given the monopolist's output and pricing choice, there are consumers who are willing to pay more than the marginal cost of production who do not receive the product. Thus, not all the gains from trade are exhausted—the outcome is inefficient. The associated loss in potential gains from trade is pictured by the triangle *cde* in Figure 6.5. Consumers, along the corresponding segment of the demand curve, value the product for more than $10, but less than $105 dollars. The firm does not lower the price to sell to these consumers because it does not want to lower the price for other customers (recall that the firm charges the same price to all customers). From the firm's standpoint, the gain from selling to additional customers is more than offset by the loss from having to charge a lower price to all customers.[5]

Monopolistic Competition

As the name implies, *monopolistic competition* is a market structure that is a hybrid between competition and monopoly. In this market structure, there are multiple firms that produce similar products. There is free exit and entry into the industry. Competition, however, is not perfect because the firms sell differentiated products. Examples of industries with these characteristics include toothpaste, cigarettes, and golf balls. For instance, Colgate and Crest toothpastes compete directly. Yet many customers do not view them as perfect substitutes, and the companies have some market power. New toothpaste firms, however, are likely to enter the industry if the existing firms are making large profits.

Monopolistic competition is similar to monopoly in that firms in both market structures face downward sloping demand curves—a toothpaste company can raise its price without losing all sales. Given that the firms face downward sloping demand curves, they strive to select the price/quantity combination that maximizes profits. The output decision is based on the same analysis as for the pure monopolist—choose the output where $MC = MR$.

The difference between monopoly and monopolistic competition is that in monopolistic competition abnormal profits invite entry. For example, if a new dimple pattern on golf balls is a hot seller, other companies will imitate the product. This entry will shift the original firm's demand curve to the left and reduce profits. Zero profits exist when the demand curve is shifted to the point where average cost equals price. Figure 6.6 shows this condition.

Entry will tend to force profits to zero. However, some brands will still be more distinctive than others. Also costs can vary because of differences in production techniques, inputs, etc. Thus, it is possible for some firms to make small abnormal profits in monopolistic competition.[6]

---

[5]This inefficiency (or *social cost*) is one reason why governments often pass regulations, like antitrust laws, to restrict the formation of monopolies. These regulations can also be motivated by concerns about the higher prices that consumers pay when they face monopolistic suppliers. While government regulation has the potential to reduce inefficiencies and wealth transfers (from consumers to firms), it is important to keep in mind that government regulation is not costless. (There are salaries for regulators and court costs, for instance.) From a societal viewpoint, the costs of government regulation should be weighed against the benefits.

[6]Monopolistic competition is inefficient for two reasons. First, as in monopoly, there is the loss from not selling to all consumers who value the product at above the marginal cost of production. Second, firms do not operate at the bottom of their average cost curves (see Figure 6.6). Lower average cost would be obtained with fewer firms, each producing more output. Nevertheless, regulation to address these inefficiencies is likely to be undesirable. Consumers value product differentiation and are probably better off with more variety at slightly higher average cost than lower variety produced at lower average cost. Second, because of competition, the monopoly power of firms is likely to be relatively small.

FIGURE 6.6   Monopolistic Competition.

In monopolistic competition, firms sell differentiated products. This figure shows the demand curve for a firm in such an industry. The curve is downward sloping. Similar to monopoly pricing, the firm selects the output where marginal revenue equals marginal cost. Monopolistic competition differs from monopoly in that abnormal profits will invite entry. Entry shifts the demand curve for the firm to the left (as some of the customers buy from the new firms). The firm makes no abnormal profits when price is equal to average cost. This condition is pictured in the figure. Monopolistic competition is inefficient in that the firm does not operate at the bottom of its long-run average cost curve. Also, as in the case of monopoly, the firm does not sell to all customers who value the product at more than the marginal cost. The inefficiencies associated with monopolistic competition, however, are likely to be relatively small, and customers benefit from the variety of brands.

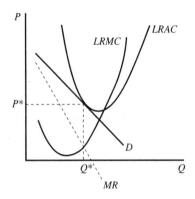

Pricing with Market Power

To this point, we have assumed that the firm sells to all customers at the same price. Firms with market power, however, can potentially increase profits by selling products at different prices to different customers.[7] In this section, we provide a brief introduction to some of the pricing policies that firms use to increase profits.

Consumer Surplus

The concept of *consumer surplus* helps to clarify the objectives of a firm's pricing policy. Consumer surplus is defined as the difference between what the consumer

---

[7]Note that there are laws that restrict the ability of firms to charge different prices to different customers. Managers contemplating the types of pricing policies discussed in this section should check with legal counsel on the legality of the proposed pricing policy.

is willing to pay for a product and what the consumer actually pays when buying it. Figure 6.7 provides an illustration of consumer surplus. The demand curve in this figure reflects what consumers are willing to pay for the product. It is never in the interests of the firm to sell the product at below marginal cost, since it can do better by not producing the product. Thus, the maximum potential gains from trade in this example are given by triangle *abc*. If the firm sold the product at marginal cost all the gains would go to consumers in the form of consumer surplus. Managers in maximizing profits try to devise a pricing policy that captures as much of this surplus as possible. We saw that when the firm charges one price to all customers that it captures some, but not all, of this surplus. The firm can potentially do better with a more complex pricing policy.

Price Discrimination

Price discrimination occurs whenever a firm's prices in different markets are not related to differentials in production and distribution costs. With price discrimination, the mark-up or profit margin realized varies across customers. Two conditions are necessary for profitable price discrimination. First, different price elasticities of demand must exist in various submarkets for the product. Otherwise, there is no point in segmenting the market. When different price elasticities do exist, it is generally optimal to charge higher prices to those customers who are less sensitive to price (if possible). Second, the firm must be able to identify submarkets and to restrict transfers among consumers in different submarkets. Otherwise, any attempt to charge differential prices to the submarkets will be undercut by resale across the submarkets. (One group of consumers can buy at the low price and sell to the other groups at a price below the firm's prices to these groups.)

First-degree price discrimination extracts the maximum amount each customer is willing to pay for the product. In this case, the producer extracts all the potential consumer surplus. This extreme form of price discrimination is rare and is possible only when the number of customers is extremely small. With first-degree price discrimination, the firm sells to all customers who are willing to pay more than the marginal cost of production. Thus, all gains from trade are exhausted and the outcome is efficient. All the gains from trade, however, go to the firm.

Second-degree price discrimination involves setting prices based on quantity purchased. Prices are often *blocked* with a high price charged for the first unit or block of units purchased, and lower prices set for successive units or blocks. Public utilities frequently price in this manner. If the quantity discounts are based solely on costs, then there is no price discrimination. However, large quantity users are likely to be more price sensitive than low quantity users, and thus block pricing allows different rates to be charged to the two groups even if per unit costs are similar.

FIGURE 6.7   Consumer Surplus.

Consumer surplus *is the difference between what the consumer is willing to pay for a product and what the consumer actually pays when buying it. This figure provides an illustration of consumer surplus. The demand curve reflects what consumers are willing to pay for the product. It is never in the interests of the firm to sell the product at below marginal cost, since it can do better by not producing the product. Thus, the maximum potential gains from trade in this example are given by triangle abc. If the firm sold the product at marginal cost all the gains would go to consumers. The firm's objective is to devise a pricing policy that captures as much of this surplus as possible. When the firm charges one price to all customers it can capture some, but not all, of this surplus. The firm can potentially do better with the more complex pricing policy.*

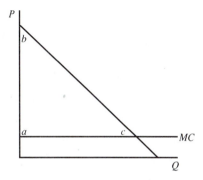

Another type of block pricing can occur in the choice of package size. For example, assume you value one hot dog at 40 cents and a second hot dog at 20 cents. If the vendor sells the dogs individually, she has to charge 20 cents or less to get you to buy two. If she sells the dogs in packs of two, she can charge 60 cents for the package, and you will buy the dogs at 30 cents apiece. (Note the fact that hot dogs tend to come in packs might also be explained by cost arguments: packaging costs increase less than in proportion to the number of hot dogs.)

Third-degree price discrimination results when a firm separates its customers into several classes and sets a different price for each class. For example, utility companies charge different rates to individual versus commercial users; computer companies give educational discounts; airlines charge different rates based on the amount of notice given for the reservation. As we will see in the following example, a firm that can segment its market maximizes profits by setting marginal revenue equal to marginal cost in each market segment.

Example of Third-Degree Price Discrimination

Consider the example of the Snowfish Ski Resort which can separate its demand into local skiers and out-of-town skiers. The marginal costs of servicing a skier of either type is $10.00. Suppose the resort faces the following demand curves:

$$\text{Out of town: } Q_o = 500 - 10P \tag{6.5}$$
$$\text{Local: } \quad Q_1 = 500 - 20P. \tag{6.6}$$

Total demand at any one price is the sum of the demands for the two types of consumers[8]:

$$Q = 1000 - 30P. \tag{6.7}$$

If the company sells all tickets at one price, profit maximization will occur at (subject to rounding error)[9]:

$$P = \$21.66, Q = 350, Q_o = 283, Q_1 = 67, \text{Profit} = \$4,081.$$

The company, however, can make higher profits by charging different prices to the two sets of skiers. The optimal prices are found by setting the marginal revenue equal to the marginal cost in each of the two market segments. Under this pricing policy, the following prices, quantities, and profits are observed:

$$P_o = \$30, Q_o = 200, P_1 = \$17.50, Q_1 = 150, \text{Profit} = \$5,125,$$

where P_o and P_1 are the prices charged to out-of-town and local skiers, respectively. Under this pricing policy, the resort charges higher prices to the out-of-town skiers, who are less sensitive to ticket prices than local skiers.

There are a number of methods that Snowfish might use to charge the two groups different prices. For example, discount coupons might be sold at supermarkets away from major resort hotels. Presumably, most of the sales at these supermarkets will be to local customers. Alternatively, discount books of tickets (nontransferable) could be sold locally prior to the start of ski season. Indeed, ski resorts use both techniques. For either of these policies to work, the resort must limit local skiers from buying the tickets at $17.50 and reselling them to out-of-town skiers at prices less than $30.

---

[8]This demand curve assumes that price is less than or equal to $25.00. At higher prices, the local skiers purchase no tickets, and the total demand curve is simply the demand curve for out-of-town skiers ($Q = 500 - 10P$).

[9]The reader should know by now that the solution to this problem is found by setting marginal revenue equal to marginal cost and solving for Q. Price can then be found from the equation for the demand curve. As a homework problem, derive the solutions to the pricing problem in this example. Note that equation 6.7 has Q on the left-hand side. This expression can be rearranged to produce the more familiar "inverse" demand curve.

The Little Mermaid
An Example of Price Discrimination

Coupons are one method that firms use to charge different prices to different consumers. Presumably customers that are relatively insensitive to price are less likely to spend time cutting coupons (because of higher opportunity costs of time). An example of a firm using coupons in this manner is the Disney corporation.

When Disney first distributed the *Little Mermaid* video tapes the tape retailed for around $20.00. However, a customer could clip a coupon (available at any store) and mail it in for a $5.00 rebate. What was going on? Why not simply sell the tapes for $15.00? Wouldn't costs be avoided? For example, it is expensive to issue and mail checks and print posters and coupons.

To illustrate the potential benefits of the policy, suppose that if the tapes were sold at same price to all customers, Disney would have priced them at $20. With this policy, Disney would lose the potential profit from selling to consumers who are willing to pay a price above Disney's production cost but less than $20. Disney's apparent objective was to find a way to sell to these consumers at a lower price without having to lower the price to other consumers. One way to partially accomplish this objective was through rebates. Presumably those willing to purchase at $20.00 had higher opportunity costs for their time (on average). This made them less likely to fill out and mail in the coupons. Customers not using the rebates paid a price of $20.00, while the customers using the rebate coupons paid $15.00.

There are a variety of issues to consider in deciding on such a rebate program. First, there is a tradeoff between the costs of administering the program and the benefits of additional sales. Also there is the loss of $20.00 sales to customers who would have purchased at $20 but now use the rebate coupons. Deciding whether or not to implement such a program requires careful analysis.

Two-Part Tariffs

A two-part tariff is another pricing mechanism that can sometimes be used to increase profits. Here the consumer pays an up-front fee for the right to buy the product and then pays additional fees for each unit of the product consumed. A classic example is an amusement park where you pay a fee to get in and then so much a ride. This type of pricing is also used by some golf and tennis clubs, computer information services, telephone companies, and similar service providers.

To illustrate this technique, consider an example where all consumers have identical demands for the product, $P = 10 - Q$. Figure 6.8 displays a demand curve for a representative consumer. The marginal cost of producing the product is $1. The potential consumer surplus that the firm could capture is shown by triangle *abc* and is equal to $40.50 (.5 × 9 × 9). Maximum profits can be extracted by charging an up-front fee equal to all the consumer surplus (or slightly less) and then charging a price equal to marginal cost, $1. Under this pricing scheme, the consumer purchases nine units.

FIGURE 6.8   **Two-Part Tariff.**

In this example, all potential customers have identical demands. The figure displays a demand curve for a representative consumer, $P = 10 - Q$. The marginal cost of producing the product is $1. The potential consumer surplus that the firm could capture is $40.50, as shown by triangle abc. *Maximum profits can be extracted by charging an up-front fee equal to all the consumer surplus (or slightly less) and then charging a price equal to marginal cost, $1. Under such a scheme, the consumer purchases nine units.*

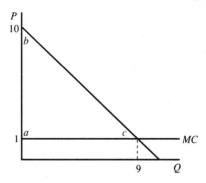

The pricing problem becomes more complicated when consumers vary widely in their demands for the product. Charging a high entry fee allows the firm to extract surplus from consumers who have a high demand for the product. However, consumers with lower demand will choose not to purchase. Solving for the optimal entry fee and price in this case is more difficult. If consumers vary widely in demand it is often best to charge a low entry fee (possibly zero) and to charge a price above marginal cost for use.

Two-Part Pricing at Xerox and IBM

Xerox originally only leased copy machines to customers. The lease contract required customers to purchase the paper from Xerox. Thus, customers had to pay two prices to use the machines, the lease price and the paper price. The price for the paper was set above marginal cost. Thus, high volume users paid more for using Xerox machines than low volume users. Similar procedures were used by IBM in computer leases (selling computer cards at above cost). One explanation for this practice is price discrimination. So long as the high volume users had less elastic demands, this was one method of charging them higher prices. The companies earned more than simply selling or leasing the machines to all users at the same price. Indeed, this practice was the subject of several key court cases. Many of these types of tying arrangements are illegal today.

Other Considerations

To this point, we have not considered the response of rivals or new entrants to pricing decisions. Indeed, the demand curve is formed by assuming that the prices of other goods (for example, competitors' prices) are held constant. The short-run profit-maximizing price (or optimal discrimination policy) is a good point to start the analysis. However, a firm must often consider competitor responses to pricing decisions. For example, a proposed price cut will be more effective if it is not followed by rival firms. Also, potential new entry is important. We have already discussed barriers to entry. In the next section, we will discuss the consideration of rival firms in more detail.

Oligopoly

Market Structure

In *oligopolistic markets,* only a few firms account for most of the production in the market. Products may or may not be differentiated. Firms can earn substantial profits. These profits are not reduced through new entry because of barriers to entry. As we will see, however, abnormal profits can sometimes be eliminated in oligopolistic industries through competition among the existing firms. Examples of oligopolistic industries include automobiles and steel in the 1950s. Currently, the top four cereal makers in the United States produce about 90 percent of the output, while the top eight account for almost all the production.

In the analysis of other market structures, we assumed that firms take the prices of their competitors as given. Thus, rival firms are not expected to respond to changes in the prices of any given firm. This assumption is not valid in oligopolistic industries. For example, when American Airlines lowers it prices on certain routes it is obviously concerned about whether United Airlines and other competitors will follow suit. In fact, firms in oligopolistic industries will generally be concerned about how other firms will react to most major policy decisions (for example, advertising campaigns or product decisions). Decision making in these industries requires *strategic thinking.* Decision makers must realize that competitors are rational parties operating in their own self-interest. Thus, it is important for decision makers to place themselves in the shoes of their rivals and consider how they might react.

Nash Equilibrium

To analyze oligopoly, we need an underlying principle to define an equilibrium when firms make decisions that explicitly take each other's behavior into account. Previously we used the concept that a market is in equilibrium when firms are doing the best they can and have no reason to change price or output. For example, in a competitive equilibrium there is no reason for new entry or exit (existing firms are making "normal" profits). No existing firm has any reason to change its output level (all are producing where $MC = MR = P$).

We can apply this same basic idea to oligopolistic markets with some modification. In our subsequent analysis, a firm does the best it can, given what its rivals are doing. In doing so, the firm anticipates that other firms will respond to its actions by doing the best that they can. The actions are *noncooperative* in that each firm makes decisions that maximize its profits, given the actions of the other firms. The firms do not collude to maximize joint profits. An equilibrium exists when each firm is doing the best it can given the actions of it rivals. We call this a *Nash Equilibrium.*

To illustrate this concept, assume that there are two firms in an industry (*duopoly*). Each independently chooses a price for an identical product. The firms either choose a high price or a low price. The payoffs are given in Figure 6.9 (the first entry in a cell is the profits for firm A; the second is the profits for firm B). For example, if both firms charge a high price, firm A's profits are 400 and firm B's profits are 200. The equilibrium is for firm A to charge a high price and firm B to charge a low price. Any other combination is unstable: given the action of one of the firms the other firm has the incentive to deviate. For instance, if both firms charge a high price it is in the interests of firm B to deviate and lower price (its profits go from 200 to 250). The other combinations of firm A charging a low price and firm B a high price and both firms charging a low price are similarly unstable—the firms have an incentive to deviate given the other firm's choice. The Nash equilibrium, on the other hand, is self-enforcing. If firm A charges a high price it is optimal for firm B to charge a low price. Similarly, if firm B charges a low price it is optimal for firm A to charge a high price. Given the choice of the other firm there is no reason for the remaining firm to alter its strategy.

The Nash Equilibrium in this example is not the outcome that maximizes the joint profits of the two companies. Combined profits would be higher if both firms charged a high price. Conceptually, the combined profits under this pricing policy could be split in a manner that makes both firms better off than under the Nash outcome. For instance, the combined profits of $600 could be split with each firm receiving $300. Thus, as this example illustrates, noncooperative equilibria are not necessarily Pareto efficient. (Often one or more firms can be made better off, without making other firms worse off, by changing the joint decisions.)

The Cournot Model

The first major economic model of oligopoly was introduced by Augustine Cournot in 1838. To illustrate this model, suppose again that there are two firms in the industry.[10] The firms produce identical products. In the *Cournot model,* each firm treats the *output* level of its competitor as fixed and then decides how much to produce. In equilibrium, neither firm has an incentive to change its output level—given the other firm's choice. (Thus, this is a Nash Equilibrium.)

---

[10]This model can easily be extended to more than two firms. The same general results hold.

FIGURE 6.9   Nash Equilibrium

In this example, there are two firms in an industry. Each independently chooses a price for an identical product. The firms either choose a high price or a low price. The payoffs are given the table (the first entry in a cell is the profits for firm A; the second is the profits for firm B). The equilibrium is for firm A to charge a high price and firm B to charge a low price. Any other combination is unstable; that is, given the action of one of the firms, the other firm has the incentive to deviate. The equilibrium is called a Nash Equilibrium.

Firm B

		High Price	Low Price
	High Price	400, 200	200, 250
Firm A			
	Low Price	40, 0	20, 40

Suppose the duopolists face the following total industry demand:

$$P = 100 - Q, \tag{6.8}$$

where $Q = Q_A + Q_B$. For simplicity assume that both firms have marginal costs of zero:

$$MC_A = MC_B = 0. \tag{6.9}$$

Each firm takes the other firm's output as fixed. Thus, the anticipated demand curve for firm i ($i = 1$ or 2) is:

$$P_i = (100 - Q_j^*) - Q_i, \tag{6.10}$$

where Q_j^* is the anticipated output of the other firm. The marginal revenue for firm i is:

$$MR_i = (100 - Q_j^*) - 2Q_i. \tag{6.11}$$

Firm i's profits are maximized by setting marginal revenue equal to marginal cost (in this case zero). Doing so, and rearranging the expression, yields the following *reaction curve:*

$$Q_i = 50 - .5Q_j. \tag{6.12}$$

The reaction curve indicates Firm i's optimal output given the output choice of firm j. Both firms have the same reaction curve in this example, except that the subscripts are reversed.

FIGURE 6.10 Cournot Equilibrium

The duopolists in this example face the total industry demand curve, $P = 100 - Q$, where Q is the sum of the two outputs. Both firms face a marginal cost of zero. The figure shows the reaction curves for each firm. The reaction curve indicates Firm i's optimal output given the output choice of Firm j (i, j, = A or B). The Cournot Equilibrium is where the two reaction curves cross. Each firm produces 33.33 units. The market price is $33.34. The output for the firms is lower and the profits greater than in the competitive equilibrium. The output for the firms is greater and the profits lower than in the collusive (monopoly) equilibrium.

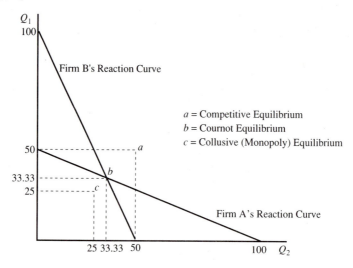

The equilibrium is where the two curves cross. At these output levels each firm is profit maximizing given the other firm's output choice. Neither firm has an incentive to alter its output. The equilibrium is pictured in Figure 6.10. In equilibrium, each firm produces 33 1/3 units for a total output of 66 2/3 units. The price is $33.34. This output level is less than with pure competition. In pure competition, the total output would be 100 units and the price would be zero (where $P = MC$). In the Cournot equilibrium, the firms make abnormal profits. Price is $33.34 and average costs are zero. Thus, each firm makes profits of $1,110.89. This profit is less than the two firms could obtain if they directly colluded and produced the monopolistic output of 50 units (for example, 25 units per firm). Here the joint profits would be $2,500 rather than $2,221.78.

Price Competition

In the Cournot model, firms focus on choosing output levels. An alternative possibility is that the firms might focus on choosing product price. Here the Nash Equilibrium is for both firms to choose a price equal to marginal cost (the competitive outcome). To see why, suppose one of the firms chooses a price, $P' > MC$. In this case, it is optimal for the other firm to charge a price just below P' to capture all the industry sales. (Customers buy the product from the firm that charges the lowest price.) Given the second firm charges a price just below P', it is optimal for the first firm to charge a slightly lower price, and so on. Only when the price is equal to marginal cost do both firms have no incentives to lower price. (Lowering price further would result in selling below cost and a loss.) Of course, both firms would like to devise a way of avoiding competition and earning higher profits. However, as we discuss below, fostering cooperation can be difficult.

Empirical Evidence

There are many different economic models of oligopoly. We have presented two of them to illustrate that economic theory does not make unambiguous predictions on what to expect in these industries. Some models yield outcomes close to pure competition—firms sell at marginal cost and make no abnormal profits. Other models yield outcomes closer to pure monopoly. What actually occurs in oligopolistic markets is an empirical issue. The existing evidence supports the hypothesis that oligopolies result in less output than purely competitive industries and that firms earn abnormal profits (at least in some industries).[11] Firms, however, sometimes compete on price to each other's detriment and do not typically earn as much in aggregate as a perfect monopolist.

Fare Wars in the Airline Industry

Firms in oligopolistic industries sometimes compete on price to each other's detriment. An example is the United States airline industry in the early 1990s. The major airlines during this period, including American, United, Delta, and Northwest, repeatedly entered into fare wars that lowered the price of air travel for consumers and lowered the combined profits of the airline industry. For instance, one company would lower its summer fares in the hope of gaining new passengers. Typically the price reduction was met by other firms within the industry within a matter of days. Outside analysts generally agreed that the firms in the industry lost profits through these price cuts. Indeed, many of these companies reported losses during the period.

Cooperation and the Prisoner's Dilemma

As we have discussed, it is in the economic interests of firms in oligopolistic industries to find ways to cooperate and to avoid losing profits through competition. Conceptually, the firms are best off if they collude and act as a single monopolist

---

[11]See Dennis W. Carlton and Jeffrey M. Perloff, *Modern Industrial Organization,* Harper Collins, 1990, Chapter 10, for a discussion of some of the relevant empirical literature.

in setting the price and output for the industry. This action maximizes joint profits, which can then be divided among the firms in the industry. The United States government understands these incentives and has passed a variety of antitrust laws to prevent firms from fixing pricing. These laws are designed to limit the inefficiencies associated with monopoly and to reduce the prices consumers pay for products. Internationally, firms tend to have more latitude in forming cooperative agreements to increase profits (for example, consider the OPEC cartel).[12]

Even when firms are free to cooperate, cooperation is not always easy to achieve. Individual firms have incentives to "cheat" and not follow agreed-upon outputs and prices. This incentive can be illustrated by the well-known *Prisoner's Dilemma*. In the Prisoner's Dilemma there are two suspects who are arrested and charged with a crime. The police do not have sufficient evidence to convict the suspects unless one of them confesses. The police place the suspects in separate rooms and ask them to confess. If neither confesses, they are convicted of a minor crime (for example, loitering) and are sentenced to two months. If both confess, they spend 12 months in jail. Finally, if one confesses and the other does not, the confessor is released immediately but the other is sentenced to 18 months in jail (12 for the crime and six for obstructing justice). The payoffs (in terms of jail time) faced by each individual are pictured in Figure 6.11.

The Nash equilibrium is for both suspects to confess. Given the payoffs, it is always in the *individual interests* of each suspect to confess (taking the action of the other party as given). For instance, if prisoner A does not confess, prisoner B is set free by confessing. Alternatively, if prisoner A confesses prisoner B reduces his jail sentence from 18 to 12 months by also confessing. Either way it is in the interests of prisoner B to confess. By symmetric logic, it is also optimal for prisoner A to confess. While it is in the individual interests of each party to confess, it is clearly in their *joint interests* not to confess. By not confessing, both parties only serve two months in jail, compared to 12 months when both confess. The Prisoner's Dilemma, however, suggests that any agreement for both to confess is likely to break down when the prisoners make their individual choices, unless there is some mechanism to enforce the joint commitment not to confess. One such mechanism is the Mafia—both prisoners have incentives not to confess if they expect to be executed by the Mob if they provide evidence to the police.

Cartels consist of formal agreements to cooperate in setting prices and output levels. (These activities are generally illegal in the U.S.) Firms trying to maintain cartels can face a Prisoner's Dilemma. For example, members can agree to restrict output to increase joint profits. However, individual firms have incentives to cheat. If all other firms restrict output, prices will not be affected significantly by the extra output of one firm. However, that firm's profits will increase from selling more. If all firms react to these incentives by increasing output the cartel breaks down. Actual

[12]In smaller countries, much of the local production of key products is exported. In this case, it can be in the countries' interests to allow the formation of cartels. Ultimately, consumers pay higher prices and there are inefficiencies. However, many of the costs are borne by people in other countries.

FIGURE 6.11   Prisoner's Dilemma.

In the Prisoner's Dilemma there are two suspects who are arrested and charged with a crime. The police do not have sufficient evidence to convict the suspects unless one of them confesses. The police place the suspects in separate rooms and ask them to confess. If neither confesses, they are convicted of a minor crime (for example, loitering) and are sentenced to two months. If both confess, they spend 12 months in jail. Finally, if one confesses and the other does not, the confessor is released immediately but the other is sentenced to 18 months in jail (12 for the crime and six for obstructing justice). The payoffs (in terms of jail time) faced by each individual are pictured. Each entry in the table lists the jail sentences for prisoner A and prisoner B, respectively. The Nash equilibrium is for both suspects to confess. Given the payoffs, it is always in the individual interests of each suspect to confess (taking the action of the other party as given).

	Prisoner B	
	No Confession	Confession
No Confession (Prisoner A)	−2,−2	−18,0
Confession (Prisoner A)	0,−18	−12,−12

cartels often unravel because of these incentives. Cartels can persist if the cartel can impose penalties on cheaters (like the Mafia in the Prisoner's Dilemma). For these penalties to be effective, cartel members must be able to observe (or accurately infer) that a firm has cheated. Also, to the extent that cartel members expect to interact on a *repeated basis,* there are increased incentives to cooperate. Repeated interactions also increase the incentives to invest in developing effective enforcement mechanisms to limit cheating. These incentives potentially can be strong enough to avoid the Prisoner's Dilemma.

Even when firms are not allowed to form cartels, there may be ways to cooperate to increase profits. For example, over time a firm might become known as a price leader. Such a firm changes prices in face of new demand or cost conditions in a way that approximates what a cartel would do. Other firms follow the price changes, thus acting like members of a cartel. Individually firms can still have short-run incentives to cheat (for example, reducing price to get more sales). However, firms might avoid this short-run temptation to foster cooperation in the long run (and hence higher long-run profits).[13]

---

[13]Indeed, economists have shown that in any long-term relationship, with no known ending date, cooperation is a *possible equilibrium*—the parties need not succumb to the Prisoner's Dilemma.

Summary

A *market* consists of all firms and individuals who are willing and able to buy or sell a particular product. These parties include those currently engaged in buying and selling the product, as well as *potential entrants. Market Structure* refers to the basic characteristics of the market environment, including: (1) the number and size of buyers, sellers, and potential entrants, (2) the degree of product differentiation, (3) the amount and cost of information about product price and quality, and (4) the conditions for entry and exit.

Perfectly competitive markets are characterized by four basic conditions: (1) a large number of buyers and sellers, (2) product homogeneity, (3) rapid dissemination of information at low cost, and (4) free entry into and exit from the market. In competitive markets, individual buyers and sellers take the market price for the product as given—they have no control over price. Firms view their demand curves as horizontal. The firm's short-run supply curve is the portion of the short-run marginal cost curve that is above average variable cost. The long-run supply curve is the portion of the long-run marginal cost curve that is above long-run average cost. In a competitive equilibrium, firms make no abnormal profits. Production is efficient in that firms produce at the low point on their long-run average cost curves. Firms in competitive industries must move fast to take advantage of transitory opportunities. They must also strive for efficient production in order to survive. Some firms in the industry can have resources that give them a competitive advantage (for example, a very talented manager). Oftentimes, however, the excess returns do not go to the firm owner, but rather to the factor of production that is responsible for the particular advantage.

While the competitive model is a reasonable approximation in many industries, there are other industries where firms have substantial market power—prices are affected significantly by the output decisions of individual firms. Market power can exist when there are substantial *barriers to entry* into the industry. Expectations about incumbent reactions, incumbent advantages, and exit costs can all serve as barriers to entry.

The extreme case of market power is *monopoly,* where there is only one firm in the industry. Here, the industry and firm demand curves are one in the same. In contrast to pure competition, consumers pay more than the marginal cost of production and the firm earns abnormal profits. Output is restricted from competitive levels. The monopolistic outcome is inefficient—not all the potential gains from trade are exhausted. One motive for government regulation of monopoly is to reduce this *social cost.*

As the name implies, *monopolistic competition* is a market structure that is a hybrid between competition and monopoly. Monopolistic competition is like monopoly in that firms in both market structures face downward sloping demand curves. The analyses of output and pricing policies are similar between the two cases. The difference between monopoly and monopolistic competition is that in monopolistic competition abnormal profits invite entry that drives down profits.

Price discrimination occurs whenever a firm's prices in different markets are not related to differentials in production and distribution costs. In maximizing profits, managers strive to capture the maximum amount of *consumer surplus* (subject to the constraint that the product is sold for more than cost). There are three degrees of price discrimination. *Two-part tariffs* are also used by some firms to increase profits.

In *oligopolistic markets,* there are only a few firms that account for most or all of the production in the market. Products may or may not be differentiated. Firms can earn substantial profits. However, these profits can be eliminated through competition among existing firms in the industry. A *Nash Equilibrium* exists when each firm is doing the best it can given the actions of it rivals. We use this concept to analyze output and pricing decisions in oligopolistic industries. In the *Cournot model,* each firm treats the *output* level of its competitor as fixed and then decides how much to produce. In equilibrium, firms make abnormal profits. However, these profits are not as large as could be made if the firms colluded and engaged in monopolistic pricing. Other models of oligopoly yield different equilibria. For instance, one model based on *price competition* yields the competitive solution—price equals marginal cost and there are no abnormal profits. Overall, economic theory makes no clear-cut prediction about the behavior of firms in oligopolistic industries. The empirical evidence suggests that in at least some oligopolistic industries firms restrict output from competitive levels and correspondingly make at least some abnormal profits.

It is in the economic interests of firms in oligopolistic industries to find ways to cooperate and to avoid losing profits through competition. Even when firms are free to cooperate, cooperation is not always easy to achieve. Individual firms have incentives to ''cheat'' and not follow agreed-upon outputs and prices. This incentive is illustrated by the well-known *Prisoner's Dilemma*. This dilemma can cause cartels to be unstable. However, firms can sometimes successfully cooperate when the members can impose penalties or sanctions on defecting firms. Also, cooperation can be sustained through the incentives provided by long-run, *repeated relationships.*

CHAPTER 7

Contracting Costs and Organizational Architecture

In 1988, the world witnessed the largest takeover in history, the purchase of RJR-Nabisco by Kohlberg, Kravis, Roberts & Company. The public accounts of this takeover highlight the lavish expenditures of RJR executives prior to the takeover. For example, Burrough and Helyar in the best seller, *Barbarians at the Gate,* write:

> "It was no lie. RJR executives lived like kings. The top thirty-one executives were paid a total of $14.2 million, or an average of $458,000. Some of them became legends at the Waverly for dispensing $100 tips to the shoeshine girl. Johnson's two maids were on the company payroll. No expense was spared decorating the new headquarters, high-lighted by the top-floor digs of the top executives. It was literally, the sweet life. A candy cart came around twice a day dropping off bowls of bonbons at each floor's reception areas. Not Baby Ruths but fine French confections. The minimum perks for even lowly middle managers was one club membership and one company car, worth $28,000. The maximum, as nearly as anyone could tell, was Johnson's two dozen club memberships and John Martin's $75,000 Mercedes."

In addition, accounts suggest that major investment decisions at RJR were often driven by the preferences of managers (for example, pet projects) rather than by value maximization. For example, it is argued that Ross Johnson, chief executive officer of RJR, continued to invest millions of dollars in developing a smokeless cigarette long after it was obvious that the project was not going to be profitable.

The behavior of RJR executives raises at least four interesting questions: (1) Were the actions of RJR executives actually inconsistent with value maximization? (2) If so, why did the owners of the firm (the shareholders) allow the actions to take place? (3) Do individuals have incentives to design firms to limit actions that reduce firm value? (4) If so, can these incentives help to explain the actual design of organizations?

In this chapter, we answer these questions. We also provide a definition of the firm that focuses on the individual as the basic unit of analysis. Such a definition is critical for a study of organizational architecture (the focus of the remainder of the book). We also discuss how reputational concerns can reduce incentive conflicts within firms.

Incentive Conflicts and Contracting

Conflicting Objectives

Firms consist of individuals engaged in joint effort. For example, shareholders and lenders provide capital to the firm. Managers operate the firm, while lower-level employees carry out other tasks. Subcontractors supply inputs to the firm.

Economic theory argues that individuals are creative maximizers of their *own utility*. Thus individuals within the firm are not likely to have objectives that are automatically aligned. For example, the shareholders of the firm want employees to work hard and be creative to produce profits (since shareholders have the legal rights to the profits). In contrast, employees are likely to prefer short work days and spending company money on high salaries, country-club memberships, expensive office furniture, fancy automobiles, and French candy.

Agency Problems

An *agency relationship* consists of an agreement under which one party, the *principal,* engages another party, the *agent,* to perform some service on the principal's behalf. Many agency relationships exist within firms. For example, shareholders appoint boards of directors as their agents to manage firms. Boards, in turn, delegate much of the operating authority to top managers, while managers assign tasks to lower-level workers. Since individuals are utility maximizers, there is good reason to believe that agents will not always act in the best interests of principals—there are *agency problems.*

Agency Problems and Contracts

Why don't agency problems destroy all potential agency relationships? For example, shouldn't the fear that managers will use all company resources for their personal benefit prevent shareholders from delegating operating authority to managers?

Agency relationships exist because agents face constraints that help to control agency problems. For example, constraints are imposed on managers by the market for corporate control—firms with inefficient managers can be taken over by other firms and the management team replaced. Indeed this is what happened at RJR-Nabisco. Managers are also constrained by product-market competition—if they don't produce efficiently in a competitive market the company will go out of business.

Agency Problems throughout the World

Agency problems are not just an American business phenomenon. Rather, these problems exist throughout the world in both the private and public sectors. For example, government officials taking bribes reflects a basic agency problem between government officials and the people they represent. In September 1993, Japanese prosecutors arrested the chairman of a leading construction company in a major bribery scandal. The chairman was alleged to have bribed the governor of the Ibaraki prefecture to favor his company's bids for public work projects. The governor was arrested for taking hundreds of thousands of dollars in bribes (*Wall Street Journal,* September 23, 1993).

A similar event occurred in China where a bureaucrat confessed to using a safe-deposit box in Hong Kong to stash away more than $1.2 million in cash bribes from companies attempting to get pieces of real-estate deals she controlled. Meanwhile, in the banking sector, the premier of China is attempting to change the common practice by bankers of ignoring credit standards and awarding loans to people ''with connections.'' In one case, eight bankers received stiff sentences, including the death penalty for accepting bribes in return for loans. (*Business Week,* July 26, 1993).

Important constraints are also imposed on agents by *contracts* between the principal and the agent. Contracts constrain agents by specifying the rights and obligations of the contracting parties and the corresponding payoffs. Since economic decisions are a function of both objectives and constraints, contracts can potentially motivate agents to make optimal choices on the behalf of the principal.

As an example, consider a top manager who has a labor contract that pays a fixed salary, *S,* as long as the manager maximizes profit. If the manager fails to profit maximize, for example by being too generous with such perquisites as club memberships, salaries, or buying French bonbons, the board reduces the compensation at year end for every dollar of lost profits. (For now, we assume that the board can observe lost profits at no cost.) One method that the board could use to implement this scheme is to pay a variable year-end bonus that is low if profits are low.

The manager gains utility from both salary, S, and perquisites, P:

$$U = f(S,P), \text{ where} \tag{1}$$

the manager's utility, *U,* is increasing in both *S* and *P*. We assume that *S* and *P* are not perfect substitutes. For example, if the manager has a high salary and few perquisites, he might be willing to give up $100 of salary for $75 worth of perquisites because perquisites are not taxed. Alternatively, if the manager has many perquisites and a low salary, he might be willing to trade $100 worth of perquisites for $75 of taxable income to have additional cash to pay the house mortgage and buy groceries. Preferences of this type can be illustrated by standard convex indifference curves.

FIGURE 7.1 Optimal Perquisite Taking.

The manager is paid a fixed salary, S, as long as the manager maximizes profits. If the manager fails to maximize profits by taking perquisites (for example, too many club memberships, paying too-high salaries to top subordinates, or buying expensive company cars), the board reduces the compensation by the amount of the lost profits. Given this compensation scheme, the manager chooses the combination (S^*, P^*). This choice is Pareto-efficient.

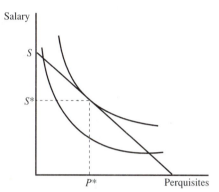

Figure 7.1 illustrates that the manager optimally chooses the combination (S^*, P^*). This combination places the manager on the highest indifference curve possible given the compensation plan. This choice is Pareto-efficient. The shareholders are indifferent to the manager's choice—they always pay the equivalent of S to the manager. The manager, however, is better off by being able to choose the combination of salary and perquisites that he most prefers.

This example suggests that some perquisite-taking by managers is likely to be optimal. (It is a less expensive way to pay the managers because of tax advantages.) Thus the perquisite-taking by RJR executives was not necessarily inconsistent with profit maximization. Evidence from the stock market, however, suggests that the behavior of RJR executives was excessive. In particular, the stock price of RJR moved from about $55/share at the beginning of the takeover contest in October 1988 to about $90/share when the company was taken over. Furthermore, the management team was subsequently replaced. (Thus the old management team does not appear to have been maximizing the value of the firm.)

Contracting Costs

Our example indicates that, in principle, contracts could be used to solve all agency problems. The example of RJR, however, suggests that contracts generally are unsuccessful in accomplishing this objective.

Contracts are not costless to negotiate, write, or enforce. For instance, in our example it is unlikely that the board of directors could actually measure the lost profits to deduct from the manager's salary. (This process requires a lot of information that is costly to acquire and process.) Also the manager might be able to convince board members not to follow through with the compensation agreement and pay S independent of the amount of perquisite-taking. Indeed, Ross Johnson at RJR tried to keep board members on his side by paying them large retainers. Shareholders could always try to elect a new board. However, this is not a costless undertaking. Legal fees alone can often be substantial for writing and enforcing contracts. For example, it is estimated that the legal profession's receipts were about $91 billion in 1991 (*Business Week,* September 6, 1993).

While contracts are not perfect in solving agency problems, the principal usually can limit the divergence of interest by establishing appropriate incentives for the agent in the contract and by incurring *monitoring costs* aimed at limiting the aberrant activities of the agent. Also the agent might incur *bonding costs* to help guarantee that she will not take certain actions or to ensure that the principal will be compensated if she does. (For example, the agent might buy an insurance policy that pays the principal in the case of theft.) Generally, however, it will not pay for either party to incur enough costs to ensure that the agent will completely follow the wishes of the principal (at some point the marginal cost is greater than the marginal benefit for making additional expenditures to increase compliance). The dollar equivalent of the loss in gains from trade that results due to the divergence of interest in the agency relationship is known as the *residual loss.* Total agency costs are the sum of the *out-of-pocket costs* (monitoring and bonding costs) and the residual loss.[1]

Example of Contracting Costs

To illustrate the concept of agency costs, consider Good Tire Company and the law firm Brown & Brown. Good Tire wants outside legal counsel for contracting and litigation as well as for general legal advice. Brown & Brown is capable of supplying these services.

Good Tire's marginal benefit, *MB,* for hours of legal services is:

$$MB = \$200 - 2L, \text{ where} \tag{2}$$

L is the hours per week of legal services provided to the firm. The marginal benefit of additional hours of legal services declines with the total number of hours provided.

Brown & Brown's marginal cost, *MC,* for providing legal services is:

$$MC = \$100. \tag{3}$$

---

[1]See M. C. Jensen and W. H. Meckling, 1976, "Theory of the Firm: Managerial Behavior, Agency Costs and Ownership Structure," *Journal of Financial Economics* 3, 305–360.

The marginal cost of providing additional hours of legal services is constant at $100/ hour.

All potential gains from trade between Good Tire and Brown & Brown are realized at the point where the marginal benefits of legal service equal the marginal costs:

$$MB = MC, \tag{4}$$
$$200 - 2L = 100,$$
$$L^* = 50 \text{ hours.}$$

It is not optimal to provide more than 50 hours of legal services because the marginal benefits are less than the marginal costs. Correspondingly, it is sub-optimal to provide less than 50 hours because the marginal costs of providing additional hours are less than the marginal benefits.

Assuming there are no agency problems, the optimal contract would call for 50 hours/week of legal services. For example, Good Tire might agree to pay Brown & Brown $6,250 a week for 50 hours of legal work. (The weekly amount is based on an hourly rate of $125.) This outcome is pictured in the graph on the left in Figure 7.2. The total gain from the exchange (surplus) is $2,500, as depicted by the triangle labeled S. At a price of $125/hour for legal services, the gains are split evenly between the two companies.[2]

However, there is a potential agency problem that can confound this relationship: It is costly for Good Tire to observe how many hours of legal work Brown & Brown actually provides to the firm. Thus, Brown & Brown might work less than 50 hours but claim they worked the full amount. Indeed the problem might be so severe that Good Tire simply does not hire Brown & Brown. In this case, the entire gains from trade are lost. This agency cost is a residual loss—the lost surplus that results because it does not pay to solve the agency problem.

More generally, the two firms might be able to promote a mutually-advantageous exchange by limiting the agency problem though expenditures on monitoring and bonding. For example, Good Tire might spend $400/week to hire an auditor to check Brown & Brown's work, while Brown & Brown might spend $400/week to document that they are actually conducting legal work for the firm. It is, however, unlikely that it will completely pay the two parties to spend enough resources to guarantee that Brown & Brown will do no overbilling. For example, the end result might be that, after the $800 expenditures on monitoring and bonding, Brown & Brown provides 40 hours of legal service and bills for 50 hours. Both parties anticipate this outcome and might negotiate a price of $5,000 for the legal service (40 actual hours * $125/hour or $100/hour for the 50 hours that are billed).

The graph on the right in Figure 7.2 illustrates this outcome. The triangle, labeled R, is the residual loss of $100—the lost surplus that results because it does

---

[2]Recall that total benefits (TB) are equal to the area under the marginal benefit curve, while total costs (TC) are the area under the marginal cost curve. Thus at 50 hours of legal service, the total surplus is $S = TB - TC$. Note that the firms might negotiate prices other than $125/hour and split the gains unevenly.

FIGURE 7.2   Agency Costs in Legal Contracting.

The left-hand graph shows the marginal benefit, MB, to Good Tire for hours of legal services, L, and the marginal cost, MC, to Brown & Brown for providing these services. Assuming no agency problems the optimal number of hours is 50. The total gains from trade, $2,500, are shown by the triangle labeled S. The right-hand graph reflects the agency problem between the two firms—Brown & Brown might bill for more hours than hours worked. The two firms spend $400 each for monitoring and bonding costs. These out-of-pocket costs are shown by the rectangle labeled O. Since it does not pay to solve the agency problem completely, we assume that Brown & Brown ends up providing only 40 hours of legal services. The triangle, R, represents the residual loss of $100. The original surplus S is reduced by the sum of the out-of-pocket costs and the residual loss. The resulting surplus is $1,600. How this surplus is split depends on the price charged for the legal services.

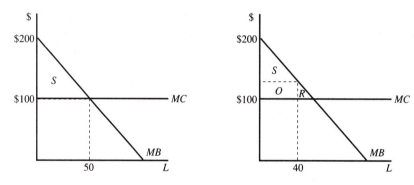

not pay to completely solve the agency problem. In addition, the two companies pay $400 each for monitoring and bonding. These payments reduce the surplus by $800 as shown by the rectangle labeled *O*. The remaining surplus is $1,600. This surplus is equal to the original surplus of $2,500 minus the total agency costs of $900—the sum of the out-of-pocket costs (monitoring and bonding costs) and the residual loss.

Incentives to Economize on Contracting Costs

It is very important to understand that both the principal and the agent have incentives to resolve agency problems in the least costly manner. By doing so, there are more gains from trade to share between the two parties. For instance, in the Good Tire example, there would be an additional $900 of surplus to split between Good Tire and Brown & Brown if the agency problem could be resolved costlessly. (If they didn't have to spend money on auditors and compliance, they could divide the savings between themselves.)

Do Companies Really Have Agency Problems with Their Law Firms?

Our example of agency problems with law firms illustrates a real-life problem faced by businesses every day: figuring out whether their lawyers are playing it straight. According to *Business Week:*

> "The task is time-consuming and often unpleasant, but for companies battling ever diminishing budgets can be fruitful. General Dynamics, for example, lopped off $186,000, or 42% from just one bill when it discovered a law firm charging for what ended up to be useless research. Motorola Inc. saved a pocketful when it confronted counsel for billing it for hours spent preparing documents that, because of a statute passed a year earlier, were no longer required."

From "The Verdict: Guilty of Overcharging," *Business Week,* September 6, 1993.

For any given scale of activity, individuals wishing to maximize self-interests minimize the agency costs in any contracting relationship.[3] Incentives exist to write contracts that provide monitoring and bonding activities to the point where the marginal cost equals the marginal gain from reducing the residual loss. This means that incentives exist within the contracting process to produce an efficient utilization of resources (at least from the standpoint of the contracting parties).

Viewing observed contracts as efficient responses to the particular contracting problem can be a very powerful tool for explaining observed organizational architectures. As a simple example, consider the difference in the way pear pickers are paid compared to workers that assemble airplanes. Agricultural workers are usually paid on a piecework basis. The more they pick, the more they get paid. Alternatively, workers that assemble airplanes often are paid straight salary. (The same salary is paid independent of output.) How can we explain this difference in observed contracts? In general, output increases if people are paid on a piecework basis. A person will pick more pears per hour if paid by the pear than by the hour. However, piecework payments generate their own set of agency problems. These payments motivate people to focus on output and to ignore quality. In fruit picking, a supervisor can monitor the quality of the output cheaply through direct inspection of the picked fruit. In the case of airplanes, quality deficiencies may not be detected until after the employee leaves his job (for example, when the airplane crashes). In this case,

---

[3]Note for the technically inclined: For this statement to be strictly true, production costs must be separable from agency costs and there must be no wealth effects. (The choices of the principal and agent are independent of their individual wealth levels.) When these conditions are violated, the individuals might not want to minimize total agency costs. However, they still have strong incentives to consider these costs in designing contracts. For our purpose it is reasonable and convenient to ignore these technical considerations.

the agency costs of piecework payments are larger than the benefits. We use this type of logic throughout the book to explain the design of organizations.

The Firm as a Nexus of Contracts

Firms are frequently referred to as if they were capable of making conscious decisions. For example, consider the following quotes from the October 26, 1993, issue of the *The Wall Street Journal:*

> ''Surgical Care Affiliates proposed to acquire Medical Care America.''

> ''General Mills named Stephen Sanger president of the packaged food concern, making him the clear favorite to become its next Chairman and Chief Executive Officer.''

Our discussion of contracts, however, emphasizes that a firm is not a decision-making entity. Rather it is individuals within the firm that make decisions. For example, the board of directors names the president and decides on major acquisitions, while lower-level managers often decide on the firm's output and pricing policies.

Treating the firm like an individual decision maker is a useful abstraction in some contexts. For example, the analysis in the last three chapters assumed the firm was an entity that acted to maximize profits. This type of analysis has proven very useful in explaining the output and pricing decisions of firms.[4] Analyzing organizational issues *within the firm,* however, requires a definition of a firm that focuses on individuals as the basic unit of analysis. A particularly useful definition is offered by Jensen and Meckling (1976)[5]:

DEFINITION

''The firm is a legal fiction that serves as a nexus of contracts.''

The firm is a legal fiction in the sense that it is a creation of the legal system. A firm, while an artificial entity, has the legal standing of an individual in that it can enter contracts, sue, be sued, and so on. *Nexus of contracts* refers to the firm always being one party to the many contracts that make up the firm. Examples of these contracts are employee contracts, supplier contracts, customer warranties, stocks,

---

[4]The assumption of profit maximization is reasonable for studying output and pricing decisions to the extent that contracts and other constraints motivate individuals in the firm to take actions to increase profits.

[5]M. C. Jensen and W. H. Meckling, 1976, ''Theory of the Firm: Managerial Behavior, Agency Costs and Ownership Structure,'' *Journal of Financial Economics* 3, 305–360.

<hr>

FIGURE 7.3   The Firm as a Nexus Contracts.

The firm is a creation of the legal system that has the standing of an individual in a court of law. The firm serves as one party to the many contracts that make up the firm.

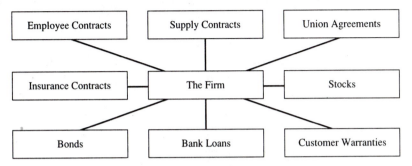

bonds, loans, leases, franchise agreements, and insurance contracts. The nexus-of-contracts view of the firm is pictured in Figure 7.3.

Some contracts are explicit legal documents, while many others are implicit. An example of an implicit contract is a worker's understanding that if a job is well done it will result in a promotion. Implicit contracts are often difficult to enforce in a court of law. Later in this chapter, we discuss how reputational concerns can help to assure that individuals honor implicit contracts.

Examples of Incentive Conflicts

We have defined the firm as a nexus of contracts and argued that contracts will tend to be designed to reduce the adverse effects of incentive conflicts within the organization. We now elaborate on some of the more important incentive conflicts that arise among contracting parties in organizations. Later in the book, we discuss how particular contract provisions and other mechanisms help to control these conflicts in a productive fashion.

Shareholder/Manager Conflicts

Shareholders have the legal rights to the residual profits of the firm (what is left over after other claimants are paid). Shareholders typically delegate the management of the firm to top executives. At least four sources of conflict arise between shareholders and managers: (1) Choice of effort—additional effort by the manager generally increases the value of the firm, but additional effort can reduce the utility of the manager. (2) Differential risk exposure—managers typically have substantial levels of human capital and personal wealth invested in the firm. This large investment can make managers overly risk-averse from the standpoint of the shareholders who typically hold only a small fraction of their wealth in any one firm. For example, the managers might forgo profitable projects because they do not want to bear the risk. (3) Differential horizons—the manager's claim on the corporation is generally limited to her tenure with the firm. The corporation, on the other hand, has an indefinite life, and stockholder claims are tradeable claims on the entire future stream of residual cash flows. Managers, therefore, have incentives to place lower values on cash flows occurring beyond their horizon than is implied by the market values of these cash flows. (4) Free-cash-flow problems—a manager might be reluctant to reduce the size of the firm by paying cash out of the firm (for example as dividends) even if the firm has no profitable investment projects. Rather the manager might prefer to empire-build.

Conflicts with Suppliers

Owners of firms want to acquire high-quality inputs at low prices. Owners of supplying firms want to provide low-cost inputs at high prices. This tension can cause conflicts between buyers and suppliers. Supplying firms worry about the buying firms demanding price concessions, while buying firms worry that suppliers will either shirk on quality (to reduce cost) or attempt to raise prices. In Chapter 15, we provide a detailed analysis of buyer/supplier relationships.

Buyer-Supplier Conflicts in the 1990s

Large firms have become increasingly aggressive at demanding price concessions from suppliers. For example, a survey of 300 large manufacturers by the National Association of Purchasing Management indicates that the average price paid to suppliers decreased by about 1% in 1992. This price decline contrasts to price increases ranging from 2% to 5% over the previous five years. Large manufacturers have also become more likely to switch suppliers in an attempt to decrease costs.

These activities have increased the strain between buyers and suppliers and have made small suppliers less likely to enter into exclusive contracts with one large firm. For example, the co-owner of a small aerospace-industry supplier that derives two-thirds of its sales from Boeing says, "Pressure from Boeing to reduce prices has gotten worse in the past couple of years. They haven't learned to cut costs internally so they are beating up on the vendors. We are looking for new customers wherever we can." In some industries, the conflicts are particularly severe. For example, according to a survey in 1992 by *Ward's Auto World,* a trade publication, more than half of 154 auto-industry suppliers say GM's cost-cutting reorganization was unfavorable to them. GM has been especially aggressive in demanding price cuts from suppliers.

Suggested by M. Selz, "Some Suppliers Rethink Their Reliance on Big Business," *The Wall Street Journal,* March 29, 1993.

Other Conflicts

Similar types of incentive conflicts are likely to arise between most contracting parties in the firm. For example, top managers worry about effort and perquisite-taking problems with lower-level workers. Shareholders and other capital suppliers can have disputes over the optimal dividend and investment policies of the firm. Managers often quarrel with labor unions. Firms can have incentives to default on warranties with customers.

Freerider Problems

Thus far we have concentrated on incentive conflicts between individuals in hier-archal relationships. (There is a principal and an agent.) Agency-like problems, however, arise in almost all cooperative undertakings where the decision maker does not bear the full wealth effect of his actions. For example, consider partners in a large law firm. The actions of each partner affect the profits of the organization which are shared among the partners. This arrangement can motivate partners to *freeride* on the efforts of others. Each partner hopes the other partners will work hard to keep the firm profitable. However, each partner has an incentive to shirk—individuals gain the full benefit of their shirking, but only bear part of the costs (their share of the reduced profits). Freerider problems are common in most group efforts, and left unchecked can greatly reduce the output of teams. We frequently refer to freerider problems throughout this book.

Experimental Evidence on Freerider Problems

"More than 50 years ago a German scientist named Ringelmann asked workers to pull as hard as they could on a rope attached to a meter that measured the strength of their efforts. Subjects worked alone and in groups of two, three, and eight.

While the total amount of force on the rope increased as group size rose, the amount of effort by each person seemed to drop. While one person pulling alone exerted an average of 63kg of force, this dropped to about 53kg in groups of three and was reduced to about 31kg in groups of eight. The greater the number of people performing the task, the less effort each one expended.

The impact or effect of any social force directed towards a group from an outside source (for example, a manager) is divided among its members. Thus, the more persons in the group, the less the impact such force will have upon each. Because they are working with others, each group member feels they will take up any slack resulting from reduced effort on their part. And since all members tend to respond in this fashion, average output per person drops sharply."

From A. Furnham, "Wasting Time in the Board Room," *Financial Times*, March 10, 1993.

Costly Information and Contracting

We have argued that contracting costs preclude costless contractual solutions to agency problems. One especially important factor that limits contractual solutions is costly information. Both pre-contractual and post-contractual information problems can limit the viability of contracts and correspondingly reduce the gains from trade from agency relationships.

Pre-contractual Information Problems

Information at the time of contract negotiations is typically *asymmetric*. For example, in negotiating a labor contract, the prospective employee typically has superior information on what wage she will accept, while the employer knows more about what he is willing to pay. Pre-contractual informational asymmetries can cause at least two major problems in bargaining.

First, asymmetric information can cause parties not to reach an agreement even when in principle a contract could be constructed that is mutually advantageous. For example, assume that a worker is willing to accept a job for as little as $2,000 per month and the human resources manager is willing to pay as much as $3,000 per month. In principle, a mutually advantageous contract could be negotiated at any price between $2,000 and $3,000. Neither side, however, is likely to know the other side's *reservation price.* In an attempt to get the best price possible, both parties might overreach resulting in a bargaining failure. For example, the worker might claim that she will not work for less than $3,500. The human resources manager, in turn, might refuse the offer and discontinue negotiations because he does not think that he can hire the worker for less than $3,000 (his reservation price). This phenomenon helps to explain the existence of labor strikes that end up hurting both labor and the company. (Strikes result in lower productivity and sales, and thus there are fewer profits to split between labor and the company.)

A second problem caused by pre-contractual informational asymmetries is *adverse selection.* Adverse selection refers to the tendency of individuals, with private information about something that affects a potential trading partner's benefits, to make offers that are detrimental to the trading partner.

As an example consider the market for health insurance. Table 7.1 displays three individuals and their expected medical costs for the year. Ann is very healthy and is expected to spend only $100 on medical expenses, while Claire is very unhealthy and is expected to spend $900. Bob is in the middle with expected expenditures of $500. The average expected expenditure for all three individuals is $500/person.

It is likely that each individual knows more about his or her health than an insurance company—the individual knows how they have been feeling and their health habits, while an insurance company is likely to have information that is restricted to the typical expenditures for the entire population (by age and sex categories). In this spirit, assume that each individual knows his or her expected expenditure, while the insurance company only knows the expected expenditure for

---

TABLE 7.1   Example of Adverse Selection in Insurance Markets

---

This table shows the expected annual medical expenditures for three individuals. If an insurance company sells insurance to all three at a price above $500/year, it expects to make a profit. However, if the company prices insurance at $500, Ann is unlikely to purchase the insurance. Bob and Claire have expected expenditures of $700/person. Thus if Bob and Claire are the sole purchasers, the company must sell the insurance at above $700 to break even. In this case, Bob might not buy the insurance. The end result can be a market failure where the company prices the insurance at $900 and sells only to Claire.

	Expected Annual Medical Expenditures
Ann	$100
Bob	$500
Claire	$900
All Three Individuals	$500/Person

the three individuals as a group—$500/person. If the company expects to make a profit, it must on average sell insurance policies at premiums above the expected expenditures of the buyers.

The information structure in this example can cause a market failure. For instance, assume that the insurance company tries to sell insurance at $510. If all three parties buy the insurance the company expects to make a profit. However, at this price Ann might not want to purchase insurance. She expects to spend only $100 for medical expenses, and so to her the insurance is very expensive. If only Bob and Claire buy the insurance, the company on average will lose money at a premium of $510. The insurance company might anticipate that healthy individuals will not buy the insurance at $510 and attempt to raise the price. For example, if it sells the insurance policies to both Claire and Bob at $710 it will make a profit. (Their average expected expenditure is $700/person.) However, at this price Bob is less likely to buy the insurance because the price is substantially above his expected expenditures of $500. In the end, the insurance company might price insurance at above $900 and sell only to Claire, the most unhealthy of the three.

The company might be able to prevent this market failure and sell insurance to all three parties by becoming better informed about the individual health of its applicants. For example, it might require a medical exam of all applicants as well as access to all their medical records. In this case, different rates could be charged depending on the health of the individual. Collecting information, however, is costly and thus there is an incentive to consider these costs in the design of the organization and its policies.[6]

---

[6]The company might also overcome the problem by selling group insurance to a company that employs all three individuals. In this case, the individuals do not select whether or not to be covered. Thus the insurance company can make a profit at a premium above $500 per person.

In some cases, adverse-selection problems can be reduced by the clever design of contracts. For example, an insurance company might be able to offer a menu of contracts with different deductibles, coinsurance requirements, and prices that would motivate the individuals to *self select* based on their private information. For example, Ann might choose a low-priced insurance contract with a high deductible, while Claire might choose a high-priced contract that provides for full insurance. In this case, the company might be able to sell insurance to all three people at a profit.

Sometimes it is possible for individuals to communicate or *signal* their private information to other parties in a credible fashion. For example, Ann might be able to convince the insurance company that she is very healthy and should be sold insurance at a low rate. (For example, she might document that she participated in ten marathon races during the year.) Ann's communication to the company will be convincing to the company only if the cost to Bob and Claire for sending the same signal is higher than Ann's. (For example, due to poor health they are unable to participate in ten marathons.) Otherwise, they could take the same action to claim they were healthy, and there would be no reason for the company to believe the claim.

Adverse-selection problems are not limited to insurance markets but occur in many settings. For example, prospective employees are likely to know more about their talents and productivity than prospective employers. Similarly, the seller of a used car knows more about the quality of the car than the buyer. Thus, at a given price, sellers are more likely to offer "lemons" than high-quality cars.[7] In these settings, traders often develop mechanisms that help to reduce adverse-selection problems. For example, used-car dealers offer warranties that guarantee that if the product is a lemon the seller will repair or exchange it at his expense. Also there are diagnostic mechanics that can provide prospective buyers additional information about the quality of a car.

Post-contractual Information Problems

In most cases, the parties to a contract cannot costlessly observe each other's actions after the contract is entered. For example, employers cannot costlessly observe the effort exerted by workers and buying firms cannot costlessly observe the quality of the production of its subcontractors. These post-contractual informational asymmetries cause *moral-hazard* problems—an individual can have incentives to deviate from the contract and take self-interested actions because the other party has insufficient information to know if the contract was honored. As we have discussed, moral-hazard problems can be reduced by setting appropriate incentives in contracts and through various types of monitoring and bonding. How organizations might be designed to reduce moral-hazard problems is a recurring topic throughout the rest of this book.

---

[7]See G. Akerlof, 1970, "The Market for Lemons: Quality Uncertainty and the Market Mechanism," *Quarterly Journal of Economics* 84, 488–500.

Battling Adverse Selection and Moral Hazard in Automobile Insurance

Robert Plan Corporation specializes in providing automobile insurance to high-risk customers in urban areas. Most insurance companies have stayed away from this market because of high risks from both adverse selection and moral hazard. Robert Plan has been successful in this market by aggressively addressing both problems.

The company carefully scrutinizes applications to assess the proper premium. It claims that about 70% of its applications are "misstated," with applicants fibbing about items like whether they drive to work or where their primary residence is. Robert Plan uses its own private investigators to check out potential fibs. They may visit applicants' homes and follow them as they drive their cars (to determine if they are driving to work).

The company is also concerned about the moral-hazard problem of excessive claims. The company is notorious for being aggressive in ensuring that it does not pay excessive claims. Company investigators say one maneuver that "works well" is letting the air out of a tire to see if someone claiming a back injury "feels well enough to change it." The top management of the company does not "condone this action and says if it is going on it will stop it." However, for the company to survive it must conduct "hand-to-hand combat with fraud."

Suggested by S. Woolley, "Smile, Cheater, You're on Candid Camera," *Business Week*, October 4, 1993.

Implicit Contracts and Reputational Concerns

Many of the contracts that make up the firm are implicit—they consist of promises and understandings that are not backed up by formal legal documents. Examples include promises of promotions and salary increases for a job well done and informal understandings that suppliers will not shirk on quality. By definition, implicit contracts are difficult to enforce in a court of law and largely depend on the private incentives of individuals to honor the terms of the contract. Given the incentive conflicts that we have discussed in this chapter, how can individuals ever depend on others to honor the terms of implicit contracts? For example, why would an employee ever trust an implicit promise by a manager to give the person a bonus for a job well done? Doesn't the manager always have incentives to default on the contract after the worker's job is complete? Not paying the worker increases profits and the manager's bonus.

The answer is that reputational concerns can act as a powerful force to motivate contract compliance. In particular, the market can impose substantial costs on institutions and individuals for unethical behavior. Thus, market forces can provide private incentives for honorable behavior.

As an example, consider a firm that has a long-run contract to provide a metal part to a manufacturing firm each month at a price of $10,000. The cost of producing this product is $9,000, so the profit per unit is $1,000. It is possible for the supplier to produce a low-quality product for $2,000. However, it has agreed to provide a high-quality product. Since the quality of the part is only known to the buyer after purchase, it would be possible for the supplier to make a profit of $8,000 by producing a low-quality part but claiming it is a high quality product. The buying firm, however, will detect the quality of the part after purchase and will discontinue future purchases if it is cheated. The supplying firm faces a trade-off. It can gain $7,000 in the short run by cheating. However, it loses a $1,000/month future profit stream. The supplier has the incentive to be honest as long as the value of the future profit stream is greater than the short-run gain from cheating.

Typically, the costs of cheating on quality are higher if the information about such activities is more rapidly and widely distributed to potential future customers. For example, in markets like the diamond trade in New York, cheating on quality is very rare. This market is dominated by a close-knit community of Hasidic Jews; thus, information about unethical activities is rapidly distributed throughout the market. In other broader markets, specialized services that monitor the market help insure contract performance. For example, *Consumer Reports* evaluates products from toasters to automobiles, the *Investment Dealer's Digest* reports on investment bankers, and *Business Week* ranks MBA programs. By lowering the costs for potential customers to determine quality, these information sources increase the costs of cheating.

Crimes, Lies, and Prudential-Bache

During the 1980s Prudential-Bache sold partnerships with Clifton S. Harrison to renovate and build commercial properties. Almost all ran into financial troubles. Amid the collapse of the deals it became public that Mr. Harrison, a man presented by Prudential executives as worthy of the highest recommendation, was a convicted criminal who had served 18 months in jail for financial fraud. The brokerage firm apparently knew this all along and decided not to tell. As of October 1993, Prudential was still negotiating with regulators to settle fraud charges. The settlement is expected to cost about $370 million. The firm also faces lawsuits from investors who say the deals destroyed their lives.

The reputation costs to Prudential have been large. To quote a former Prudential broker, "It's the nearest thing to a disaster I ever encountered . . . our friends have been our clients, and our clients have been our friends. Now we have been deprived of both." Today Prudential is trying to regain the trust of customers. As their recent campaign slogan says: "The most important thing we earn is your trust."

Suggested by K. Eichenwald, "Crimes, Lies and Prudential-Bache," *New York Times*, October 10, 1993.

More generally, reputational concerns are most likely to be effective in promoting contract compliance when (1) the gains from cheating are small, (2) the likelihood of detecting cheating is large, and (3) the payoffs from maintaining a good reputation are large. When these conditions are not met, reputational concerns cannot be expected to motivate contract compliance. In many settings, however, reputational concerns are very important in promoting cooperation and honesty. The ability to enter into self-enforcing agreements can significantly reduce the costs of contracting in an organization. (Fewer resources are used for negotiating and enforcing formal contracts.) Later in Chapter 18 of the book, we will see that it is sometimes possible to design organizations in ways that increase the likelihood that reputational concerns will promote honorable behavior.

Summary

An *agency relationship* consists of an agreement under which one party, the *principal,* engages another party, the *agent,* to perform some service on behalf of the principal. Many agency relationships exist within firms. Since individuals are creative maximizers of their own utility there are likely to be incentive conflicts. Agents do not always act in the best interests of principals; there are *agency problems.*

Contracts can help mitigate agency problems. Economic decisions are a function of both objectives and constraints. Contracts can potentially motivate agents to make optimal choices on behalf of the principals by setting the appropriate constraints and incentives.

Contracts are not likely to resolve agency problems completely because contracts are costly to negotiate, write, and enforce. The principal, however, can usually limit the divergence of interest by establishing appropriate incentives for the agent in the contract and by incurring *monitoring costs* aimed at limiting the aberrant activities of the agent. Also, the agent might incur *bonding costs* to help guarantee that she will not take certain actions or to ensure that the principal will be compensated if she does. Generally, it does not pay to completely resolve the incentive conflict. The dollar equivalent of the loss in the gains from trade that results due to the divergence of interest in the agency relationship is known as the *residual loss.* Total agency costs are the sum of the *out-of-pocket costs* (monitoring and bonding costs) and the residual loss.

Parties to a contract have incentives to resolve agency problems in the least costly manner. By doing so, there are more gains from trade to share between the parties. Viewing observed contracts as efficient responses to the particular contracting problem can be a very powerful tool for explaining organizational arrangements.

Treating a firm like an individual decision maker is a useful abstraction in some contexts. For example, in previous chapters we analyzed output and pricing decisions by assuming the firm was an entity that acted to maximize profits. Analyzing organizational issues within the firm, however, requires a definition of a firm that focuses on individuals as the basic unit of analysis. A particularly useful definition is that *the firm is a legal fiction that serves as a nexus of contracts.* The firm is a legal fiction in the sense that it is a creation of the legal system with the legal standing of an individual. Nexus of contracts refers to the firm always being one party to the many contracts that make up the firm.

Much of the discussion in this chapter concentrates on incentive conflicts between individuals in hierarchal relationships. Agency-like problems, however, arise in almost all cooperative undertakings where the decision maker does not bear the full wealth effects of his actions. In particular, the members of a team can have incentives to *freeride* on the efforts of teammates.

One especially important factor that limits contractual solutions to agency problems is imperfect information. Typically there are *informational asymmetries* at the time of contracting. Informational asymmetries can cause breakdowns in bargaining. *Adverse selection* refers to the tendency of individuals, with private information about something that affects a potential trading partner's benefits, to make offers that are detrimental to the trading partner. Adverse selection can cause market failures. Pre-contractual information problems, however, can be mitigated by information collection, clever contract design, credible communication, and mechanisms such as warranties.

In most cases, there is also imperfect information post-contract—parties to a contract cannot perfectly observe each other's actions. These post-contractual informational asymmetries cause *moral-hazard* problems—an individual can have incentives to deviate from the contract and take self-interested actions because the other party has insufficient information to know if the contract was honored. How organizations might be structured to reduce moral-hazard problems is a recurring topic throughout this book.

Many of the contracts in firms are *implicit contracts,* rather than formal legal documents. Implicit contracts are hard to enforce in a court of law and largely depend on the private incentives of individuals for enforcement. *Reputational concerns* can provide incentives to honor implicit contracts. These concerns are most likely to be effective when (1) the gains from cheating are small, (2) the likelihood of detecting cheating is large, and (3) the payoffs from maintaining a good reputation are large. It is sometimes possible to structure organizations in ways that increase the likelihood that reputational concerns will promote honorable behavior.

CHAPTER 8

Introduction to Organizational Architecture

In 1984, ITT Corporation was the largest manufacturer of telecommunications equipment in the world, operating in over 80 different countries. It was also broadly diversified with operations in industrial and consumer products, insurance, automotive parts, telephone service, natural resources, food processing, and utilities. ITT, however, faced a variety of market pressures that made 1984 an especially poor year. To quote *Moody's Handbook of Common Stocks* (Winter 1984–85):

> ITT's telecommunications operations continued to suffer from soft market conditions in the U.S., a personal computer glut and competitive pricing. European operations are being hurt by the strength of the U.S. dollar.

In 1984, earnings per share at ITT were only $2.97 per share, compared to $4.50 a year earlier. Dividends were cut by nearly $1.00 per share. ITT was rumored to be a potential target for a takeover.

Part of ITT's problem was that it had become too large and diversified. Decision making in the organization was highly formalized and bureaucratic. This system made it difficult for ITT to respond rapidly to changing customer demands and competitive pressures. The inability to act quickly was especially problematic given the dramatic changes occurring in telecommunications and computers.

ITT responded by announcing that it planned to sell over $2 billion in assets in order to focus on its core strengths and major lines of business. As one example of this "asset redeployment program," ITT sold O. M. Scott & Sons Company in a divisional leveraged buyout in December 1986.[1] Scott, the largest producer of lawn-care products in the United States, was originally acquired by ITT in 1971.

---

[1] Our discussion of O. M. Scott relies heavily on a paper entitled "Organizational Changes and Value in Leveraged Buyouts: The Case of the O. M. Scott & Sons Company," by George P. Baker and Karen H. Wruck, *Journal of Financial Economics,* December 1989.

141

The buyout was accompanied by organizational changes at Scott that were designed to enhance performance. These changes involved three important dimensions of the organization that we refer to as the firm's *organizational architecture*[2]:

1. The assignment of decision rights (rights to decide and take actions) among individuals.
2. The reward system.
3. The performance-evaluation system.

In particular, after the buyout managers at Scott were given substantial authority to make and implement decisions. In contrast, as part of ITT these managers often had to seek approval from executives at a number of levels at ITT headquarters and approval was frequently denied. To motivate value-enhancing decisions, coverage under the bonus plan was expanded to include additional managers. Payouts for exceeding performance targets were increased substantially from the old plan. For example, average bonuses as a percent of salary for the top ten managers increased from 10 percent and 17 percent in the two years before the buyout to 66 percent and 39 percent in the two years after. In addition, employees had substantial financial interests in the firm through stock ownership. Post-buyout, employees owned 17 percent of Scott's equity. Employees had virtually no stock ownership in the company before the buyout. Correspondingly, the performance-evaluation was changed to place a heavy emphasis on financial performance. Specific targets for corporate, divisional, and individual performance were established.

These changes in organization at Scott were accompanied by a dramatic increase in operating performance. For example, in the two-year period following the buyout, earnings before interest and taxes increased by 56 percent. Over the same time period, sales increased by 25 percent. These increases were not caused by a reduction in either R&D expenditures or expenditures on marketing and distribution. In fact, expenditures in both categories increased, as did spending on capital projects. In addition, there was no major layoff of employees; employment decreased from 868 to 792 over the period. One likely explanation for the improved performance at Scott is that the changes in architecture provided managers with decision rights and incentives to make value-increasing decisions.

The example of O. M. Scott illustrates that organizational architecture is an important determinant of the success or failure of firms. The purpose of this chapter is to introduce the concept of organizational architecture and to provide a broad overview of the factors that are likely to be important in designing the optimal

---

[2]These three features, which we define as the *organizational architecture,* emphasized have been in the literature from both economics and management. For example, see M. C. Jensen, 1983, "Organization Theory and Methodology," *The Accounting Review* 58, 319–339; M. C. Jensen and W. H. Meckling, "Specific and General Knowledge and Organizational Structure," in *Contract Economics,* Lars Werin and Hans Wijkander, eds., Basil Blackwell Ltd., Oxford, U.K., 1992, chapter 9; and P. Milgrom and J. Roberts, *Economics, Organization & Management,* Prentice-Hall, Englewood Cliffs, New Jersey, 1992. A representative example, from the management literature is D. Robey, *Designing Organizations,* Richard D. Irwin Inc., Burr Ridge, Illinois, 1991.

architecture for a particular organization. The next six chapters contain a more in-depth discussion of each of the three components of organizational architecture.

Understanding organizational structure provides managers with powerful tools for affecting firm performance. As we will see, however, managers must be careful and thoughtful in how they use these tools or the results will be nonproductive. This book presents material that will help managers be more productive users of these tools.

We begin by discussing the basic economic problem facing firms and markets. We then examine how the organizational architecture can help solve this problem.[3]

Economic Problem

The basic economic problem facing individuals, firms, and the overall economy is the same: how to make the most out of limited resources. For example, individuals maximize utility given budget constraints. Firms strive to produce marketable products at the lowest possible cost. A primary goal of any economic system is to produce the preferred output in an efficient manner.

The economic problem within firms and economic systems is complicated by the fact that important information for economic decision making is generally held by many different individuals. Furthermore, this information is often expensive to transfer. (The information is *specific*.) For example, a scientist is likely to know more about the potential of particular research projects than people higher up in the firm. Similarly, a machine operator may know more about how to use a particular machine than his supervisor. In both cases, the information is likely to be costly to transfer.

A second complication is that decision makers might not have appropriate incentives to make efficient decisions even if they have the relevant information. (There are *agency problems*.) For example, a scientist might want to complete a research project out of scholarly interest even if the project is unprofitable. Similarly, machine operators might not want to use machines efficiently if efficient use means more work for them.

Thus the economic problem in firms and economic systems involves trying to assure that: (1) decision makers have the relevant information to make good decisions and (2) decision makers have incentives to use the information productively.

Architecture of Markets

As discussed in Chapter 3, the price system helps solve the economic problem in markets. In market economies, individuals have private property rights. If a person owns a resource (for example, a piece of property, automobile, building, etc.), she

---

[3]Our development in the first part of this chapter draws heavily on M. C. Jensen and W. H. Meckling, ''Specific and General Knowledge and Organizational Structure,'' in *Contract Economics,* Lars Werin and Hans Wijkander, eds., Basil Blackwell Ltd., Oxford, U.K., 1992, chapter 9.

decides how to use it. Furthermore, the right can be sold to others. If someone else knows how to make better use of the resource, the owner can sell it and keep the proceeds. Owners have strong incentives to use resources productively because they bear the wealth effects.

Using our vocabulary, the market provides an architecture that promotes efficient resource use. First, through market transactions, decision rights for resources are rearranged so that they are held by individuals with the relevant specific knowledge. Second, the market provides a mechanism for evaluating and rewarding the performance of resource owners—owners bear the wealth effects of their actions. This mechanism generates important incentives to take efficient actions. A powerful feature of the price system is that this architecture is created automatically with little conscious thought or human direction.

Organizational Architecture in Firms

Within firms there are no automatic systems for either assigning decision rights to individuals with information or motivating individuals to use information to promote firm objectives. Rather the organizational architecture has to be created. For example, at both ITT and O. M. Scott the architecture was designed and implemented by senior management.

Resources within firms tend to be allocated by administrative decisions rather than by prices.[4] For example, the CEO of a company typically transfers a manager from one division of the company to another by a simple command. Similarly, the utilization of a plant can be changed by administrative order. The top management of a firm must decide how to partition the decision rights among employees. For instance, does the top management make most major decisions or are these decisions delegated to lower-level managers? As another example, can machine operators deviate from procedures outlined in company manuals?[5]

Through the delegation of decision rights, employees are granted authority over how to use company resources. Employees, however, are not owners—they cannot sell company property and keep the proceeds. Therefore, employees have fewer incentives to worry about the efficient use of company resources than the owners. To help control these agency problems, the firm must develop a *control system* (the reward and performance-evaluation systems). As we discuss below, the optimal control system depends on how decision rights are partitioned in the firm and vice versa.

---

[4]Recall from Chapter 3 that one of the reasons for the existence of firms is that conducting transactions through the price mechanism can be expensive. In Chapter 14, we discuss how some firms use internal transfer prices in resource-allocation decisions.

[5]In small firms, top management and owners are often the same. In large firms, owners (the shareholders) delegate most decision rights to the board of directors and the CEO. These parties are charged with developing the architecture for the firm. In this chapter, we treat top managers and owners as the same. In subsequent chapters, we expand our analysis to discuss potential agency problems between top management and shareholders.

Once the firm grows beyond a basic size, the top manager is unlikely to have the relevant information for all major decisions. Consequently, the manager faces three basic alternatives in designing the organizational architecture. First, the top manager can make most major decisions even if he does not have the relevant information. In this case, there are limited agency problems and the development of a detailed control system is not critical. However, the manager is likely to make suboptimal decisions. Second, the manager can attempt to acquire the relevant information to make good decisions. This option can enhance decision making. However, obtaining and processing the relevant information can be very costly and time-consuming. Third, the manager can decentralize decision rights to individuals with better information. This option, links decision-making authority with specific information. However, there are agency problems. Control systems have to be developed. Also it is often important to transfer information from top management to decentralized decision makers to coordinate the efforts of employees and to enhance decision making.

Organizational Architecture at Century 21

Century 21 International is the largest real estate firm in the world accounting for 10 percent of all U.S. residential real estate transactions in 1990. Century 21 operates throughout the United States and in ten countries, including Japan, the United Kingdom, and France. In 1990, Century 21 brokers and sales associates assisted over 800,000 families in buying or selling properties, translating into an estimated $80 billion in real estate worldwide and approximately $2.2 billion in commissions.

Given the geographic and cultural diversity facing Century 21, it would not be productive for the U.S. headquarters to make all major decisions. This centralized decision making would be especially problematic for the international operations, where laws and cultures can be far different than in the United States. To quote Century 21's management:

> "We provide the international regions with whatever knowledge we possess on how they can help their franchisees develop better offices. What they use is basically up to them and will reflect their housing market and real estate traditions. We allow our master subfranchisors a great deal of flexibility in running their regions, and internationally we want them to be able to accommodate their services to their culture. We are not going overseas with our system and saying, 'This is the way it is, you can't change it.' We wouldn't get very far that way. There has to be some flexibility."

Decentralized decision making, however, requires a control system that promotes productive effort. At Century 21, most of the local operators are franchisees. Franchisees are essentially owners of their units and keep a large share of their units' profits. This ownership provides strong incentives to increase sales and value. Also Century 21 reserves the right to terminate individual franchises that fail to maintain acceptable levels of service.

Suggested by C. Shook and R. L. Shook, *Franchising: The Business Strategy that Changed the World,* Prentice Hall, Engelwood Cliffs, NJ, 1993.

Of course, managers can choose a mix of these basic alternatives. For example, top managers might want to make some decisions and delegate others. The optimal choice among the many possibilities depends on the particular circumstances facing the firm. For instance, in some firms top managers have most of the relevant information for decision making (or the information can be acquired at low cost). Here relatively centralized decision making is more likely to be the preferred option. In contrast, in other firms top managers lack sufficient information to make many decisions. In this case, decision rights are more likely to be decentralized with corresponding control systems used.

Determinants of Organizational Architecture

Our discussion indicates that the optimal architecture is likely to vary across firms. Figure 8.1 summarizes some of the factors that are important in determining the optimal architecture. At the top of the figure are three important factors in the firm's business environment: *technology, markets,* and *regulation.* These three factors help to determine the firm's *business strategy* (what the firm is trying to accomplish) and its corresponding asset structure, customer base, and the nature of knowledge creation. The business strategy, in turn, affects the optimal organizational architecture. The architecture provides incentives for individuals to take particular actions, which impacts firm value.

Figure 8.1 treats the business environment as *exogenous* (beyond the managers' control). Business strategy and architecture are policy choices made by the management in response to the business environment. (They are *endogenous* variables.) Under this analysis, changes in technology, markets, and regulation translate into potential changes in the optimal business strategy and architecture.

As an example of how changes in the business environment can promote changes in business strategy and architecture, consider the case of increased foreign competition in the 1980s and 1990s. For years, many large American Companies (for example, ITT, IBM, General Motors, Eastman Kodak, and Xerox) faced limited competition in their product markets. Indeed, many of these companies had substantial market power. They correspondingly had little incentive to focus on rapid product development, high-quality production, or competitive pricing. Their organizations were highly bureaucratic with very centralized decision making and limited incentive compensation. Many of these firms experienced a dramatic increase in foreign competition over the past decade (for example, from the Japanese). This competition forced these large firms to rethink their basic strategies. In particular, firms increased their emphasis on quality, customer service, and competitive pricing. To accomplish these objectives, firms often had to change their architectures. For instance, firms pushed decision rights lower in the organization, where specific knowledge about customer demands was located (recall the example of O. M. Scott). They also increased their use of incentive compensation and developed performance-evaluation systems that focused on quality and customer service.

FIGURE 8.1   The Determinants of Business Strategy, Organizational Architecture, and Firm Value.

Market conditions, technology, and government regulation are important determinants of business strategy, which in turn help to determine organizational architecture. Two-way arrows are drawn because there are feedback effects. Both business strategy and architecture affect the incentives and actions of agents within the firm and thus help to determine firm value.

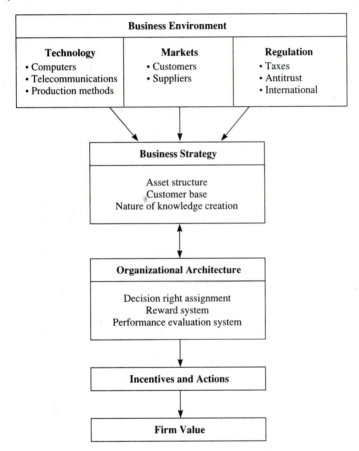

In some ways, Figure 8.1 provides an overly simple view of the determinants of strategy, architecture, and firm value. For instance, the figure ignores potential feedback effects among the environment, business strategy, and organizational architecture. Consider, for example, how the architecture at Microsoft encourages innovation that, in turn, alters the basic technology facing the firm. Large firms also often have political power that can be used to influence government regulation. While these types of feedback effects can sometimes be important, in most circumstances managers essentially must take the business environment as given. This environment, in turn, largely determines what the firm can expect to accomplish (its business strategy) and its organizational architecture. The value of Figure 8.1 is that it provides managers with a structured way of thinking about the factors that are likely to affect the firm's optimal architecture. We use this structure throughout the book for analyzing organizational decisions.

Changing Organizational Architecture

This discussion suggests that the optimal architecture for a particular firm can change with shifts in the firm's environment. Changes in architecture market conditions (for example, a new competitor), technology, or government regulation can affect optimal design. For instance, changing markets in telecommunications and computers played a part in motivating ITT to restructure and to sell divisions such as O. M. Scott.

Changing Organizational Architecture at J.C. Penney

Purchasing decisions at J.C. Penney used to be relatively centralized. For example, buyers in New York would decide on the company's clothing lines for the year. Unfortunately, this procedure did not incorporate much of the relevant specific information about what products would sell best at particular stores in different parts of the country. In the 1980s, Penney's invested in satellite communications that provided the firm with closed circuit television. This technology allowed central buyers in New York to display goods to local store managers, who could stock their stores based on their specific knowledge of local tastes and fashions. This type of decentralized decision making was made feasible by the new communications technology.

Suggested by H. Gilman, "J.C. Penney Decentralizes Its Purchasing: Individual Stores Can Tailor Buying to Needs," *The Wall Street Journal,* May 8, 1987.

It is important to note, however, that changing architecture can be costly. First, there are direct costs. The new architecture has to be designed and communicated to employees throughout the company. Moreover, changes in architecture frequently require costly changes in the firm's accounting and information systems. Often what appears to be a straight-forward change in the performance-evaluation system is a major and costly project for the firm's data processing and accounting departments. Literally hundreds of computer programs might have to be changed to alter the accounting and information systems.

Second, and perhaps more important are indirect costs. Changes in organizational architecture are likely to affect some employees positively (for example, by increasing their responsibility and possibilities for rewards) and other employees negatively. Thus, the attitudes toward change are likely to vary among employees. Dealing with the associated politics of implementing change in a firm can be expensive. In addition, frequent changes in architecture can have undesirable incentive effects. For instance, workers have limited incentives to invest in learning new job assignments, devising more efficient production processes, and developing relations with coworkers, if they expect to change assignments in the near future. In general, frequent restructuring within a firm causes uncertainty about job assignments and will promote actions that focus more on short-run payoffs and less on long-run investments.

Changing Organizational Architecture Requires Careful Analysis

At any point in time, there are a set of prominent management techniques that are touted as the key to success. For example, in the 1990s popular techniques include reengineering, benchmarking, total quality management, broadbanding, worker empowerment, and skill-based pay. Most of these techniques involve fundamental changes in organizational architecture. For example, advocates of total quality management commonly recommend delegating decision rights to teams and not paying incentive compensation based on individual performance.

Adopting the most recent "business trend" or "fad" can get a firm in trouble unless the change is warranted by the actual circumstances facing the firm. Unfortunately, many firms appear to adopt changes without a careful analysis of the relevant costs and benefits. To quote *The Wall Street Journal* (July 6, 1993), "Many companies try management fads, only to see them flop." In fact, surveys indicate that a majority of companies are dissatisfied with the results of organizational changes.

The basic point is that companies should not change the organization simply because it is the current fad. Certainly, some organizational changes can enhance value. However, companies should carefully consider whether the benefits of a change are larger than the costs given their particular circumstances.

Changing the Organization Too Frequently: Not a New Phenomenon

"We trained hard, but it seemed that every time we were beginning to form into teams we would be reorganized. I was to learn later in life that we tend to meet any new situation by reorganizing, and what a wonderful method it can be for creating the illusion of progress while producing confusion, inefficiency, and demoralization."

Petronius Arbiter 210 B.C.

Interdependencies in the Organization

It is important to understand that the components of organizational architecture are highly interdependent. The optimal control system depends on the allocation of decision rights and vice versa. For example, if decision rights are decentralized it is important to have a control system that provides incentives for employees to make value-enhancing decisions. In particular, reward and performance-evaluation systems have to be developed that compensate the worker on performance outcomes. Similarly, if a firm adopts a compensation plan to motivate employees, it is important to grant workers decision rights so that they can act on these incentives. In this sense, the components of organizational architecture are like *three legs of a stool*. It is important that all three legs be designed so that the stool is level. Changing one leg without careful consideration of the other two is typically a mistake. For example, it is unlikely that O. M. Scott would have been as successful after the buyout if managerial decision rights had been changed without accompanying changes in the firm's compensation plan.

When the Legs of the Stool Don't Balance

Hammer and Champy (1993) give an example of a major airline company where the three legs of the stool did not match. In this example, a plane was grounded for repairs at a given airport. The nearest qualified mechanic was stationed at another airport. The decision right to allow the mechanic to work on the airplane was held by the manager of the second airport. The manager's compensation, however, was tied to meeting his own budget rather than to the profits of the overall organization. The manager refused to send the mechanic to fix the plane immediately because the mechanic would have had to stay overnight at a hotel and the hotel bill would have been charged to the manager's budget. The mechanic was dispatched the next morning so that he could return the same day. A multi-million dollar aircraft was grounded, costing the company thousands of dollars. The manager, however, avoided a $100 hotel bill. Presumably the mechanic would have been dispatched immediately had the manager been rewarded on the overall profit of the company or alternatively if the decision right had been held by someone else with this objective.

Suggested by M. Hammer and J. Champy, *Reengineering the Corporation*, Harper Business, New York, 1993.

Organizational architecture involves a number of interrelated policies and systems within the firm. For example, incentive compensation schemes for lower-level managers are often based on accounting performance for their particular units. Changing the unit structure and associated compensation schemes can therefore require changes in the firm's accounting system. Similarly, it might be optimal to pay the manager of a subsidiary based on the stock-market performance of the subsidiary. But, for this policy to be implemented, the subsidiary must be publicly traded. Thus, there can be interdependencies between the organizational architecture and the firm's financing policies. As another example, consider the design of the firm's organizational architecture and its computer/information systems. For instance, new computer programs provide "expert systems" that allow low-skilled workers to complete complicated tax returns, assess the qualifications of mortgage applicants, and perform other tasks which previously required extensive training. These programs have allowed companies in financial services to decentralize additional decision rights to lower-level workers. For example, some firms have granted lower-level employees the rights to approve mortgage applications without supervisor approval if the computer program indicates that the applicant is qualified.

Marmots and Grizzly Bears

Business writers, consultants, and government regulators frequently claim that existing business practices are inefficient and propose changes that would allegedly improve productivity. The principle of survival of the fittest, however, suggests that many of these claims are likely to be misguided. In a competitive world, if organizations survive over the long run with a particular architecture, it is unlikely that there is some *obvious change* that could be implemented to increase profits. Sometimes the reasons for survival of a particular practice might not be clear to an outside observer. Existing practices, however, should not be deemed inefficient without careful analysis.

The interaction between marmots and grizzly bears serves to illustrate this point. Marmots are small ground hogs and are a principal food source for certain bears. Zoologists studying the ecology of marmots and bears observed bears digging and moving rocks in the autumn in search of marmots. They estimated that the calories expended searching for marmots exceeded the calories obtained from consuming marmots. Thus searching for marmots appears to be an inefficient use of the bear's limited resources. Given Darwin's theory of natural selection, bears searching for marmots should become extinct. A well-meaning consultant or government regulator, therefore, might recommend that bears quit searching for marmots.

Fossils of marmot bones near bear remains, however, suggest that bears have been searching for marmots for a long time. An explanation is that searching for marmots provides benefits to bears in addition to calories. For instance, bears sharpen their claws as a by-product of the digging involved in hunting for marmots. Sharp claws are useful in searching for food under the ice after winter's hibernation. Therefore, the benefit of sharpened claws and the calories derived from marmots offset the calories consumed gathering the marmots. The moral is that in biology or business, an outside observer should be very careful in concluding long-standing practices are inefficient without careful study.

Suggested by J. S. McGee, 1980. "Predatory Pricing Revisited," *Journal of Law & Economics*, 289–330.

Survival of the Fittest

Firms compete along many dimensions including organizational design. The competitive process selects which firms survive much like the process of "natural selection" in the theory of evolution—the strong survive. This principle of Economic Darwinism implies that companies have the greatest chance of survival if they are organized efficiently given their particular economic environment. The company that is best organized among its competitors will tend to be the most profitable and thus most likely to survive.

Less successful companies will tend to imitate the more successful companies. This process will tend to move companies with similar economic settings into similar organizational architectures. Successful organizations will be imitated whether the original innovator was smart or simply lucky in designing a superior organization. For example, in 1984, ITT found it difficult to compete with smaller companies which were more responsive to changing markets and consumer demands. In response, they sold assets in order to reduce the size of the company and to focus on major lines of business.

Survival of the Fittest: The Case of Franchising

In the 1950s most quick-service restaurants in the U.S. were local "mom and pop" businesses. Similarly, small independent businesses tended to dominate industries such as motels, convenience stores, and auto repair shops. Individual businesses in these industries competed with one another, and the most profitable tended to survive. Nevertheless, there was room for improvement. In particular, the quality across businesses was not uniform and consumers bore risks trying new establishments. (For example, vacationers were not sure what to expect when patronizing out-of-town restaurants and motels.)

Entrepreneurs responded to this opportunity by developing a relatively untried form of organization—franchising. For example, during the 1950s Ray Kroc, Bill Rosenberg, and Kemmons Wilson founded McDonald's, Dunkin' Donuts, and Holiday Inn, respectively. Other franchise companies formed during this period include H&R Block, Midas Muffler, and Pizza Hut, to name a few. The idea in each case was to establish a national chain that provided customers with uniform quality and service at all outlets.

One benefit of franchising is that franchisees are highly motivated to increase sales and profits (since they get to keep most of the profits). Also franchising has the advantage of group affiliation for national advertising, large quantity discounts for input purchases, and quality control. The success of franchising has been immense. There are now over 500,000 franchised units operating in this country with sales of nearly $800 billion. These sales represent about one-third of the nation's retail sales.

Franchising now dominates many industries such as fast food, auto repair, and motels. In these industries, franchise companies proved to be generally stronger than independent small businesses. Thus, many small companies were either driven out of business by franchise companies or motivated to join franchise systems themselves.

The concept of survival of the fittest has important implications. First, existing organizational architectures are not random. For example, as we will discuss in subsequent chapters, there are sound economic explanations for the existing architectures in most industries. Second, surviving organizations at a point in time are optimal in a *relative* sense—they are best among the competition and not necessarily the best possible. These points suggest that improvements in organizational design are potentially possible. However, a manager should not be too quick to condemn prevailing organizations without careful analysis. Understanding why particular types of organizations survive in alternative settings can be important background knowledge for analyzing the consequences of organizational change.

Corporate Culture

Corporate culture is one of the more frequently used terms in the literature on organizations. Corporate culture usually encompasses the ways work and authority are organized, the ways people are rewarded and controlled, as well as organizational features such as customs, taboos, company slogans, heroes, and social rituals. Managers are encouraged to develop high-powered, productive cultures. However, little concrete guidance is provided on how to accomplish this goal.

Our focus on organizational architecture is consistent with the concept of a corporate culture. Indeed, our definition of organizational architecture corresponds to key aspects of what is frequently defined as corporate culture. For example, the architecture specifies how authority (decision rights) is distributed among workers and how rewards are determined. The advantage of this approach is that it defines the key components of a firm's corporate culture and analyzes how managers might affect culture by conscious action.

As an example, recall our discussion of Sears Auto Centers in Chapter 2. The old corporate culture at Sears Auto Centers could be characterized as an environment where dishonest salespeople customarily misled customers. After the scandal became public, Sears had to find a way to change this corporate culture. This approach provides direct guidance on how this change might be accomplished—in this case by changing the compensation scheme.

Most organizations do not write down all the features of their organization in detailed procedures manuals. Rather, the features are communicated to employees in less formal and potentially less costly ways. In this sense, aspects of the corporation such as slogans, role models, and social rituals can be viewed as methods of communicating organizational architecture to workers in a low-cost fashion. For example, a slogan like ''At Ford, quality is job 1'' emphasizes that workers are expected to focus on quality and that this focus will be rewarded by the company. Similarly social rituals, such as training sessions and company parties, can help to disseminate information by increasing the interaction among workers who might not see each other on a frequent basis. Singling out role models or heroes for special awards is another way of communicating what the company values.

Corporate Culture at Mary Kay Cosmetics

Total sales at Mary Kay Cosmetics increased from about $198,000 in 1963 to over $613 million in 1993. Mary Kay has built a sales force of 300,000 and has helped to create 74 millionaires (women who have earned commissions of $1 million or more over their careers). A typical sales director earns about $35,000 year, while a national sales director averages about $200,000.

The organizational structure at Mary Kay focuses directly on sales. All sales consultants purchase products directly from Dallas at the same price. Rewards are based solely on sales and recruiting additional sales consultants. There is no cap on what sales consultants earn. As sales and the recruiting of consultants rise, so do commissions. Past resumes and credentials are unimportant—"You say you were a brain surgeon in your last job? Fine. Get a beauty case and start dialing."

What is interesting about Mary Kay is how many features of the firm's culture reinforce each other in a consistent manner. For example, stories of role models are prevalent throughout the organization. Almost every employee knows the story of Mary Kay Ash who started out as a young saleswoman for Stanley Home Products. She was so poor that she had to borrow $12 to travel from her Houston home to Stanley's 1937 convention in Dallas. Through hard work, she built the Mary Kay Cosmetic Company and amassed a family fortune of over $300 million. Stories of other successful sales consultants permeate the organization. These stories reinforce the rules of the game and help motivate hard work and increased sales. The company is also famous for lavishly rewarding its successful sales consultants in a very public manner. The annual sales meeting is an extravaganza where individuals are rewarded with complementary pink Cadillacs, jewelry, color-coded suits, badges, emblems, and being crowned as "queens."

The message at Mary Kay is clear. Success is measured by sales and recruiting efforts. Do these things well and you will be rewarded, both financially and through public recognition. This message is consistently communicated through compensation plans, stories of role models, company rituals and ceremonies.

Suggested by A. Farnham, "Mary Kay's Lessons in Leadership," *Fortune*, September 20, 1993.

Less tangible features of organizations, such as rituals and role models, can be important in reinforcing and communicating organizational architecture. They, however, can also affect the costs of changing architectures. Managers can change formal evaluation and compensation schemes and clearly communicate these changes to the relevant employees. Getting employees to change their heroes, customs, and social rituals can be more difficult.

Case Study:
Eastman Kodak

For many years, Eastman Kodak had a virtual monopoly in film production. This market power resulted in large profits. It also permitted Kodak to control the timing for introducing new products to the market place and in responding to changes in consumer demands.

By the 1980s, Kodak's market environment had changed greatly. The Fuji Corporation produced high-quality film that eroded Kodak's market share. Increased competition also came from generic store brands. In addition, the 1980s witnessed a technological explosion. Improved communications, design capabilities, and robotics allowed companies to bring new products to market within months rather than years.

These changes in the market environment placed significant pressure on Kodak. Kodak's stock price dropped from over $85 per share in 1982 to just over $71 in 1984. This 16 percent decline in stock price appears particularly poor when it is compared to the substantial increase in stock prices for the market as a whole. Earnings per share at Kodak also dropped substantially. The company realized it had to change its organization to regain profits and market share. To quote Colby Chandler, former CEO of Kodak, at the 1984 annual meeting:

> "Like many companies, we are not used to working in an environment where there is rapid technological transfer from laboratory to the marketplace. But we know that will be important in our future."

During 1984, Kodak undertook a major corporate restructuring. Prior to the restructuring, decision making at Kodak was very centralized. Top-level approval was required for most major decisions. The restructuring created 17 new business units with profit-and-loss responsibility. Business-unit managers were given increased decision-making authority for new products, pricing, and other important policy choices. By decentralizing decision rights, top management hoped to make the company more responsive to changing customer demands and market conditions. To quote the 1984 annual report:

> "In short, Kodak is finding new ways to stimulate the innovative nature of its people. The result: a spirit of independence, new ideas and a quickened pace in the process which turns new ideas into commercial realities."

Unfortunately for Kodak, changing the *assignment of decision rights* did not have a significant impact on the company's performance. In response, Kodak adopted the Management Annual Performance Plan (MAPP) in 1987. Under this plan, the base salary of management employees was reduced by 10 percent and replaced with a variable bonus. The bonus was to average 10 percent ranging from 0 to 20 percent. Bonus payments were based on individual, unit, and company objectives.

Case Study Eastman Kodak continued

The idea behind MAPP was that changing the *performance-evaluation and reward systems* would motivate managers to be more creative and industrious. The plan, however, did not have a large impact on managerial incentives or corporate profits. In fact, in 1993 Kodak officials were quoted as saying that (1) management had not really been held accountable for not delivering results, (2) management had to develop tougher work standards and demote failing employees, and (3) that in the past managers who advanced at Kodak had excelled in office politics but not necessarily leadership (*Democrat and Chronicle,* Rochester, NY, 6/27/93). Frustrated by the continued lack of success, Kodak's board of directors fired its CEO in late 1993.

Discussion Questions

1. What factors motivated Kodak to change its organizational architecture?
2. What mistakes did Kodak make in changing its architecture?
3. What might it have done differently?
4. How does this example relate to the concept of the survival of the fittest?

Overview of Chapters 9–14

The next six chapters provide a detailed discussion of the three components of organizational architecture. Chapters 9 and 10 analyze the assignment of decision rights. Through the assignment of decision rights, firms create jobs. Two important characteristics of jobs are the variety of the assigned tasks and the authority in making decisions on how to complete these tasks. Chapter 9 examines the issue of decision authority, while Chapter 10 focuses on the assignment of tasks.

Once jobs are created, firms must design reward systems that are sufficient to attract qualified workers. Chapter 11 analyzes the level of pay and the components of the compensation package (mix between salary and fringe benefits). The focus in this chapter is how to design pay packages that allow firms to attract and retain qualified workers at the lowest cost. While, the level of pay attracts workers to jobs, it is incentive compensation that provides a primary motivation for employees to complete the assigned tasks. Chapter 12 provides a detailed analysis of incentive compensation.

Incentive plans base their payoffs on measures produced by the performance-evaluation system. Chapter 13 focuses on performance measurement of individual workers, while Chapter 14 examines the performance measurement of subunits within the firm (for example, divisions and subsidiaries).

Summary

The *organizational architecture* includes three important components of organizational design, which are major determinants of the success or failure of firms:

1. The assignment of decision rights (rights to decide and take actions) among individuals.
2. The reward system.
3. The performance-evaluation system.

The basic economic problem facing both firms and economic systems involves trying to assure that decision makers have the relevant information to make good decisions and that these decision makers have appropriate incentives to use information productively. The price system provides an architecture that helps solve this problem in markets. Through market transactions, decision rights are transferred to individuals with the relevant knowledge. The market also provides a mechanism for evaluating and rewarding the performance of resource owners—owners bear the wealth effects of their actions. A powerful feature of markets is that this architecture is created automatically with little conscious thought or human direction.

Things are different within firms. There is no automatic system for either assigning decision rights to individuals with information or motivating individuals to use information to promote firm objectives. Rather, organizational architecture has to be created. The optimal architecture depends on the environment facing the firm. For example, in some firms top management will have most of the relevant information for decision making. In this case, relatively centralized decision making is more likely to be adopted. In contrast, in firms where lower-level workers have the relevant information, decision rights are more likely to be decentralized. In this case, reward and performance-evaluation systems must be developed to control agency problems and to promote better decision making.

The factors that are likely to be particularly important determinants of a firm's organizational architecture are *market conditions, technology,* and *government regulation.* These three factors interact to determine the firm's optimal business strategy and architecture. The business strategy and architecture, in turn, are major determinants of firm value.

Changes in these three basic factors can motivate changes in the firm's organizational architecture. Changing architecture, however, is costly. In addition to the direct costs of designing and implementing new procedures, there are potentially important indirect costs. These costs include the costs of dealing with the politics of change and the adverse incentive effects that occur if a company restructures too frequently. (For example, employees have reduced incentives to consider the long-run consequences of their actions if they expect to change jobs in the near future.) Thus changing the organization should be done only after careful analysis.

The components of organizational architecture are highly interdependent. They are like three legs of a stool. Changing one leg without careful consideration of the other two is usually a mistake. Organizational architecture is also related to other policies and systems within a firm, including the accounting and information systems, marketing and financial policy.

Firms compete along many dimensions including architecture. The competitive process selects which firms survive much like the process of natural selection in the theory of evolution. Companies have the greatest chance of survival if they are organized efficiently given their particular economic environments. This principle does not rule out the possibility of improvements in organization. However, it does suggest that long-standing business practices should not be rejected without careful study. Also, understanding why particular types of organizations survive in particular settings provides important background knowledge for analyzing organizational issues.

Corporate culture is a frequently used term. Corporate culture is usually meant to encompass the ways work and authority are organized and the ways people are rewarded and controlled, as well as organizational features such as customs, taboos, company slogans, heroes, and social rituals. Our focus on organizational architecture is consistent with the concept of a corporate culture. Indeed, our definition of architecture corresponds to key aspects of what is frequently defined as corporate culture. The advantage of this approach is that it defines the key components of corporate culture and analyzes how managers might affect this culture through conscious action. It also helps to explain why the corporate cultures of firms vary systematically across industries—different environments motivate different architectures.

The purpose of this chapter was to introduce the concept of organizational architecture and to provide a broad overview of the factors that are likely to be important in determining the optimal architecture for a particular organization. The next six chapters contain a more in-depth discussion of each of the three components of organizational architecture: the assignment of decision rights, the reward system, and the performance evaluating system.

The Assignment of Decision Rights:

The Level of Empowerment

Honda Motor Company was founded in 1948 by Soichiro Honda.[1] Initially, decision making in the company was quite top down. In fact, Mr. Honda made virtually all product and design decisions, while finance and marketing decisions were made by his partner Takeo Fujisawa.

In 1973, Mr. Honda retired. Successors adopted a more decentralized decision system. Major decision-making authority was spread among nearly 30 senior executives who spent much of their time gathered at conference tables hammering out policies in informal sessions called *waigaya,* a Honda word meaning "noisy-loud." Engineers in research and development had significant control of the design of new automobiles. Under this so-called "Honda System," the company grew and prospered.

By the late 1980s, however, Honda's growth had stalled and profits declined. Honda lost market share in the Japanese auto market, falling from third to fourth behind Mitsubishi. Part of Honda's problem was that it failed to respond to changing tastes in the Japanese auto market. Many Japanese consumers wanted to purchase sporty cars with distinctive styling. Yet Honda concentrated on producing four-door family sedans.

In April 1991, the new CEO, Nubuhiko Kawamoto announced that he was radically changing the decision-making system at Honda by taking direct control of

---

[1]Our discussion of Honda Motor Company is based largely on: 1) Clay Chandler and Paul Ingrassia, "Just as U.S. Firms Try Japanese Management, Honda is Centralizing," *The Wall Street Journal,* April 11, 1991 and Michael Williams, "Redesign of Honda's Management Faces First Test with Unveiling of New Accord," *The Wall Street Journal,* September 1, 1993.

the company's automotive operations in Japan. He reasoned that the company had grown too large for group decision making. To quote Mr. Kawamoto:

> "We'd get the people from research, sales, and production together and everyone would say 'not this' or 'not that.' We'd talk but there would be no agreement. Product planning would be on a tight schedule but we would have another discussion, another study and more preparation. Finally, the decision would come months later."

The centralization of decision rights at Honda was seen as a "cultural revolution." Even after Mr. Kawamoto obtained the retired Mr. Honda's support for the radical change, Honda employees resisted. In spite of this resistance, the system was changed. As of 1993, powerful "car czars" ran the development of new models, middle managers had clear job responsibilities, and according to some insiders Mr. Kawamoto's power even exceeded that once held by Mr. Honda.

The first real test of the new management structure was the unveiling of the 1994 Accord in the fall of 1993. The vehicle was priced very competitively and was generally viewed as a success. In fact, the Accord was named as one of the top ten cars of 1994 by *Car and Driver Magazine* and import car of the year by *Motor Trend Magazine*.

Honda is just one of many firms that changed the assignment of decision rights within their organizations in the 1990s. However, in contrast to Honda, many firms decentralized decision rights, for example, through the *empowering* of workers. An example, again from the automobile industry, is Fiat, which announced in 1992 that it was decentralizing certain decision rights, assigning them to the operating levels and reducing management positions. Other firms decentralizing decision rights in the 1990s include General Electric, Eastman Kodak, Motorola, United Technologies and Xerox, to name but a few. A common action has been to decentralize decision rights to teams of workers rather than to individuals. The financial press is replete with stories about how companies have improved profits, quality, and customer satisfaction through worker empowerment and other changes in their decision systems.

These examples raise a number of important organizational questions: Can altering the assignment of decision rights really have an important impact on productivity and value? What factors affect the optimal partitioning of decision rights within the firm? When is it optimal to delegate decision rights to a team of workers rather than to specific individuals? The purpose of Chapters 9 and 10 is to address these and related questions. This chapter focuses on a single decision right and asks where the right should be located within the firm. Chapter 10 considers multiple decision rights and examines how combinations of rights are bundled into jobs and subunits (for example, divisions) of the firm.

This chapter begins by providing a more detailed discussion of the problem of assigning tasks and decision rights within the firm. We then present a simple example that illustrates some of the factors that are important in determining the optimal assignment of a decision right. We use this example to discuss centralization versus decentralization, as well as the placement of a right among employees within the same hierarchal level. We also use this example as a springboard to discuss the

---

FIGURE 9.1   Dimensions of Job Design.

Two important dimensions of job design are the variety of tasks and decision authority. This figure illustrates four possible combinations. Traditionally, many firms have created jobs like Point 1, which involve few limited tasks and low in decision authority. Lately there has been a trend towards jobs, like Point 4, which involve many tasks and broad decision authority. It, however, is easy to give examples of jobs like Point 2 that involve many limited tasks and decision authority—for instance, certain clerical jobs. Similarly, it is easy to point to examples of jobs like Point 3 that involve few tasks and broad authority—for instance, certain sales jobs.

tradeoffs between assigning a decision right to an individual versus a team of individuals. Next we consider the decision process in more detail and define the terms *decision management* and *decision control*. These terms are especially helpful in making the concept of empowerment more precise. Finally, we examine how the incentives of employees to try to influence decision makers can affect the optimal assignment of a decision right within the firm.

Assigning Tasks and Decision Rights

Firms transform inputs into outputs which are sold to customers. This *process* typically involves many *tasks*. For example, at Honda Motor Company vehicles have to be designed, assembled, painted, sold, and delivered. An important element of organizational architecture is the partitioning of the totality of tasks within the organization into smaller blocks and assigning them to specific individuals and/or groups.

Through the process of designing the organization, specific *jobs* are created. For example, if a set of clerical tasks is bundled together and assigned to an individual, a secretarial job is created. Jobs have at least two important dimensions: (1) the *variety of tasks* that the employee is asked to complete and (2) the *decision authority* that is granted to the individual to complete the tasks.

Jobs vary substantially in terms of the variety of tasks and decision authority. Figure 9.1 pictures four possibilities. Point 1 displays a combination of few tasks and limited decision authority. An example is a typist in a typing pool who concentrates on a single task and has limited discretion on what to do or how to do it. Point 2 shows a combination of many tasks and limited decision authority. For instance, clerical jobs typically involve numerous tasks (filing, typing, answering the phone, scheduling meetings, for example), but limited decision authority. Point 3 pictures few tasks with broad decision authority. As an example, consider a salesperson who has many decision rights concerning which customers to call, what sales pitch to make, what prices to charge, and so on. Yet, the person concentrates on one principal task—selling products to customers. Recently, there has been a trend towards creating jobs, like Point 4, that are less specialized and where employees have broader decision authority. The reasons for this trend will become evident as we proceed through the next two chapters.

As a manager moves up in the corporation, design issues consume larger amounts of the manager's time. For example, the manager of a purchasing department plays an important role in defining the tasks each employee in the department performs. Unfortunately, the problem of partitioning tasks into jobs is extremely complex. It involves the assignment of literally thousands of tasks and decision rights. It also involves simultaneous consideration of other corporate policies, such as performance evaluation and compensation policy. Although economic theory is not sufficiently well developed to provide a detailed solution to this general problem, through some relatively simple examples it can provide important insights. In this chapter, we present such an example to study the issue of decision authority. The next chapter considers the problems of *bundling* tasks into jobs and jobs into subunits of the firm. Thus this chapter concentrates on the horizontal axis in Figure 9.1 (the breadth of decision authority), while Chapter 10 concentrates on the vertical axis (variety of tasks).

Our primary example in this chapter involves Bob's Auto Company, a firm which sells automobiles in two cities. As pictured in Figure 9.2, the management of the firm consists of Roberta (Bob) Morris, the CEO, and two local managers. The local managers oversee the operations in the two cities. We concentrate on one specific task/decision right, pricing. Assigning an individual the right to set prices at a local unit increases that person's decision authority. For example, if Bob grants the local managers the right to set prices, she reduces her decision authority and correspondingly increases the decision authority of the local managers.[2]

The issue of *centralization versus decentralization* focuses on which level of the firm's hierarchy to place the decision right. The firm is said to have centralized decision making if the right is assigned to Bob and decentralized decision making if the right is assigned to the local managers. A second issue is choosing *where in a given hierarchical level* a decision should be made. The decision authority of both

---

[2]Initially, we assume that either Bob sets the prices at the local units or she grants the right to set prices to the local managers. In reality, Bob can grant the local managers some decision authority without giving them full pricing rights. For example, Bob might allow the managers to set prices within a given range. We consider these additional possibilities later in the chapter.

FIGURE 9.2   Organizational Structure of Bob's Auto Company.

Bob's Auto Company markets automobiles in two cities. Roberta (Bob) Morris is the CEO. The two local managers oversee the operations in the two cities. The one important decision right in this example is the pricing decision. The first question involves centralization vs. decentralization. Should Bob make the pricing decisions or should they be decentralized to the local managers? The second question involves horizontal placement of decentralized decision rights. If pricing decisions are decentralized, should Bob: (1) grant each manager the pricing right for his own location, (2) grant both decision rights to one manager who makes all pricing decisions, or (3) grant the decision rights for the two locations to both managers and ask them to work as a team?

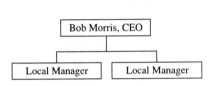

Bob's Auto Company

local managers is increased if both are given decision rights for pricing. Alternatively, Bob might decide to increase the decision authority of only one of the local managers, for example, by letting that manager make all pricing decisions. We begin by discussing centralization versus decentralization. We subsequently consider the lateral issue of where in a hierarchy to place the right.

Centralization versus Decentralization

Most of the economic analysis of assigning decision rights has focused on the question of whether to centralize or decentralize decision rights.[3] We utilize Bob's Autos to illustrate the major implications of this analysis. The basic question is should Bob set the prices at the two locations or should the pricing decisions be decentralized to the local managers? The answer to this question depends on the benefits and costs of decentralized decision making.

---

[3]See Kaplan, Robert S., *Advanced Management Accounting,* Prentice-Hall, Englewood Cliffs, New Jersey, 1989 as an example of the standard treatment of this topic. Also see Michael C. Jensen and William H. Meckling, "Specific and General Knowledge, and Organizational Structure," *Main Currents in Contract Economics,* Lars Wein and Hans Wijkander, eds., Blackwell Press, Oxford, 1992 and Christie, Andrew A., Marc P. Joye, and Ross L. Watts, "Decentralization of the Firm: Theory and Evidence," 1993, working paper, University of Rochester, Rochester, NY.

Benefits of Decentralization

Better use of local knowledge.   The local managers are likely to have important information about the local markets. For example, they are likely to have better information than Bob about the demands of particular customers. This information is potentially costly to transfer. If Bob makes all pricing decisions, either the firm incurs information-transfer costs or bears the cost of making decisions without the relevant knowledge. Decentralizing decision rights links decision-making authority with local specific knowledge and thus can reduce the costs of information transfer and processing. The improved use of local knowledge is thus one of the major benefits of decentralized decision making.

Timeliness of response.   Centralized decisions require local managers to seek permission to change prices. Local information has to be transferred to Bob (or be ignored). Subsequently, Bob has to deliberate and convey her decisions back down to local managers for implementation. This process takes time and decision making is relatively slow. The result can be lost sales. Granting decision rights to the local managers promotes rapid decision making and quicker responses to changing market conditions.

Conservation of management time.   Having Bob making local pricing decisions, can involve substantial opportunity costs—using top-management time for decision making means the time cannot be used for some other purpose. Often it is better to decentralize operating decisions to local managers and focus the top manager's attention on other issues, such as long-run strategy (for example, what car lines to sell and how to promote them).

Training and motivation for local managers.   It is important for firms to attract talented workers and to train them as eventual replacements for top management. Decentralizing decision rights promotes both objectives. Granting responsibility helps to attract and retain talented, ambitious local managers (who are likely to value this aspect of the job). It also provides experience in decision making that is important training for more senior positions.

Costs of Decentralization

Agency costs.   Decentralizing decision rights marries authority with local specific knowledge. However, the local managers do not necessarily have strong incentives to act in the best interests of the firm. For example, the managers may choose to sell cars to their friends at low prices or attempt to obtain "kickbacks" from customers in return for selling at low prices. Developing an effective control system to motivate desired actions is not always easy or inexpensive. Also there are residual losses because it generally does not pay to resolve agency problems completely. Usually agency problems are larger the further down in the organization decision rights are placed.

Improving Performance through Decentralization: The Zebra Team

Eastman Kodak manufactures about 7,000 black-and-white-film products, which are used for a variety of purposes, such as printing, X-rays, and even spy satellites. Annual sales of these products are about $2 billion. Prior to 1989, Kodak used a very centralized decision-making process for manufacturing film. Manufacturing was divided into functions such as emulsion mixing (used for coating film), film coating, and film finishing. People in each of these functions reported up the line to functional managers.

In the late 1980s, poor performance motivated Kodak to reorganize the manufacturing of black-and-white film. Primary responsibility for the entire ''flow'' of the process was decentralized to a team of managers. A key feature of the new organization was the use of self-directed work teams.

The results of this reorganization were impressive. The ''Zebra Team'' cut production costs by some $40 million and inventory by about $50 million. In finishing, what had taken four to six weeks was accomplished routinely in two days. In film coating, what had taken 42 days was done in less than 20. New products were brought to market in half the time.

A good example of how the Zebra Team made effective use of local specific knowledge is the development of ''Cholach's Chariot.'' *Accumax* is a film product used in the manufacturing of circuit boards. Any dust on the film translates into a broken wire on a circuit board and thus makes the film worthless. Accumax is finished and slit into final products in a high-tech, ultra-clean room. Unfortunately, the old supply cart used to transport the film to storage was not dust free and thus much film was wasted. Bob Cholach was a slitter operator with specific knowledge about how the problem could be fixed—an airtight transport cab. Through his efforts, such a cab was designed and built, resulting in significant benefits to the company. Comparing the new empowered work environment with the old system, Mr. Cholach noted:

> ''In the old days I'd have been told, 'That's not your job—don't worry about it.'' But here I was given the power and finances to design and build something that would help my teammates. It wasn't like dropping a piece of paper into a suggestion box, either. They let me run with it from start to finish.''

Suggested by Frangos, Stephen J. (with Steven J. Bennett), *Team Zebra*, Oliver Wight Publications, Essex Junction, VT, 1993.

Ideally Bob would like to measure the market value of the decisions made by the local managers. In this case, it is relatively easy to use compensation schemes to motivate value-maximizing behavior. Unfortunately, observing market values for individual decisions within the firm is usually impossible. Compensation schemes can be based on performance measures, such as internal accounting numbers. For example, the local managers might be paid based on total profits for their units. However, as we will discuss in Chapters 11 through 14, developing effective compensation schemes and performance measures is difficult. The firm can use other mechanisms, such as direct monitoring, to reduce agency problems, but none of these techniques is costless.

Coordination costs.   If the two local managers set prices independently, they can ignore important interaction effects. For instance, lowering the price in one city might divert sales from the other city (if they are nearby). It can also be wasteful for both managers to conduct the same type of market analysis to decide on their pricing policies if their markets are similar. For instance, most of the important information might be obtained by conducting one survey rather than two.

Costs of transferring central information.   It is also possible that local managers do not have all the relevant information to make good pricing decisions. For example, Bob might have important information about product costs, upcoming promotions and new products from the automobile manufacturer; Bob also might have important knowledge and expertise for solving pricing problems. Often central managers obtain important information from observing the effects of various policies implemented through time and at multiple locations. In contrast, local managers generally have more limited experience and obtain direct information from only one location.

This discussion implies that an important role of central management in a decentralized decision system is to promote information flows and coordination among decision agents in the firm. These activities are likely to be costly. For instance, transferring information to local decision makers can be expensive. Coordination and information costs will be lowest when the product demands and costs for the local units are independent (for example, the locations are far apart) and the relevant knowledge for decisions is held by the local managers.

The Benefits and Costs of Decentralized Decision Making

Benefits

Better use of local knowledge.
More rapid decision making.
Conservation of the time of top
  management.
Training and motivation for local
  managers.

Costs

Agency costs.
Coordination costs.
Costs of transferring central
  information.

Graphical Illustration of the Tradeoffs

To illustrate the basic tradeoffs in this example, assume that the pricing decision can be decentralized to the local managers in varying degrees. We use D to represent the degree of decentralization of the pricing decision. When $D = 0$, all pricing decisions are made by Bob; as D increases the local managers are granted more decision rights. For example, at a low level of D the managers might have the authority to alter centrally determined prices within a 5 percent band. At a sufficiently high D, the local managers have full authority to set prices. For simplicity, assume that D is continuous. Also assume that the benefits of decentralization can be written:

$$\text{Benefits} = B \times D, \tag{1}$$

where B is a positive constant. The benefits include better use of local knowledge, increased response times, conservation of top-management time, and training/motivation for local managers.

There are, however, costs associated with decentralization. For instance, there are increased agency problems and the decisions of the local managers have to be coordinated. Also there are the increased costs of having to transfer central information to local decision makers. Assume the costs of decentralization are:

$$\text{Costs} = (A \times D) + (C \times D^2), \tag{2}$$

where A and C are positive constants. The first term, AD, represents the agency costs from decentralization and the second term, CD^2, represents the coordination/information costs. This formulation assumes that coordination/information costs increase at an increasing rate with decentralization. For example, it becomes more and more difficult to coordinate decisions as decision rights become more decentralized.

The objective of the firm is to choose D to maximize the net benefits, where:

$$\text{Net Benefits} = \text{Benefits} - \text{Costs} = BD - AD - CD^2. \tag{3}$$

Figure 9.3 contains a graph of the benefits and costs of decentralization. Net benefits are maximized where the vertical distance between the benefits and the costs is greatest. This condition occurs at:

$$D^* = (B-A)/2C. \tag{4}$$

As is standard in economic problems of this type, D^* is the point at which the marginal benefits of decentralization equal the marginal costs.[4] At this point, the

---

[4]The solution to this maximization process can be obtained through elementary calculus. Alternatively, equation (3) is quadratic, and thus you can use the quadratic formula to solve for the roots of the equation. The two roots, 0 and $(B-A)/C$, are where net benefits equal zero. The parabola is at a maximum midway between the two roots: $(B-A)/2C$. Note that the optimal point, D^*, is where the vertical distance between the benefits and costs is greatest. This point occurs where the slope of the benefit curve is equal to the slope of the cost curve. The slope of the benefit curve is the marginal benefit, while the slope of the cost curve is the marginal cost. Thus the optimal point is where the marginal benefit of decentralization equals the marginal cost.

FIGURE 9.3   **A Graphical Illustration of the Tradeoffs between Centralization and Decentralization of Decision Making at Bob's Auto Company.**

In this example, the local managers have important specific knowledge that is valuable for decision making, and timeliness of response is important. The benefits of decentralization are given by Benefits BD, where D is the level of decentralization of pricing decisions and B is a positive constant. These benefits include better use of local knowledge, increased response times, conservation of the time of top management, and training/motivation for local managers. The costs are given by Costs AD + CD², where the first term, AD, represents the increased agency costs from decentralization and the second term, CD², represents the increased coordination costs (A and C are positive constants). The optimal level of decentralization is D* = (B−A)/2C. At this point, the marginal benefits and the marginal costs of decentralization are equal. (The slopes of the total benefit and costs curves are the same.)

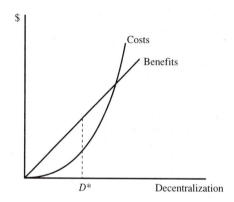

additional benefits from more informed decision making and timeliness of response are just offset by the increased agency and coordination/information costs. (The slopes of the cost and benefit curves are equal.)

Over time, it is likely that the costs and benefits of decentralization will change. For example, the importance of rapid decision making can change with changes in competition in the industry and shifts in consumer demand. Technological changes can significantly reduce the costs of transferring information and controlling agency problems (for example, consider fax machines and network computers). Changes in the benefits of decentralization can be represented by changes in B, the coefficient in the benefits equation. For example, if the benefits of a timely response increase with more global competition, B increases. Equation (4) and Figure 9.3 indicate that increases in B are associated with increases in the optimal amounts of decentralization. Changes in the agency and coordination/information costs of decentralization can be represented by changes in A and C, respectively. Both equation (4) and Figure 9.3 indicate that an increase in these costs is associated with a decrease in the optimal level of decentralization.

Our graphical illustration simplifies the centralization/decentralization decision in many ways. For example, the analysis is much more complicated if the assignment of more than one decision right is considered. Also, the example takes the divisional structure of the firm as given (two operating divisions and a headquarters). More generally, the unit structure is determined along with the assignment of decision rights. (We discuss this issue in the next chapter.) It is particularly important to emphasize that when a firm changes its decision system, it is generally optimal to make simultaneous changes in other organizational features, such as the performance-evaluation and reward systems (As we noted in chapter 8, these aspects of organizational architecture are like three legs of a stool, and it is important to keep them in balance). For example, it is often desirable to accompany decentralization with an increased emphasis on performance and incentive compensation (in order to motivate decentralized decision makers). Our illustration is incomplete in that it does not consider simultaneous changes in other organizational variables. (We discuss these issues in chapters 11 through 14.) Despite these limitations, the example highlights some of the important trade-offs in deciding on the degree of decentralization.

Our analysis of centralization versus decentralization also helps us to understand the changes in the assignment of decision rights at Honda Motor Company in 1991. Recall that after Mr. Honda retired in 1973, Honda Motors adopted a relatively decentralized decision system. When Honda Motors was small, this system worked well. The relevant specific knowledge for decision making was spread among many executives, making the benefits of decentralization high. At the same time, the firm was small enough to control the agency and coordination/information problems at low cost. In the context of our example, Honda could be viewed as operating with an optimally high level of decentralization. By 1991, however, Honda had grown tremendously and this highly decentralized system no longer worked effectively. As Mr. Kawamoto, the new CEO, analyzed, group decision making was too slow given current market conditions. Also Mr. Kawamoto had been a Honda engineer and had detailed specific knowledge about designing automobiles—thus the benefits of decentralization were lower than in the past. Mr. Kawamoto reduced the amount of decentralization. In the context of our example, there had been a reduction in the benefits of decentralization, B, and an increase in coordination costs, C, resulting in a lower D^*, the optimal level of decentralization.

Recent Trends

In contrast to Honda Motors, the general trend over the last decade has been toward greater decentralization. In Chapter 8, we argued that changes in organizational architecture are motivated by changes in the basic economic environment. What factors have changed in the environment to motivate decentralization?

In the past decade, global competition has increased tremendously in many industries. Consider, for example, the automobile, film, and computer industries. This competition has increased pressure on firms to cut costs, produce higher quality products, and meet the demands of customers in a more timely fashion, and correspondingly has increased the benefits of decentralization.

In this context, technology is important for at least two reasons. First, the rate of technological innovation has increased dramatically. Firms must either respond quickly to the resulting changes in market conditions and production technologies or lose profits. Second, new technologies have significantly altered the costs of information transfer (for example, cellular phones and fax machines). In many cases, these changes have worked to promote decentralization. For example, computers and telecommunications systems (satellites and fiber optics) have reduced the costs and time of transferring central information to local decision makers to coordinate and enhance decentralized decisions.[5] Computers have also made it less expensive to track the sales and production costs of individual products. This reduction in costs has increased the feasibility of developing more precise performance standards for local decision makers which can be used in incentive compensation plans.

Computers and Information Transmission: The Rapid Response Team at McKinsey & Company

Decentralized decision making takes advantage of local specific knowledge. However, local decisions need to be coordinated. Also, these decisions can often be enhanced by providing local decision makers with useful information from other parts of the organization. An example of the importance of computers in transferring information to local decision makers involves McKinsey & Company.

McKinsey & Company is one of the most prominent management-consulting firms in the world. In 1989, it had over 2,000 professionals working at over 50 offices spread across five continents. It is important for McKinsey to have relatively decentralized decision making because of the vast amounts of local specific knowledge held by on-site professionals. Nevertheless, for McKinsey to deliver consistent and state-of-the-art products it is important to communicate throughout the organization.

In 1989, McKinsey formed the Rapid Response Team. The purpose of this team was to respond to requests about the best current thinking and practice by providing access to both documents and experienced consultants in a short time frame. This activity requires a computerized database that catalogs printed material and the experience profiles of consultants throughout the organization. In 1991, the Rapid Response Team responded to over 1,000 requests for information and assisted nearly a quarter of the firm's consultants and clients throughout the world. The service has been viewed very positively at McKinsey & Company.

Suggested by Katzenbach, Jon R. and Douglas K. Smith, *The Wisdom of Teams,* Harvard Business School Press, Boston, 1993.

---

[5]In some cases, the effect has been in the opposite direction—local information has become less expensive to transfer to central headquarters thus favoring centralized decision making. For example, computerized cash registers allow central tracking of inventory and can increase the benefits of centralized purchasing.

Technological advances have also allowed many firms to flatten their management structures. Traditionally, firms have relied on *middle managers* to transmit information and orders from top management to lower-level workers. Middle managers have also played an important role in coordinating and monitoring the actions of these workers. Newer computer technology, by facilitating communication between top management and lower-level employees, has reduced the demand for middle managers.

Computer Technology and Busting the Bureaucracy: Cypress Semiconductors

Computer technology has allowed top managers to communicate more directly with lower-level workers. As a result, this technology makes it less expensive for top managers to control and coordinate the actions of workers, and thus has reduced the demand for middle managers, who traditionally have played an important role in transmitting information from the top of the organization to lower levels. An example of the use of computer technology in this context is Cypress Semiconductors. T. J. Rodgers, CEO of Cypress, uses a computer system to track the daily objectives of every company employee. The company essentially has no middle management. To quote an article from *Fortune:*

> "The computer system allows the CEO to stay abreast of every employee and team in his fast-moving organization. Each employee maintains a list of 10 to 15 goals like 'Meet with marketing for new product launch,' or 'Make sure to check with Customer X.' Noted next to each goal is when it was agreed upon, when it's due to be finished and whether it's finished yet or not.
>
> This way, it doesn't take layers of expensive bureaucracy to check who's doing what, whether someone has got a light enough workload to be put on a new team, and who's having trouble. Rodgers says he can review the goals of all 1,500 employees in about four hours, which he does each week."

Suggested by Dumaine, Brian, "The Bureaucracy Busters," *Fortune*, June 17, 1991, page 46.

Assigning Decision Rights across a Hierarchal Level

While discussion of decision rights often focuses on centralization versus decentralization, lateral issues also can be important. For instance, in our auto dealership example, if Bob decentralizes decision rights she can either: (1) grant each manager the pricing decision for his own location, (2) grant both decision rights to one manager who makes all pricing decisions, or (3) grant the decision rights for pricing at the two locations to both managers and ask them to work as a team in deciding on the pricing policy. Similar to the centralization versus decentralization problem, the relevant factors in making this choice include the distribution of knowledge and the costs of coordination and control. For example, granting decision rights to the managers separately takes full advantage of local specific knowledge. However, pricing at the two locations is not necessarily well coordinated. Alternatively, granting all decision rights to one manager assures coordinated decision making and takes advantage of any economies of scale in having one person make both decisions, but it comes at the potential expense of less effective utilization of the other manager's local knowledge. There might also be differences in agency costs between the two alternatives. For example, it might be less expensive to monitor the decisions of one person than two. The value of the third option, granting decision rights to a team of managers, depends on a number of factors which we discuss in the next section. Which of the three options is best depends on the specific circumstances facing the firm. For instance, having the two managers make independent decisions is likely to dominate when the two markets are more independent and more of the relevant knowledge for pricing is at the individual unit level.

Questions relating to the lateral placement of decision rights frequently arise within organizations. For example, should personnel decisions be made within each individual division or should these rights be granted to a separate human resources department? Should a divisional manager be in charge of R&D or should this function be performed elsewhere in the organization? Can a college of business operate its own placement center or must it rely on the placement services of the central university?

Assigning Decision Rights to Teams

The Use of Teams

Our analysis of Bob's Auto suggests that a firm might want to assign a decision right to a team of workers rather than to one individual. Indeed, firms grant decision rights to teams of workers for at least three basic purposes:[6] (1) to manage activities, (2) to recommend actions, and (3) to make products. Teams that manage activities are often comprised of several individuals from different functional areas. These teams tend to be relatively permanent. The assignment is to manage some particular business or subprocess. Teams that recommend actions focus on specific projects and disband when the task is complete. An example is the "Silver Bullet Team" formed at Eastman Kodak to reduce the use of silver in film making.[7] (Silver is the most expensive ingredient in making film; Kodak is the world's largest user of silver.) Teams that make products are often at the plant level. For example, some firms have granted teams of production workers the right to set their own work schedules and assignments and organize the basic production process.

---

[6]See Katzenbach, Jon R. and Douglas K. Smith, *The Wisdom of Teams*, Havard Business School Press, Boston, 1993.

[7]See Frangos, Stephen J., *Team Zebra*, Oliver Wight Publications, Essex Junction, VT, 1993.

Casual evidence suggests that firms are making increased use of team decision making.[8] This increase in the use of teams has been motivated by the same two factors that have motivated the trend toward decentralization, increased global competition and changes in technology. Competition has forced firms to become more efficient and pay more attention to quality and customer service. Teams of workers with specific knowledge about different functional areas are sometimes able to provide better customer service and higher quality products than if they work independently (for example, through better communications and more rapid actions). Technology has enhanced the ability of teams by providing important information at low cost. For example, a team charged with reducing inventory levels benefits greatly from timely information on the levels of inventory under its control. Computerized information systems make it less expensive than in the past to track inventory. Information systems have also reduced the costs of generating detailed cost and revenue data for evaluating team performance.

When Will Teams Work Best?

Some argue that team decision making is almost always better than individual decision making. Economics, however, suggests that this argument is not correct. Rather, three basic conditions must be met for teams to be productive. First, there must be potential synergies from working as a team.[9] The use of teams involves costs such as coordinating the activities of team members, taking time to reach consensus (recall the problems with the team-oriented system at Honda Motors), and free-rider problems. There is no reason to incur these costs unless there are offsetting benefits. Second, team members must either have or be able to acquire at low cost the relevant specific knowledge for making good decisions. Finally, it must be possible to control free-rider problems at relatively low cost.

Conditions for Productive Use of Teams

1. There must be potential synergies from working as a team.
2. Team members must either have or be able to acquire at low cost the relevant specific knowledge for making good decisions.
3. It must be possible to control free-rider problems at relatively low cost.

---

[8]Sometimes the popular press would have you believe that teams are a new idea in business. Businesses, however, have always used teams for decision making. The evidence does suggest an increased use of teams.

[9]See Alchian, A. and H. Demsetz, 1972, "Production, Information Costs, and Economic Organization," *American Economic Review* 62, 777–95.

To illustrate the importance of these conditions, consider fruit picking. In fruit picking, there are at least two basic ways to organize workers. The most common method has a foreman decide who picks which trees. Individuals pick the fruit on their own trees and are compensated based on their own output. In the second method, decision rights for a section of an orchard are assigned to a team of workers. The team assigns tasks to individual team members. Often several individuals work on the same tree at once. Total pay for the team is based on team output. The team decides how to allocate this pay among members. What circumstances favor one form of organization over the other?

For team production (the second method) to be productive there must be synergies from working as a team. For instance, productivity might be enhanced by having short people pick the bottom of trees, while tall people pick the tops of trees. Alternatively, it might be optimal for some workers to pick fruit, while others take loads of fruit to bins. If, in contrast, it is best for individuals to work on separate trees with little interaction, there is no reason to form a team. The team would have to spend time assigning tasks and pay to workers. However, these tasks might be more efficiently performed by a foreman. In this case, there are few benefits to offset the increase in costs.

It is also important that the members of a fruit-picking team have specific knowledge about the talents of each worker, the ripeness of the fruit in different parts of the orchard, etc. For example, if the workers do not know the ripeness of the fruit, they might pick the trees in the wrong order and waste fruit. If the knowledge of the ripeness of the fruit and the lay of the land is held by the foreman, team production is less desirable. Sometimes the relevant knowledge can be acquired by team members through education and training. Indeed, some firms that have had bad experiences with teams have found success after proper training was provided.

Team-Based Organization: Hallmark Greeting Cards

It used to take about two years for Hallmark to bring a new card to market. A new card had to move through the various functional areas (for example, art, design, production, and marketing). Some of these functions were located in separate buildings. All this took time. Now Hallmark uses teams and organizes around specific holidays. For example, one team might work on Mother's Day and another team on Valentine's Day. Teams are given most of the decision rights for the design and marketing of particular cards. Teams consist of individuals from across the various functional activities. Through this process, Hallmark has cut its time to market for new cards in half.

Suggested by Stewart, Thomas, 1992, "The Search for the Organization of Tomorrow," *Fortune Magazine* (September 22), 92–98.

Free-rider problems of team production have to be controlled. Individual members of a fruit-picking team will have incentives to shirk and free-ride on the efforts of others. For example, if all team members but one work hard output will be high. However, the shirking worker benefits from exerting less effort. As we discussed in Chapter 7, this logic tends to promote significant problems in team efforts. Free-rider problems can be controlled most effectively if the group is small and if team members can observe each other's effort. Presumably, teams are given the rights to allocate pay among members because it allows the team to punish workers who shirk by reducing pay.

Optimal Team Size

This discussion suggests that free-rider problems will limit the optimal size of teams. Indeed, Katzenbach and Smith (1993) argue that their research indicates virtually all effective teams that they observed had no more than 25 members and many were much smaller (ranging from 2 to 25). Free-rider problems, however, are not the only determinants of optimal team size. At least two other factors are important. First, as the team size increases, so does the knowledge base of the team. Indeed, many teams are formed specifically because more than one individual holds the relevant knowledge for the activity. Second, adding team members can have both positive and negative effects on the productivity of other team members. For example, a team of three workers can potentially move many more pianos than a team of two workers. (The productivity of the two workers increases greatly with the addition of the other team member.) In contrast, as team size continues to grow it can become difficult to make decisions and work in a coordinated fashion. The optimal team size depends on all these agency, information, and productivity factors.

Organizational Structure for Teams

Delegating decision rights to teams of workers does not resolve the basic agency problems associated with decentralized decision making. Therefore, while higher-level managers do not usually take an active role in assigning tasks and rewards within a team, they still have an important role in setting the rewards and the evaluation criteria for the team as a whole. For instance, to mitigate potential agency problems, top managers commonly evaluate and reward teams based on team output. These higher-level managers also have a role in providing technical assistance and advice to teams. Finally, they serve as a court of last resort when a team is unable to handle internal problems (such as members not being able to get along with one team member or significant shirking by team members).

Since the organization within the team is not normally dictated by higher-level managers, it is important for new teams to establish their own internal architecture. For example, what is the team trying to accomplish? How are decision rights and tasks assigned to individual members? How will individual and team performance be evaluated? How will the tendency to shirk and free-ride be controlled?

Are there ways to reward individual team members for following through on commitments and exerting effort for the team?[10]

The Wisdom of Teams

Jon Katzenbach and Douglas Smith of McKinsey Corporation undertook a study to analyze what lessons might be learned from actual teams at real companies. The results are published in a popular book entitled *The Wisdom of Teams.*

Katzenbach and Smith define a team as, "a small group of people (typically fewer than twenty) with complementary skills who are committed to a common purpose, performance goals, and approach for which they hold themselves mutually accountable." Closely aligned with our concept of organizational architecture, they argue that successful teams are characterized by a strong emphasis on measurable performance and mutual accountability. To quote them:

> "Teams do not spring up by magic. Nor does personal chemistry matter as much as most people believe. Rather, we believe that by persistently applying the definition offered here, most people can significantly enhance team performance. And focusing on performance— not chemistry or togetherness or good communications or good feelings—shapes teams more than anything else (page 61)."

Suggested by Katzenbach, Jon R. and Douglas K. Smith, *The Wisdom of Teams*, Harvard Business School Press, Boston, 1993.

Decision Management and Control

Thus far our characterization of decision making has been rather simplified. In particular, we have generally assumed that either an agent has a decision right or does not. In reality, some aspects of a decision can be decentralized, while other aspects can be maintained at a higher level. For example, at Bob's Autos the managers might be granted the right to set prices within some range, but have to ask approval from Bob on larger price changes. Thus the decision authority of an employee can be increased (see Figure 9.1) without granting the employee all rights to a particular decision.

---

[10]Sometimes higher-level managers play a role in reducing shirking among team members. For example, some companies require team members to evaluate each other. This information is then used in individual pay and promotion decisions made by higher-level managers. The idea is the specific knowledge of individual performance is held at the team level. This process is intended to incorporate this information in the performance-evaluation and reward system to motivate individuals to work harder. We will discuss this in more detail in subsequent chapters.

A useful characterization of the decision process is provided by Fama and Jensen.[11] In particular, they divide the decision-making process into four steps:

1. *Initiation*—generation of proposals for resource utilization and structuring of contracts;
2. *Ratification*—choice of the decision initiatives to be implemented;
3. *Implementation*—execution of ratified decisions; and
4. *Monitoring*—measurement of the performance of decision agents and implementation of rewards.

Often, firms assign initiation and implementation rights to the same agents. Fama and Jensen refer to these functions as *"decision management."* They use the term, *"decision control"* to refer to the ratification and monitoring functions.

Definition

Decision Management:	The initiation and implementation of decisions.
Decision Control:	The ratification and monitoring of decisions.

Employees do not normally bear the full wealth effects of their actions—there are agency problems. Granting an agent both decision management and control rights for a decision will typically lead to suboptimal behavior. For example, in the case of Bob's Autos, if the local managers make pricing decisions and there is no monitoring or other control, the managers will almost assuredly use the decision rights for their own benefit. For instance, the managers might sell cars to family and friends below cost. Based on this logic, Fama and Jensen argue that whenever decision makers are not owners, decision management and decision control will be separated. Only when the decision maker is also the major residual claimant does it make sense to combine decision management and control.[12]

Basic Principle of Allocating Decision Rights

If decision makers do not bear the major wealth effects of their actions, decision management and decision control will be held by separate decision makers.

---

[11]See Fama, Eugene F., and Michael C. Jensen, 1983, ''Separation of Ownership and Control,'' *Journal of Law and Economics* 26, 301–326.

[12]Residual claimants have the legal rights to the profits of the enterprise once all the fixed claimants of the firm (e.g., bondholders, employees, etc.) are paid. Without limited liability residual claimants are also responsible for making up short-falls in the payments to fixed claimants (when profits are insufficient to cover expenses).

A prominent example of separating decision management and decision control is the presence of a board of directors at the top of all corporations. In large corporations, the residual claimants are shareholders. The management of the firm is largely the responsibility of the CEO who typically owns less than one percent of the firm's stock. To mitigate potential agency problems, shareholders grant major decision-control rights to the board of directors. The board ratifies major decisions initiated by the CEO. The board also has monitoring authority and the rights to fire and compensate the CEO.

Should the Positions of CEO and Chairman of the Board Be Separated?

Many commentators complain that boards of directors of U.S. companies fail to provide adequate discipline of top managers. Of particular concern is the common practice of combining the titles of CEO and Chairman of the Board. On the surface, this practice seems to violate the principle of separating decision management and decision control. Benjamin Rosen, Chairman of Compaq Computer, voiced this concern succinctly:

> "When the CEO is also Chairman, management has *de facto* control. Yet the board is supposed to be in charge of management. Checks and balances have been thrown to the wind." (*USA Today*, April 22, 1993.)

Large shareholder associations and pension funds have in recent years sponsored proposals at Sears Roebuck and other large firms calling for separation of the titles. Government officials have considered regulations to force this change.

Contrary to the allegations of reformers, combining the CEO and Chairman titles does not necessarily violate the principle of separation of decision management and decision control. The extreme case of no separation exists only when the board has the CEO as its only member. Indeed the boards of several large U.S. companies, including American Express, Eastman Kodak, General Motors, IBM, and Westinghouse, have fired their CEO/Chairman in recent years.

Estimates indicate that the titles are combined in over 80 percent of U.S. firms. In the vast majority of the remaining cases, the Chairman is the former CEO. Proponents of regulations to force firms to appoint outsiders as Chairman are essentially arguing that almost all major firms in the United States are inefficiently organized. While this assumption may be correct, reformers have presented no cogent argument for how such an important corporate-control practice can be wealth-decreasing and still survive in the competitive marketplace for so long across so many companies.

Suggested by Brickley, James A., Jeffrey L. Coles, and Gregg Jarrell, "Leadership Structure: On the Separation of the Positions of CEO and Chairman of the Board," University of Rochester, 1993.

The principle of separation of decision management and control helps to explain the frequent use of hierarchies in organizations. In hierarchies, decision management is formally separate from decision control; that is, decisions of individuals are monitored and ratified by individuals that are above them in the hierarchy. The same agent may have decision-control and decision-management functions; for example, divisional managers might have approval rights over certain initiatives of lower-level employees and at the same time have to request authorization for the division's capital expenditure plan. The important thing is that one agent not have both decision management and control rights for the *same decision*. In smaller organizations, where one person (or a small number) has the relevant knowledge to make decisions, it is expensive to separate decision management from decision control. In this case, the two functions are often combined. In such cases, however, the decision maker also tends to be the major residual claimant to avoid agency problems. (For example, the company is organized as a sole-proprietorship, partnership, or closely-held corporation.)

Separation of Decision Management and Control: Not a New Concept

The English merchant guilds were formed during the 12th century. These precursors to the modern corporation were chartered by the crown and given a monopoly to conduct trade within their own towns, usually in return for a payment to the crown. Each guild would specialize in a particular trade (carpenters, stone cutters, pewterers, etc.). The guilds held property and elected officials to manage the trade and property. Incorporation by the crown created a legal entity that could conduct business.

In order to protect the members of the guild from embezzlement and mismanagement by their elected officers, the charters of the guilds contained provisions for the election of auditors from the general membership to audit the financial records of the guild. For example, The Worshipful Company of Pewterers of the City of London was audited by the members. The Book of Ordinances of 1564 contains the following "order for ye audytors":

> "Also it is agreed that there shalbe foure Awdytours Chosen euery yeare to awdit the Craft accompte and they to parvese it and search it that it shall be perfect. And also to accompt it Correct it and allowe it So that they make an ende of the awdet therof between Mighelmas and Christmas yearely and if defaute be made of ffenishinge thereof before Christmas yearely euery one of the saide Awdytours shall paye to the Craft box vj s. viij d. a pece."

Audits by members of the guild are early examples of separating decision management from control. The guild officers had decision management rights, but decision control rights in the form of annual monitoring of financial transactions were vested in member auditors.

Suggested by Boyd, Edward, "History of Auditing," in *History of Accounting and Accountants*, Richard Brown, ed., 1905, p. 79. Also see, Ross Watts and Jerold Zimmerman, "Agency Problems, Auditing, and the Theory of the Firm: Some Evidence," *Journal of Law and Economics* 26, October 1983, pp. 613–633.

While management and control rights for a decision are often granted to individuals at different levels in the organization, they are sometimes granted to separate individuals at the same level of the corporate hierarchy. For example, the quality of the output of a manufacturing division is sometimes monitored by a quality unit with equal status in the organization. Similarly, internal auditors often monitor units on the same hierarchal level.

The concept of decision management and control is also useful in making the term *empowerment* more precise. Managers are sometimes unclear about what rights are being granted when they say they are empowering workers. This ambiguity can lead to disputes and conflicts between management and employees—for example, when management reverses the decisions of workers who thought they were empowered. The principle of separation of decision management and control suggests that empowerment should not mean that a worker has all rights to a particular decision. For example, an empowered worker might have increased rights to initiate and implement decisions. However, there is still an important role for managers to ratify and monitor decisions. Ratification does not necessarily mean that a worker must seek approval for every decision. In some cases, managers might want to pre-ratify decisions within a particular range (*"boundary setting"*). For instance, at Bob's Autos, the managers might have authority to set prices within some range. In any case, Bob would want to maintain monitoring rights over the decision. Often conflicts over empowerment can be avoided by a careful discussion about what rights are actually being delegated to the employee.

Influence Costs

To this point, we have assumed that decision-making authority is either granted to an individual or a team within the firm. Once the right is granted, the agent or team is actively involved in decision making (subject to ratification and monitoring from others). Sometimes, however, firms use bureaucratic rules that purposely limit active decision making.[13] For example, airlines allocate routes to flight attendants based on seniority—there is no supervisor who decides who gets which route. Similarly, some firms base promotions solely on years worked with the firm. Some universities do not permit grade changes, once the grade is recorded.

One potential benefit of limiting discretion in making decisions is that it reduces the resources consumed by individuals trying to influence decisions. Employees are often very concerned about the personal effects of decisions made within the firm. For example, flight attendants care about which routes they fly. Employees are not indifferent to which colleagues are laid off in an economic downturn. These concerns motivate politicking and other potentially nonproductive *influence activities.* For instance, employees might waste valuable time trying to influence decision makers. In vying for promotions, employees might take dysfunctional actions to make other employees look bad.

---

[13]See, Milgrom, Paul, 1988, "Employment Contracts, Influence Activities and Efficient Organization Design," *Journal of Political Economy* 96, 42–60.

Not assigning the decision right to a specific individual lowers *influence costs*—there is no one to lobby. This policy, however, can impose costs on an organization. For example, consider individuals who are competing for a promotion. These individuals have incentives to provide evidence to their supervisor that they are the most qualified for the promotion. This information is often useful in making better promotion decisions. However, the information comes at a cost—workers spend time trying to convince the supervisor that they are the most qualified rather than on some other activity such as selling products. It makes sense to run the "horse race" as long as the marginal benefits from better information are larger than the marginal costs of the influence activity. The horse race should be stopped at the point where the marginal value of additional information about individual qualifications is equal to the marginal cost of additional influencing activity.

In some cases, the firm's profits are largely unaffected by decisions that greatly affect individual employee welfare. For example, firm profits might be invariant to which flight attendant gets the Hawaii route vs. the Sioux Falls route. It is in this setting that bureaucratic rules for decision making are most likely. The firm benefits from a reduction in influence costs, but is little affected by the particular outcome of the decision process.

Influence Costs at Reynolds Tobacco

"After a century of 'one-for-all,' the Sticht (the CEO) succession scramble split Reynolds into warring camps. No longer did people pull together for the company. Now they looked after the interests of the executive they hitched their star to: Wilson, Horrigan, or Abely. Preparing for a financial analysts' meeting, Wilson and Abely quarreled over who would speak first, a squabble Sticht finally had to settle. At a rehearsal for presentations to a companywide conference, Abely had run over his allotted time when Horrigan stomped into the room. 'What's that——doing up there?' he stormed. "It's my time." Abely ordered a feasibility study on spinning off Sea-Land. Wilson, to whom Sea-Land reported, got wind of it and confronted John Dowdle, the treasurer, who was doing the study. 'I'm sorry, I can't tell you about that,' Dowdle said. 'Abely will fire me if I tell you.' Horrigan hired a public relations firm to get him nominated for the right kinds of business and humanitarian awards to enhance his resume. Horrigan's big score: a Horatio Alger Award."

Suggested by Bryan Burrough, and John Helyar, *Barbarians at the Gate*, Harper Perennial, New York, 1990, p. 58.

Summary

Firms engage in the *process* of transforming inputs into outputs which are sold to customers. An important element of organizations is partitioning the totality of *tasks* of the organization into smaller blocks and assigning them to individuals and/or groups within the firm. Through the design process, jobs are created. Jobs have at least two important dimensions, *variety of tasks* and *decision authority*. This chapter focuses on decision authority. The next chapter focuses on the bundling of tasks.

In *centralized decision systems,* most major decisions are made by individuals at the top of the organization. In *decentralized systems,* many decisions are made by lower-level workers. Decentralized decision making has both benefits and costs. Potential benefits include better use of local knowledge, more rapid decision making, conservation of management time, and training/motivation for lower-level manager. Potential costs include agency and coordination costs. The optimal degree of decentralization depends on the marginal benefits and the marginal costs. These costs and benefits vary across firms and over time. There has been a recent trend toward greater decentralization motivated in part by increased competition and changes in technology.

Decision rights are not just assigned to a hierarchal level, but to particular positions within the hierarchial level. Similar to the centralization versus decentralization problem, relevant factors in making this horizontal choice include the distribution of knowledge and the costs of coordination and control.

Sometimes firms assign decision rights to *teams* of workers rather than to specific individuals. Firms assign decision rights to teams for at least three basic purposes: to manage activities, recommend actions, and make products. The use of teams can sometimes increase productivity; however, this is not always the case. Three basic conditions must be met for teams to be productive: (1) there must be potential synergies, (2) team members must either have or be able to acquire at low cost the relevant knowledge for good decision making, and (3) it must be possible to control free-rider problems at relatively low cost. This last condition suggests that small teams are likely to work better than large teams. However, the distribution of knowledge and other productivity/size effects are also important in determining optimal team size.

Higher-level managers have an important role in setting the rewards and evaluation criteria for teams as a whole. For instance, to mitigate agency problems, managers commonly evaluate and reward teams based on team output. Higher-level managers also have a role in providing technical assistance and advice to teams and in serving as court of last resort for solving disputes among team members. Since the organization within teams is not generally set by higher-level managers, it is important for new teams to establish their own internal architecture.

Decision management refers to the initiation and implementation of decisions, while *decision control* refers to the ratification and monitoring of decisions. When agents do not bear the major wealth effects of their decisions, it is generally important to separate decision management from decision control. A prominent example of this principle is the presence of a board of directors at the top of all corporations. This principle also helps to explain the presence of *hierarchies* in most organizations. It can also help to make the concept of empowerment more precise.

Sometimes firms adopt rules that limit the discretion of decision makers. For example, airlines assign routes to flight attendants based solely on seniority. One benefit of limiting discretion is that it reduces the incentives of individuals to engage in costly *influencing activity* (for example, politicking). Some influencing activity, however, is valuable in that it produces information that improves decision making. Firms are, therefore, most likely to limit discretion when firm profits do not depend heavily on the decisions, but where the decisions are of significant concern to employees (as in the case of assigning routes to flight attendants).

The Assignment of Decision Rights:

Bundling Tasks into Jobs and Jobs into Subunits

IBM Credit Corporation is a wholly-owned subsidiary of IBM. Its major business is the financing of installment-payment agreements for IBM products. If IBM Credit were a stand-alone company, it would rank in the *Fortune 100* finance companies with assets valued at over $10 billion. In 1993, IBM Credit was touted in the financial press for decreasing the time required to process a credit application from six days to four hours.[1] This decrease in cycle time was achieved through a substantial rebundling of the tasks performed by individual workers. Prior to *re-engineering,* individuals performed narrowly assigned tasks. For example, one employee would check the applicant's credit, while another employee would price the loan. Workers were grouped based on functional specialties to form the basic subunits of the firm (for example, the credit and pricing departments). After the re-engineering, applications were handled by "case workers" who were assigned most of the tasks involved in processing the application. The basic subunit structure of the company was correspondingly altered.

The results at IBM Credit suggest that the bundling of tasks into jobs and subunits of the firm is an important policy choice that can dramatically affect a firm's productivity. The primary purpose of this chapter is to examine this bundling decision. We begin by analyzing the problem of how to bundle tasks into jobs. We then consider the problem of combining jobs into subunits of the firm. We conclude the chapter by discussing recent trends in the assignment of decision authority (the

---

[1]For example, see Michael Hammer and James Champy, "The Promise of Reengineering," *Fortune Magazine,* May 3, 1993, pp. 94–97.

FIGURE 10.1   Tasks at Financial Software Incorporated.

Financial Software Inc. (FSI) is a hypothetical distributer of financial software. Its customers include individual consumers and businesses. Within FSI, there are two primary activities or functions, *selling software and after-sales service (helping customers install the software on their systems and interfacing it with other programs for instance). As displayed in the figure, FSI must perform four basic tasks—sales and service for each of the two customer groups.*

Financial Software Inc. (FSI)		
	Function	
Customer Type	Sales	Service
Individuals	Task 1	Task 2
Businesses	Task 3	Task 4

---

topic of Chapter 9) and the bundling of tasks (the topic of this chapter). We expand on the example of IBM Credit to illustrate these trends. Later in the book, in Chapter 17, we discuss the topic of process re-engineering in more detail.

Bundling Tasks into Jobs

Specialized versus Broad Task Assignment

In Chapter 9, we discussed how jobs have at least two important dimensions—decision authority and variety of tasks. We then analyzed the topic of decision authority in greater detail. We now turn to the second dimension, the bundling of tasks. The problem of how to bundle tasks is obviously quite complex; unfortunately limited formal analysis of the topic exists. Nevertheless, as was the case in studying decision authority, important insights can be gained through the examination of relatively simple examples.

Financial Software Inc. (FSI) is a hypothetical distributer of financial software. Its customers include individual consumers and businesses. Within FSI, there are two primary activities or *functions,* selling software and after-sales service (helping customers install the software on their systems and interfacing it with other programs). Thus, as displayed in Figure 10.1, FSI must perform four basic tasks—sales and service for each of the two customer groups. Of course, these four basic tasks could be subdivided into a much larger number of smaller tasks. To keep the analysis for instance tractable, however, we ignore this finer partitioning and assume that the firm has only four tasks. The insights from our analysis readily extend to more general cases.

FSI operates at multiple locations throughout the country. At a particular location, each of the four tasks take four hours per day to complete; thus the firm must hire two full-time employees in this office. In structuring the two jobs, the most obvious alternatives are to: (1) have each worker specialize in one function (either selling or service) which is performed for both customer groups or (2) have one worker provide both sales and service to individual consumers and the other worker perform both functions for business customers. We refer to the first alterative as *specialized task assignment* and the second as *broad task assignment*. Below we discuss their relative benefits and costs.

Benefits of Specialized Task Assignment

There are several potential benefits that can arise from using specialized rather than broad task assignment:

Exploiting Comparative Advantage. Specialized task assignment allows the firm to match people with jobs based on skills and training and correspondingly has workers concentrate on their particular specialties. For example, FSI can hire sales-people to sell and technicians to provide service. The principle of comparative advantage (see Chapter 3), suggests that this specialization will often produce higher output than having individuals perform a broad set of tasks.

Adam Smith on the Economies of Specialization

With specialized-task assignment, workers concentrate on performing a narrow set of tasks. Adam Smith, an important 18th century economist and philosopher, was among the first to recognize and promote the potential gains from this type of specialization. In his famous book, *The Wealth of Nations,* he argued how a number of specialized workers each performing a single step in the manufacturing of pins could produce far more output than the same number of generalists making whole pins. Smith presents the following description of a pin factory using specialized workers:

> "One man draws the wire, another straightens it, a third cuts it, a fourth points it, a fifth grinds it at the top for receiving the head; to make the head requires two or three distinct operations; to put it on is a peculiar business, to whiten the pins is another; it is even a trade by itself to put them into the paper."

Smith notes that a small factory with 10 specialized workers could produce about 48,000 pins a day, while 10 independent workers could not have produced 20 pins per day.

Suggested by Adam Smith, *The Wealth of Nations*, 1776.

Lower Cross-Training Expenses. With specialized task assignment, each worker is trained to complete one basic function. With broad task assignment workers are trained to complete more than one function, which can be expensive. For instance, at FSI suppose the service function requires a skilled technician with an advanced college degree, while the sales function requires an individual with only a high-school diploma. Specialized task assignment allows FSI to hire one person with an advanced degree and one person without an advanced degree. With broad task assignment, the level of education required is usually the highest level for the assigned tasks. Thus, broad task assignment requires FSI to hire two people with advanced degrees and train them to perform both functions. Assuming it costs more for FSI to hire a person with an advanced degree than a person with only a high-school diploma, broad task assignment is more expensive than specialized task assignment.

Relative Ease at Motivating Workers to Perform a Narrow Set of Tasks.   At FSI, a worker concentrating on sales can be motivated by commissions, while a worker concentrating on service can be motivated by a bonus based on customer satisfaction. Also each worker can be monitored by specialists with similar training and knowledge. If, in contrast, workers are assigned a broad set of tasks, the company will want to design compensation plans and monitoring systems that motivate the workers to exert the correct balance of effort across the tasks. Developing such compensation plans and systems is frequently quite difficult.[2] For example, if FSI pays too high a sales commission, workers will concentrate on sales at the expense of providing good after-sales service to customers. Alternatively, if FSI pays too high a bonus for customer satisfaction, the worker will concentrate on after-sales service at the expense of reduced selling.

Costs of Specialized Task Assignment

While specialized task assignment has advantages relative to broad task assignment, it also has drawbacks. Some of the primary costs of specialized-task assignment are:

Lost Complementarities from Performing Few Functions.   Sometimes performing one function can lower the cost of performing the other function. For example, important information about a customer's service requirements might be gained through the sales effort. This information is less likely to be utilized optimally if sales and service are conducted by two separate people; it can be costly to transfer the information to the other worker. As another example, consider the case of two workers on an automobile assembly line. The first attaches the door to the car frame, and the second attaches the latching mechanism and makes sure the door latches to the frame. If the first does not align the door properly, the second will have more difficulty getting the door to latch. Combining both tasks into one job causes the person attaching the door to be sure of proper alignment before the latch is attached.

---

[2]See Bengt Holmstrom and Paul Milgrom, "Multitask Principal-Agent Analyses: Incentive Contracts, Asset Ownership and Job Design, 1991," *Journal of Law Economics and Organization* 7, 24–52. We discuss this point in more detail in the next chapter.

Functional Myopia.   With specialized task assignment, workers tend to concentrate on their individual functions, rather than on the overall process of providing good sales and service to customers. For example, a salesperson, who is compensated primarily through commissions, will have incentives to sell software to customers even if the sale imposes large service costs on the company, as when the software is not a good match with the customer's existing computer system.

Reduced Flexibility.   Not cross-training workers has costs as well as benefits. For example, if only one person is trained to perform a particular function, what happens if the person is sick? Also, having only one person trained to do a job in a firm can place the firm at a disadvantage when bargaining with the worker over salary and other benefits.[3] These problems are likely to be greatest in small companies, since in large companies several people are likely to be trained to perform any given task.

Incentive Issues.   We discussed how it is often easier to motivate people to perform a narrow set of tasks than to motivate them to strike the appropriate balance among a variety of tasks. In some cases, however, producing an output requires the coordinated execution of several separate tasks, which individually are hard to access. Here, it can make sense to assign all the tasks to one individual who is accountable for the final product. For instance, in our example of attaching doors and latches to automobiles, assigning both tasks to one individual makes it easy to identify who is to blame if the door does not close.

Optimal Bundling of Tasks

This discussion suggests that there are tradeoffs in choosing between specialized and broad task assignment. Obviously, specialized task assignment will be optimal in environments where the benefits are high relative to the costs, and broad task assignment will be preferred in other environments. Our analysis indicates that one variable that is likely to be of particular importance in determining this choice is the relative degree of complementarity among tasks within versus across functional areas. For instance, at FSI the magnitude of the benefits of specialized task assignment depend largely on how related are the selling efforts between the two customer groups. If there are only minor differences between selling to individuals and businesses, training employees to do one makes them well suited to do the other. In contrast, if the tasks are very different, little is gained by training one employee to perform the two selling tasks over training separate workers. Similarly, the costs of specialized task assignment at FSI depend on the importance of complementarities across functional areas. When these complementarities are low (for instance, little valuable information is gained about service through the selling effort), little is lost by having employees concentrate on one function.

---

[3]See Lars A. Stole and Jeffrey Zwiebel, 1993, Organizational Design and Technology Choice with Nonbinding Contracts, working paper, University of Chicago.

Ultimately, the optimal bundling of tasks into jobs depends on how specialized knowledge is created and the costs of transferring knowledge. Ideally, an individual performing a task should have the relevant specific knowledge to complete the task successfully. To accomplish this objective, either the relevant information can be transferred to the person performing the task or the task can be assigned to a person who has the specific knowledge. The preferred option depends on the original distribution of knowledge and the costs of knowledge transfer.

Our example of FSI is highly simplified and in most settings more complicated task divisions are feasible. For instance, the selling function might have two phases— the initial contact and closing the deal. The initial contact requires less specialized product and service knowledge than closing the deal, but is potentially more time consuming. Here it might be optimal for a salesperson to handle the initial contact and have a joint call with both the salesperson and service person to close the deal. As another example, at some locations more complete specialization might be feasible. For instance, an employee at an office with a larger sales volume could concentrate solely on selling to individuals or to businesses. While our basic example of FSI abstracts away from these more complicated considerations, it nevertheless identifies some of the key considerations in deciding on how to divide tasks into jobs.

Bundling of Jobs into Subunits

Firms group jobs together to form the basic subunits of the firm (for example, divisions and subsidiaries). These basic building blocks of the organization are the work groups which define and characterize what each part of the firm does. Firms form subunits by grouping jobs by function, product, geography, or into some combination of the three. In this section, we discuss these basic ways to organize. We focus on the firm level—how the overall firm might be divided into major subunits. The next section provides a brief discussion of how this analysis extends to the subunit level. Chapter 14 presents a more detailed analysis of how firms evaluate the performance of subunits.

Grouping Jobs by Function

General Description.   One common method of grouping jobs is by functional specialty. Figure 10.2 displays an organizational chart for FSI under this type of functional grouping. Individual jobs are characterized by specialized-task assignment. All the sales jobs in the organization are grouped together to form a sales department, while the service jobs are grouped together to form a service department. These departments are charged with managing their particular functions for the firm's entire product line. The CEO's office plays an important role in defining the organizational architecture coordinating activities across departments, making key operating decisions, and setting corporate strategy. Typically, the CEO appoints a committee of top-level managers (including the senior department managers) to focus on coordination and planning issues.

FIGURE 10.2.   Financial Software Incorporated (FSI) with Functional Organization.

This figure displays an organizational chart for FSI, where jobs are grouped by functional specialty. These jobs are characterized by specialized-task assignment. All the sales jobs in the organization are grouped together to form a sales department, while the service jobs are grouped together to form a service department. These departments are charged with managing their particular functions for the firm's entire product line. The CEO's office plays an important role in defining organizational architecture coordinating activities across departments, making key operating decisions, and setting corporate strategy.

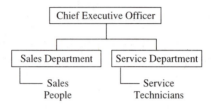

Benefits of Functional Subunits. There are at least three major benefits from grouping jobs by function. First, this grouping helps to promote effective coordination within the functional areas. For instance, a supervisor in service can assign workers to specific projects based on current work load and expertise. It is also relatively easy for functional specialists to share information since they are in the same department. For example, if a service technician develops a new solution to a problem, his supervisor can help promote its use by training other workers in the department. Second, this grouping helps to promote functional expertise. Individuals focus on developing specific functional skills and are directly supervised by knowledgeable individuals who can help with this development. Third, there is a well-defined promotion path for employees. Employees will tend to work their way up within a functional department (for example, from salesperson, to local sales manager, to district sales manager).

Problems with Functional Subunits. While functional grouping has advantages, it also has disadvantages. First, there is the opportunity cost of using valuable senior management's time for coordinating functions and making operating decisions. This time might be better spent on activities such as long-range planning (deciding what businesses the company should be in, planning strategies to be successful in these businesses, and implementing the firm's organizational architecture, etc.). Second, "handoffs" across departments can take significant time. For example, when a sale is made by the sales department at FSI, the order has to be communicated to the service department, which in turn must schedule the required customer service. This process can cause lengthy delays in serving the customer. Third, there can be significant coordination problems across departments. For instance, a salesperson might promise rapid installation to a customer without having good information about the workload of the service department. Moreover, important information can be lost in the transfers between departments. Fourth, employees sometimes concentrate on their functional specialties rather than the process of serving customers. For instance, the sales department might focus on achieving department goals, even if it imposes costs on other departments in the firm.

Concentrating on Functions at Cadillac

Some of the coordination problems that can arise with functional organization are highlighted by a former process that Cadillac used for developing new products. Under this process, engineers were grouped by narrow functional specialty and charged with completing a related set of tasks:

> "The designer of the car's body would leave a hole for the engine, then the power-train designer would try to fit the engine into the cavity, then the manufacturing engineer would try to figure out how to build the design, and finally the service engineer would struggle to invent ways of repairing the car. The results were predictable. On one model, the exhaust manifold blocked access to the air-conditioning compressor, so seasonal maintenance meant removing the exhaust system. On another model, the connection between the spark plugs and the spark plug wires was so tight that mechanics tended to break the wires when they pulled them off to check the spark plugs."

Automobile companies have been able to reduce problems of this type by moving to a system of "concurrent engineering" where everyone affected by design participates in the process as early as possible. Often companies use development teams that are charged with the entire process. Development teams group jobs by product rather than by function.

Suggested by William H. Davidow and Michael S. Malone, *The Virtual Corporation,* Harper Business, New York, 1993.

Where Functional Subunits Work Best.   Functional grouping works best in small firms with a limited number of products. In these firms, it is relatively easy for senior managers to coordinate operating decisions across departments in a timely and informed fashion. For large firms, with more diverse product offerings, top management is less likely to have the specific knowledge for making operational decisions for the company. In addition, the opportunity cost of having top management concentrate on operating and coordination issues rather than major strategic issues for the firm can be large.[4]

These arguments suggest that young firms will often start with functional subunits and will switch their organizational architectures as they grow. Evidence of

---

[4]See Oliver E. Williamson, 1975, *Markets and Hierarchies,* Free Press, New York.

this trend is seen in the historical experience of U.S. firms. The first large firms in the U.S. were the railroad companies which started to emerge around 1850.[5] These firms initially organized around basic functions, such as finance, pricing, traffic, and maintenance. As the incidence of large firms increased in other industries in the late 1800s (such as steel, tobacco, oil and meatpacking), most followed the lead of the railroads and organized around basic functions. As companies like DuPont, General Motors, and General Electric continued to expand (both geographically and in the number of product lines) in the early 1900s, they began faring poorly in product markets against smaller competitors. In response, these companies began experimenting with different organizational forms. After significant experimentation, many large companies adopted the *multidivisional form (M-form) of organization,* which groups jobs by product or geography.[6] Modern firms continue to display this transitional pattern, moving from functional subunits to M-form corporations.

Alfred Chandler on the Limitations of Functional Grouping

Alfred Chandler, a prominent economic historian, summarizes the problems that functional subunits create as a company becomes large and diverse in the following way:

> "The inherent weakness in the centralized, functionally departmentalized operating company . . . became critical only when the administrative load of the senior executives increased to such an extent that they were unable to handle their entrepreneurial responsibilities efficiently. This situation arose when the operations of the enterprise became too complex and the problems of coordination, appraisal, and policy formulation too intricate for a small number of top officers to handle both long-run, entrepreneurial, and short-run, operational administrative activities."

From: Alfred D. Chandler Jr., *Strategy and Structure,* Doubleday & Company, New York, 1966, pp. 382–383.

Another variable that is likely to affect the desirability of functional subunits is the rate of technological change in the industry. Here, we define technological changes broadly to include new products, new production techniques, and organizational innovations. Functional subunits are more effective in environments with stable technology, since frequent communication across functional departments and specialists is less important and interactions can be handled through routine rules and procedures. In addition, higher-level management is likely to possess the relevant specific knowledge to coordinate the functional areas. In less stable environments, direct communication across functional areas is more important and new

---

[5]See Alfred D. Chandler Jr. 1977, *The Visible Hand: The Managerial Revolution in American Business,* Belnap Press of Harvard University Press, Cambridge, Mass.

[6]For a fascinating account of the development of the M-form corporation, see Alfred D. Chandler Jr., *Strategy and Structure,* Doubleday & Company, New York, 1966.

situations are likely to arise that will challenge established coordination procedures. In turn, higher-level managers are less likely to have all the relevant specific knowledge to address these challenges. Rather the specific knowledge is more likely to be spread across workers throughout the firm. For example, the frequent introduction of new products increases the benefits of communication among salespeople and design engineers about customer demands and preferences. Similarly, it is important for development and manufacturing personnel to share information when production techniques and technologies are frequently changing. Thus, when an environment is dynamic the desirability of a product-orientated organization increases.

Grouping Jobs by Product or Geography

General Description.   The typical M-form corporation is organized into a collection of business units based on product or geographic area. Operating decisions such as product offerings and pricing are decentralized to the business-unit level. Top management of the firm is responsible for major strategic decisions, including the optimal architecture and the allocation of capital among the business units. Figure 10.3 shows how FSI would look organized around product or geography. In the first case, the company is divided into a Business Products Division and a Consumer Products Division. Each of these divisions has its own sales and service departments which focus on the particular products of the division (often jobs within the business units are grouped by functional area). Organized geographically, the company is divided into a West Coast Division and an East Coast Division. In this case, the sales and service departments within each business unit serve both individual and business customers within their geographic areas.

Benefits of Product/Geographic Subunits.   The M-form corporation was perhaps the most significant organizational innovation in the first half of the 20th century. An advantage of the M-form of organizing for large corporations (especially in dynamic environments) is that decision rights for operations are assigned to individuals lower in the organization where the relevant specific knowledge is more likely to be located. Managers of business units are compensated based on the performance of their units; this provides incentives to use this specific knowledge more productively. Decentralizing decision rights to business-unit managers also frees senior management to concentrate on other issues. The separation of the corporate office from operations focuses top executives of the firm on the overall performance of the corporation rather than specific aspects of the functional components.

Problems with Product/Geographic Subunits.   Business-unit managers tend to focus on the performance of their own units. This focus is consistent with the maximization of firm value as long as product demands and costs are independent across business units. In this case, firm value is simply the sum of the values of the individual units. Frequently, however, there are interdependencies among units that must be taken into account if firm value is to be maximized. For example, there is

---

FIGURE 10.3   Financial Software Incorporated (FSI) with Product and Geographic Organization.

This figure shows how FSI would look organized around product or geography. In the first case, the company is divided into a Business Products Division and a Consumer Products Division. Each of these divisions has its own sales and service departments which focus on the particular products of the division (often jobs within the business units are grouped by functional area). Organized geographically, the company is divided into a West Coast Division and an East Coast Division. In this case, the sales and service departments within each business unit serve both individual and business customers within their geographic areas.

Product Organization

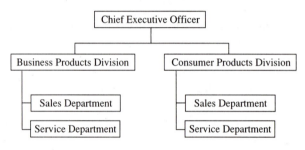

Goegraphic Organization

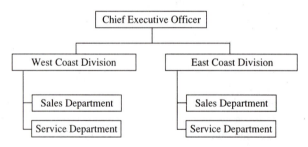

likely to be some overlap in customers, intermediate products are often transferred between subunits, and the units share common resources. If managers focus on their own units and do not consider these interdependencies, overall firm value is reduced. For example, the West and East Coast divisions of FSI might compete against one another over a national customer and reduce overall firm profits by selling products at a lower price than if they coordinated their marketing. As we discuss in Chapter 14, this problem can be mitigated by forming *groups* of interrelated business units and paying unit managers based on overall group performance. However, developing a compensation scheme that appropriately motivates unit managers is not easy.

The Formation of Multidivisional Firms in the Oil Industry

In the 1950s most of the *Fortune 500* oil companies were organized into functional departments. These companies were not performing well relative to smaller corporations. Oil companies began experimenting with their organizational architectures. The design that appeared to work best was the multidivisional form of organization. Some of the firms organized around geographic areas, while other firms organized around product lines. Companies that switched to the M-form early outperformed other companies that did not switch as soon. By the middle 1970s most of the large oil companies had switched to the multidivisional form of organization. Those that did not switch tended to be smaller companies which performed well under the old structure.

H.O. Armour and D. Teece, 1978, "Organizational Structure and Economic Performance," *Bell Journal of Economics* 9, 106–22.

Matrix Organizations

General Descriptions.   Some firms maintain an overlapping structure of functional and product/geographic subunits.[7] In these *matrix organizations,* there are functional departments such as finance, manufacturing, and development. Individuals from these functional departments are also assigned to subunits organized around product, geography, or some special project. Matrix organizations are characterized by intersecting lines of authority. Individuals report to both a functional manager and a product manager. Functional departments usually serve as the primary mechanism for personnel functions and professional development. The functional managers typically have the primary responsibility for performance reviews. Product managers, however, provide input into these reviews.

Matrix organization is often used in such industries as defense, construction, and management consulting. These industries are characterized by a sequence of new products or projects (for example, building a new airplane or a new shopping mall). Individuals are assigned to work on particular projects and are reassigned to new projects after the initial projects are completed. Given the nature of the projects in these industries, it is important for individuals across functional areas to communicate and to work together closely. For example, it is very important for all parts of an airplane to fit together properly and meet the demands of the customer. This

---

[7]For a more detailed discussion of matrix organizations, see Walter F. Baber, *Organizing for the Future,* The University of Alabama Press, 1983.

characteristic promotes the use of product-oriented teams. These projects, however, also benefit from a high level of functional expertise, which is promoted by maintaining functional areas. For instance, it is very important that the plane be aerodynamically sound.

Intel Corporation: A Matrix Organization

Intel Corporation's organizational structure in 1992 provides an example of a matrix organization. The company organized around five major product groups including entry-level products, Intel products, microprocessor products, multimedia and super-computing components, and semiconductor products. Intel staffed these groups with people from the basic functional groups of corporate business development, finance and administration, marketing, sales, software technology and manufacturing. Thus, individual workers were members of both product and functional groups. The term matrix refers to the intersecting lines of authority that result from such an organizational arrangement.

Suggested by ''Intel Corporation: Going into OverDrive,'' Harvard Business School Case #9–593–096, May 1993.

Figure 10.4 shows how FSI might look if it were organized as a matrix organization. The firm maintains functional departments of sales and service. Individuals from these departments are simultaneously assigned to either the business product or consumer product subunits (''teams''). The functional managers focus on managing the particular function across both products, while the product managers focus on the management of particular products across functions.

Benefits and Costs of Matrix Organizations

A potential advantage of matrix organization, relative to functional organization, is that individuals are more likely to focus on the overall business process than on their own narrow functional specialty. But when functional supervision is maintained, there is a mechanism for helping to assure functional excellence and for providing opportunities for advancement and development.

Potential problems with the matrix form of organization arise from the intersecting lines of authority. Individuals who are assigned to product teams do not necessarily have strong incentives to cooperate or to be concerned about the success of the team. Rather, individuals are likely to be concerned about how their functional supervisors view their work (since functional supervisors do the performance reviews). Also employees often see their roles as being representatives for their functional areas. For example, individuals can be overly concerned about how the decisions of a product team impact their particular area. These problems can be

FIGURE 10.4   Financial Software Incorporated (FSI) with Matrix Organization.

This figure shows how FSI might look if it were organized as a matrix organization. The firm maintains functional departments of sales and service. Individuals from these departments are simultaneously assigned to either the business-products or consumer-products subunits ("teams"). In particular, salesperson 1 and service technician 1 serve on the business products team, while salesperson 2 and service technician 2 are on the consumer-products team. The functional managers focus on managing the particular function across both products, while the product managers focus on the management of particular products across functions.

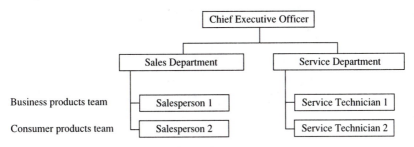

reduced by appropriate design of the performance-evaluation and reward systems (discussed in subsequent chapters). For instance, individuals will be more concerned about the output of a product team if their compensation depends on this output. A related problem with matrix organizations is the potential for disputes between functional and product managers.

Organizing the Subunit

We have examined the decisions concerning partitioning the firm into major subunits. The same analysis applies to grouping jobs within subunits. For example, deciding whether to group jobs within a business unit by function, product, or geography depends on the same types of costs and benefits that we discussed at the firm level. Grouping jobs into functional departments at a business-unit level is most likely to be effective when the unit is small and has a limited range of products. In contrast, in large business units with diverse product offerings, organizing by product or geography can be the preferred alternative. Product/geographic organization is also likely to be more desirable in rapidly-changing business environments, since senior management is less likely to have the relevant specific knowledge to make operating and coordination decisions.

Organization at Chase Manhattan Bank

We have discussed several ways that firms group jobs into subunits of the firm. Often firms use more than one method in forming subunits. For example, Chase Manhattan Bank uses three types of subunits. Chase Delaware handles all the credit card business. The business for individuals and middle-market firms is organized geographically. Large business customers are served by specific teams that generally operate out of New York City. Frequently, these teams are set up by industry.

Recent Trends in the Assignment of Decision Rights

F. W. Taylor on Iron Workers

Frederick Winslow Taylor, an industrial engineer at beginning of the 20th century, is known as the father of Scientific Management. His views were very influential in affecting the assignment of decision rights in many firms. In particular, he argued that the attributes of lower-level workers dictated that they be granted limited decision authority and a narrow set of tasks. In his words:

> "Now one of the very first requirements for a man who is fit to handle pig iron as a regular occupation is that he shall be so stupid and so phlegmatic that he more nearly resembles in his mental make-up the ox than any other type. The man who is mentally alert and intelligent is for this very reason entirely unsuited to what would, for him, be the grinding monotony of work of this character. Therefore the workman who is best suited to handling pig iron is unable to understand the real science of doing this class of work. He is so stupid that the word 'percentage' has no meaning to him, and he must consequently be trained by a man more intelligent than himself into the habit of working in the accordance with the laws of this science before he can be successful."

Many modern managers do not think that this view of lower-level workers is accurate in today's environment. The work force of today is better educated than in Taylor's time, and modern production technologies often call for increased education and less brawn. Correspondingly, many managers have empowered lower-level workers by giving them broader decision authority and a less specialized set of tasks.

Suggested by Frederick Winslow Taylor, *The Principles of Scientific Management*, Harper and Brothers Publishers, 1923, page 59.

Traditionally, many firms have created jobs that specify limited decision authority (the topic of Chapter 9) and narrow task assignments. In turn, these jobs have tended to be grouped by functional specialty (either at the overall firm level or at the business-unit level). During the 1990s there has been a significant trend toward granting workers broader decision authority and less specialized task assignments. Many companies have also shifted away from functional subunits toward more product-oriented organizations.

Bundling of Tasks into Jobs and Jobs into Subunits in the Manufacturing of Copy Machines

In this chapter, we have argued that firms must make two interrelated but separate organizing decisions. First, each employee must be assigned a set of tasks; second, employees must be grouped into work teams to form subunits of the firm. Employees can be given a narrow set of tasks and asked to specialize in only these tasks or they can be given a variety of tasks. Employees can be grouped into major subunits based on function, product, or geography. Major subunits subdivide into additional subgroups.

To illustrate the separate but related nature of these two organizing decisions, consider the manufacturing of a wiring bundle for a copy machine. The bundle contains several hundred wires and connectors that provide the circuits connecting the paper-flow units, scanner, and photo receptor to the internal computer logic. The wire harness is plugged into various components during the assembly process. One person can be responsible for one task, for example, connecting one of the many connectors or testing the completed wire harness. Alternatively, one individual can be assigned the task of producing and testing a completed harness. In either case, a group of workers are assigned individual tasks that produce wire harnesses for a particular copier.

Now suppose the firm manufacturers 10 different copiers, each with its own wire harness. There can be 10 subgroups of wire-harness makers. These 10 subgroups can be placed in one wire-harness department. Alternatively, these 10 subgroups can each be assigned to and report to a manager responsible for a particular copier. Placing each wire-harness team into one wire-harness department is a functional organization. Assigning each team to a product manager is a product organization. If the same copier is produced in both the U.S. and Germany, there can be one harness-wiring group supplying wire bundles for both assembly sites or separate wire-harness groups in the two countries. The latter case is a geographic organization. Whether wire-harness production is organized by function, product, or geography, within each wire-harness team tasks can be handled narrowly where each worker performs just one or two tasks (attaching one type of connector) or tasks can be assigned broadly (each worker producing an entire harness and testing it). Major variables in determining both the bundling of tasks into jobs and the grouping of employees into subunits are the costs of acquiring and transferring specialized knowledge.

These trends in the assignment of decision rights have been motivated by at least three important factors. First, the rate of technological change in most industries has increased dramatically. As previously discussed, this change is likely to promote a more product-oriented organization. A second factor is increased competition. World-wide competition has increased in many industries and has placed pressure on firms to deliver high-quality service and products to customers. Product-oriented organizational structures tend to focus workers on customer demands. The third factor is improvements in information technology. An important example is the development of "expert systems" which enable workers, who are not functional specialists, to obtain the relevant technical knowledge for making decisions at lower cost. For example, at FSI the development of more sophisticated computer programs could enable salespeople to configure software with various computer systems and programs without the aid of highly-skilled technicians. ("Smart" software could essentially configure itself.)

David Kearns on Increased Foreign Competition

Over the past few decades, competition has increased in many industries. This increased competition has been motivated by such things as lost patent protection, reduced transportation costs, deregulation, and improved technology throughout the world. David Kearns was CEO of Xerox during the 1980s. During his tenure, Xerox faced a substantial increase in foreign competition. This increased competition motivated Xerox to improve customer service and the quality of its products. To achieve this objective Xerox substantially reassigned decision rights by empowering workers and moving away from functional organization. In Kearn's words:

"About the only consoling factor was that I knew we weren't the only ones in the soup. Global competition had set upon this country, and everyone was vulnerable. American business was threatened not only by Japan and Korea. Europe was mobilizing into a potent force that demanded serious consideration. And yet, as I looked around me, I saw that so many great and admired companies were doing nothing but sitting on their hands. Like us, they were kissing away their businesses and laying the groundwork for their own destruction.

After my string of trips to Japan and after deep introspection about Xerox's strengths and flaws, the solution began to point in one direction. Our only hope for survival was to urgently commit ourselves to vastly improving the quality of our products and service. This was something a lot of corporations talked about, but it was extraordinarily difficult to do. It meant changing the very culture of Xerox from the ground up. Everyone from the cleaning people to the chairman would have to think differently."

Suggested by David T. Kearns *Prophets in the Dark*, Harper Business, New York, 1992, pp. xv–xvi.

For a specific example of the types of changes that are occurring in firms, we shall take a more detailed look at IBM Credit Corporation. Figure 10.5 lists the basic functions that IBM Credit must perform to process a credit application.[8] The credit of the applicant has to be checked; the deal must be priced (an interest rate must be

---

[8]See Michael Hammer and James Champy, 1993, *Reengineering the Corporation,* Harper Business, New York. Note that our discussion of IBM Credit abstracts from many of the details of the actual operation of the company. For example, we do not consider the company's credit-collection activities and the organizational chart is highly simplified. This simplification allows us to illustrate the main points of our analysis without becoming bogged down in less relevant detail.

FIGURE 10.5   Functions at IBM Credit.

This figure lists the basic functions that IBM Credit must perform in order to complete the process of transforming credit applications into formal credit offers.

IBM Credit
___

1. Credit Checking
2. Contract Preparation
3. Pricing
4. Document Preparation

FIGURE 10.6   IBM Credit with Functional Organization.

Under functional organization, the firm is divided into functional departments including credit, pricing, contracts, and documents. Employees are typically assigned a specialized set of tasks within their functional areas.

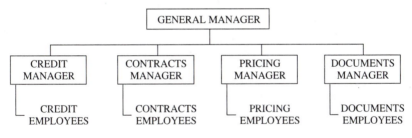

IBM Credit with Functional Organization

chosen); formal contracts have to be written; and final documents have to be compiled and sent to the applicant.

Prior to re-engineering, IBM Credit was organized around these four basic functions. Figure 10.6 shows an organizational chart for IBM Credit under this functional structure. The firm was divided into functional departments including credit, pricing, contracts, and documents. Employees, in turn, were typically assigned a specialized set of tasks within their functional areas and given limited decision authority on how to complete them. For example, a clerk in the credit department might have the simple task of logging applications using prescribed procedures. Coordination across functional departments was accomplished by higher-level management, often through formal rules and procedures. For example, IBM had procedures for transferring credit applications among the various functional departments. Department heads served together on committees to assist in the coordination process. Under this organization, customers received relatively poor service. For instance, IBM

FIGURE 10.7　IBM Credit's Revised Organization.

Under the revised structure, individual case workers have the primary decision rights and responsibility for completing all the steps in the credit-granting process. Each financing request is assigned to a case worker who checks the applicant's credit, prices the deal, completes the contracts, etc. There are some functional specialists in the firm (not shown on the chart) who help the case workers when difficult or unusual circumstances arise.

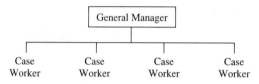

IBM Credit's Revised Organization

Credit took about six days to process a credit application, and it was difficult to provide timely information to the customer about the status of an application.

During the 1990s increased competition placed competitive pressures on IBM Credit to shorten the required time to process a credit application and to provide better customer service. Improved information and computer technology was developed to enable organizational change. For instance, some of the necessary information for processing a credit application was previously stored in a manual filing system. Given this system, it made sense to assign certain tasks to workers who had familiarity and proximity to the information data base. Computerization of this information allowed workers throughout the firm to access this information directly and made it feasible for the firm to reassign tasks.

In response to these pressures and new technologies, IBM Credit completely changed their assignment of decision rights. Under the new structure, pictured in Figure 10.7, individual *case workers* have the primary decision rights and responsibility for completing all the steps in the credit-granting process. Each financing request is assigned to one case worker who checks the applicant's credit, prices the deal, and completes the contracts. Employees have significant decision authority in completing these tasks, and the functional subunits of the firm have largely been abandoned.[9] With this organization, IBM Credit is able to process a credit application in about four hours. Customer satisfaction has correspondingly increased.

---

[9]There are still some functional specialists in the organization who help the case workers when difficult or unusual circumstances arise.

Recent Trends in Organization: GTE

During the 1990s there has been a trend toward more product-oriented organization. An example of a firm that reorganized around along these lines is the telephone company, GTE. Traditionally, GTE had been organized into functional departments such as repair, billing, and marketing. This structure often frustrated customers, who had difficulty locating which person in the company was responsible for addressing particular problems. Due to increased competitive pressures, GTE decided that it had to offer dramatically better customer service to its telephone customers. Rather than making incremental improvements in each of its functional departments, GTE decided to reorganize around the basic process of providing customer service. In particular, customers wanted one-stop shopping—for example, one number to fix an erratic dial tone, question a bill, sign up for call waiting, or all three, at any time of the day. GTE began meeting this demand when it set up its first pilot "customer care center" in Garland Texas in 1992. GTE management states that preliminary data from these pilot projects indicates a 20 percent to 30 percent increase in productivity. Customers also obtain better service.

Stewart, Thomas, 1993, "Reengineering: The Hot New Management Tool," *Fortune,* August 23, 41–48.

IBM Credit and GTE are just two examples of the many firms that have undertaken similar restructurings in the 1990s. The success stories from these restructurings have led some management consultants to advocate wide-scale change for all firms throughout the world. The analysis in Chapters 9 and 10, however, indicates that a firm should not restructure without carefully considering whether a reassignment of decision rights is warranted given its particular business environment. While changes in technology and competition have shifted the optimal assignment of decision rights in many firms, these shifts have not occurred in all industries. For instance, the benefits of narrow task assignment and functional specialization are still likely to be high for many firms in relatively stable industries. Consider, for example, a small coal-mining operation. Here it is likely to continue to make sense to have some workers concentrate on mining the coal, while other employees sell it, and other employees deliver it.

Summary

The bundling of tasks into jobs and subunits of the firm is an important policy choice that can dramatically affect a firm's productivity. The primary purpose of this chapter is to examine this bundling decision.

We distinguish between two types of jobs, those with *specialized-task assignment* and those with *broad-task assignment*. With specialized-task assignment the worker is assigned a narrow set of tasks related to one functional specialty (for example, sales). With broad-task assignment the worker is assigned a greater variety of tasks. The benefits of specialized-task assignment relative to broad-assignment include exploiting comparative advantage, lower cross-training expenses, and relative ease in motivating workers to perform a narrow set of tasks. The costs of specialized-task assignment include lost complementarities from not performing multiple functions, functional myopia, and reduced flexibility. The optimal bundling of tasks depends on the magnitude of these costs and benefits. One variable that is likely to be of particular importance is the relative degree of complementarity among tasks within versus across functional areas. Specialized-task assignment is favored when the complementarity of tasks within a functional area is relatively high.

Firms can group jobs into subunits based on functional specialty, product, geography, or some combination of the three. *Functional subunits* group all jobs performing the same function into the same department (for example, a sales department). The CEO's office plays a major role in coordinating these departments and in making operating decisions. The benefits of functional organization are promotion of coordination and expertise within functional areas and provision of a well-defined promotion path for employees. The problems with functional organization are the high opportunity cost of using top-management time to coordinate departments and make operating decisions; handoffs across departments that can take significant time; coordination failures across departments; and workers concentrating on their own functional specialties rather than the customer. Functional subunits are likely to work best in small firms with a limited number of products and in relatively stable environments.

Larger, more diverse firms, often find it desirable to form subunits based on product or geography. In the *multidivisional (M-form) firm,* operating decisions are decentralized to the business-unit level. Top management of the firm is responsible for major strategic decisions, including finding the optimal organizational architecture and allocating capital among business units. A primary benefit of the M-form corporation is that decision rights for operations are assigned to individuals lower in the organization where the relevant specific knowledge is located. Managers of business units are compensated based on the performance of their units so as to provide incentives to use this specific knowledge productively. Decentralizing decision rights to business-unit managers also frees top executives to concentrate on other issues. Problems with the M-form of organization arise because business-unit managers often have incentives to take actions that increase the performance of their business units at the expense of other units in the firm. These problems can be mitigated through careful design of business units and by paying business-unit managers based on *group performance* (where the group consists of profit centers with interrelated costs and demands). It is usually difficult, however, to avoid this problem completely.

Some firms maintain an overlapping structure of functional and product/geographic subunits. These *matrix organizations* have functional departments, such as finance and marketing. Members of these departments are assigned to cross-functional product teams (subunits). Team members report to both a product manager and a functional supervisor. Generally, performance evaluation is conducted by the functional supervisor. Matrix organization is common in project-oriented industries, such as defense, construction, and consulting. An advantage of matrix organization, in contrast to pure functional organization, is that individuals are more likely to focus on the overall business process than on their own narrow functional specialty. Potential advantages over pure product organization are that the functional departments help to assure functional excellence and provide additional opportunities for advancement and development. Potential problems with the matrix organization arise from the intersecting lines of authority. A worker is likely to have loyalties divided between the goals of the project team and the goals of the functional department. This problem can be mitigated by appropriate design of the performance-evaluation and reward systems. However, as we will see in subsequent chapters, accomplishing this objective can be a difficult task.

Decisions on how to group jobs must be made at many levels in the organization. Our analysis of the costs and benefits of alternative groupings of jobs focuses at the overall firm level (how to form major subunits). The same basic analysis, however, applies to the grouping of jobs at the subunit level of the firm.

Traditionally, many firms have created jobs that are low in decision authority and narrow in task assignment. Lately there has been a trend toward granting workers more decision authority and broader task assignment. Many companies have also shifted away from functional subunits toward more product-oriented organizations. These trends can be explained by increases in the rate of technological change, increased competition, and improvements in information technology.

CHAPTER 11 The Level and Mix of Compensation

Nature Aid Corporation is a small firm located in Seattle, Washington. In the fall of 1994, the company published the following advertisement in a local newspaper:

Vice President of Manufacturing

"Fast growing vitamin & beauty aid manufacturer. Required industry experience 5 years or more, formulation, purchasing, inventory management, packaging. Salary $50K +, good fringe benefits. Profit sharing. The position is located in the Pacific Northwest, renown for its quality of life."

Like thousands of other position announcements published everyday throughout the world, the ad lists the qualifications for the job and gives information about compensation. The ad also emphasizes the desirability of living in the Pacific Northwest.

Summarized in this ad are three important decisions that all firms must make with respect to compensation policy: (1) the level of compensation—how much to pay, (2) the composition of the pay package—the salary/fringe-benefit mix, and (3) the form of any incentive-based compensation. In the case of Nature Aid, the company has decided to offer the new vice president at least $50K in salary, high fringe benefits, and profit sharing.

These three compensation decisions are critically important for most firms. First, they determine the likelihood that a firm will be able to attract and retain qualified workers. Compensation is a major reason people work. Thus the number of applicants for job openings and the quit rate among existing employees are likely to be heavily influenced by the level of compensation. Second, compensation-related expenses are a major cost for most firms and play a major role in determining profits and losses. Therefore, designing compensation packages that allow a firm to attract and retain desired employees at the lowest cost manner is important for long-run survival. Third, the form of the compensation contract is likely to be important in determining how hard employees work once they are hired. For instance, employees are likely to work harder if they receive incentive compensation. The form of incentive compensation also determines the specific activities to which they will devote their effort.

In the next two chapters, we examine compensation policy. This chapter considers how firms choose the level of pay and the mix between salary and fringe benefits. The next chapter analyzes incentive compensation. We begin this chapter by discussing the classical model of employment and wages from economics. The managerial implications of this analysis are stressed. We then discuss how job characteristics, such as the risk of danger and the length of the commute, can affect the level of pay through compensating differentials. Next we consider internal labor markets and how pay in these markets varies from the classical analysis. Finally, we analyze the choice of the mix between salary and fringe benefits. The chapter concludes with a summary.

The Level of Pay—The Classical Model

In the classical economic model of wages and employment, firms have *no discretion over the wages they pay to workers*; rather, wages are determined by supply and demand in the market place. There are no long-term contracts. Rather all labor is hired in the "spot" market for a single period. As shown in Figure 11.1, individual firms continue to hire workers up to the point where the marginal revenue product equals the market-determined wage rate (see Chapter 5). Until this point, hiring additional workers brings more revenue into the firm than it costs to hire the workers. Past this point, the costs of hiring additional workers are larger than the benefits. The hiring decisions of all firms in the market determine the demand curve for the particular occupation. The supply curve, in turn, is determined by the decisions of individual workers on whether to accept the given wage rate, stay at home, go to school, or work in another occupation. The market wage rate equates supply and demand. All workers are assumed to be equally skilled and of the same quality.

The implications of this analysis are that if a firm pays too little (below the market wage rate), it will not be able to hire qualified workers, or it will have high turnover. Alternatively, a firm that pays too much will have long queues for job openings and low turnover. In addition, the firm will do poorly in the market place relative to firms that do not overpay, and in a competitive market will eventually go out of business.

In most labor markets, however, market prices are not readily observable. Workers vary in characteristics and are not typically perfect substitutes. Thus, observing the wage for one worker does not provide full information on what it takes to hire another worker. In addition, firms do not share complete information about their levels of compensation. The difficulty in observing the market price for

**FIGURE 11.1   How Firms Choose Employment and Wages in the Classical
Model.**

*In the classical model, firms have no discretion over the wages they pay to workers; rather
the wages are determined by supply and demand in the market place. As shown in the
figure, individual firms continue to hire workers up to the point E*, where the marginal
revenue product equals the market-determined wage rate. Until this point, hiring
additional workers brings more revenue into the firm than it costs to hire the workers.
Past this point, the costs of hiring additional workers are larger than the benefits.*

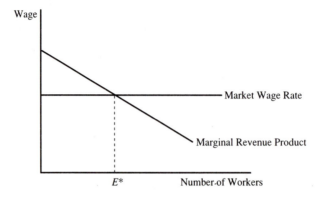

labor means that it is not always easy to tell if a firm is underpaying or overpaying
its workers.

Paying the Wrong Level of Pay
at Salomon Brothers

"In the first year out of the training program, 1983, Howie Rubin made $25 million for
Salomon Brothers in the new activity of mortgage-backed securities. The several-hundred
million dollar question was first raised by Howie Rubin: Who really made the money, Howie
Rubin or Salomon Brothers? Salomon Brothers decided it was the company and refused to
pay Rubin more than the normal pay scale. In his first year, Rubin was paid $90,000, the
most permitted a first-year trader. In 1984, his second year, Rubin made $30 million trading.
He was then paid $175,000, the most permitted a second-year trader. In the beginning of
1985 he quit Salomon Brothers and moved to Merrill Lynch for a three year guarantee: a
minimum of $1 million a year, plus a percentage of his trading profits."

After 1985, Salomon Brothers lost much of its market share in mortgage-backed
securities to other firms such as Merrill Lynch.

Suggested by Michael M. Lewis, 1989, *Liar's Poker*, Norton Press, New York, 126.

Our discussion to this point suggests that two important indicators of whether a firm is paying the market wage rate are: (1) the number of applications it receives for job openings and (2) the quit rate for existing employees. If a firm is inundated by *qualified applicants* when it advertises a job opening, and the turnover rate among existing employees is low, it is likely that the firm is paying above the market wage rate.[1] In contrast, if the applicant rate is low and turnover is high, the firm is probably paying below the market rate.

In choosing the rate of pay, it is important to consider the tradeoffs between incremental compensation and turnover costs. Turnover costs include the costs of recruiting employees, training expenses, and reduced productivity from employing inexperienced workers. In addition, if employees expect that they will work for the firm for only a short time, they are less likely to be concerned about how their actions affect the long-run cash flows of the firm. For instance, a salesperson might push to make a sale to collect a commission, knowing that the customer will be unhappy with the product and will reduce future purchases. Sometimes employees who leave a firm take customers and trade secrets to competing firms. Some turnover, however, is likely to benefit the firm—for example, by adding "new blood" and fresh ideas to the organization.

Paying Too Much at Nucor?

"When Nucor's mill in Darlington, South Carolina, advertised to fill eight openings last fall, over 1,300 applicants showed up, creating such a traffic jam that state police had to be called out. Unfortunately, the force was a bit thin—three officers were already at Nucor applying for jobs."

It is possible that the number of applications at Nucor includes many unqualified candidates. But the size of the applicant pool certainly motivates the questions, whether Nucor is paying too much or whether it wants to pay more than the market wage rate for particular jobs?

Suggested by Nancy J. Perry, "Here Come Richer, Riskier Pay Plans," *Fortune,* 12/19/88, p. 58.

Outside job offers made to existing employees are also indicative of market rates. While these offers provide important information about the market value of existing employees, firms must be careful in deciding whether to match these offers. Failure to match can result in losing valued employees. A policy of matching outside offers, however, encourages employees to spend time generating offers. This activity takes time away from work and also increases the likelihood that employees will obtain offers that entice them to leave the firm.

---

[1] Paying above the market wage rate will typically place the firm at a competitive disadvantage. As we discuss below, however, there are several reasons for why some profit-maximizing firms might want to pay above the market wage rate.

Compensating Differentials[2]

The classical analysis does not consider differences in working conditions across jobs. (In fact the concept of a job is not defined.) In reality, however, jobs vary in many dimensions, among them the quality of the work environment, the geographic location, the length of the commute, the risk of danger, the characteristics of co-workers, the degree of monotony on the job. Holding the salary level constant across job offers, an individual will choose the job with the most desirable characteristics (such as low risk of injury and a nice location). To attract workers to undesirable jobs, firms must increase the level of pay.[3] The *extra* wage that is paid to attract a worker to an undesirable job is called a *compensating wage differential*. Recall that in advertising its job opening, Nature Aid Corporation stressed that it was located in the Pacific Northwest. Given the desirability of this location, the firm can attract workers at a lower wage rate than that paid to otherwise identical workers in many other parts of the country (where compensating differentials must be paid to attract workers).

The prediction that unpleasant jobs pay more than pleasant jobs *holds other factors constant*. Variation in job requirements for education, skills, and training also can account for differences in pay. For example, an office job in a pleasant work environment might pay more than the relatively unpleasant job of garbage collector because the skills required for the office job are higher. Garbage collectors, however, will be paid more than similar unskilled labor in more pleasant jobs. Correspondingly, jobs in large cities usually pay more than similar jobs in small cities because employers must compensate for the higher cost of living in large cities.

The best evidence of the existence of compensating wage differentials is provided by studies that relate wages to the risk of fatal injury on the job.[4] Using data from around the world, wages were found to be positively associated with the risk of being killed on the job, holding other factors constant. The estimates of the magnitude of the compensating differential are relatively imprecise and vary across studies, but indicate that workers receive between $20 and $300 more per year for every one-in-ten-thousand increase in the risk of being killed on the job. These estimates imply that a firm with 1,000 employees could save between $20,000 and $300,000 in wage costs per year by increasing the level of safety enough to save one life every 10 years.

---

[2]In this section, we discuss the key points of the theory of compensating differentials as they relate to managerial decision making. For an expanded discussion of compensating differentials, see Ronald G. Ehrenberg and Robert S. Smith, *Modern Labor Economics,* 3rd Edition, Scott Foresman and Company, Glenview, Illinois, 1988, Chapter 8.

[3]This prediction assumes that employees can obtain relatively good information about important characteristics of the job either before or shortly after employment. This assumption is likely to be valid in many cases. For instance, an applicant for a firefighter position in an arid location is likely to know that the job is hazardous. The applicant can also observe the quality of the fire station and equipment. The applicant can collect other information about the work environment from current or past employees.

[4]See Ronald G. Ehrenberg and Robert S. Smith, *Modern Labor Economics,* 3rd Edition, Scott Foresman and Company, Glenview, Illinois, 1988, pp. 266–270.

Compensating Differentials for Working at Night

Many production workers in the United States work night shifts. Since most workers prefer to work during the day, firms have to pay compensating differentials to attract enough workers to staff their night shifts. Research suggests that in 1984 night workers in manufacturing plants received about 30 cents more per hour than day workers. The average manufacturing wage in 1984 was $9.18.

Suggested by S. L. King and H. B. Williams, ''Shift Work Pay Differentials and Practices in Manufacturing,'' *Monthly Labor Review* 108, December 1985, 26–33.

Compensating wage differentials perform at least two important functions. First, all societies have unpleasant jobs that must be done (for instance, most have morticians and garbage collectors). Compensating differentials serve to attract people to these jobs and reward them for their efforts. Workers who accept unpleasant jobs are likely to be the ones who bear the lowest cost for performing them. For example, if a wage premium is offered for working in a noisy factory, the people most likely to apply are those least bothered by noise. Individuals who are significantly averse to noise would choose to work in a quiet environment at a lower wage. Second, the existence of compensating differentials imposes a financial penalty on employers who have unpleasant work environments. Employers can reduce this penalty by enhancing their work environments. This possibility implies that the firms that provide better work environments will be those firms that can do so at the least cost (since the marginal cost of providing a pleasant environment is low relative to the marginal benefit of reducing the penalty).

This discussion suggests that there is a job-matching process in labor markets where firms offer and workers accept jobs in a manner that makes the most of their strengths and preferences. An organization that finds it very expensive to reduce the risk of injury will offer risky jobs and wage premiums. In turn, the people who take these jobs are likely to be the most tolerant toward risk. For example, fishing companies often find it too expensive to reduce the risk of injury beyond some standard, and thus must offer wage premiums to crews of fishing boats. Individuals applying to work on these boats are likely to be among those most willing to place their lives at risk on the job. In contrast, a firm that can provide a safe environment at a low cost will offer low-risk jobs and lower wages; these positions will be filled by more risk-averse workers.

Internal Labor Markets

In the classical model, there are no long-term labor contracts. Firms adjust their levels of employment and wages whenever the value of the marginal product of labor or the market wage rate changes. In addition, firms do not invest in general-purpose training.[5] The gains from general-purpose training go to the worker, not the firm—if the firm does not pay the worker the market price for the new skills, the worker will move to another firm that is willing to pay.

Labor Secretary's Bid for Plant Safety Runs into Skepticism

In the summer of 1994, Labor Secretary Robert Reich charged a Bridgestone Tire subsidiary with 107 safety violations. He also levied a fine of $7.5 million. The Labor Secretary ostensibly took this action on behalf of the workers at the tire plant. To quote the Secretary, "American workers are not going to be sacrificed at the alter of profits." The Secretary, however, was "amazed" when the workers and local community did not support his action. Indeed workers were generally skeptical and nonsupportive of his claims. For example, one worker indicated that the Secretary "didn't know what the hell he was doing."

The lack of worker support for this action can be explained by the theory of compensating differentials. Dangerous jobs pay a premium over jobs in safer environments. Workers who accept dangerous jobs consider themselves better off than working at lower wages in safer environments. Thus, regulations that force firms to provide safer work environments and lower wages (wages have to be reduced to remain competitive) can make employees worse off. In addition, the company might lay off workers if it is too expensive to comply with the regulations.

While workers can be harmed by this type of regulatory action, there are at least two arguments that might justify government intervention. First, the workers might not have good information about the level of danger. For example, they might think that a plant is safer than it really is. Why the government, however, would be better informed about the level of safety at a plant than the workers is not obvious. Second, there are other parties that have to be considered. For example, workers who get hurt on the job can impose costs on society through subsidized medical care and disability payments. While the overall costs and benefits of this type of regulation are hard to estimate, it is clear that workers do not always benefit.

Suggested by Asra Q. Nomani, "Muffed Mission: Labor Secretary's Bid to Push Safety Runs into Skepticism," *The Wall Street Journal*, August 19, 1994, page 1.

While the classical model provides a relatively good description of some labor markets, such as the market for unskilled agricultural workers, it does a poor job describing employment and wages in many other cases. For example, in contrast to

---

[5]General-purpose training refers to improving skills that are equally useful to a wide variety of different firms, for example, obtaining an MBA degree, learning general principles of engineering, or learning popular word-processing programs. Below, we will discuss another type of training, firm-specific, where the new skills are of more benefit to the existing firm than other firms.

the model, many firms rarely reduce worker pay and frequently invest in general-purpose training (such as paying for an employee to obtain an MBA).

Many firms are better characterized as having *internal labor markets,* wherein outside hiring is done only at entry-level jobs and most other jobs are filled from within the firm. Firms with internal labor markets establish *long-term relationships* with employees. For instance, it has been estimated that in 1991 the typical worker between 45 and 54 had been with his or her current employer for ten years. Another study found that over half of all men and one fourth of all women in the United States find employers for whom they will work for at least 20 years.[6]

Established career paths and the prospect for promotions play important roles in firms with internal labor markets. These firms interact with outside labor markets only on a limited basis. Rather than simply reflecting outside market conditions, the rates of pay (discussed in more detail below) and job assignments in internal labor markets are often determined by administrative rules and implicit understandings. Firms can have more than one internal labor market. For example, the internal market for white-collar workers can have little interaction with the internal market for blue-collar workers. In addition, firms with internal labor markets typically offer some jobs that are well described by the classical model, for instance, certain low-skilled positions.

Internal Labor Markets in Japan

Large companies in Japan make extensive use of internal labor markets. Many Japanese executives have spent their entire careers with the same firm. Senior executives almost never move from one major firm to another. Firms rarely go outside the firm to hire for any position other than entry-level jobs. Turnover is extremely low. Pay is tied largely to seniority, and the differences in pay among employees are small relative to the differences in American companies.

Small pay differentials would be difficult to maintain if there were an active outside labor market in Japan. Market pressures would tend to bid up the salaries of the strong performers. Recently, poor performance has placed pressures on Japanese firms to reconsider their policies of lifetime employment guarantees. If many firms abandon this policy, the outside labor market is likely to become more active.

Suggested by Masahiko Aoki and Ronald Dore, editors, *The Japanese Firm,* Oxford University Press, Oxford, England, 1994.

Agreements between employers and employees concerning compensation and responsibilities are contracts. Firms, however, generally do not enter into formal

---

[6]See James Aley, ''The Myth of the Job Hopper,'' *Fortune Magazine,* September 19, 1994, 32 and Robert E. Hall, ''The Importance of Lifetime Jobs in the U.S. Economy,'' *American Economic Review* 72, September 1982, 716–24.

written agreements (*explicit contracts*) with nonunion employees. Rather most employees work under *implicit contracts* (a set of shared, informal understandings about how firms and employees will respond to contingencies).[7] Implicit contracts differ from explicit contracts in that they are less enforceable in a court of law. Firms and employees, however, often have strong economic incentives to honor implicit contracts to protect their reputations (see Chapter 7). A primary reason for the frequent use of implicit contracts is that it would be very costly to list all possible contingencies and associated responses in a formal document.

Reasons for Long-Term Employment Relationships

There are at least three factors that help to explain the widespread use of the long-term employment relationships found in internal labor markets. These factors include firm-specific human capital, employee motivation, and information about employee attributes.

Firm-Specific Human Capital.   Firm-specific human capital consists of knowledge, skills, and personal relationships that make an employee worth more to a current employer than to alternative employers. This type of human capital can significantly enhance the productivity of workers. For example, a manager who knows the firm's customers and the particulars of its accounting, personnel, customers, and information systems will be more productive than a manager who does not. Long-term relationships provide incentives for employers and employees to invest in firm-specific training. If employers and employees expect that their relationships are short-term, there are limited incentives to make this investment. Correspondingly, long-term relationships allow firms and employees to capture the benefits of accumulated firm-specific human capital.

Employee Motivation.   The prospect of a long-term relationship with a firm can provide powerful incentives to employees to work on behalf of their employers. Employees who are considering shirking, stealing, and other nonproductive activities must weigh the benefits of these actions against the costs of losing future benefits should they be caught and fired. Since there is more to lose in long-term relationships than in short-term relationships, the incentives to engage in productive activities are higher in long-term relationships.[8] Also, as we discuss below, long-term relationships increase the flexibility that a firm has in designing compensation packages to motivate employee effort.

---

[7]See Sherwin Rosen, "Implicit Contracts," *Journal of Economic Literature* 23, September 1985, 1144–75.

[8]This statement assumes that an employee cannot costlessly replicate the same stream of benefits by changing to a new employer. For example, the new job might pay lower compensation, the worker might incur moving costs, there might be a period of unemployment, etc.

Learning of Employee Attributes.   Over time, managers receive significant information about the skills, work habits, and intelligence of individual workers. Employers then can use this information in matching employees and jobs within the firm. For example, firms with internal labor markets have fewer surprises in filling higher-level jobs than firms that rely on outside labor markets.

Costs of Internal Labor Markets

Not all firms have internal labor markets. Rather some firms rely heavily on outside markets to fill positions at all levels. For instance, in our initial example, Nature Aid Corporation advertised in a public newspaper to fill the position of vice president of manufacturing. The observation that some firms do not have internal labor markets suggests that the costs of these markets can be larger than the benefits. One potentially important problem with internal labor markets is the restricted competition for higher-level jobs in the organization. If a firm only considers internal candidates for higher-level jobs, it will not always hire the most qualified person (who may be from outside the firm). The likelihood of finding a desirable candidate in the outside labor market is highest when the job does not require firm-specific training (since experience with the firm does not create an advantage in the job). Thus, theory suggests that firms are more likely to use internal labor markets where firm-specific training is important. Indeed, firms in the steel, petroleum, and chemical industries, where complicated production technologies take significant time to learn, tend to rely on internal labor markets, while firms in the shoe and garment industries do not.[9] Firm-specific skills (or at least industry-specific skills) are arguably less important in garment and shoe manufacturing.

Pay in Internal Labor Markets
Careers and Lifetime Pay

Employees who take jobs at firms with internal labor markets often have expectations that they will spend their entire *careers* at the same firm. Thus, in considering an entry-level job, a perspective employee will generally focus on the entire stream of earnings over the anticipated career path. For example, a worker might accept a job at Firm A that pays thousands of dollars less than some other job offered at Firm B because the worker anticipates faster compensation growth at Firm A.

The fact that individuals tend to base employment decisions on career earnings gives firms with internal labor markets flexibility over setting the level and sequence of pay. In contrast to the classical model, firms do not need to pay the market wage rate (or equivalently, in equilibrium, the value of the marginal product) at each point in time. Rather, firms can vary compensation over a career path, as long as the

---

[9]See Peter Doeringer, and Michael Piore, *Internal Labor Markets and Manpower Analysis*, D.C. Heath, Lexington, Mass., 1971.

overall value of the remaining stream is competitive at each point in time (valued
as highly by workers as streams offered by competing firms in the labor market).
Firms, of course, are also constrained by product-market competition, since paying
too much to workers over the long run can drive companies out of business.

Hiring an Outside CEO at Eastman Kodak

Eastman Kodak had a long history of filling senior positions exclusively with long-
time employees. An advantage of this policy is that senior executives have significant
experience with the firm and detailed specific knowledge of the company. The prospect
of promotion and long-term employment also provides important motivational effects.
A disadvantage, however, is that sometimes the best people for senior jobs are
outsiders.

During the late 1980s and early 1990s, shareholders placed intense pressure on
Kodak's board to appoint outsiders to senior positions. Many shareholders thought
that hiring outsiders was necessary to bring new skills and visions into the firm. On
October 1993, Kodak announced that it had hired George Fisher, CEO of Motorola,
as the new CEO. The stock market greeted this announcement with an 8 percent increase in Kodak's stock price (from the close of the market on the 26th to the close
on the 28th). This reaction represented a $1.6 billion increase in overall value of the
company.

Economists have identified at least three ways that firms can use their flexibility
in setting the level and sequencing of pay to enhance employee motivation. These
methods include the payment of efficiency wages, upward sloping earnings profiles,
and tying major pay increases to promotions. As we will discuss, however, influence
costs can affect the desirability of taking full advantage of this flexibility.

Efficiency Wages

In many jobs, it is difficult to monitor employee actions. It is also difficult to devise
incentive compensation schemes that motivate desired behavior. For example, manufacturing companies want factory workers to work hard. In most cases, however,
it is difficult to measure employee effort with much precision. In addition, the payment of piece rates or other output-based compensation can motivate workers to
shirk on quality.

One potential way to motivate workers in these cases is to pay compensation
above the market rate. Paying a premium for workers obviously increases labor
costs. However, it can also have the desirable effect of motivating workers not to
shirk. Workers who are paid a wage premium are likely to reduce their shirking
because they are afraid that if they are caught and fired they will lose the premium.
(They will be unemployed or have to accept a lower-paying job.) This effect will

be greatest for workers who have long time horizons with the firm, since they have more to lose. Wage premiums of this type are often referred to as *efficiency wages.*[10]

Economists debate whether the use of efficiency wages is widespread. While the empirical evidence is inconclusive, some studies suggest that firms in some industries use efficiency wages with relatively high frequency. For example, the authors of one study find systematic wage differences across industries after controlling for many job and worker characteristics.[11] In addition, they find a negative relation between turnover and industry wage differentials, suggesting that workers in high wage industries receive wage premiums. The authors interpret this evidence as consistent with the hypothesis that efficiency wages are paid in certain industries.

Motivating Honesty in the Local Police Force

Economists Gary Becker and George Stigler were asked to consider ways to reduce the corruption in the Chicago police force. The recommendation of these Nobel laureates was to pay the police more than the market wage rate. With sufficiently high premiums, the police would have incentives not to take bribes from criminals. For this condition to hold, the immediate gains from taking bribes must be offset by the expected loss in wage premiums given the possibility of being caught and fired. Thus, the required premium to prevent cheating depends on the size of the bribes and the likelihood of getting caught. Higher bribes and lower likelihood of getting caught translate into higher required premiums.

Paying wage premiums will entice a large number of people to apply for job openings. To reduce the surplus of applicants, Becker and Stigler suggested that the jobs be sold to workers. The price of jobs would reflect the expected premiums. Under this scenario, the payment for a job can be considered as a bond posted by an officer not to cheat. If the officer is honest, the officer gets the bond back in the form of the premium wage. If the officer cheats and gets caught the bond is lost.

The suggested wage premiums are very similar to the concept of efficiency wages. In more modern theories of efficiency wages, however, workers do not purchase jobs. The concept of buying jobs may seem unusual. However, many people essentially do this when they pay money to manage the outlet of a franchise company.

Suggested by Gary S. Becker and George J. Stigler, "Law Enforcement, Malfeasance, and Compensation," *Journal of Legal Studies* 3, January 1974, 1–18.

---

[10]For a more detailed analysis of efficiency wages, see George A. Akerlof, "Gift Exchange and Efficiency Wages: Four Views," *American Economic Review* 74, May 1984, 78–83; Carl Shapiro, and Joseph E. Stiglitz, "Equilibrium Unemployment as a Worker Discipline Device," *American Economic Review* 74, June 1984, 433–44; and Janet Yellen, "Efficiency Wages Models and Unemployment," *American Economic Review* 74, May 1984, 200–208. Note that if all firms in an industry pay efficiency wages, there will be unemployment. (The supply of labor will exceed demand.) The threat of unemployment can provide incentives for workers not to shirk.

[11]Alan B. Krueger, and Lawrence H. Summers, "Efficiency Wages and the Inter-Industry Wage Structure," *Econometrica* 56, March 1988, 259–293.

FIGURE 11.2   An Example of an Upward-Sloping Earnings Profile.

This figure displays a possible growth pattern of the value of the marginal product and compensation for a representative worker in a given firm. Within this particular firm, both the value of the marginal product and compensation increase as the worker becomes more experienced. Compensation, however, increases at a faster rate. In the early years, the worker is paid below the value of the marginal product, while in later years the worker is paid more. The worker is underpaid in early years, but is willing to work for the firm because of the anticipation of being overpaid in subsequent years. Under this compensation scheme, a young worker has incentives to work hard to avoid being fired and losing future wage premiums. An older worker, in turn, does not want to get fired because of being paid more than can be earned at other firms.

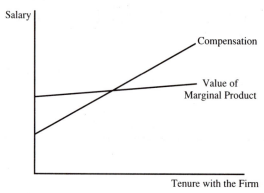

Job Seniority and Pay

Compensation typically increases with seniority within the firm. Part of this increase is explained by increases in productivity that come from experience. In many firms, however, compensation increases faster than productivity as the employee ages. Firms frequently offer attractive retirement packages to encourage older workers to retire, and (unless precluded by law) often have mandatory retirement.[12] For example, the employee must retire at age 65.

One explanation for these age-related policies is that they provide increased incentives to employees to work in the interests of the firm.[13] To see how, consider the example pictured in Figure 11.2. This figure displays the growth patterns of the value of the marginal product and compensation for a representative worker within a particular firm. Both the value of the marginal product and compensation increase as the worker becomes more experienced. (The analysis does not change if we allow

---

[12]Amendments made to the Age Discrimination Employment Act in 1978 and 1986 have precluded mandatory retirement for most workers in the United States.

[13]See Edward Lazear, "Why is there Mandatory Retirement?" *Journal of Political Economy* 87, December 1979, 1261–84.

for declines in productivity in later years.) Compensation, however, increases at a faster rate. In the early years, the worker is paid below the value of the marginal product, while in later years the worker is paid more. The worker is underpaid in early years, but is willing to work for the firm because of the anticipation of being overpaid in subsequent years. Under this compensation scheme, a young worker has incentives to work hard to avoid being fired and losing future wage premiums. An older worker, in turn, does not want to get fired because of being paid more than can be earned at other firms.

Firms that employ this type of compensation policy have short-run incentives to fire older workers, since older workers are being paid more than they are worth. Unjustified firings of older workers, however, can be against the long-run interests of firms because they reduce the incentive effects of the compensation plan—workers will not believe that hard work will lead to premiums when they get older. Most firms, however, cannot continue to pay premiums to all older workers and stay in business. Thus, these firms will want to have policies that help to assure that older workers will retire when they reach a particular age. For example, a retirement age could be chosen where the present value of the underpayments in the early years is exactly offset by the overpayments in the later years. Thus, over their careers, workers are simply paid the values of their marginal products (as in the classical model). Such a condition can be necessary for a firm to survive in a competitive market place.

Promotions

Firms are typically partitioned into hierarchial levels, where the jobs at a given level pay more than positions at lower levels. Workers move up the hierarchy through promotions. Since workers compete for promotions, promotions can be viewed as contests or tournaments among employees.[14] Workers exert effort trying to win these contests.

Promotions obviously play an important role in providing incentives in many organizations. One benefit of using a promotion-based incentive scheme is that it commits the firm to serious performance reviews of its workers. Promoting the wrong person to a job can impose a significant cost on a firm. Firms have incentives to conduct in-depth performance reviews to reduce the likelihood of making this mistake. Another primary benefit is that promotion contests help to filter out random shocks in evaluating performance. Typically, the worker with the best *relative performance* is chosen for promotion. As we discuss in Chapter 13, there are potential risk-sharing benefits that come from using relative performance measures rather than absolute performance measures.* In particular, workers are less likely to be rewarded or penalized for factors beyond their control—common shocks that affect all the contestants in the promotion contest are filtered out of the decision.

---

[14]See Edward Lazear, and Sherwin Rosen, ''Rank Order Tournaments as Optimal Labor Contracts,'' *Journal of Political Economy* 89, October 1981, 841–64.

*Relative performance measures are based on how a worker performs compared to a peer group. Absolute performance measures compare the worker's performance to some predetermined standard.

A Horserace at General Electric

Sometimes firms "run horseraces" among internal candidates. Under this procedure, the candidates are notified that they are competing for a job with higher pay and prestige. The contest provides significant incentives for the candidates to perform since the prize for winning can be very large. General Electric ran such a horserace to fill the CEO position, when Reginald Jones retired in 1981. The winner was Jack Welch. In 1993, Welch was paid $4 million in salary and bonuses. The next highest paid person in the firm received $1.7 million.

Suggested by Richard Vancil, *Passing the Baton*, Harvard Business School Press, Boston, 1987.

Promotion-based schemes, however, have several significant drawbacks that make their widespread use somewhat puzzling.[15] First, judging people on relative performance can undermine worker cooperation, and workers might even sabotage the work of others. Second, there can be serious conflicts between matching people for jobs and providing incentives. For instance, the so-called "Peter Principle" argues that employees keep getting promoted until they reach jobs that they cannot handle. Third, promotions seem like a rather crude tool for providing incentives. Promotions only occur at discrete intervals, and either the employee is promoted or not. Monetary incentives, such as bonus payments, are much more flexible. Fourth, employees do not always value promotions. For example, professors and research scientists often do not want administrative positions. Fifth, promotion contests can subject decision makers to significant influencing activities.

Despite these drawbacks, promotions are a widely-employed method for motivating workers throughout the world. Lately, however, the prospect for promotion in many firms has fallen due to an overall reduction in middle-management positions and a slowing in growth rates. This development has lowered the incentives of many employees, who think that the chances for promotion are low, even if they do a good job. In response, many firms have tried to restore worker incentives by adopting more explicit pay-for-performance plans. The American Productivity and Quality Center reports that 75 percent of employers in the United States have an incentive plan (such as a profit or gain-sharing plan) for rank-and-file workers, and that roughly 80 percent of these plans have been adopted since 1983.[16]

Influence Costs

Co-workers frequently compare compensation levels. Differences in pay among co-workers motivate employees to seek explanations for compensation decisions.

---

[15]See George P. Baker, Kevin J. Murphy, and Michael C. Jensen, "Compensation and Incentives: Practice and Theory," *Journal of Finance* 43, May 1988, 593–616.

[16]See Nancy J. Perry, "Here Come Richer, Riskier Pay Plans," *Fortune*, December 19, 1988, 50–58.

Workers also use information about the pay of other employees to lobby for pay increases. It is frequently conjectured that firms reduce the differentials in pay to cut down on this type of influencing activity. This policy, however, comes at a cost because under-performing workers are likely to be paid too much, while better workers are likely to be under-compensated and leave the firm. Influence costs also help to explain why many firms try to keep their compensation decisions confidential. In many cases, however, it is difficult to prevent co-workers from sharing information on compensation.

Influence Costs and Pay in Universities

The potential for influencing activity is especially high in firms where workers have common knowledge about each other's pay. Our discussion suggests that these firms might limit the differences in pay to reduce influence costs. One study provides empirical evidence on this issue by examining compensation levels in academic departments at about 2,000 colleges. Common knowledge about pay is more likely in small departments, in departments where the members frequently interact on a social basis and in public institutions (where public disclosure of pay is often required). Consistent with the influence-cost arguments, the study found that all three factors were associated with reductions in the dispersion of pay.

Suggested by Jeffrey Pfeffer and Nancy Langton, "Wage Inequality and the Organization of Work: The Case of Academic Departments," *Administrative Sciences Quarterly* 33, 1988, 588–606.

The Salary/Fringe-Benefit Mix

To this point, we have focused on the overall level of compensation paid to workers. To highlight the relevant issues, we have treated the specific components of the compensation package as if they were all cash payments. Most workers, however, receive a significant amount of their compensation in the form of *fringe benefits*—compensation that is either in-kind or deferred. For instance, recall how Nature Aid stressed that they paid "good fringe benefits" in their advertisement for a vice president of manufacturing.

Examples of in-kind payments are health insurance and membership in a company recreation center, where the employee receives an insurance policy or a service rather than cash. Payments to pension plans and Social Security are examples of deferred compensation. For the typical American worker, about 75 percent of the total compensation package is pay for time worked, while about 25 percent is fringe benefits. Based on the cost to the employer, the most important fringe benefits are pensions and insurance, pay for leave time (vacations and sick or other leave), and mandated contributions to Social Security and Workers Compensation. Many employees also receive benefits such as company-paid education, dental care, discounted meals, and subsidized recreation programs.

FIGURE 11.3   Employee Preferences for Salary and Fringe Benefits.

This figure pictures an employee's preferences for salary and fringe benefits using standard indifference curves. The convexity of the curves implies that the employee is willing to substitute a relatively large amount of money for additional fringe benefits when the employee is paid primarily cash (possibly due to tax considerations). However, this willingness to substitute declines as the employee receives more fringe benefits. (The employee wants cash for other purposes.)

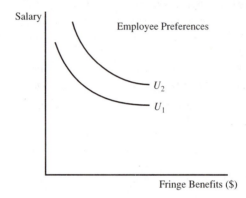

Employee Preferences

Salary and fringe benefits typically are not perfect substitutes from an employee's viewpoint. One reason is taxes. For example, an employee who wants to purchase a $5,000 insurance policy would prefer the firm to provide the policy rather than $5,000 in cash. Since insurance policies are purchased with after-tax dollars, an employee in a 33.33 percent tax bracket would have to receive $7,500 in salary to purchase the policy. The employee might also want the firm to purchase fringe benefits because the benefits can be purchased by the firm at lower prices. For example, a firm might be able to provide group insurance at a lower cost per employee than if employees individually purchased the insurance. On the other hand, employees often prefer $5,000 in cash to $5,000 in fringe benefits, since the cash gives them more flexibility in selecting their purchases.

In our initial analysis, we do not break fringe benefits into finer categories. Rather we consider the choice between salary and overall fringe benefits. Later, we discuss the mix of fringe benefits. Figure 11.3 pictures an employee's preferences for salary and expenditures by the firm on fringe benefits using standard indifference curves. The convexity of the curves implies that the employee is willing to substitute a relatively large amount of salary for additional expenditures on fringe benefits when the employee is paid primarily cash (possibly due to taxes considerations). However, this willingness to substitute declines as the employee receives more fringe benefits. (The employee wants cash for other purposes.)

FIGURE 11.4   Employer Preferences for Paying Salary or Fringe Benefits.

This figure displays isoprofit curves for a representative firm, under the assumption that it does not care whether it pays the worker cash or uses the same amount of cash to provide fringe benefits. Each curve is a straight line with a slope of −1; the firm is indifferent between paying a dollar for salary or a dollar for fringe benefits. Along any isoprofit curve, the profits for the firm are the same. The firm would like to be on the lowest isoprofit curve possible (since lower isoprofit curves mean that less money is being spent on labor).

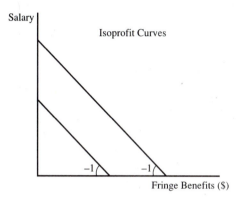

The employee, of course, would like to be on as high an indifference curve as possible. A firm, however, will be able to hire the worker, as long as the compensation package meets the worker's *reservation level of utility.* If the compensation package provides this level of utility, the worker is better off working at the firm than working for alternative employers or not working at all. For example, the reservation utility of the worker in Figure 11.3 might be pictured by the indifference curve labeled U2. The reservation utility of the worker increases as the compensation packages offered by other employers become more attractive.

Employer Preferences

Initially, suppose that the firm does not care whether it pays the employee cash or uses the same amount of cash to provide fringe benefits. For instance, both expenditures might be deductible for tax purposes and so it costs the firm the same amount in either case. Figure 11.4 displays isoprofit curves for a representative firm under this assumption. Each curve is a straight line with a slope of −1; the firm is indifferent between paying a dollar for salary or a dollar for fringe benefits. Along any isoprofit curve, the profits for the firm are the same. The firm would like to be on the lowest isoprofit curve possible (since lower isoprofit curves mean that less money is being spent on labor).

FIGURE 11.5 The Optimal Mix Between Salary and Fringe Benefits.

This figure pictures an indifference curve for the reservation utility *of a representative worker that the firm is trying to hire. The firm can hire the worker using any compensation package along this curve. The figure also shows selected isoprofit curves for the firm. The objective of the firm is to choose the compensation package that meets the reservation utility of the worker at the lowest cost. The optimal choice is [S*,F*] where the indifference curve is tangent to the isoprofit curve. The firm could choose other combinations along the indifference curve. However, these combinations are more expensive. The firm could also offer combinations that are less expensive than [S*,F*]. However, these combinations would not meet the worker's reservation utility.*

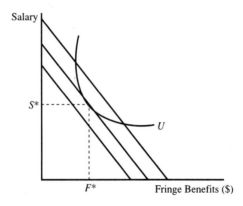

The Salary/Fringe-Benefit Choice

Initially, assume that all employees that the firm wants to hire have similar preferences for wages and fringe benefits. Figure 11.5 pictures an indifference curve for the reservation utility of a representative worker. The firm can hire the worker using any compensation package along this curve. The figure also shows selected isoprofit curves for the firm. The objective of the firm is to choose the compensation package that meets the reservation utility of the worker at the lowest cost. The optimal choice is [S*,F*] where the indifference curve is tangent to the isoprofit curve. The firm could choose other combinations along the indifference curve. However, these combinations are more expensive. The firm could also offer combinations that are less expensive than [S*,F*]. However, these combinations would not meet the worker's reservation utility.

This analysis suggests that it is in the interests of firms to listen to employee preferences about fringe benefits. If workers prefer the company to buy a dental policy over paying them the same amount in cash, the firm should buy the dental policy. Buying the dental policy makes the employees better off and the firm no worse off. Indeed, if the change results in paying workers more than their reservation utilities, the firm can lower cash wages further and share in the gains. (The firm might do this by giving lower raises in the following year.) Thus, designing more efficient contracts allows the firm to attract and retain workers at a lower cost.

Paying for Fringe Benefits at Lincoln Electric

The willingness of firms to listen to the preferences of workers suggests that workers pay for their own fringe benefits. For instance, most companies would be willing to pay higher salaries if workers did not want health insurance. Workers, therefore, face an opportunity cost of lost salary when they receive fringe benefits. Lincoln Electric, a manufacturing company in Cleveland, makes this tradeoff very clear to workers. Workers at Lincoln receive about half their compensation in the form of annual bonus payments. Fringe-benefit costs are taken out of this bonus payment and are shown on the employees' pay stubs. On several occasions, Lincoln employees have voted against dental plans because the majority of workers prefer cash.

We have assumed that the firm is indifferent between paying a given amount of cash to employees and spending the same amount on fringe benefits. While this assumption is likely to be valid in many cases, there are at least two complicating factors. First, taxes at the firm level can be important. For example, the firm might have to pay Social Security taxes on wages but not fringe benefits. This tax changes the slope of the firm's isoprofit curves. For example, assuming a tax rate of 6 percent, the firm would be indifferent between paying $1.00 for salary or $1.06 for fringe benefits. The slope of the isoprofit curve is $-.943$. As pictured in Figure 11.6, it is optimal to offer higher fringe benefits and lower salary than without the tax. Note that personal taxes are incorporated in the employee's indifference curves, while firm taxes are incorporated in the isoprofit curves of the firm. Thus, our analysis suggests that in designing compensation packages the firm should consider the *total* tax bill for the employee and the firm.[17] Reducing overall taxes means that there is more money to split between the firm and the employee. It is generally not optimal to consider the taxes of only one party (for example, firm taxes).

The second complication is that fringe benefits can affect employee behavior in ways that affect firm profits. For example, sick leave can motivate absenteeism. Similarly, liberal insurance coverage can reduce employee incentives to worry about prices for medical care. These types of incentive effects can affect the optimal compensation package. For example, some firms have reduced insurance coverage to workers for the expressed purpose of providing workers with incentives to negotiate with doctors over price. Presumably workers do not like to bargain with doctors and will ultimately be paid higher wages to offset this increased cost (assuming they were being paid their competitive wage in the first place). However, the costs to the firm will be reduced if the increase in wages is less than the reduction

---

[17]See Myron S. Scholes and Mark A. Wolfson, *Taxes and Business Strategy*, Prentice Hall, Englewood Cliffs, NJ, 1992.

FIGURE 11.6   Optimal Choice of Salary and Fringe Benefits with Payroll Taxes.

This figure illustrates how payroll taxes can affect the optimal choice of salary and fringe benefits. In the first case, the firm does not pay payroll taxes (such as Social Security) on wages or fringe benefits. The optimal choice is [S*,F*]. In the second case, the firm pays payroll taxes on wages, but not fringe benefits. This tax flattens the isoprofit curves for the firm, and the optimal choice is [S',F']. In the second case, the firm pays lower salaries and higher fringe benefits.

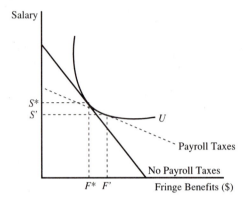

in insurance costs. These considerations can shift the slope of the isoprofit curves in either direction and thus can either increase or decrease the optimal amount of fringe benefits.

Using Fringe Benefits to Attract Particular Types of Workers

Firms often care about the personal characteristics of the workers that they hire. For example, firms concerned about the high costs of turnover might favor hiring people with families since they are less likely to quit. Alternatively, firms in intense work environments, such as investment banks in New York City, might favor hiring single people because they are likely to work longer hours. Firms are constrained in using salary offers to attract a particular type of labor force. For example, firms are likely to violate discrimination laws if they offer people with families more money than people who do not. Firms, however, can sometimes use the mix between fringe benefits and salary to attract particular types of workers.[18] Figure 11.7 pictures an example. The figure displays an isoprofit curve for the firm and indifference curves representing the reservation utilities of people who are single and people who have

---

[18]Our objective in this section is to describe how firms use the salary and fringe benefit mix to attract particular types of individuals. We are not arguing that this policy is necessarily ethical, just, or legal in all cases.

FIGURE 11.7   Using the Mix between Salary and Fringe Benefits to Attract Particular Types of Workers.

The figure displays an isoprofit curve for the firm and indifference curves representing the reservation utilities of people who are single and people who have families. In this example, people with families have a higher preference for fringe benefits (for example, health insurance) than single people who prefer cash. If the firm wants to attract individuals with families, it will offer high fringe benefits and low wages, [$2,F2]. In this case, only people with families will apply for the job. Single individuals will not apply because the package does not meet their reservation utilities. If instead, the firm wants to hire single people, it will offer high salary and low fringe benefits, [$1,F1].

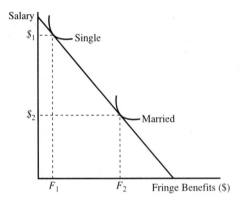

families. In this example, people with families have a higher preference for fringe benefits (for example, health insurance) than single people who prefer cash. If the firm wants to attract individuals with families, it will offer high fringe benefits and low wages, [$2,F2]. In this case, people with families are more likely to apply for the job. Single individuals are less likely to apply because the package does not meet their reservation utilities. If instead, the firm wants to hire single people, it will offer high salary and low fringe benefits, [$1,F1].

The Mix of Fringe Benefits

Our basic analysis of the choice between fringe benefits and salary also applies to the choice of the mix of fringe benefits. For example, it typically makes sense to provide employees with disability insurance, rather than dental insurance, whenever the workers prefer the disability insurance (assuming the same cost to the company). In this spirit, many companies have shifted toward menu or *cafeteria-style* benefit plans, where individual employees allocate a fixed-dollar fringe-benefit allowance among a variety of choices. The potential benefit of these plans is that different workers value different benefits differently. By allowing them to choose, they will work for the firm at a lower overall cost.

Cafeteria plans, however, entail costs that can limit their desirability. First, they are more expensive to administer. For example, employees must be informed of all their options and an administrative system has to be established to record choices, make the appropriate payments to suppliers, allow for changes in choices, and complete the appropriate tax forms. Second, cafeteria plans can generate adverse-selection problems that increase the cost of benefits. Adverse selection is likely to be a particular problem in the case of health insurance. As discussed in Chapter 7, individuals know more about their likelihood of getting sick than an insurance company. This asymmetric information is less a problem if the insurance company provides the benefits to all employees as a group. However, when free to choose, the people who are most likely to buy insurance are those who find it a good deal at the quoted price. Thus, at any given price, the insurance company is likely to attract a clientele that causes it to lose money. To reduce the likelihood of losing money, the insurance company can do things like demand physical examinations and investigate past medical records before agreeing to insure an applicant. However, these actions increase the costs of providing the benefit. To reduce the adverse-selection problem, companies often allow workers to opt out of health insurance only if they can document that their spouse has coverage at another firm. This policy limits the amount of discretion that employees have on whether to buy health insurance, and therefore helps to assure that the insurance company will have both high and low health risks in the pool. Also, a cafeteria plan is more likely to be valued by two-career families since, for example, one family member can acquire dental insurance, while the other obtains health insurance.

Summary

Firms make three important policy decisions with respect to compensation policy: the level of pay, the composition of the pay package, and the form of incentive compensation. This chapter considers the level and composition of the pay package. The next chapter examines incentive compensation.

In the *classical model* of wages and employment, firms have no discretion over the wages paid to workers; rather wages are determined by supply and demand in the market place. If a firm pays too little, it will have trouble attracting employees to job openings and will have high turnover. A firm that pays too much will have numerous job applicants and low turnover. In addition, the firm will have high costs and will compete poorly in the product market. It is not always obvious whether a firm is paying the market wage rate to employees. Important indicators are the applicant and quit rates and the nature of outside job offers made to existing employees.

The classical model does not consider differences in the working conditions across jobs. (In fact, the concept of a job is not defined.) In reality, however, jobs vary in many dimensions, such as geographic location and the risk of danger. Holding other factors constant, unpleasant jobs must pay a *compensating differential* to attract workers. Compensating differentials attract workers to unpleasant jobs and give companies incentives to enhance the work environment whenever it is cost effective.

The classical model provides a good description of some labor markets, such as the market for unskilled agricultural workers. It does a poor job in describing employment and wages in many other cases. Many firms are better characterized as having *internal labor markets,* where outside hiring is done only at entry-level jobs and most other jobs are filled from within the firm. Internal labor markets are characterized by *long-term relationships* between the worker and the firm. Long-term relationships can be beneficial because they give employers and employees incentives to invest in *firm-specific training,* provide incentives for employees to work in the interests of the firm, and allow firms to take advantage of information about employee attributes. One cost of using internal labor markets, however, is that it is not always desirable to hire people from within the firm for higher-level positions.

Employees taking jobs in internal labor markets evaluate *career earnings.* Thus, firms with internal labor markets have flexibility in setting the level and sequencing of pay. Firms can vary compensation over the career path, as long as the overall stream of earnings is competitive at each point in time relative to the streams offered by other firms in the same labor market. Economists have identified at least three ways that firms can use their flexibility in setting the level and sequencing of pay to enhance employee motivation. These methods include the payment of *efficiency wages, upward sloping earnings profiles,* and tying major pay increases to *promotions. Influence costs,* however, can affect the desirability of taking full advantage of this flexibility. Indeed, firms potentially reduce the dispersion of pay among coworkers to limit these costs.

The typical American worker receives about 25 percent of total compensation in the form of *fringe benefits,* such as vacation time, insurance coverage, and contributions to retirement plans. Salary and fringe benefits are not perfect substitutes for most workers. Tax benefits and the fact that the company can often purchase fringe benefits more cheaply can favor fringe benefits. The desire for flexibility in making purchases can favor cash payments. Employers have incentives to listen to the preferences of workers when it comes to the choice between salary and fringe benefits. By listening to these preferences firms can design compensation packages that attract and retain workers at the lowest cost. Firms can sometimes use the salary/fringe-benefit mix to attract particular types of workers. For example, offering liberal insurance coverage is more likely to attract people with families than single individuals, who likely prefer cash payments. Firms also have incentives to listen to employee preferences when it comes to choosing the mix of fringe benefits. This incentive has motivated many firms to consider *cafeteria-style* benefits. Widespread use of these plans, however, is limited due to administrative costs and *adverse-selection problems.*

CHAPTER 12 Incentive Compensation

The Fibers Division is the largest of Du Pont's chemical businesses, with 1989 sales of nearly $6 billion. It has departments ranging from automobile seat covers to apparel. In October 1988, this division announced ''one of the most ambitious pay-incentive programs in America.''[1] The plan covered nearly all of the division's 20,000 employees, including both management and rank-and-file workers.

Under the plan, employees placed a portion of their pay into an ''at-risk pool.'' If the business exceeded its profit goals for the year, the employees would get a multiple of the at-risk monies as a bonus. If not, the workers stood to lose the money in the pool. The intent was to eventually have as much as 6 percent of the annual pay at risk. Initially, the plan was adopted for a three-year trial period. Many other companies indicated that they planned to watch this experiment carefully to see what they could learn about incentive pay. To quote Robert C. Gore, a vice president at Towers Perrin Company (a major compensation consulting firm), ''The attention that the American business community has given to the Du Pont program is tremendous.''

In 1990, the division had to achieve a target of 4 percent real-earnings growth for the workers to recover their at-risk pay. Profits for the first nine months, however, were off 26 percent, due largely to a bad economy. For instance, demand for the division's products had significantly declined due to weak housing and automobile markets. By the fall of 1990, it was obvious that the workers were likely to lose this money. Employee discontent was very high—they were facing significant financial losses, due largely to factors beyond their control. In October 1990, Du Pont suddenly cancelled the incentive program with more than a full year to go in the trial period. In the words of the Fibers Division chief, ''I have to conclude it was an experiment that didn't work.''

---

[1]The details of this example come from two articles: Laurie Hays, ''All Eyes on Du Pont's Incentive Program,'' *The Wall Street Journal,* December 5, 1988, p. B–1, and Richard Koening, ''Du Pont Plan Linking Pay to Fibers Profit Unravels,'' *The Wall Street Journal,* October 25, 1990, p. B–1.

Given the widespread interest in this experiment, it is important to understand why the Du Pont plan failed. Is incentive pay, as some critics claim, simply a bad idea? In this case, any firm adopting a large-scale incentive plan is making a mistake and likely to experience the same fate as Du Pont. Alternatively, can the failure of this scheme be traced to basic design problems that could have been avoided by more careful planning? This chapter analyzes the economics of incentive compensation. The analysis suggests that Du Pont's failure was largely due to problems with the plan. Correspondingly, the analysis provides insights into how companies might design better compensation plans.

We begin this chapter by providing a more detailed discussion of incentive problems. We then examine how ownership can solve some of these problems by providing strong incentives to individuals to take efficient actions. Next, we consider one important limitation of ownership in controlling incentive problems, inefficient risk bearing. The implications of risk bearing for the design of compensation contracts are emphasized. Next, we review some of the key insights about incentive compensation contained in the economics literature. We begin by discussing the standard principal/agent model. We then extend this basic analysis by considering the informativeness principle, group incentive pay, multi-task principal/agent problems, alternative forms of incentive pay, and the role of incentive pay in self selection. Towards the end of the chapter, we discuss the debate on whether incentive pay works, and we provide a case study on CEO compensation to allow the reader to apply some of the concepts we have developed on compensation policy. The chapter concludes with a summary.

The Incentive Problem

As described in Chapter 7, incentive problems exist in firms because owners and employees have different objectives. For example, an insurance company wants its salespeople to sell products to customers, but the salespeople might prefer playing golf. Similarly, a research company might want its scientists to develop marketable products, while the scientists might prefer to work on more interesting, but less marketable, ideas. Presumably, the employees at Du Pont's Fibers Division have other interests than simply making and selling fibers products.

Consider the example of the American Assembly Corporation (AAC), a small company that assembles parts for several large manufacturing firms. As in many companies, there is a basic conflict between the aims of the owners and the aims of the employees. The owners would like employees to work hard, while the employees would prefer longer coffee breaks or working at a slower pace.

To add concreteness to the discussion, focus on the problem of motivating one representative worker at AAC, George Smith. George's preferences toward wealth and work are portrayed by the following utility function:

$$U = W - e^2, \tag{1}$$

where W is his total level of wealth and e is the number of units of effort exerted (for example, hours spent actually assembling parts). This utility function, which measures utility in dollar equivalents, indicates that he becomes better off as his total wealth increases, but becomes worse off as he exerts more effort on behalf of the firm. As George exerts effort, he suffers decreased utility because he would rather engage in other activities. His reservation utility is $1,000. The firm must provide George with this level of utility or he will not work for the firm.

The firm benefits from George's effort since more parts are assembled. The benefits to AAC from his effort are:

$$B = \$100e. \tag{2}$$

Initially, assume that his effort is perfectly observable. In this case, the firm can offer George a compensation contract that pays him a sum of money if, and only if, he provides a specified level of effort. He will accept this contract, as long as he is paid his reservation utility. To meet this condition, the firm must pay him a wage of $1,000 + e^2. If he is paid $1000 + e^2, then his utility is $U = (\$1,000 + e^2) - e^2 = \$1,000$, and he is receiving his reservation utility. Thus, the profits to the firm from his efforts are:

$$\Pi = \$100e - (\$1,000 + e^2). \tag{3}$$

The firm's objective is to choose the e that maximizes profits.

Figure 12.1 provides a graphic illustration of this problem. The figure pictures both the benefits to the firm ($100e) and the costs ($1000 + e^2). Profits are the difference between the two. As the figure indicates, maximum profits occur at $e = 50$. At this effort level, George is paid $3,500 and the profits for AAC are $1,500. This outcome is the efficient bargaining solution for the two parties. He is indifferent among the possible effort choices (he is paid his reservation wage in all cases), while firm profits are maximized at 50. The firm could get him to provide additional effort by paying him more. However, the costs to the firm are higher than the benefits. At the optimal effort level of $e = 50$, the marginal costs of effort are equal to the marginal benefits, where all the benefits and costs to both parties are considered.

Thus far, we have assumed that George's effort is perfectly observable. In many cases, however, e will not be observable by either the firm or a court of law. In addition, the firm might not be able to tell whether he worked hard by simply observing his output. Often output is difficult to measure and is affected by factors beyond the employee's control.[2] In this case, there is a standard agency problem.

If George promises to provide 50 units of effort and is paid a straight salary of $3,500, he will have the incentive to renege on his promise and provide a lower

---

[2] In our example, the firm can infer e from observing B, George's output. More generally, B would be affected by factors that are beyond the control of the worker. For example, the following relation might hold: $B = \$100e + \mu$, where μ is a random error term. Random factors that might affect his output include the quality of raw materials and equipment failures. With the random error term, the firm cannot infer e from observing B.

FIGURE 12.1   The Optimal Effort Choice at AAC.

This figure pictures both the benefits and the costs to the American Assembly Corporation (AAC) from the efforts of a given employee. Profits are the difference between the two. Maximum profits occur at e = 50. This example assumes that the employee will exert the agreed upon effort, as long as he is paid his reservation utility. To meet this constraint, the firm must pay a wage of $1,000 + e^2. This payment meets the reservation wage of $1,000 and reimburses the worker for his disutility of effort. Benefits to the firm are $100e. At the optimal effort level, e = 50, $5,000 in gross benefits are generated. The worker is paid $3,500 and firm profits are $1,500. The firm can get the worker to exert more effort by paying him more. However, the costs are larger than the benefits. The effort choice is efficient—the worker is indifferent among the possible choices (since he is paid his reservation utility in each case) and the profits for the firm are maximized at this level.

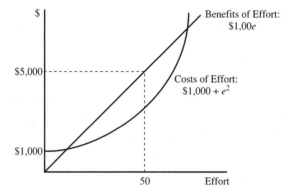

amount of effort. He gets paid anyway and is better off by not working as hard. The firm might suspect that George did not work hard. However, it would not know for sure. In this case, a straight salary of $3,500 does not provide him with the optimal incentives. Rather AAC must devise some other type of incentive contract that motivates him to provide more effort.

This simple example illustrates three important points about incentive problems. First, incentive problems exist because of conflicts of interest between employers and employees. If the interests of employees and employers were perfectly aligned, there would be no reason to worry about incentives. Second, incentive conflicts do not cause problems when actions are observable. Firms can choose the optimal actions and pay workers only if these actions are taken. For instance, if the actions of employees at Du Pont were perfectly observable, there would be no reason for the firm to have a profit-based plan for employees. Rather the employees could be optimally motivated by simpler contracts. Third, in a competitive labor market, employees must be compensated for undertaking undesirable actions. (There are compensating differentials.) Thus, it is not usually optimal to have employees work as hard as physically possible. Rather, in choosing the optimal action, there is a tradeoff between the benefits of the action for the firm and the personal costs to the employees.

Incentives From Ownership

In some cases, there is a surprisingly simple way to solve incentive problems even when the actions of employees are unobservable. The solution is to sell each employee the rights to his total output. The agency problem is caused by the fact that most of the costs of exerting effort are borne by employees, while many of the gains go to the employer. By selling employees their output, both the benefits and costs of exerting effort are internalized by employees and thus employees will make optimal choices. For instance, in the AAC example, the firm could sell George the rights to the value of his output ($100e) for a price of $1,500. In this case, AAC makes the same profits as when effort was perfectly observable. George's objective, in turn, is to maximize his personal utility given by:

$$U = (\$100e - \$1,500) - e^2, \tag{4}$$

where the first term represents the wealth from exerting effort (the value of the output minus the $1,500 payment to the company) and the second term represents the disutility of effort. Given this problem, George will choose to exert 50 units of effort and will have utility of $1,000.[3] This outcome is the same as in the perfect information case. It is achieved, however, even though his effort is unobservable.

This discussion highlights the strong incentive effects that come from ownership. Indeed this type of incentive mechanism is often used in practice. For example, about one-third of all retail sales in the United States are made through franchised outlets. In franchising, the future profits of each unit are sold to franchisees, who as owners have strong incentives to maximize value.[4] As another example, in the 1980s there were a large number of managerial buyouts of firms and divisions of firms, where the managers went from the status of employees to owners. The empirical analysis of these buyouts indicates that the managers operated the units more efficiently when they became owners.[5]

There are, however, at least three important factors that limit the use of ownership in solving incentive problems. First, there is the problem of wealth constraints. For instance, while the top managers at Du Pont might act more like owners if they owned the company, few management groups in the world would have enough money to make the purchase. Second, it is often impossible to measure the profit contribution of a given worker. In most firms there are production synergies, where the total output is greater than the sum of what each worker could produce by herself. Identifying the individual contributions when there is this type of "team

---

[3]This solution can be found using elementary calculus or a graphical analysis, as in Figure 12.1. We will present a more detailed analysis of the employee's effort choice later in this chapter.

[4]See Paul H. Rubin, 1978, "The Theory of the Firm and the Structure of the Franchise Contract," *Journal of Law and Economics* 28, 223–233, and James A. Brickley, and Frederick H. Dark, 1987, "The Choice of Organizational Form: The Case of Franchising," *Journal of Financial Economics* 18, 401–420.

[5]See Steven Kaplan, "The Effects of Management Buyouts on Operating Performance and Value," *Journal of Financial Economics* 24, 217–254.

production'' is problematic. The firm could be owned jointly by the workers. However, this solution does not solve the agency problem—there is the standard freerider problem discussed in Chapter 7. Third is the problem of risk. Typically, employees do not have full control over their outputs. Rather, outputs usually depend on random outside events, as well as employee efforts. For example, Du Pont's profits are affected by changes in the oil, housing, and automobile markets. Ownership, in making employees fully accountable for their actions, also makes them fully responsible for output fluctuations that are beyond their control. Under the reasonable proposition that employees do not like to bear risk, employee ownership entails a risk-bearing cost. As we discuss below, this cost must be considered in designing optimal incentive contracts.

Optimal Risk Sharing

To illustrate some of the basic principles of efficient risk-sharing, consider the simple example of Bob and Cindy. Bob receives a monthly income from a trust fund. Depending on the performance of the fund, this income can either be $0 or $10,000, each with a probability of .5. Bob's expected income is $5,000.[6] However, the income stream is risky—half the time Bob gets $0. Cindy also has a trust fund with the same income possibilities. Half the time she gets $0, the other half $10,000. The income flows for Bob and Cindy are *independent*. (That is, regardless of the outcome for Bob, the probability is still .5 that Cindy will get $0.)[7] In this case, the joint distribution of outcomes for Bob and Cindy is (incomes in brackets; p = probability of the outcome):[8]

[$0;$0]	$p = .25$
[$0;$10,000]	$p = .25$
[$10,000;$0]	$p = .25$
[$10,000;$10,000]	$p = .25$

Assuming that Bob and Cindy do not like risk (that is, they are **risk averse**), they can both be made better off by agreeing to split the combined income. The possible payoffs for each individual, given an even split, are:

$0	$p = .25$
$5,000	$p = .25$
$5,000	$p = .25$
$10,000	$p = .25$

---

[6]The expected income is the *average* amount that Bob will receive in a month. It is calculated by adding together each possible income multiplied by the respective probability: ($10,000 × .5) + ($0 × .5) = $5,000.

[7]We assume that the flows are independent to simplify the calculations in the example. The basic insights of this analysis hold as long as the two flows are not perfectly positively correlated.

[8]A joint outcome [$X,$Y] refers to Bob receiving X dollars, while Cindy receives Y dollars. Since the events are independent, the probability of any joint outcome is the probability of the first event (that Bob receives $X) multiplied by the probability of the second event (that Cindy receives $Y). For example, the probability that both will receive $0 is .5 × .5 = .25.

The expected income per individual is still $5,000. By sharing the risks, however, the variability of their individual incomes has been reduced. The variability is reduced because the likelihood that both Cindy and Bob will be lucky or unlucky is less than the likelihood that only one of them is lucky or unlucky. For example, by sharing the risks the probability of getting nothing is only .25, compared to .5 with no risk-sharing. Holding the expected value constant, risk-averse individuals prefer income streams that are less volatile. (Ideally they would like income streams that are certain.) It is this reduction in volatility from pooling risks that drives the purchase of insurance, as well as the purchase of diversified portfolios (for example, mutual funds).

People often vary in their attitudes toward risk. For instance, some people are relatively willing to take huge financial gambles, while others are not. An efficient allocation of risk takes these differences in preferences into account. For example, assume that Bob is *risk-neutral,* while Cindy is risk-averse. (A risk-neutral person cares only about the expected payoff and does not care about the risk.) Bob will value each of the two random income flows at $5,000 (the expected value), while Cindy will not. For example, Cindy might be willing to accept a certain payment of $4,000 for her risky income flow. Here there are gains from trade by having Bob buy Cindy's income. For example, a payment of $4,500 would split the potential gains of trade between the two parties. Each party would be better off by $500.

The common stock of large corporations is typically held by many investors with well-diversified portfolios. Because of this diversification, investors are not overly concerned about the fortunes of any one company. (Things tend to balance out over their entire portfolios; that is, one firm is lucky while another firm is unlucky.)[9] Workers, in contrast, receive large fractions of their incomes from single companies and can care greatly about the fortunes of single firms. This difference in outlook implies that employees of a firm can often be viewed as being more risk-averse than the owners of the firm. Note that we are not saying that workers necessarily have fundamentally different preferences than owners. Rather it is the differential ability to hedge firm-specific risk that makes shareholders in large corporations less concerned about risk.

Assuming that the owners of the firm are essentially risk-neutral, it is optimal from a risk-sharing standpoint to pay employees straight salaries and let the total risk of random income flows be borne by the shareholders. By paying straight salaries, the firm avoids having to pay a compensating differential for risk (a *risk premium*) to attract and retain the desired work force.

This discussion suggests that one problem with Du Pont's incentive plan was inefficient risk bearing. From a risk-sharing standpoint, it would be better for Du Pont shareholders to maintain the risky claim and pay the employees a straight salary. The expected value of the payouts to employees could have been reduced

---

[9]For example, see William F. Sharpe, 1964, "Capital Asset Prices: A Theory of Market Equilibrium under Conditions of Risk," *Journal of Finance* 19, 179–211.

by paying straight salaries, without making employees worse off. Therefore, for Du Pont's plan to be beneficial there must be offsetting benefits, such as increased incentives. Later in this chapter, we discuss the likely magnitude of these incentive effects.[10]

Basic Principle
Optimal Risk Sharing

Assuming the owners of the firm are essentially risk neutral, it is optimal from a *risk-sharing standpoint* to pay employees a straight salary and let the risk of random income flows be borne by owners (for example, shareholders in large corporations).

Optimal Incentive Contracts

Our discussion to this point suggests that compensation contracts serve at least two important functions. First, they are used to motivate workers. Second, they are used to share risk more efficiently. Unfortunately, there is a tradeoff between these two objectives. Efficient risk sharing suggests that it is optimal to pay employees straight salaries, while incentive considerations suggest that it is best to tie pay to performance. An optimal compensation contract strikes an appropriate balance between these two considerations.

Basic Principle:
Tradeoffs between Incentives and Risk Sharing

Optimal risk sharing implies that workers should be paid straight salaries. Straight salaries, however, do not provide strong incentives. Therefore, there is a tradeoff between paying incentive compensation to increase effort and the associated costs of inefficient risk bearing. Often the optimal contract consists of a fixed salary and some variable component based on output.

Economists have devoted significant resources to studying how to design optimal compensation contracts. In this section, we summarize some of the more important findings from this research. We begin with the most basic model in the

---

[10]Another possible benefit of some performance-based compensation plans is decreased tax payments to the government. In this chapter, we do not consider the tax consequences of incentive plans. Readers interested in this topic should consult Myron S. Scholes and Mark A. Wolfson, *Taxes and Business Strategy,* Prentice Hall, Englewood Cliffs, New Jersey, 1992.

economics literature, the standard principal/agent model. We then extend the basic analysis by considering the informativeness principle, group incentive pay, multi-task principal/agent problems, types of incentive pay, and the role of incentive pay in self selection.

Principal/Agent Model

The Basic Model.   Economic analysis of incentive compensation begins with the basic principal/agent model.[11] This model presents a relatively simple characterization of the contracting process. However, it illustrates the tradeoffs between risk sharing and incentives and provides a number of useful insights for designing better compensation plans. In this model, there is an employer (the principal) who wants the employee (the agent) to work on her behalf. The employer is risk-neutral, while the employee is risk-averse. The most basic analysis focuses on one employee. Concerns about teamwork do not arise in the basic model. The agent's output, Q, is a function of his effort, plus some random effect, μ (with expected value 0 and variance, σ^2). For instance assume:

$$Q = \alpha e + \mu, \tag{5}$$

where output is defined as the market value of the production. The model does not consider the possibility of manipulating or gaming the observed output level (for example, by the employee "cooking the books").

In this formulation, if the employee increases effort by one unit, output goes up by α units. Thus α is the marginal productivity of the worker—the higher the α, the higher the marginal productivity. The random effect, μ, reflects factors that can affect output, but are beyond the worker's control (for example, equipment failures). The higher σ^2 the more likely it is that the output will experience significant random shocks.

Optimal risk sharing suggests that there are benefits from having the employer bear the output risk and paying the employee a straight salary. For example, the worker might agree to put forth effort level, e^*, and be paid a fixed salary, W, for this effort. The employer would maintain a claim on the difference between the value of the output and W.

$$\text{Principal's payment} = [\alpha e + \mu] - W. \tag{6}$$

There is, however, an agency problem with this arrangement if the employer cannot observe the effort level of the worker or μ, the random shock. The worker has the incentive to agree to e^* as an effort level and then exert less effort. The employer will tend to observe lower outputs when the worker shirks. However, the employee can claim the result is due to bad luck (that is, μ was negative).

---

[11]One of the first presentations of this model is Bengt Holmstrom, 1979, "Moral Hazard and Observability," *Bell Journal of Economics* 10, 74–91.

Employee's Effort Problem.   Incentives can be provided to the worker by basing part of the compensation on realized output. For example, consider the worker's incentives under the following contract:

$$\text{Compensation} = W_o + \beta Q, \tag{7}$$

where $0 \leq \beta \leq 1$. This contract pays the worker a fixed wage, W_o, plus a proportion, β, of the output, Q.[12] To illustrate the employee's effort choice, assume $W_o = \$1,000$, $\beta = .2$, $Q = \$100e + \mu$, and $C(e) = e^2$, where $C(e)$ is the employee's cost of effort in dollar equivalents. Given these values, the compensation contract is:

$$\text{Compensation} = \$1,000 + .2[\$100e + \mu]. \tag{8}$$

The benefit to the worker from exerting effort is that it increases compensation—each unit of effort increases compensation by $20 (.2 × $100). Random shocks due to μ affect total compensation, but do not affect the benefits of exerting effort. For any realization of μ, compensation is always $20 higher for every extra unit of effort provided. Thus in choosing the optimal effort level the employee can ignore μ. (It does not affect the costs or benefits of effort).[13] The cost to the worker from exerting effort is e^2. The employee's objective is to choose the effort level that maximizes the net benefits.

Figure 12.2 displays how the employee's compensation and personal costs increase as the employee exerts more effort. As shown in the figure, the optimal effort choice is 10. Note that the figure shows total costs and benefits. It can be shown that marginal benefits and marginal costs at any effort level are equal to the slopes of the total curves at that point. The difference between total costs and benefits is greatest when the slopes of the total curves are equal. Thus at the optimal choice ($e = 10$), the marginal costs of effort are equal to the marginal benefits, and net benefits are maximized.

Figure 12.3 shows how the employee's effort choice changes with changes in the fixed wage, W_o, and the incentive coefficient, β. Changing the fixed wage from $1,000 to $2,000 results in a parallel shift in compensation, but the employee still chooses $e = 10$. The fixed wage *provides no incentives* for the employee to work harder since it does not affect the *marginal benefits* of effort. Marginal benefits are $20, regardless of the fixed wage. In contrast, when the incentive coefficient is increased, the employee selects a higher effort level. For instance, with $\beta = .3$, the employee selects 15 units of effort. In this case, marginal benefits increase to $30 and the worker exerts more effort. The implications of this analysis conflict with

---

[12]For simplicity, we restrict our attention to linear compensation contracts. These contracts are commonly observed in practice and can be justified theoretically under certain assumptions. See Bengt Holmstrom, and Paul R. Milgrom, 1987, ''Aggregation and Linearity in the Provision of Intertemporal Incentives,'' *Econometrica* 55, 303–28.

[13]Note for the technically inclined: Throughout our analysis, we assume constant absolute risk aversion. Relaxing this assumption means that the worker will consider an additional effect in choosing the effort level. In particular, the effort choice will affect the utility of the worker by altering the costs imposed on the worker from bearing risk. We ignore this potential effect because it complicates the analysis without providing substantially more insights.

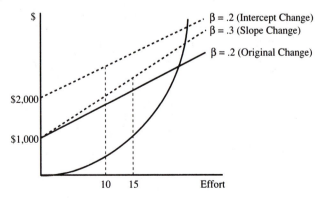

FIGURE 12.2   The Employee's Effort Choice.

*This figure shows how the compensation and personal costs increase as the employee
exerts more effort. The compensation function is $1,000 + $20e. The cost function is e^2.
The objective of the employee is to choose the effort level that maximizes the net benefits.
This maximization occurs at e = 10. At this point, the marginal benefits of effort ($20) are
equal to the marginal costs. The employee's expected compensation is $1,200.*

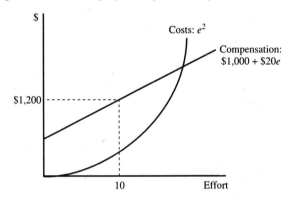

FIGURE 12.3   How the Employee's Effort Choice Changes with Changes in
the Fixed Wage and Incentive Coefficient.

*The initial contract is: Compensation = $1,000 + .2($100e). The picture shows that
increasing the fixed wage from $1,000 to $2,000 causes a parallel shift in the
compensation function, but does not alter the effort choice. (It stays at 10.) Changing the
incentive coefficient (β) from .2 to .3 changes the slope of the line and increases the
amount of effort to 15.*

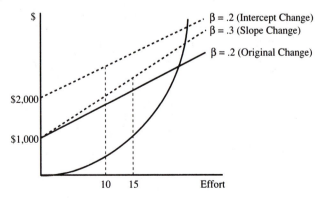

the common argument that well-paid employees work harder because they are happier on the job. According to this analysis, higher pay does not provide incentives unless it is tied to good performance.

It is important to note that this analysis focuses on a single time period. In a multi-period setting, a high level of pay can motivate workers if the *likelihood of being fired is contingent on performance.* (See the discussion in the last chapter on efficiency wages.) In this case, the contract is a method of tying pay to performance. High pay and guaranteed tenure with the firm, however, provide no incentive effects.

Motivating Workers at Allen-Edmonds Shoe Company

Agency theory argues that tying pay to performance motivates workers more than fixed salaries. Allen-Edmonds Shoe Company learned this principle the hard way. Allen-Edmonds is a manufacturer of high-priced shoes. For years, it paid its factory workers based on individual output through a piece-rate system. In 1990, acting on the advice of quality experts, the company abandoned the piece-rate system and started paying workers fixed hourly wages. The intent was to encourage workers to focus on quality and teamwork. Productivity plummeted as workers were observed taking more breaks and ''fooling around.'' After the company lost $1 million in 1990, it reinstated piece-work payments. Productivity and profits immediately ''shot back up.'' An executive of the company stated, ''Our people needed the discipline that the piecework system gives to them.''

Barbara Marsh, ''Allen-Edmonds Shoe Tries 'Just-In-Time' Production,'' *Wall Street Journal*, March 4, 1993, B-2.

The Optimal Contract.   We have shown how the employee will choose effort under any given compensation contract. The firm's problem is to choose the specific compensation contract that maximizes expected profits, given the employee's anticipated effort choice. The primary choice variable is β. Given this choice, W_o can be adjusted up or down to meet the reservation utility of the worker. Selecting a contract with a high β benefits the firm because it increases the effort exerted by the worker. However, choosing a high β also involves costs for the firm. In particular, the expected compensation that the firm must pay to the worker increases with β for two reasons. First, as discussed above, the worker must be compensated for exerting more effort. Second, increasing β imposes additional risk on the worker—the variable portion of compensation increases. As risk increases, so does the compensating differential that must be paid to attract and retain the worker. The optimal contract involves an appropriate consideration of these costs and benefits. Usually, it is optimal to choose a contract that motivates the employee to exert less effort than would be the case if effort were perfectly observable. When effort is observable, the contract can call for a high level of effort without imposing risk on the worker.

FIGURE 12.4   Implications of the Principal/Agent Model.

The basic model does not provide strong guidance on exactly how firms should shape their compensation plans. The analysis, however, does suggest that the four factors listed in this figure are likely to be particularly important in determining how strongly to base pay on performance.

Factors That Favor High Incentive Pay

---

1. The employee's output is sensitive to his effort.
2. The employee is not very risk averse.
3. The level of risk that is beyond the employee's control is low.
4. The worker's response to increased incentives is high. (The worker exerts a lot more effort.)

Incentive Pay and Expected Compensation

A study of earnings of workers in 500 U.S. firms in the footwear and clothing industries found that piece-rate workers on average were paid 14 percent more than workers paid straight salaries. This premium was found after controlling for union status, sex, and other variables that might affect compensation. Economic theory suggests at least three reasons for this wage premium. First, people work harder under piece rates than under fixed salaries and must be compensated for the extra effort. Second, piece-rates impose risk on workers—output is affected by random factors such as equipment failures. Thus firms using piece rates must pay a compensating differential for risk. Third, piece-rates are likely to attract more highly skilled and productive workers since they will earn more under piece-rates than under fixed salaries. Firms have to pay more for skilled workers than for unskilled workers.

Suggested by Eric Seiler, 1984, "Piece Rate vs. Time Rate: The Effect of Incentives on Earnings," *Review of Economics and Statistics* 66, 363–76.

Implications.   Economists have used the mathematics of optimization to study the general solution to this contracting problem.[14] The results do not provide strong guidance on exactly how firms should shape their compensation plans. The analysis, however, does suggest four factors that are likely to be important in selecting how strongly pay should be tied to performance. These factors are summarized in Figure 12.4. The first factor is the sensitivity of output to additional effort from the employee. In our formulation, this factor is captured by α in equation (5). A high α

---

[14]The basic model assumes that the employer has the relevant knowledge to solve this problem, including knowledge of the production function, the worker's utility function, and the variance of the random error term. For a mathematical derivation of the results in this section, see Chapter 7 of Paul Milgrom and John Roberts, *Economics Organization & Management*, Prentice Hall, Englewood Cliffs, New Jersey, 1992.

implies it is optimal to pay high incentive pay (holding other factors constant) since the benefits of motivating effort are high. A second factor is the risk aversion of the employee. Higher risk aversion implies a higher cost from inefficient risk bearing and thus a lower optimal amount of incentive pay. The third factor is the level of risk that is beyond the employee's control (σ^2). When the level of risk is low, output is determined primarily by the employee's effort, and it makes sense to pay high levels of incentive compensation. When the risk is high, output is a noisy measure of effort, and incentive compensation imposes high costs for inefficient risk bearing. The fourth factor is how much additional effort the employee exerts as incentives are increased. If the worker is nonresponsive to increased incentives, high incentive compensation imposes risk on the worker without inducing additional effort. Thus, there is no reason to pay high incentive pay. As suggested in Figure 12.3, the response rate depends on the personal costs to the employee for exerting additional effort. For instance, changing the cost function in the graph from e^2 to e^3 would make the employee less responsive to changes in incentives. With the original cost function, the worker increases effort by 5 units as β is increased from .2 to .3. The increase is .58 under the second cost function.[15]

The principal/agent model points to at least two problems with the Du Pont plan. Both problems stem from using divisional profits as an output measure. First, while these profits are affected by the collective efforts of all divisional employees, *individually* workers have little effect on the measure. For example, a given worker out of 20,000 can increase his work effort substantially and have almost no effect on divisional profits. Thus the individual α's are low and the plan provides limited incentives for workers to exert effort. (They bear costs from exerting effort but gain few personal benefits.) The limited incentives are due to the classic *freerider problem* discussed in Chapter 7. We discuss this issue in greater detail below under the topic of group incentives. The second problem is one that we have already mentioned. Divisional profits are affected by many random factors (σ^2 is high), and thus the compensation plan imposes a high degree of risk on the workers.

Informativeness Principle

As we have seen, incentive problems exist because of imperfect information. If the actions of employees were observable, it would be easy to write contracts to motivate optimal behavior. It follows that the inefficiencies that result from incentive problems can be reduced by improvements in information. The standard principal/agent model assumes that there is only one indicator of an employee's effort, the worker's output. In most cases, however, there are other sources of information that can be used to determine whether or not the employee worked hard. For instance, Du Pont was able to tell that the decline in profits in 1990 was not due to a lack of effort on the part of divisional employees by observing the performance of other

---

[15]Note for the technically inclined: It is the second derivative of the cost function that is important in determining the response rate. Larger second derivatives (or equivalently steeper marginal cost curves) translate into lower response rates.

companies and gathering information such as government reports on unemployment. Appropriate use of this type of information increases the precision by which employee effort is measured, and when included in the compensation contract (with the appropriate weights) reduces the costs of inefficient risk bearing. Theoretically, it is optimal to include all indicators that provide additional information about the employee's effort in the compensation contract (assuming the measures are available at low cost). This basic idea is called the *informativeness principle*.[16]

Informativeness Principle

In designing compensation contracts, theory suggests that it is optimal to include all performance indicators that provide additional information about the employee's effort (assuming the measures are available at low cost). Measuring the employee's effort with more precision reduces the costs of inefficient risk bearing and can make it feasible to motivate a more efficient effort choice.

One important source of information about an employee's effort level is the output of co-workers performing similar tasks. For instance, if a salesperson's performance is bad in a given year, was the person unlucky or lazy? If average sales in the company declined substantially over the same time period, it is likely that the employee was simply unlucky. In contrast, if other salespeople had great years, the salesperson is likely to have been lazy. The informativeness principle, therefore, indicates that information about other employees' sales should be included in the compensation contract as a benchmark (that is, to use a *relative-performance contract*).[17]

The informativeness principle is based on the assumption that the worker cannot manipulate or "game" any of the performance indicators. In small groups, however, relative-performance schemes can motivate collusion, sabotage, and a general lack of cooperation. These actions lower the performance benchmark and thus enhance measured performance of the worker. In large groups, these problems are likely to be less important, since it is harder to enforce collusive agreements and sabotaging a limited number co-workers does little to affect the benchmark.

The informativeness principle indicates that it is optimal to include any low-cost indicator in the compensation contract that improves the measurement of the worker's performance. It can also be desirable for the firm to expend additional resources on developing even more precise measures of performance. Here, there is a tradeoff between the costs of developing better performance measures and the benefits of improved risk sharing and effort motivation.

---

[16]See, Bengt Holmstrom, 1982, "Moral Hazard in Teams," *Bell Journal of Economics* 13, 324–40.

[17]Chapter 13 includes a more detailed discussion of relative-performance evaluation. It also includes an appendix on how to choose the appropriate weight for a performance benchmark.

The informativeness principle suggests another potential problem with the Du Pont plan. The company could have reduced the risk imposed on the workers by including other indicators in the contract. For instance, rather than using an absolute performance standard (such as 4 percent real earnings growth), the target could have been set relative to the growth of other firms in the same industry. This type of contract might have avoided the problems that the company faced in 1990, when employees were likely to lose money under the plan due to no fault of their own.

Group Incentive Pay

In the basic principal/agent model workers are motivated by being paid based on their *own output*. Many firms, however, base incentive pay on *group performance*. For example, of 425 companies responding to a 1987 survey by the Hay group, 87 percent offered some type of incentive pay in addition to base salary.[18] The most common forms of incentive pay were profit-sharing plans and other types of group incentive plans (based on productivity improvements, etc.).

There are at least three reasons why firms might favor group incentive plans over individual plans. First, individual performance is often difficult to measure, while the performance of a group of workers can be measured at low cost. For example, the owner of a small grocery store can tell whether the overall business is doing well from the store's profits. Measuring the performance of each of the employees is much more difficult. Second, group pay emphasizes cooperation and team work, while some individual incentive plans (depending on design) motivate more self-centered actions. Third, group plans can motivate workers to monitor each other for bad performance. Mutual monitoring is beneficial because the specific knowledge about individual performance is often held by co-workers.

Standard freerider arguments, however, provide a strong reason to question whether group plans provide powerful incentives, particularly when the group is very large. In Du Pont's Fibers Division with 20,000 employees, the contributions of individual workers have almost no effect on the overall bottom line. In this case, profit-sharing plans would appear to have limited incentive effects. Does paying a janitor on overall company performance really motivate the person to push the broom harder or to complain when other janitors shirk on their jobs? These arguments suggest that large-group incentive plans (like Du Pont's) impose risk on workers and have limited benefits.

While many economists find the freerider arguments to be very compelling, there are some offsetting considerations that potentially help to explain the widespread popularity of group plans. First, it might be beneficial to increase the awareness of employees about the stock-price performance and profitability of the company. By focusing on these measures, employees learn how managerial and employee actions affect the bottom line. For instance, employees might be less likely

---

[18]See Laurie Hays, ''All Eyes on Du Pont's Incentive Program,'' *The Wall Street Journal,* December 5, 1988, p. B–1.

to complain about a corporate restructuring when they see that it increases stock price. Indeed, it does not take much stock ownership to motivate most workers to monitor the stock price on a frequent basis. Hence these benefits can be obtained without shifting too much risk on the workers. Second, workers might experience disutility from taking actions that harm other members of a group that they closely identify with. Thus, employees might not want to harm co-workers by shirking on the job, when the group receives incentive pay. In this case, feelings like "guilt" and "shame" might motivate workers, even if they do not face direct financial consequences from shirking.[19] Third, paying workers on stock-price performance and profits sends signals to workers about what is valued in the company. These signals serve to reinforce a performance-based "corporate culture" (see Chapter 8). To be most effective, however, they must be complemented by other features in the organizational architecture that provide more direct incentives.

Multitask Principal/Agent Problems

In the standard principal/agent model, effort is one dimensional—the firm only cares about how hard the employee works. Most jobs, however, involve a variety of tasks. For instance, workers on an assembly line can spend time increasing output, perfecting quality, performing preventative maintenance, or helping co-workers. Similarly, professors at universities allocate their time among teaching, research, consulting, and administrative duties. Thus, managers usually have to be concerned not only with how hard employees work, but also with how they allocate their time among assigned tasks, university officials are not indifferent about how professors allocate their time.

Motivating a worker to strike the appropriate balance among tasks is not easy.[20] A complicating factor is that some tasks are more easily measured than others. For example, university officials can observe teaching ratings, while the quality of administrative service is harder to measure. Compensating the worker based on what is measurable will encourage the worker to exert effort on the compensated tasks and shirk on other tasks. For example, paying professors based solely on teaching ratings will encourage effort on teaching, at the expense of administrative service, consulting, and research. Similarly, paying an assembly worker based on output will encourage the worker to produce more units, but to ignore quality and helping co-workers. These multitask considerations suggest that firms might often want to avoid paying workers based solely on measurable outputs.

Given enough time, however, managers are likely to obtain information about the overall performance of workers. For example, deans have the opportunity to observe the service of professors on committees; they hear comments on faculty

---

[19]See Eugene Kandel and Edward P. Lazear, 1992, "Peer Pressure and Partnership," *Journal of Political Economy* 100, 801–817.

[20]See Bengt Holmstrom and Paul Milgrom, 1991, "Multitask Principal-Agent Analysis: Incentive Contracts, Asset Ownership and Job Design," *Journal of Law Economics and Organization* 7, 24–52.

research from colleagues; they talk to students about teaching quality. Incentives can be provided to workers by basing promotions, terminations, and periodic pay adjustments on this type of information. Indeed, universities rely heavily on these mechanisms to motivate faculty. Evaluating this information, however, usually requires *subjective judgments* on the part of managers. To provide proper incentives to workers, managers must develop reputations of being impartial and objective. To be most effective, firms must establish performance measures and rewards that motivate managers to develop these reputations. Chapter 13 provides an expanded discussion of subjective performance evaluation.

Forms of Incentive Pay

Typically the term *incentive pay* conjures up images of piece-rates, commissions, and cash bonus plans, where the worker is paid based on measurable output. This image is not surprising given that more than a quarter of the workers in the U. S. manufacturing sector receive at least part of their income through these types of incentive plans.[21] Our discussion in this chapter, however, suggests that mechanisms like tying promotions and salary adjustments to performance are also incentive pay. Broadly speaking, any compensation contract (explicit or implicit) that rewards employees for good performance or punishes employees for bad performance can be considered incentive pay. Under this definition all of the following are incentive compensation:

1. Bonuses for good performance.
2. Salary revisions based on performance.
3. Piece-rates and commissions.
4. Stock ownership and profit-sharing plans.
5. Prizes for winning contests (for example, vacations).
6. Promotions and titles for good performance.
7. Firings and other penalties for bad performance.
8. Unvested pensions that are lost upon dismissal.
9. Preferred office assignments for good performance.

It is important to note that rewards *do not have to be monetary*. Rather rewards can consist of anything that the employee values. For example, managers in some organizations have little flexibility in what they pay employees. Nevertheless, incentives can be provided by rewarding good-performing employees with better offices, trips to training sessions at nice locations, preferred parking spaces, special honors, and desirable job assignments.

---

[21]See John McMillan, 1992, *Games Strategies, & Managers,* Oxford University Press, New York City, page 93.

Incentive Compensation and Self-Selection

The basic principal/agent model assumes that the employer and employee have the same information at the time of initial contract negotiations. In some contracting situations, however, this pre-contractual information is asymmetric. For example, a prospective employee is likely to know more about the likelihood of quitting over the next year than the prospective employer. Similarly, sales representatives are more likely to know about the sales potential of their territories than higher-level managers.

Imaginative Incentives to Reduce Absenteeism

During the 1940s one company successfully reduced absenteeism by holding a daily raffle. The prizes were various products that were especially hard for workers to obtain during the shortage-prone war years. Employees had to be present to win.

In a second scheme, adopted by an automobile company, employees were awarded points for each day that they were present at the factory. The points could be redeemed for prizes, such as tickets to popular vacation attractions. The interesting feature of the plan was that the points were not given to the worker, but to the worker's spouse! Reports indicate that with the spouse helping to monitor worker attendance, the absenteeism rate declined significantly.

Suggested by Ronald G. Ehrenberg and Robert S. Smith, 1988, *Modern Labor Economics*, Scott Foresman and Company, Glenview Illinois, p. 417.

Sometimes it is possible for the firm to induce employees to reveal their private information by clever design of the compensation contract. Consider the example of Onex Copy Company. This company uses sales representatives throughout the country to sell copy machines to customers. Each salesperson is assigned a specific territory. Some territories have better sales potential than others. For simplicity, assume that there are only two types of territories, good and bad. Good territories have the potential to generate $2 million in sales, while bad territories have the potential to generate only $1 million in sales. The sales representatives know the quality of their own territories. Central managers, however, cannot distinguish which territories are good and bad.

The firm would like to use information about whether specific territories are good or bad to evaluate the performance of the sales representatives. The company also wants accurate forecasts to plan production cycles and to make other decisions. The company could simply ask the sales representatives to state the quality of their territories. The sales representatives with good territories, however, are likely to lie—if the firm thinks that a good territory is bad, the representative will look good when sales are high. (Alternatively the representative can generate the expected bad sales with limited effort.)

In this example, the firm can induce the representatives to tell the truth by offering the following menu of contracts. Sales representatives who state that their territories are good receive compensation contracts that pay 2.6 percent of sales. Sales representatives who state that their territories are bad receive a flat wage of $50,000. Given this choice it is in the interests of all sales representatives to tell the truth—representatives with bad territories would prefer the $50,000 wage contract, while people with good territories would prefer the contract that pays 2.6 percent of sales (for them, a $52,000 payout). The key to making the scheme work is that the compensation for each type of employee is higher when the information is correctly reported than when it is not.

In this example, there are many potential compensation schemes that can induce truth telling. The problem of the firm is to choose the most profitable contract. Onex is likely to want the compensation contract to provide strong performance incentives, as well as to induce truth-telling. Thus, it might choose to pay commissions to both types of workers, but structure alternative commission rates to induce truth-telling.

There is no systematic evidence on how frequently firms actually consider these types of information problems in contract design. We are aware of one example, IBM Brazil.[22] During the 1970s, this company experimented with offering a menu of contracts to motivate truthful sales forecasting and employee effort. According to executives from this company, these experiments were successful.

Does Incentive Pay Work?

Throughout this chapter, we have argued that compensation plans motivate workers. While this argument is readily accepted by many people, it is not without controversy. For instance, quality guru, W. Edward Demmings has gone so far as to assert that "pay is not a motivator." In the same spirit, psychologist Alfie Kohn in a controversial article on the merits of incentive pay states, "Bribes in the workplace simply can't work."[23]

Critics of incentive pay rely on two basic arguments. The first is that money does not motivate workers. As support for this view, it is pointed out that workers usually rank money relatively low when it comes to factors that make a job attractive. Factors such as the nature of work and quality of colleagues appear more important. The second, more prominent criticism is that it is difficult (if not impossible) to design an effective incentive compensation scheme. Support for this argument is provided by the many examples of flawed compensation schemes that have produced unwanted behavior (for example, the case of Sears Automotive Centers discussed in Chapter 2). Interestingly, the two lines of criticism are somewhat at odds with one another. If money did not motivate people, incentives schemes

---

[22]See Jacob Gonik, 1978, "Tie Salesmen's Bonuses to Their Forecasts, *Harvard Business Review* 56, 116–23.

[23]See Alfie Kohn, 1993, "Why Incentive Plans Cannot Work," *Harvard Business Review,* September/October, 54–63.

would not produce the dramatic changes in behavior that proponents of the second argument cite. In making a similar point, economist George Baker notes, "The problem is not that incentives can't work but that they work all too well."[24]

The Power of Incentives—
Evidence from Chinese Agriculture

One especially interesting piece of evidence on the effectiveness of incentive pay comes from one of the largest economic experiments in history—reforms in Chinese agriculture in the early 1980s. Between 1952 and 1978, the Maoist period, Chinese agriculture revolved around the "commune system." Under this system, workers were divided into production teams. There were some attempts to tie pay to performance. However, these attempts were relatively weak, and there was a tendency to base pay on family size, independent of effort. From 1980 to 1984, under the rule of Deng Xiaoping, the commune system was gradually replaced by the "household-responsibility system." Under this system each peasant family was given a long-term lease on a plot of land. The family had to deliver a quota of agricultural products to the government each year, but could keep any production in excess of the quota. This additional output could be consumed by the family or sold to others.

Economic theory argues that the ownership of residual claims on output provides strong incentives. Thus, this theory predicts higher productivity under the household-responsibility system than the commune system. Empirical studies support this prediction. For instance, one study estimated that productivity in Chinese agriculture increased by nearly 50 percent over the period of the Dengist reforms.

Suggested by John McMillan, *Games Strategies and Managers*, Oxford Press, New York, 1992, 96–98.

Certainly it is easy to point to many examples of compensation schemes that have caused dysfunctional behavior among employees. We have done so throughout this book. (Recall our example of Sears Auto Centers.) Incentive schemes also involve administrative costs, such as keeping track of output and explaining the system to workers. The important question, however, is not whether incentive plans entail costs (which they certainly do), but whether it is possible to design incentive plans where the benefits are larger than the costs. Examples like the Lincoln Electric Company (discussed in Chapter 13) suggest the answer is yes. Also, the fact that incentive plans (commissions, piece-rates, and bonus plans) have survived so long in a competitive market place suggests that the net benefits of incentive pay are often positive.

---

[24]See George P. Baker, III, letter in "Rethinking Rewards," *Harvard Business Review*, November/December, 44–45.

Case Study:
The Debate over CEO Compensation

The most visible and highly-paid person in most corporations is the chief executive officer (CEO). CEO compensation is particularly important to firms for two reasons. First, the compensation package is likely to be important in attracting and retaining good CEOs. Second, employees throughout the organization carefully watch CEO pay. Important morale problems can occur when employees think that the CEO is overpaid. For instance, employees complain bitterly when they are asked to take pay cuts because the company is in trouble and the CEO at the same time gets a big raise.

Controversy over CEO pay has increased significantly in recent years. One charge is that the *level* of CEO pay is too high. It is easy to point to many CEOs who report compensation in the millions of dollars (reported compensation figures typically include salary and bonus payments, as well as gains from exercised stock options). For example, in 1991 Stephen Wolf was paid over $18 million as CEO of UAL. To quote Professor Edward E. Lawler, III, ''CEO pay just seems to get more absurd each year. What is outrageous one year becomes a standard for the next.''

The second major criticism of CEO pay concerns *how* CEOs are paid. Critics argue that CEOs are agents of stockholders and that CEO pay should be based heavily on stock-price performance. Jensen and Murphy (1990) provide the most detailed evidence on this topic. They find that for the typical CEO a $1,000 change in the value of the company stock results in about a $3.25 change in CEO wealth. They argue that this relation (which is equivalent to the CEO owning .325 percent of the common stock) is too small and that most companies would be better off if they increased incentive pay for CEOs. Some support for this view seems to come from studies that document an increase in stock price when companies announce that they are increasing incentive pay for CEOs.

Using the concepts discussed in Chapters 13 and 14 answer the following questions:

1. Do you think that most American CEOs are paid too much? Justify your answer.

2. Do you think that most American companies should increase the amount of incentive compensation for CEOs? Justify your answer.

Useful references: John Byrne, ''The Flap Over Executive Pay,'' *Business Week* (May 6, 1991, 90–112; Michael C. Jensen and Kevin J. Murphy, 1990, ''CEO Incentives—It's Not How Much You Pay, But How,'' *Harvard Business Review* (May–June), 138–153; Joseph G. Haubrich, 1994, ''Risk Aversion, Performance Pay, and the Principal-Agent Problem,'' *Journal of Political Economy* 102, 258–276; James A. Brickley, Sanjai Bhagat, and Ronald C. Lease, 1985, ''The Impact of Long-Range Compensation Plans on Shareholder Wealth,'' *Journal of Accounting and Economics* 7, 115–29.

Unfortunately, the scientific evidence on this debate is limited.[25] There are numerous studies indicating that tying pay to performance has a positive impact on

---

[25]See George T. Milkovich, and Jerry M. Newman, *Compensation,* Fourth Edition, Irwin Press, Homewood, IL, Chapter 8.

employee performance. Other studies, however, reach the opposite conclusion. Since many of the studies on this topic have serious flaws, it is difficult to draw strong conclusions from the evidence. Our overall reading of this literature indicates that incentive compensation can be value-enhancing, if properly designed and implemented. Our intent is to provide insights into how managers might accomplish this task.

Summary

Incentive problems exist because of conflicts of interest between employers and employees. These problems are easily resolved when actions are observable. Firms can choose the optimal actions for employees and pay workers only if these actions are taken. In most situations, however, employee actions are not perfectly observable. Here, firms can motivate workers through incentive compensation.

In a competitive labor market, workers must be compensated for undertaking undesirable actions. (There are compensating differentials.) Thus, it is not usually optimal to have workers work as hard as physically possible. Rather, in choosing the optimal action there is a tradeoff between the benefits of the action for the firm and the personal costs to the workers.

Sometimes, there is a surprisingly simple way to solve incentive problems even when the actions of employees are unobservable. The solution is to sell each employee the rights to his/her total output. The agency problem is caused by the fact that most of the costs of exerting effort are borne by employees, while many of the gains go to the employer. By selling employees their output, both the benefits and costs of exerting effort are internalized by employees and thus employees will make optimal choices. We observe this solution being used in franchising and managerial buyouts. There are, however, at least three important factors that limit the use of ownership in solving incentive problems: wealth constraints, team production, and the costs of inefficient risk bearing.

Risk-averse individuals do not like to bear financial risks and thus prefer income flows with less volatility. Risk-averse individuals can benefit from sharing risks because it lowers the volatility of the individual cash flows. People often vary in their attitudes towards risk. For instance, some people are relatively willing to take financial gambles, while others are not. An efficient allocation of risk takes these differences in preferences into account. If one party is risk-neutral while another party is risk-averse, it is optimal to have the risk-neutral party bear all the risk and the other party to receive a fixed payment.

Stockholders of firms often hold diversified portfolios and can be considered essentially risk-neutral when it comes to the fortunes of a given firm. (Good luck by some firms tends to be offset by the bad luck of other firms in a diversified portfolio.) Workers, in contrast, have a large fraction of their human capital invested in one firm and can be viewed as risk-averse. Thus, from a risk-sharing standpoint, it is optimal to pay employees straight salaries and to let the total risk of random income flows be borne by the shareholders. Straight salaries, however, provide limited incentives for workers to exert effort—*there is a tradeoff between optimal risk sharing and optimal incentives.*

Economic analysis of incentive compensation begins with the basic *principal/ agent model*. This model presents a relatively simple characterization of the contracting process. It, however, illustrates the tradeoffs between risk sharing and incentives and provides a number of useful insights for designing better compensation plans. In particular, the model suggests that firms should pay more performance-based pay when: (1) the sensitivity of output to additional effort from the employee is high, (2) the employee is not very risk averse, (3) the level of risk that is beyond the employee's control is low, and (4) the employee responds to increased incentives by exerting substantially more effort.

According to the *informativeness principle,* it is optimal to include all indicators that provide additional information about employee effort into the compensation contract (assuming these indicators are available at low cost). Including these indicators in the contract reduces the randomness of payouts and thus the costs of inefficient risk bearing. One important source of information about an employee's effort is the output of co-workers performing similar tasks. The informativeness principle, therefore, suggests that it is optimal to use *relative-performance evaluation*. Problems of sabotage and collusion, however, can make relative-performance evaluation undesirable, especially in small groups.

In the basic principal/agent model, workers are motivated by being paid based on their own output. Many firms, however, base incentive pay on *group performance*. Standard freerider arguments provide a strong reason to question whether group plans provide powerful incentives, particularly when the group is large. There are, however, at least three factors that might help to explain the widespread popularity of these plans. First, it can be beneficial to increase the awareness of employees about stock-price performance and profitability (assuming employees can be motivated to monitor these measures by relatively small plans that do not shift much risk on to the workers). Second, workers might suffer feelings of ''guilt'' or ''shame'' from shirking and imposing costs on co-workers who are compensated on group performance. These feelings might motivate workers, even if the direct financial consequences are small. Third, paying workers on firm performance sends a strong signal to workers about what is valued in the company. To be most effective, however, these signals must be reinforced by other parts of the organizational architecture that provide more direct incentives.

Most jobs involve a variety of tasks. Motivating a worker to strike the appropriate balance among tasks is not easy. A complicating factor is that some tasks are more easily measured than others. Compensating the worker based on what is measurable will encourage the worker to exert effort on the compensated tasks and shirk on other tasks. These *multi-task considerations* suggest that firms might often want to avoid paying workers based solely on measurable outputs. Given enough time, managers are likely to obtain information about the overall performance of workers. Incentives can be provided to workers by basing promotions, terminations, and periodic pay adjustments on this information. Often, this information is not quantifiable but is based on the subjective opinions of supervisors.

The term *incentive pay* conjures up images of piece-rates, commissions, and cash bonus plans, where the worker is paid based on measurable output. Broadly speaking, however, any compensation contract (explicit or implicit) that rewards employees for good performance or punishes employees for bad performance can be considered incentive pay. Rewards *do not have to be monetary*. Rather rewards consist of anything that the employee values.

The basic principal/agent model assumes employers and employees have the same information at the time of initial contract negotiations. In some contracting situations, however, precontractual information is asymmetric. Sometimes it is possible for the firm to induce employees to reveal their private information by clever design of the compensation contract. For such a scheme to work, the payoffs to workers must be higher when they are honest than when they misreport information.

Throughout this chapter, we have argued that compensation plans motivate workers. While this argument is accepted by many it is not without controversy. Critics of incentive pay rely on two basic arguments. The first is that money does not motivate workers. The second, more prominent criticism, is that it is difficult (if not impossible) to design an effective incentive compensation scheme. The first argument seems inconsistent with the many examples where monetary incentives have dramatically affected employee behavior. The second argument is correct in that developing an appropriate incentive scheme is not always easy. The important question, however, is whether plans can be designed where the benefits are larger than the costs. Examples, such as Lincoln Electric, suggest it can be done. Our intent is to provide insights into how managers might design value-maximizing contracts.

CHAPTER 13 Individual Performance Evaluation

Introduction

Lincoln Electric Company, headquartered in Cleveland, Ohio, was founded in 1895 to manufacture electric motors and generators.[1] In the early part of the 20th century, the firm became the premier supplier of electric arc welding machines and welding disposables (electrodes). In 1993, it had 22 plants in 15 countries. Prior to expanding manufacturing operations outside of the United States, Lincoln Electric had an almost unbroken string of profitable operations and is often put forward as the model of productivity gains and cost savings.

At the heart of Lincoln Electric's success is a strategy of building quality products at a lower cost than its competitors and passing the savings on to the customer by continuously lowering prices. Lincoln has been able to implement this strategy through an employee incentive system that fosters labor productivity increases arising from a pay-for-performance compensation plan. Wages are based entirely on piecework. In addition, a year-end bonus averages close to 100 percent of regular compensation.

A key element of Lincoln's organizational architecture, and the topic of this chapter, is the performance-evaluation system. There are two components of performance evaluation: pieces produced and merit rating. The first component of Lincoln's performance evaluation is an explicit performance measure for each production worker—the number of good units produced. The worker's wage is equal to the piece rate times the number of good units produced. (Workers are not paid

---

[1]N. Fast and N. Berg, "The Lincoln Electric Company," Harvard Business School Case 376–028 (1975). Lincoln Electric is a widely cited case study. See Paul Milgrom and John Roberts, "Complementarities and Fit: Strategy, Structure, and Organizational Change," *Journal of Accounting and Economics* (1994).

for defects.) The piece rates, set by the Time Study Department, allow workers producing at a standard rate to earn a wage comparable to those for similar jobs in the local labor market. However, by working hard and through lunch and coffee breaks, employees can double and sometimes triple their pay. Moreover, no piece rate is changed because a worker is making too much money. Any worker who has been at Lincoln for at least two years is guaranteed employment of at least 75 percent of the standard 40-hour week.

The second component of Lincoln's evaluation scheme is the employee's merit rating. These ratings are used to determine the worker's share of the bonus pool. The size of the bonus pool is about the same as wages and about twice Lincoln's net income after taxes, although there is substantial annual variation in the size of the pool. Each employee's merit evaluation is based on worker "dependability," "quality," "output," and "ideas and cooperation," as assessed primarily by the worker's immediate supervisor.

Two interesting observations emerge from Lincoln Electric. First, the performance-reward system uses as an input, the output from the performance-evaluation system. (The two systems are linked.) Second, the firm uses both highly objective, explicit measures of performance (piecework) and subjective measures ("ideas and cooperation").

What makes the performance-evaluation system interesting and a non-trivial aspect of the firm's organizational architecture is the observation that "performance appraisal is a process by which humans judge other humans."[2] Employee performance is evaluated for at least two reasons. First, performance evaluation provides workers with feedback on job performance which provides important information on how to improve job performance. Second, performance evaluation is used in determining rewards and sanctions (salary increases, bonuses, promotions, and firings). The issues that arise in studying performance evaluation can differ between the two purposes. For example, if an evaluation is used solely to provide feedback, workers are unlikely to take non-productive efforts to distort the evaluation to make themselves look better. But distortions to improve reported performance are more likely if workers are compensated based on performance.

In this chapter, we focus primarily on the second reason for performance evaluation—as input for setting rewards/sanctions for workers. This chapter describes the third leg of our three-legged stool that comprises the firm's organizational architecture, the performance-evaluation system. Performance evaluation involves evaluating both individuals and sub-units of the firm. This chapter focuses on individual performance evaluation; the next chapter examines various issues in evaluating sub-units of the firm.

The remaining sections of this chapter discuss two major topics. In the next section, explicit versus subjective performance measures are described followed by a discussion of how Equal Employment Opportunity laws affect performance evaluation. The following section describes various mechanisms for establishing

---

[2]G. Milkovich, and A. Wigdor, *Pay for Performance,* (National Academy Press, Washington, D.C., 1991).

performance benchmarks. These include absolute-performance evaluation and relative-performance evaluation. Another issue addressed is benchmarking performance of workers in teams. The last section summarizes the chapter.

Japanese Car Makers Adopt Performance Evaluations

The large Japanese automobile companies are beginning to adopt traditional Western performance evaluation systems and linking compensation and promotion more closely to individual performance.

Honda and Toyota have been examples of lifetime employment in Japan's auto industry. But in 1993 and 1994 both companies announced plans to change this practice. In 1993, Honda became the first Japanese car company to adopt a merit pay plan that ties the manager's pay to achieving performance goals. In 1994, Toyota announced that it would depart from its seniority-based pay and promotion system. Mazda and Nissan announced they were adopting merit pay systems for their managers in the summer of 1994.

Source: R. Johnson, ''Advance or Perish, Honda Tells Managers,'' *Automotive News* (March 18, 1994)

Explicit Vs. Subjective Performance Evaluation

A well-designed performance evaluation should have the following characteristics:[3]

- Improve employee development by communicating goals and providing feedback.
- Enhance the processes for setting wages, promotions, and terminations.
- Predict future success of the worker.
- Insure low cost of developing the appraisal process and of performing the evaluations.
- Provide an accurate (unbiased and low variance) assessment of workers' actual performance.

This section describes the two polar extremes (and indicates the continuum between them) used for performance evaluation, explicit and subjective evaluation systems. As we will see, these two extremes differ in terms of the above ideal characteristics. *Explicit performance measures* consist of items like output and sales that can be objectively measured. Explicit measures can be used in formal contracts between the worker and the firm. *Subjective performance measures* consist of non-contractible judgments about employee performance (the year-end evaluation from a supervisor).

---

[3]G. Milkovich and J. Newman, *Compensation* (Homewood, IL: Richard D. Irwin, 1993), pp. 304–306.

Few firms' performance measures are purely explicit or purely subjective, but include mixtures of both. In many cases, organizations that use explicit measures also use subjective measures to evaluate the same employee (for example, Lincoln Electric).

Explicit Performance Evaluation

The primary benefit of explicit performance measures is that they can be used in concrete agreements or contracts between the worker and the firm. For example, the worker receives a bonus if sales exceed $1 million. The worker knows what is expected and what will happen under different outcomes. In addition, the worker's evaluation is not subject to the potential biases and whims of a particular supervisor.

The use of explicit measures also involves potential costs:

Gaming. Explicit measures can motivate the worker to engage in nonproductive efforts to improve the evaluation. For example, a sales person might offer customer discounts to shift sales from one evaluation period to another. A worker paid based on output might reduce quality to increase output. A divisional manager compensated on weight of output might substitute toward heavier inputs (lead instead of aluminum). At Lincoln Electric, typewriters had counters to record the number of characters typed, and secretaries were paid on this basis. But piecework for secretaries was abandoned when one secretary who earned much more than the others was found staying at her desk during lunch and coffee breaks typing the same character as fast as she could.

Externalities. It is usually difficult to construct an explicit measure of how the efforts of one worker affect the productivity of other workers. Evaluating workers on narrow measures of individual output (which can often be explicitly measured) will not necessarily encourage teamwork and cooperation. One complaint by workers at Lincoln Electric is that their pay suffers when workers ahead of them on an assembly line are unable to keep them supplied with work. Their amount of piecework falls as well as their pay.

Unbalanced effort. Generally it is important for a worker to expend effort across a variety of tasks. For example, a worker might be expected to sell products to existing customers, contact potential new customers, and fill out reports. Some activities are easily measured, such as sales to existing customers. On the other hand, others, like the value of contacts with potential new customers, are more difficult to assess. If workers are heavily evaluated on what can be measured (sales), they will concentrate their efforts on these activities. A worker will not allocate an optimal amount of time to the other unmeasured activities.[4]

---

[4] Bengt Holmstrom and Paul Milgrom, "Multitask Principal-Agent Analysis: Incentive Contracts, Asset Ownership and Job Design," *Journal of Law Economics and Organization* 7 (1991). Note that this problem can affect optimal job design. For example, in some cases a firm might want to have certain workers concentrate on sales to current customers. These workers could then be evaluated on sales. Other workers would concentrate on contacting new customers and correspondingly be evaluated on other dimensions.

Measurement costs. Costs are incurred in generating performance measures. For example, cost accounting systems must be developed and maintained to keep track of divisional profits. Computer systems and software that can produce detailed reports are more complicated. Since the measures are used for performance evaluation, management and clerical time is spent making sure the numbers are ''right,'' and when they are ''wrong,''fixing them.

Horizon problems. Explicit evaluations tend to be short-run measures because of the difficulty of objectively measuring consequences that might occur in the future. Short-run, explicit performance measures cause workers about to change jobs or leave the firm to concentrate their efforts on producing results that will favorably influence their appraisals before they move. For example, consider a 64-year-old salesperson paid on commission and facing mandatory retirement at age 65. This person will invest little time developing new customers for whom sales are not expected within the year.

Gaming Objective Performance Evaluation Schemes

This example illustrates how one manager successfully gamed the performance evaluation system used in deciding when to close unprofitable mines.

''In this particular company, mines were shut down after the yield per ton of ore dropped below a certain level. One old marginal mine managed to stay open for several years because of the strategic behavior of its management. It happened that the mine contained one very rich pocket of ore. Instead of mining this all at once, the management used it as its reserve. Every time the yield of the ore it was mining fell below an acceptable level, it would mix in a little high grade ore so the mine would remain open.''

Suggested by E. Lawler and J. Rhode, *Information and Control in Organizations* (Santa Monica, Calif.: Goodyear Publishing, 1976), pp. 87–88.

Subjective Performance Evaluation

Most employees are not evaluated exclusively through explicit measures. Rather their performance evaluations tend to include subjective elements. For example, most workers receive annual performance reviews from supervisors. These reviews often form the basis for setting salaries and promotions. Even when compensation is based entirely on explicit measures (piece rate in agriculture), the firm reserves the right to fire employees for low-quality production, tardiness, the inability to get along with co-workers, or other undesirable behavior. Lincoln Electric bases factory workers' wages entirely on piecework, which is an explicit performance measure. But in addition to this objective measure, Lincoln also uses a subjective merit evaluation to set the employee bonus, which is about the same magnitude as wages.

A potential benefit of subjective performance evaluation is that an employee's performance can be evaluated on a comprehensive basis (i.e, aspects of the job that are not easily measured can be considered along with more easily measured activities). For example, the supervisor can consider the employee's efforts at being cooperative, being part of a team, being nice to potential customers or filling out reports accurately. The Lincoln Electric merit-pay evaluation is based on "dependability, quality, output," and "ideas and cooperation."

There are two widely used subjective performance appraisal systems: standard-rating-scale systems and goal-based systems. Goal-based systems tend to be more explicit and objective than standard-rating-scale systems. Standard rating scales require the evaluator to rank the employee on a number of different performance factors using a five-point scale: far exceeds requirements, exceeds requirements, meets all requirements, partially meets requirements, does not meet requirements. The different performance factors judged vary across firms and positions within firms but often include the following:

Achieves forecasts, budgets, objectives.

Sets and attains high performance goals for self and group.

Organizes effective performance through oral and written communications.

Emphasizes teamwork among subordinates.

Updates knowledge of job-related skills.

Identifies problems and resolves problems.

Evaluates subordinates objectively.

Ensures equal opportunities for all subordinates.

After ranking the subordinate on these criteria, the evaluator then assigns an overall job rating: excellent, better than satisfactory, satisfactory, needs further improvement, and unsatisfactory. Most subjective performance appraisals contain a section where the supervisor provides detailed comments on the employee's strengths and weaknesses and offers specific recommendations for improvement and further employee development.

In a goal-based system, each subordinate is given a set of goals for the year. For example, one goal might be to hold training sessions for all employees in the department by November 1. Another objective is to hire four additional qualified members of minority groups. These goals tend to be more explicit and easier to measure than the more vague performance factors used in the standard rating scales such as "emphasizes teamwork." Nevertheless, these goals are still more subjective than explicit piecework measures. At the end of the year, the supervisor writes an essay detailing the extent to which each goal is met. An overall, subjective evaluation of the worker is based on the extent to which the goals are achieved.

After the supervisor has rated the employee using either standard rating scales or a goal-oriented system, the supervisor usually first reviews the evaluation with his supervisor. This helps ensure the accuracy of the review and promotes consistency of criteria across employees. Next the supervisor gives a copy of the evaluation to the worker and meets with the subordinate to review the evaluation. The employee is given the opportunity to respond in writing to the evaluation, including the expression of formal disagreement with any of the specifics in the appraisal. Finally, the evaluator and his supervisor review the feedback provided by the evaluator and the employee's response.

In the vast majority of cases, the employee's immediate supervisor does the performance evaluation. In a few cases, firms have experimented with peer evaluations, especially in situations where teams are important. The benefit of peer evaluations is that peers have a better understanding of typical performance in group assignments and the actual contribution of the individual to the team. Offsetting the better specific knowledge of peers is the fact that everyone in the team requires costly training in performing evaluations. Moreover, peer evaluation can increase the tensions generated within the team. The team might decide to collude to give everyone a high performance rating. A subsequent section discusses performance evaluations within teams more fully.

360-Degree Performance Reviews

This example demonstrates that peer review systems are not new. What is new is the jargon invented to make peer review systems appear to be a recent innovation. The current jargon includes the phrase ''360-Degree Performance Reviews.''

Privately-held W.L. Gore & Associates employs 5,600 workers and manufactures Gore-Tex waterproof fabric. All workers are called associates. There are no ''bosses,'' but each worker is assigned a ''sponsor'' who acts as a mentor.

Gore has been using 360-degree performance feedback since 1958. Under their system, annual evaluations are gathered on all associates from the individual's peers, subordinates, and superiors. The evaluations are anonymous and rate workers on their contributions to the success of the business during the past year. All ratings on each employee receive equal weight. Compensation committees composed of sponsors with specialized knowledge of the area use the rankings to award pay increases or performance warnings.

Boeing Company, the aircraft manufacturer headquartered in Seattle, Washington, began using 360-degree reviews in 1992.

Source: J. Lopez, ''A Better Way?'' *The Wall Street Journal Supplement* (April 13, 1994) p. R6.

There are at least three potential problems with subjective performance evaluation. First, there is the potential that the firm will renege on promises to workers to reward good performance.[5] For example, management might promise to give raises to those who perform well. Afterward, management might unjustifiably say that work is poor to avoid higher payments. It is less likely that a worker will be

---

[5]George Baker, Robert Gibbons, and Kevin Murphy, ''Subjective Performance Measures in Optimal Incentive Contracts,'' *Quarterly Journal of Economics,* (forthcoming).

successful in a lawsuit involving subjective performance measurement than when the worker can document that a firm reneged on an explicit contract. The incentive to renege on implicit contracts will be largest for firms in financial difficulty (near bankruptcy). Yet reneging also can occur when a supervisor has a short horizon with the firm and is compensated on unit profits. (Unit profits might be increased in the short run by not granting raises to employees.) Managers in ongoing firms, however, will often have incentives to maintain good reputations for honoring contracts. We discuss these issues further in Chapter 18.

A second potential problem with subjective measures is bias or favoritism among supervisors.[6] Supervisors do not bear the full wealth effects of their decisions. Therefore, there is the potential agency problem that supervisors will not be objective and careful in performance evaluation. For example, a supervisor might tend to rate all performance highly to avoid conflict with subordinates. Alternatively, the supervisor might rank workers based on the supervisor's personal likes and dislikes rather than on job performance. Bias adds noise to the performance-evaluation system and typically reduces morale and the employees' incentives to work hard, thereby lowering overall firm output.

Indirect empirical evidence suggests managers tend to assign relatively uniform performance ratings to workers. In a study of 7,000 performance ratings of managers and professionals in two firms, the researchers report that 95 percent of all appraisals were in just two categories: Good and Superior (Outstanding).[7] A survey of employee attitudes at Merck & Company, a large U.S. pharmaceutical firm, reported the following attitudes:[8]

- Managers are afraid to give experienced people a 1, 2, or 3 rating. It's easier to give everyone a 4 and give new people a 3.

- Charlie's been in that job for 20 years. He hasn't done anything creative for the last 15 years. Do you think my boss would give him a 3 rating? No way! Then he'd have to spend 12 months listening to Charlie complain.

This evidence suggests that supervisors bear nonpecuniary costs from low-rated, disgruntled workers. In response, supervisors bias their evaluations and hence performance ratings are inaccurate appraisals of the employee's true performance. Biased, inaccurate appraisals reduce the incentive of employees to improve their performance by working harder and can cause less qualified people to be promoted to job openings. The problem does not lie in the evaluation system per se, but rather in the incentives of the evaluators.[9]

---

[6]Candice Prendergast and Robert Topel, "Discretion and Bias in Performance Evaluations," working paper, University of Chicago (1993) and C. Prendergast, "An Agency Approach to Bias in Organizations," working paper, University of Chicago, 1992.

[7]J. Medoff and K. Abraham, "Experience, Performance, and Earnings," *Quarterly Journal of Economics* 95 (December 1980), pp. 703–736.

[8]Quotes excerpted from a 1985 Merck report by Kevin Murphy, "Performance Measurement and Appraisal: Motivating Managers to Identify and Reward Performance," in *Performance Measurement, Evaluation, and Incentives,* W. Bruns, ed., (Boston: Harvard Business School Press, 1992), pp. 37–62.

[9]See Kevin Murphy (1992).

To overcome the tendency to rate all employees above average, some firms require a forced distribution where a fixed fraction of employees are assigned to each category (i.e., the supervisor must rank a certain percentage of the employees as poor). However, forced distributions may not accurately reflect the true distribution of performance in each work group. Forced ranking systems can cause problems, especially when the size of the group being evaluated is small. For example, having to rank one of four workers as poor might force the supervisor to rate a good-performing worker as poor. The inaccuracies from the forced distribution might be larger than those from a biased supervisor. Moreover, forced distributions do not reduce the nonpecuniary costs imposed on the supervisor. Under a forced distribution, supervisors might assign ratings based on the nonpecuniary costs employees will impose on them and not based on the employee's true performances.

Explicit and Subjective Performance Evaluation at Fiat

This example illustrates how one very large company, Fiat, combines both explicit and subjective performance reviews into a single, integrated system.

The Italian firm, Fiat, is one of the world's largest corporations with over 250,000 employees in 16 operating sectors. While automobiles are its largest product, Fiat also has operating units in railway systems, aviation, publishing and communications, and financial and real estate services.

In the 1980s Fiat introduced a formal management-by-objectives (MBO) evaluation program for their 500 highest level managers. Under the MBO program, annual bonuses of up to about 30 percent of their base salary are awarded for meeting objectives.

Each manager has a set of objectives tailored to the specific situation. Managers in charge of profit centers have profit and debt objectives. Profit targets are defined in terms of net profit before taxes. Because Fiat had a dangerously high level of debt in the 1980s, profit center managers also were given objectives to lower their group's borrowings. Besides these specific financial objectives, managers have other performance indicators such as increasing sales in particular markets, completing an acquisition, improving quality or customer service, and introducing new products or processes.

Even though each manager meets the objectives, unless the manager's larger group achieves its goals, no bonus would be paid. For example, the Fiat Group has 16 sectors headed by a manager. If the entire Fiat Group fails to meet its objectives, none of the 16 sector managers receive their bonuses even though some of them achieved their goals.

Each manager has a set of weightings attached to each objective. Unless the manager achieves a minimum level of profits before taxes, no bonus is paid. Once this threshold profit level is achieved, then the weights attached are 20 to 40 percent on profits, 10 to 20 percent on reducing debt, 10 to 15 percent for each of three or four other performance targets. Each objective is scored on a five point scale with three being the minimum acceptable score.

Explicit and Subjective Performance Evaluation at Fiat—Continued

Superiors set the targets for each objective. In setting the performance targets, the following probabilities of achieving each target are supposed to be used:

Performance Level	Ideal Probability of Achievement
3 (threshold)	90%–99%
4 (good)	50%–60%
5 (excellent)	10%–20%

For example, suppose "install new production-control system" is an objective that has a weighting of 20 percent. If the system is installed by November it is judged as a "3" threshold. To achieve a "4," installation must be completed by October. And a "5" is earned if completed by September. If actual completion is October, a 4 is earned with a weighting of 20 percent and 0.80 (4 × 20 percent) is added to the manager's other performance objectives to compute an overall grade, say 3.69.

A performance rating of 3 receives a bonus of 12 percent of salary. Ratings below 3 receive no bonus. A rating of 4 receives an 18 percent bonus, and a 5 receives a 30 percent bonus. Fractional ratings are scaled (e.g., a 3.69 receives 12 percent + 0.69 × [18 percent − 12 percent] or 16.14 percent). The median manager's rating is between 4.1 and 4.4. In any given year about 10 percent of the managers are rated below 3.0 and about 15 percent are rated 4.9 or better.

The performance-evaluation system at Fiat is similar to those used by large U.S. corporations.

Source: K. Merchant and A. Riccaboni, "Evolution of Performance-Based Management Incentives at the Fiat Group," in *Performance Measurement, Evaluation, and Incentives,* W. Bruns, ed., (Boston: Harvard Business School Press, 1992), pp. 63–96.

Supervisors will have increased incentives to do a good job if they are evaluated and compensated on the job they do in evaluating lower-level employees. Problems of bias are likely to be lower if the supervisor is held accountable for the future performance of individuals that are promoted based on the supervisor's recommendation. If bias is a problem, job supervisors' discretion over performance evaluations can be limited.

Third, there are costs that arise from employees trying to influence the decisions of supervisors. Influence costs were discussed in Chapter 9. One potential method of reducing these costs is to rotate supervisors or employees more frequently (getting on the good side of one supervisor is of limited benefit). Rotation of supervisors or workers, however, can limit potential synergies and cost reductions that arise with repeated interaction between a given manager and employee. New supervisors have limited knowledge of employees' specialized skills.

We have pointed out potential problems with explicit and subjective performance measures. When these problems are large, an alternative is not to rely heavily on performance evaluations for setting rewards and punishments. Paying workers straight salary and giving simple cost-of-living raises to all employees will lead to predictable shirking and other agency problems. However, in some cases the costs of trying to address these problems might be less than the benefits. But a manager should consider carefully the alternatives before choosing no incentive compensation (given the obvious agency problems associated with this choice).

Equal Employment Opportunity

The preceding discussion described individual performance evaluation by firms as though the markets for labor (including managerial labor markets) are unregulated. The discussion so far assumed the only constraints faced by firms regarding their performance evaluation and reward systems are those of supply and demand for labor. But government regulates labor markets and hence imposes another set of constraints. Since the 1960s, Federal laws in the United States dealing with affirmative action and equal employment opportunity (EEO) have had a major effect on both the performance-evaluation systems and the reward and punishment systems. The legislation and court actions have forced companies to document their compensation and promotion decisions to demonstrate their actions were related to performance and were not influenced by the employee's race, color, religion, sex, age, or national origin.

EEO has had a significant impact on the performance appraisal systems. In deciding cases involving alleged discriminatory employment practices, the courts look more favorably at companies with the following characteristics:[10]

- Similar individuals in the firm are treated equally and consistently.
- The firm's job descriptions are clearly written and well-defined.
- The appraisal system has clear criteria for evaluating performance such as written objective scales and dimensions.
- There are specific written instructions on how to complete the performance appraisal.
- Employees are provided feedback about their performance appraisal.
- Higher level supervisors' evaluations are incorporated into the appraisal system.

While the preceding characteristics appear sensible and even worthwhile, EEO has had negative side effects. The presence of possible legal scrutiny of the firm's performance-evaluation systems cause these systems to become more formal, more explicit, with less reliance on subjective appraisal. Every action and appraisal must be documented. The firm's personnel (human resources) department assumes the role of ensuring the firm is complying with the labor laws. The performance appraisal system that meets EEO criteria would not necessarily be the optimum system without that regulation. For example, many Japanese managers try "to make

---

[10]Milkovich and Newman, *Compensation* (Homewood, IL: Richard D. Irwin, 1993), pp. 316–318.

everybody feel that he is slated for the top position in the firm''[11] by delaying performance appraisals and differentiating among cohorts for 12 to 15 years after joining the firm. Such lack of annual feedback to employees would potentially run afoul of the affirmative-action laws in the United States and thus would be strenuously opposed by the personnel departments at most large corporations. Thus, U.S. firms find it more difficult to use less-formal, less-structured performance-evaluation systems than their foreign competitors, even though such systems might be firm-value enhancing in a less regulated setting. Moreover, EEO regulations cause U.S. firms to spend more money than they would otherwise on appraisal systems that document to a court's satisfaction the firm's compliance with affirmative-action regulations. Thus, EEO regulations likely cause some U.S. firms to adopt different performance appraisal systems. This is another example of how regulation can affect the firm's optimal choice of organizational architecture.

Establishing a Performance Benchmark

In assessing performance, a benchmark or standard is required. If an employee is to be judged as superior, excellent, or below normal, some notion of "normal" or "average" performance is required. If a salesperson is being evaluated and sells $135,000 worth of products this month, is this level of sales good or bad? In Lincoln Electric, workers are paid on a piece rate. But how much should each piece be paid? If a workers' job is assembling welding machines, how much should he be paid for each defect-free assembled welder? To illustrate the issues involved with choosing a performance benchmark or piece rate, consider the following simplified example.

Craig Cook can assemble a particular model of welder at the following daily rate:

$$\text{Units assembled} = 5\,h + u,$$

where h = the number of hours of normal effort worked, and u is a random error term. If Craig works 8 hours at a normal effort level, $h = 8$; then on average 40 welders (5×8) are assembled. On average the error, u, is zero. If he works 8 hours but at a faster, more strenuous pace, $h > 8$, say $h = 12$; then 60 units per day are assembled on average. If he slacks off and takes numerous short breaks, h might only be 5 and 25 units on average are assembled. If h, the effort expended over the work day, is observable and verifiable by the firm, then it would be optimal to pay Craig by the amount of effort expended. But in our example, assume h is not verifiable.

While the average error, u, is zero, the number of units assembled is subject to potentially large shocks which means that the variance of u is not zero. For example, if low-quality parts or subassemblies have been purchased or produced, the number of units assembled will be down even though Craig expended normal amounts of

---

[11]N. Hatvany and V. Pucik, "Japanese Managerial Practices and Productivity," *Organizational Dynamics*, (Spring, 1981), p. 13. Also, see M. Aoki, *Information, Incentives and Bargaining in the Japanese Economy* (Cambridge: Cambridge University Press, 1988).

effort ($h \geq 8$) because more time is required to fit together the slightly out-of-specification parts. Or perhaps Craig is idled for a few minutes each hour waiting for delivery of parts. In these cases, u is negative. Alternatively, he might get lucky and assemble more than $5h$ units because of an unusually good set of parts, ample parts inventory, good tools, or few distractions.

Using the simple facts in the above example, we illustrate several mechanisms commonly used to set the benchmark of expected or normal performance. All the benchmarking methods can be classified into either absolute performance evaluations or relative performance evaluations.

Absolute Performance Evaluation

The assembly department in the preceding example could establish the benchmark of 40 units assembled per worker per day. Production above 40 is considered good performance and less than 40 is considered poor performance. The standard of 40 is absolute in the sense that it is fixed and known before the worker exerts effort. Management, however, might not know exactly the relation between effort and production (Units assembled = $5h + u$) nor that the average worker exerts 8 units of effort a day. Thus, to use this type of absolute benchmark, the output of the average assembler must be estimated. There are at least two ways to do this: motion and time studies and using past production data.

Motion and Time Studies.   In motion and time studies industrial engineers estimate how much time a particular task or work activity requires with the goal of determining the preferable work method. Motion studies involve the systematic analysis of work methods considering the raw materials, the design of the product or process, the process or order of work, the tools, and the activity of each step. Besides estimating how long a particular activity should take, industrial engineers are often able to redesign the product or process to reduce the required time. Time studies employ a wide variety of techniques for determining the duration a particular activity requires under certain standard conditions. Work sampling, one type of time study, involves selecting a large number of observations taken at random intervals and observing how long workers take performing various components of the job. Motion and time studies are often expensive in terms of engineering time used in the studies. They also suffer from potential bias because of employees' incentives to under perform during the study period to set lower quotas.

Past Performance.   Using data on past performance is a very common mechanism for setting absolute performance goals. Unfortunately, it leads to perverse incentives called the *ratchet effect*. The ratchet effect refers to basing next year's standard of performance on this year's actual performance. However, performance targets usually are adjusted in only one direction: upward. A bad year usually does not cause subsequent years' targets to fall. This "ratcheting up" of standards cause workers to avoid exceeding the quota so as not to raise the standard next period. In the old Soviet Union, central planners would set a plant's production quota based on past experience. Plant managers meeting their targets received various rewards and those missing the target were punished. This created incentives for managers to just barely meet the quota.

Basing performance targets on past performance also creates incentives for managers to smooth or defer good performance. For example, companies often base a salesperson's bonus on meeting target sales where the target is based on last year's sales. If sales people expect an unusually good year, they will try to defer some sales into the next fiscal year. They may take the customer's order but not turn it in to the company until the next fiscal year. In one large automobile engine assembly plant, a labor-productivity performance goal was mandated each year. Each department's target was based in part on last year's performance. This created incentives for managers to defer making big productivity improvements in any one year, preferring instead to spread them over several years.[12]

Lincoln Electric avoids the dysfunctional problems of the ratchet effect by having a policy that the piecework rate cannot be changed because the worker is making too much money. Once a piecework rate is set by the Time Study Department, it is never changed until production methods or processes are changed or unless the worker challenges the rate and a new time study is conducted. By committing to not changing the piecework rate, Lincoln Electric avoids the perverse incentives due to the ratchet effect.

Another way to reduce the problems caused by ratcheting up each year's performance targets is more frequent job rotation. If you know that next year someone else has to meet your sales figures for this year, you will sell more now. However, job rotation destroys job-specific human capital such as customer-specific relations.

Relative Performance Evaluation[13]

Even if the company can get a good estimate of average performance, there are problems with an absolute benchmark. In particular, employees are evaluated in part on factors beyond their control. For example, if Craig in assembling welders exerts average effort of $h = 8$, he expect to produce 40 units. However, some days he will assemble more and receive positive evaluations, and some days he will assemble less and receive negative evaluations. If the variation in the random error term is large, actual output can deviate substantially from what he expected. In a well-controlled manufacturing setting, the variance of the random errors will be small. But in other settings, such as a salesperson facing considerable uncertainty from competitors and other economy-wide factors (e.g., interest rates, economic growth, tax rates), the variance of the random errors can be large.

---

[12]Robert Kaplan and Amy Sweeney, "Peoria Engine Plant (A)," Harvard Business School Case 9–193–082 (June 1993).

[13]See Bengt Holmstrom, "Moral Hazard in Teams," *Bell Journal of Economics,* Autumn 1982, pp. 324–40 and Robert Gibbons and Kevin Murphy, "Relative Performance Evaluation for Chief Executive Officers," *Industrial and Labor Relations Review,* February 1990, pp. 30S–51S.

In the presence of large uncontrollable factors, absolute performance evaluations violate one of the desirable characteristics of a well-designed appraisal system: providing an accurate (unbiased and low variance) assessment of workers' actual performance. When uncontrollable factors enter the performance evaluation additional risk is imposed on the employee. Since people are risk-averse, they must be compensated to bear the risk. Everything else equal, if comparing two identical sales jobs, the one with fewer random fluctuations in performance will be the preferred job. The other job will have to pay the worker a compensating differential to entice her to bear the additional risk. Thus, it is in the firm's interest to reduce the risk workers face from factors beyond their control.

Management can reduce the risk from uncontrollable factors if they can accurately estimate u, the random, uncontrollable common shock. For example, suppose the sales-person's sales target is 8,800 units. If management thinks u was negative in a given month, it can adjust the target downward and not penalize the employee for negative factors beyond her control. If management believes u is $+300$ for the month, the benchmark performance is raised to 9,100. In assigning course grades, many instructors "curve" the grades. Instead of awarding A's for scores of 94 to 100, the top 15 percent of the class receives A's. Curving the grades controls for unusually easy or hard exams and is a way of removing some of the risk from students.

The advantage of adjusting the benchmark performance for uncontrollable shocks is that it reduces the risk the worker bears. This improves the risk-averse employee's welfare. Everything else held constant, the employee does not have to be compensated for bearing this risk, and total compensation expense is reduced. Thus, firms have incentive to reduce risks borne by employees.

Sometimes management can acquire information on u, the uncontrollable factors, by observing the output of workers in similar situations (either inside or outside the firm). If these other workers are exposed to the same random events as the workers we wish to benchmark (both groups sell products to the same customers), then management can make inferences about u from observing the actual performance of the comparison group. Reference groups can be formed using workers in the same firm or similar workers in different firms. For example, publicly-traded firms must select a benchmark reference group of other firms and report how their firm has performed relative to that benchmark. This is an example of selecting a reference group outside the firm. When evaluating professors for tenure, most universities compare the candidate's teaching and research record to recently-promoted peers in the same department. This is an example of a within-firm reference group.

Within-Firm Comparisons.   Using sales people in the same firm to estimate u has the benefit that the reference group is likely to be subject to similar shocks. They all sell the same products and face the same competitors and economy-wide factors. However, forming a reference group from workers inside the same firm has some drawbacks. In many cases, workers' jobs are dissimilar. Some salespeople have large established territories, others small developing ones. Customer types can vary dramatically across sales territories.

If an internal reference group is formed and its group average is used to assess normal performance, the group has incentives to punish high-producing workers who raise the average. In a classic research study known as the Hawthorne experiments, workers were observed physically hitting those colleagues who exceeded the commonly accepted output rate.[14] Thus, worker collusion to hold down the benchmark can occur. Also, instances of sabotage are observed in relative-performance evaluations. Instead of working hard and increasing performance, co-workers sabotage their peers in the reference group. Alternatively, employees might try to get themselves classified into a reference group that has weak performance so they will appear above average.

Relative-performance evaluation also affects recruiting incentives. Workers often are involved in interviewing and selecting potential colleagues. If paid based on relative performance, such workers have incentive to sabotage recruiting by hiring less competent new workers. This raises the relative performance of the older workers.

Potential Costs of Relative Performance Evaluations

Individuals gaming performance evaluation systems are not uncommon. This example illustrates the lengths some people go to sabotage others when their advancement is based on relative performance evaluations.

> I was recently talking to a friend of mine who works at a big bank. When I asked him about his new promotion, he told me how he got it. He managed to crack the network messaging system so that he could monitor all the memos. He also sabotaged the work group software and set back careers of a few company-naive souls who didn't realize that someone was manipulating their appointment calendars. They would miss important meetings and be sent on wild-goose chases, only to look like complete buffoons when they showed up for appointments that were never made. By the time any of these bumpkins knew what hit them, they had a new vice president.

Source: John C. Dvorak, "New Age of Villainy." *PC Magazine* (September 27, 1988).

Across-Firm Performance.   To overcome a lack of an internal reference group or to avoid the pernicious actions of sabotage and collusion, some firms employ external benchmarking. Firms either exchange information directly or do so through a trade association that aggregates across several firms to mask individual firm information. Thus, average performance in other firms is used as the reference group. Among the disadvantages of this method is that the workers in other firms may not be subject to the same common shocks as our workers. Thus, a firm might

---

[14]H. M. Parsons, "What Happened at Hawthorne?" *Science* 183 (March 8, 1974), p. 927.

increase the uncontrollable risk to which its workers are exposed. External bench-marking is often precluded by data availability. Other firms view their performance data as proprietary and highly confidential. Even if firms are willing to share data, if the firms are in the same industry such cooperation potentially is viewed as illegal under the antitrust laws. For example, in the early 1990s Ivy League colleges had to defend themselves for alleged antitrust violations because they shared faculty salary data.

Ideally, firms should try to shield workers from as much uncontrollable risk as possible. This implies that using both within-firm and across-firm comparisons where possible will reduce the risk workers face better than using either method exclusively.

Evidence exists supporting the use of relative-performance evaluation by certain companies. One study examines whether the CEO's compensation (salary plus bonus) and turnover likelihood depend on relative performance evaluation.[15] The authors use 2,214 CEOs serving in 1,295 large publicly-traded U.S. corporations from 1974 to 1986. They find that the CEO's compensation is positively related to his own stock return performance and negatively related to the stock return in the market and industry. That is, compensation is higher when the CEO's own firm's stock return is higher and when the market or industry stock return is down. Finally, the authors study the likelihood the CEO is replaced. Executive turnover is lower the larger the firm's own stock price return and the lower the industry return. If the industry is performing poorly, the CEO is more likely retained. Another study fo-cuses on subsidiary bank managers in multibank holding companies.[16] Turnover of these managers is greater when their own bank's performance is poor and when the median bank's performance in the same holding company is high. Both studies' findings are consistent with industry risk being filtered out of compensation and retention decisions.

In summary, relative performance evaluation has benefits and costs. The benefits include shielding workers from common risks, thereby reducing the risk premium these workers must be paid. The costs of relative performance evaluation include the costs of calculating the common shock and the costs of the dysfunctional incentives created by relative performance evaluation including collusion and sabotage. A model of relative performance evaluation is provided in the appendix at the end of the chapter.

Evaluating Teams

As discussed in Chapter 9, there has been a recent movement toward using teams at all levels of the organization. Companies are finding that in many applications, the potential for team production exceeds what can be produced by individuals

---

[15]ibbons and Murphy (1990).

[16]David Blackwell, James Brickley, and Michael Weisbach, "Accounting Information and Internal Performance Evaluation: Evidence from Texas Banks," *Journal of Accounting and Economics* 17 (May 1994), pp. 331–358.

working independently. Teams are often formed because they are more successful at assembling specialized knowledge for decision making than at trying to pass the knowledge through the traditional hierarchy. If the firm uses teams, again a performance benchmark is required.

Calling a group of individuals a team does not necessarily increase productivity. If individuals are evaluated only on individual performance there will be limited incentives to worry about team output. To promote joint effort and teamwork, it is usually important to evaluate team members, at least in part, on team output. Using team output focuses team members on a common objective and helps promote co-operation. One of the key roles of management in forming teams is choosing appropriate evaluation measures. Often it is appropriate to choose the team as the basic unit of performance evaluation.

Peer Review Performance Ratings of Teams

This example describes the specific areas and skills evaluated for individuals working on teams.

One small company is organized around nine management teams. Each team member rates all other team members on a five point scale on each of the following topics:

- Expresses opinions freely.
- Comes to meetings prepared.
- Takes initiative.
- Accepts criticism.
- Listens to others.
- Delegates authority.
- Shares information freely.
- Bases decisions on sound data.
- Values all customers.
- Recognizes others' contributions.

These individual peer ratings are then averaged across team members and items to arrive at an overall peer evaluation for each team member.

Pay and promotion decisions as well as future team assignments are based on these evaluations along with the team's overall performance.

Consider the case of student project teams in courses. Such projects build leadership skills and teach students how to work more effectively in teams. Such projects also enhance learning by allowing students to share their understanding and helping all students on the team to learn more than if they each did the project individually. Instructors assigning projects to study teams generally give the same grade to all members of the team. Thus, the team is evaluated based on the team's joint output.

Individual performance of team members, however, must also be evaluated or else members of a team will have strong incentives to free-ride. Often individual performance is evaluated by the team members, themselves, who have specific knowledge on the work effort of the individual. Team members can then impose penalties on shirking team members. (They can ask for an individual to be removed from the team.) One of the key functions of new teams is to develop the internal rules of the game for the team. Decision rights and work efforts must be partitioned among the team. Accordingly, team members must decide on how to evaluate the work efforts of team members. Finally, team members must decide on the rewards and punishments for members of the group. (Sometimes the rewards/punishments are social—e.g., a shirking member may be ostracized, etc.)

Returning to the student case project, instead of assigning all the members of the team the same project grade, the total project grade can be apportioned among the team members based on their peer reviews where unequal team grades are possible. Thus, while the overall project's grade might be a B+, some team members might receive an A− and others a B as long as the average across the team is a B+. Providing the team with the decision rights to evaluate each other reduces the free-rider problem and increases team production. But it can also reduce morale and lead to increased influence costs as team members lobby each other for better evaluations.

Peer Pressure in Teams

Levi Strauss, maker of Levi jeans, installed 39 multitask teams in one of its sewing plants. Each team has 20 to 30 workers responsible for completing individual orders by assembling full pairs of pants, instead of each worker specializing as zipper sewers or belt-loop attachers. In essence, at this plant jobs were redesigned from being functional to being more multitask and process-oriented (recall Chapter 10 discussion).

Worker incentive compensation is based on team output which creates incentives to free-ride. This has caused absenteeism and shirking, which caused tempers to flare. Supervisors on the plant floor spend more time intervening to prevent "big fights." The plant manager reports, "Peer pressure can be vicious and brutal." Before installing the multitask teams, each worker received two weeks of training in group dynamics and an additional one-day seminar in "let's-get-along sessions" with private consultants. These training sessions have not resolved the conflicts.

Suggested by "Managing by Values," *Business Week* (August 1, 1994), p. 50.

Summary

Performance evaluation is conducted for both individuals within the firm and subunits of the firm. How did Sally perform and how did Harry perform? Such questions require individual performance evaluations. Sally and Harry are in the automotive products group. How did this group perform? Answering this second question requires divisional performance measures. Individual performance-evaluation systems are the focus of this chapter and divisional performance evaluation is discussed in Chapter 14. Individual performance-evaluation systems differ in their degree of subjectivity. While objective, explicit schemes are desirable, most jobs involve multiple, difficult-to-measure outputs. Explicit evaluations, while offering concrete, contractible numbers, have several disadvantages, including gaming, interactions (externalities) among workers, measurement costs, and horizon problems. Most performance evaluations that contain explicit, objective measures also contain subjective measures.

Subjective evaluations can be based on either standard rating scales (usually five or seven points) for a number of different areas or goal-based schemes. Standard rating scales have the appearance of objectivity, but entail subjective judgments by the evaluator. Goal-based schemes set performance targets at the beginning of the year that the evaluator uses at the end of the year to determine an overall, subjective evaluation.

Subjective performance measures allow workers' effort to be evaluated on a comprehensive basis. But subjectivity also comes at a cost. It becomes easier for a manager or the firm to renege on the promise to reward good performance because it is harder to define what is ''good.'' There is more latitude to introduce favoritism and bias in subjective measures. Finally, subjective systems generate more influence costs as workers try to lobby for better ratings.

The equal employment opportunity laws in the United States have had a pronounced effect on performance-evaluation systems. Defending oneself against affirmative action lawsuits has caused firms to adopt more explicit, objective appraisal systems than they otherwise would have chosen voluntarily.

Evaluating performance also requires performance benchmarks. There are two general types of performance targets: absolute targets and relative targets. Absolute performance benchmarks are set at the beginning of the period and rarely adjusted for random, unusual events. Lincoln Electric sets the piece rates and hence the absolute performance benchmark when the job is established and sticks with it. These absolute benchmarks can be estimated using motion and time studies or by using past performance. If absolute performance benchmarks are estimated using past performance, dysfunctional incentives due to the ratchet effect will result. Workers will limit output if they expect next period's target benchmark will be raised.

Relative performance evaluation requires the firm to establish a reference group of workers to use as the benchmark. The reference group can either be within the same firm or outside the firm. Relative performance uses the reference group to filter out some of the common risk borne by workers. This reduces the firm's compensation bill because workers need no longer be paid to bear this risk. But relative performance evaluations can lead employees to collude or sabotage co-workers to improve their evaluations. Moreover, establishing the appropriate reference group and measuring its performance is costly.

Finally, evaluating teams of employees usually requires a measure of team performance while still recognizing individual contributions to the team. Individual performance is rewarded to overcome free-rider problems. In some cases, each team member's bonus is based on individual performance, but the bonus is only paid if the entire team meets or exceeds its cost, revenue, profit, or return on investment goal.

The next chapter completes the discussion of performance evaluation by describing divisional performance evaluation.

APPENDIX TO CHAPTER 13

THE OPTIMAL WEIGHT IN A RELATIVE-PERFORMANCE CONTRACT[17]

In this chapter we argued that it can be optimal to base a worker's pay on performance *relative* to some benchmark group, such as workers within the same organization who perform similar tasks. The advantage of this type of system is that it filters out common shocks in the evaluation of workers and thus reduces the costs of inefficient risk bearing. In this appendix, we consider how a risk-neutral firm might optimally weight the performance of such a benchmark group in a compensation contract.

For simplicity, we restrict our attention to simple linear compensation contracts of the following form:

$$\text{Compensation} = a + \beta(Q - \lambda Q_a), \tag{A1}$$

where a and β are fixed parameters, Q is the worker's own output, and Q_a is the average output of the benchmark group (for example, similar workers in the firm). We are interested in how to choose the optimal λ. Note that if $\lambda = 0$, average output receives no weight and thus is left out of the contract. In contrast, if $\lambda = 1$, then compensation is based on a simple difference between own output and average output. As we will see, however, the firm might well want to choose other values for λ.

We begin by showing that, under certain assumptions, the worker's effort choice is independent of λ. In this case, the firm can choose λ without being concerned about how it might affect worker productivity. In particular, suppose that the worker's cost of exerting effort is given by the function $C(e)$, which expresses the disutility of effort in dollar equivalents. The worker's certainty equivalent can be approximated by the following formula:[18]

$$\text{Certainty Equivalent} = E[a + \beta(Q - \lambda Q_a)] - .5\rho s^2 - C(e), \tag{A2}$$

---

[17]This appendix requires elementary knowledge of statistics, decision theory and calculus. The basic model in this section is similar to the model used in Paul Milgrom and John Roberts, *Economics Organization & Management*, Prentice Hall, Englewood Cliffs, New Jersey, 1992, chapter 7.

[18]A certainty equivalent is the amount of cash that employees would require with certainty to make them indifferent between this certain sum and the uncertain income stream. The approximation of the certainty equivalent in equation (A2) is a basic result in decision theory. It holds when the risk is small and the utility function is sufficiently smooth. See, for example, Jonathan E. Ingersoll, *Theory of Financial Decision Making*, Rowman & Littlefield, Totowa, New Jersey, 1987, page 38.

where E denotes the expectation operator, ρ is the coefficient of absolute risk aversion, and s^2 is the variance of compensation. In this expression, the first term on the right-hand side represents expected compensation, the second term is the risk premium (the worker discounts the expected value because she is risk averse), and the last term is the cost of effort. We make two additional assumptions: (1) the effort of the employee does not affect the average output of other workers and (2) ρ does not vary with the wealth of the worker (that is, the worker has constant absolute risk aversion). The worker wants to maximize her certainty equivalent with respect to the effort choice, e (which is equivalent to maximizing her utility). Conceptually, the maximizing effort level is found by taking the partial derivative of the certainty equivalent with respect to effort, e, and setting it equal to zero. The first order condition is therefore:

$$\beta Q' = C'(e), \tag{A3}$$

where Q' and $C'(e)$ are partial derivatives with respect to e. This expression indicates that the employee chooses the effort level which equates marginal benefits and marginal costs. The marginal benefit is the extra compensation that the worker receives from exerting more effort and the marginal cost is the extra disutility that she experiences from working harder. Note that λ does not enter into this equation, since average output does not depend on her effort. Thus the firm can choose any value for λ without affecting her effort level.

Choosing a λ that is not equal to zero does affect expected compensation to the worker. In particular, from equation (A2) it changes expected compensation by $-\beta\lambda E[Q_a]$. This change, however, can easily be offset by adjusting a by the same amount.

What then determines the optimal λ? The answer is the optimal λ is the one that minimizes the variance of compensation. Note from equation (A2) that the worker is made better off by reducing the variance of compensation. (It lowers the discount for risk.) The firm, on the other hand, is not harmed by this choice because the worker exerts the same effort level under any λ and a can be adjusted to keep expected compensation the same. Indeed, the firm can potentially share in the gains from the risk reduction to the worker by paying a lower expected value of compensation (since the firm can meet her reservation wage with a lower expected value of payout).

Basic statistics allows us to express the variance of compensation [equation (A1)] as:

$$\text{Var(compensation)} = \beta^2[\text{Var}(Q) + \lambda^2\text{Var}(Q_a) - 2\,\lambda\text{Cov}(Q, Q_a)]. \tag{A4}$$

Figure 13.A1 shows a picture of this quadratic function. The optimal weight is λ^* at the bottom of the parabola. Using basic calculus, we can easily show that:

$$\lambda^* = \text{Cov}(Q, Q_a)/\text{Var}(Q_a). \tag{A5}$$

Equation (A5) has a very intuitive interpretation. The numerator of the expression, $\text{Cov}(Q, Q_a)$, is a measure of the association between her own output and the average output of other workers. The higher this association, the more information average output contains about random shocks that affect the worker's output (the better is the "signal"). For example, if this covariance is zero, average sales contains no information about these shocks and should not be included in the compensation contract. The denominator of the expression is the variance of average output. The higher this variance, the more "noise" there is in average

---

FIGURE 13.A1   Choosing the Optimal Weight in a Relative-Performance Contract.

This figure reflects a simple linear contract of the form: Compensation = a + β(Q − λ Q$_a$), where a and β are fixed parameters, Q is the worker's own output, and Q$_a$ is the average output of the benchmark group (for example, similar workers in the firm). Pictured is the variance of compensation as a function of λ. Given the assumptions in the analysis, the optimal weight, λ* = Cov(Q, Q$_a$)/Var(Q$_a$). This is the value that minimizes the variance of compensation.

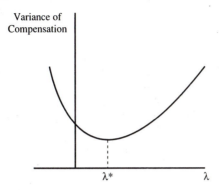

output and the less information it contains about the worker's effort. The optimal weight, λ*, can be estimated using a time series of observations on own output and average output.[19]

Firms sometimes base compensation on the simple difference between own output and average output. This measure is equivalent to choosing λ = 1. Our analysis indicates that this choice is not always optimal and in some cases can be worse than not including average output in the contract at all. (For example, when the covariance between the two variables is small.) Indeed, the optimal weight would be negative if the two variables were negatively correlated.

---

[19]Those readers familiar with linear regression analysis should note that the right-hand side of equation (A5) is the formula for the slope coefficient in a simple linear regression, where the worker's output is the dependent variable and average output of other workers is the explanatory variable. Thus this formula can be estimated through a simple regression.

Appendix Problem

Data:

Assume a salesperson has the following annual compensation package:

$$C = \$15{,}000 + .2(\text{Own Sales}).$$

This compensation plan induces the worker to exert a given level of effort in selling. Given this effort level, expected sales are \$30,000/year.

Below are 10 years worth of data for the individual's sales and the average sales for other employees in the company. The expected value of average sales is also \$30,000. However, in any given year average sales might rise or fall depending on general economic conditions, etc. Some of these same conditions affect the sales of the individual. The salesperson has no impact on the average sales for other workers.

Year	Own Sales	Average Sales
1	30000	30000
2	24000	27000
3	36000	28500
4	27000	27000
5	33000	36000
6	30000	33000
7	25500	27000
8	24000	24000
9	34500	30000
10	36000	36000

Questions:

1. Based on the 10 years of data, calculate the average annual pay and standard deviation for the salesperson under the existing compensation scheme.

2. Calculate the average pay and standard deviation for the salesperson under the alternative plan:

$$\$21{,}000 + .2(\text{Own Sales} - \text{Average Sales})$$

Note: We adjust the intercept of the pay plan by \$6,000 to reflect the average loss imposed on the worker by subtracting .2(Average Sales) from the compensation. This adjustment keeps expected pay the same as before. (Also note that the sample mean of average sales over a ten-year period need not equal its expected value of \$30,000.)

3. Does including the average sales in the pay package alter the incentives of the employee to work hard? Explain. (Assume the worker cannot affect the average by collusion, sabotage, etc.)

4. Is this pay plan superior to the original plan from a risk-sharing standpoint?

5. Devise an even better plan using the more general form:

$$C = a + .2(\text{Own Sales} - \lambda \text{ Average Sales}).$$

Note: Remember to adjust the intercept to keep expected compensation the same.

6. Calculate the average pay and standard deviation for this plan.

14 Divisional Performance Evaluation

Introduction

CSX is a large freight railroad with a fleet of locomotives, containers, and railcars and total revenues in 1994 of $9 billion. CSX transports freight in containers connecting trucks and/or cargo ships. In 1988 CSX changed the way it evaluated internal divisions. It adopted Economic Value Added. EVA®[1] is the after-tax operating profit of the division minus the total annual cost of capital invested in the division. One of its major division's EVA® was a negative $70 million. This means that in this division, the cost of capital invested in the division exceeded its operating profits by $70 million. The CEO of CSX informed the managers of this division that if they could not raise their EVA® to break even by 1993 their division would be sold.[2]

By 1993 after reorganizing and measuring these managers' performance using EVA®, freight volume was up 25 percent, the number of freight trailers dropped from 18,000 to 14,000, and the locomotive fleet fell from 150 to 100. Instead of allowing the trailers and containers to sit idle, managers now had incentives to use them or reduce their numbers. Under the previous performance evaluation system, managers were not charged for the cost of capital investments, and they treated containers and trailers as "free." By 1993 containers and trailers were loaded and back on the tracks in five days rather than sitting idle for two weeks in terminals. This division's 1993 EVA® was about $30 million. CSX's stock price rose from $28 in 1988 when EVA® was adopted to $75 in 1993.

The last chapter described individual performance evaluation systems. This discussion is extended in this chapter to evaluating the performance of subunits or divisions of the firm, as in the CSX example. As described in Chapter 10, firms are

---

[1] EVA® is a registered trademark of Stern-Stewart and Company.
[2] Tully, "The Real Key to Creating Wealth," Fortune (September 20, 1993), pp. 38–50.

organized in a variety of ways: functionally, by product line, by process or by teams. In essence, all organizations partition decision rights to subunits within the firm. This chapter describes various ways organizations measure the performance of these subunits. The next section describes the commonly-used cost centers, expense centers, revenue centers, profit centers, and investment centers. These subunits are allocated different sets of decision rights and accordingly use different performance-evaluation metrics (costs, revenues, profits). Because subunits of the organization interact with each other and often exchange goods or services among themselves, the reported performance of each center involved with the exchange depends on the rules used to value the exchange. Divisional performance evaluation of subunits exchanging goods or services requires establishing an internal transfer price for these exchanges. The following section discusses these transfer pricing issues. Finally, because most firms rely on their accounting systems to measure some of the performance of the subunits, the subsequent section discusses some general issues involving use of the accounting system in measuring performance. A chapter summary follows.

Measuring Divisional Performance

The central idea underlying this book is that because of people's limited information-processing capacities, all organizations are divided into subunits, each given some decision rights, and then each rewarded based on performance objectives for that subunit. The performance-evaluation and reward systems should be consistent with the decision rights allocated to the subunit manager. (The three legs of the three-legged stool should be matched.) Chapter 10 described alternative organizational structures: U-form, M-form, matrix (or process) organizations. In the U-form, one unit might be responsible for manufacturing, another unit for R&D, another marketing, and so forth. These basic building blocks of the organization are the work groups which define and characterize what each part of the firm does. Top management attempts to evaluate the performance of these various subunits both for setting rewards for lower-level managers, as well as for making business decisions (which units to expand). Whether the firm is organized as U-form, M-form, or some other design, each business unit generally can be categorized into one of five categories based on the decision rights it has and the way its performance is evaluated: (1) cost centers, (2) expense centers, (3) revenue centers, (4) profit centers, and (5) investment centers.[3] These subunits differ in terms of the decision rights that are granted to unit managers. Correspondingly, they also differ in terms of how performance is evaluated. CSX, the railroad example, began evaluating one of its divisions as an investment center.

---

[3]See M. Jensen and W. Meckling, ''Divisional Performance Measurement,'' Harvard Business School working paper (June 1986).

Cost Centers

Cost centers are established whenever a subunit is assigned the decision rights to produce some output and the unit's efficiency in achieving this objective is to be measured and rewarded. Cost-center managers are granted decision rights for determining the mix of inputs (labor, outside services, and materials) used to produce the output.

Managers of cost centers are evaluated based on the their efficiency of applying inputs to produce outputs. They do not have the decision rights to set prices for their output. Therefore, they are not held responsible for profits.

To evaluate the performance of a cost center, its output must be measurable. Moreover, some higher unit in the organization with the specialized knowledge and decision rights must specify the department's output or budget. Manufacturing departments in plants like the gasoline engine assembly department at Lincoln Electric are usually cost centers. The output of the engine assembly department is measured by counting the number of engines completed. Besides manufacturing settings, cost centers are also used in service organizations such as CSX's railcar maintenance department (number of railcars maintained), check processing by a bank (number of checks processed), or food services in a hospital (number of meals).

There are various objectives used for evaluating cost center performance. Three are:

1. Minimize costs for a given output.
2. Maximize output for a given budget.
3. Minimize average costs.

In the first situation, the cost-center manager minimizes total costs while producing a fixed quantity of output. For example, the manager of railcar maintenance department at CSX is told to service 100 railcars per day of a fixed specification and quality. The manager is evaluated on meeting the production schedule and on reducing the cost of servicing the 100 railcars. In the second situation, the manager has a fixed budget ($27,500 per week) and is evaluated based on the number of railcars serviced that meet quality specifications within the fixed budget. In the third situation, the manager's performance is judged by the average unit cost of servicing railcars. In all three cases, the cost-center manager usually has authority to change the mix of inputs. In the first two cases, the manager is constrained by either total output or budget. In the third case, the manager is unconstrained and can alter the number of units produced.

In all three cases, the cost-center manager has the decision rights to change how inputs are combined to produce the output. Only the first two typically are consistent with profit maximization ($MR = MC$). The first two objectives are optimal if the central management chooses (1) the profit-maximizing output level or (2) the correct budget for efficient production of this output level. Under both cost-center arrangements, the cost-center manager has incentives to reduce costs (or increase output) by lowering quality. Therefore, the quality of products manufactured in cost centers must be monitored.

Profit maximization need not occur at the point where average costs are minimized (case 3). For example, suppose a cost center has some fixed costs and constant marginal costs. Then average unit costs continue to fall with increases in output. To illustrate, assume total costs are:

$$TC = \$300{,}000 + \$6\,Q.$$

Fixed costs are $300,000 and marginal costs are a constant $6 per unit. Given the equation for total costs, average costs are derived by dividing both sides of the equation by Q to get

$$AC = \frac{TC}{Q} = \frac{\$300{,}000}{Q} + \$6.$$

With constant marginal cost, as quantity produced, Q, increases, AC falls. In this situation a cost-center manager who is evaluated based on minimizing average unit costs will push to increase output, even as inventories mount up. In general, focusing on average costs can provide incentives for cost-center managers to either overproduce or underproduce (depending on how the profit-maximizing output level compares to the quantity where average costs are minimized). In general, minimizing average unit cost is not the same as maximizing profits. Maximum profits occur where marginal costs and marginal revenues are equal, which need not be where average unit costs are lowest.

The firm's internal accounting system is used to measure the costs incurred by the cost center. The accounting system traces all the direct costs (materials, services, and labor) used by the cost center plus all the cost center's controllable costs (supervisory salaries and occupancy charges). The question always arises as to what other costs should be allocated to the cost center and how they should be allocated. For example, should the central personnel department's costs or corporate overhead be allocated to the cost center, even though these costs are not directly controllable by the cost-center manager? These questions are beyond the scope of this book, but are issues managers face when using their accounting system to help measure performance.[4]

Cost centers work most effectively if (1) the central managers can measure quantity and know the optimum output level, (2) the central managers have a good idea of the cost functions so as to set appropriate rewards, (3) the central managers can observe the quality of the cost center's output, and (4) the cost-center manager has specific knowledge of the optimal input mix.

Expense Centers

Cost centers are a common way of organizing manufacturing units. Activities such as personnel, accounting, patenting, public relations, and research and development,

---

[4]See J. Zimmerman, *Accounting for Decision Making and Control* (Burr Ridge, IL: Richard D. Irwin, 1995), chapter 6.

however, are also often organized along the lines of cost centers. In particular, units charged with these activities are given fixed budgets and asked to maximize service/output. A major difference between the organization of these activities and standard cost centers is that output is measured more subjectively than objectively. An expense center is a cost center that does not produce an easily measurable output.

The difficulty in observing the output of an expense center has several implications. The expense center is given a total budget and told to provide as much service as possible. Because the cost per unit of output cannot be calculated, the users of the center often are not charged for the center's services. These units thus tend to overconsume the services and the expense center is always asking for a larger budget. The central corporate budget-granting organization has difficulty determining the budget that maximizes firm profits (the point where the marginal cost of the last unit of service equals its marginal benefit to the firm). Expense-center managers usually perceive larger benefits from managing larger staffs (empire building) which reinforces the tendency of these centers to grow faster than the firm as a whole. If the central budget office tries to cut the expense center's budget, the expense center's manager might threaten to cut those services that are most highly valued by the users to enlist their help lobbying the budget-granting managers not to cut the budget.

There are a number of devices used to control the size of expense centers. One is to benchmark their budgets with those of similar sized firms. Another is to reorganize the firm and place the expense center under the control of the largest user who then has specialized knowledge of the expense center's value and the decision rights to set the expense center's budget. But this reorganized structure has the disadvantage of causing other units to get too little of the service, to the extent that the other users of the expense center are charged more than marginal cost. If there is no charge-back system for the expense center's services, then outside users may get none of its services. Another alternative is to outsource the service to another firm and have each user buy the services outside. Outsourcing is examined more fully in Chapter 16.

Revenue Centers

Revenue centers are used to organize the marketing activities of selling, distributing, and sometimes servicing finished products received from manufacturing. The idea behind a revenue center is to compensate the manager for specializing in selling a set of products. For example, a regional sales office might be evaluated as a revenue center. The regional sales manager is given a budget for personnel and expenses and has decision rights as to how to deploy the budget to maximize revenue. Revenue-center managers usually have limited discretion in setting the selling price; typically they have to keep the price within a prescribed range.

Similar to a cost center there are various objectives that can be used in evaluating revenue-center performance. Three are:

1. Maximize revenue for a given price and budget for personnel and expenses.

2. Maximize revenue for a given quantity and budget.

3. Maximize total revenue.

Note that the third objective is usually inconsistent with profit maximization. To maximize revenue, the manager goes to the point where marginal revenue equals zero and not marginal cost. Since marginal cost usually is greater than zero, the firm loses money on the last units sold. The other two criteria are consistent with profit maximization if the firm chooses the correct price or quantity.

Revenue centers work best if (1) the central managers have the knowledge to select the correct price/quantity, (2) the central managers have the knowledge to select the optimal product mix (otherwise the salesperson shifts effort towards selling higher-revenue-generating products rather than selling products that generate higher profits), and (3) the sales managers have specialized knowledge of the demand curves of the customers in their sales district.

Profit Centers

Profit centers are often composed of several cost, and possibly expense and revenue, centers. Profit-center managers are given decision rights for input mix, product mix, and selling prices given a fixed capital budget. Profit centers are set up when the knowledge required to make the product mix, quantity, pricing, and quality decisions is specific to the division and costly to transfer.

Managers rely on their internal accounting systems to provide performance measures for profit centers. Profit centers usually are evaluated on the difference between actual and budgeted accounting profits for the division. While measuring the profits of profit centers is seemingly straight forward, two complications often consume managers' attention: how to price transfers of goods and services between business units (transfer pricing) and which (if any) corporate overhead costs to allocate to business units. Managers in every firm are constantly debating these two issues. The transfer-pricing problem is discussed in the next section.

Motivating individual profit centers to maximize profits will not generally maximize profits for the firm as a whole when there are interdependencies among business units. For example, individual units focusing on their own profits will often ignore how their actions affect the sales and costs of other units.[5] One division can free ride on another division's quality reputation thereby reaping short-run gains at the expense of the other division. For example, Chevrolet and Buick are two profit centers in General Motors. Suppose Chevrolet, in pursuit of maximizing their profits, decides to raise the quality of its cars. This can affect consumers' perceptions of the average quality of all General Motor cars, including Buick's perceived quality. An enhanced reputation for all General Motors cars helps Buick. But if Chevrolet does not receive any credit for Buick profits, they tend to ignore the positive externality they generate for Buick and will tend to underinvest in quality

---

[5]Conceptually, other units could offer money to take these effects into account. However, in the presence of transaction costs these offers are likely to be limited.

enhancements. To help managers internalize both positive and negative externalities their actions impose on other profit-center managers, firms often base incentive compensation not just on the manager's own profit center profits but also on a group of related profit centers' profits and/or firm-wide profits. Unless the entire firm makes a certain profit target, no individual profit-center manager earns a bonus.

Investment Centers

Investment centers are similar to profit centers. However, they have additional decision rights for capital expenditures and are evaluated on measures such as return on investment. Investment centers are useful where the manager of the unit has specific knowledge about investment opportunities as well as information relevant to making operating decisions for the unit.

Investment centers are often composed of several profit centers. They have all the decision rights of cost and profit centers as well as the decision rights over the amount of capital to be invested. For example, suppose the consumer electronics group of an electronics firm is comprised of three profit centers: television division, VCR division, and stereo division. Consumer electronics has decision rights over the amount of capital invested in the group and is evaluated based on the return on the capital invested. There are two commonly used measures of performance for investment centers: return on investment and residual income.

Accounting ROI.   Return on investment (ROI) is the most commonly used investment-center performance measure. ROI is the ratio of net income generated by the investment center to the total assets invested in the investment center. It has intuitive appeal because ROI can be compared to external market-based yields to provide a benchmark for a division's performance. However, using ROI creates problems. ROI is not a measure of the division's economic rate of return because accounting income (the numerator) is not a measure of economic profit and "investment" (the denominator) is not the market value of the division's investment. Economic profit is the change in value over the period. Accounting net income excludes some value increases and includes some value declines. For example, accounting net income excludes land value appreciation until the land is sold, but includes market value declines even though the land has not been sold. Accounting net income tends to be conservative: recognize all losses and defer all gains. Also, accounting depreciation, which is deducted from accounting profits, does not necessarily reflect the change in the value of fixed assets.

Managers have incentives to reject profitable projects with ROIs below the mean ROI for the division because accepting these projects lower the division's ROI. For example, suppose the division has an average ROI of 19 percent which is above its 15 percent cost of capital. A new investment project which is 10 percent the size of the existing division investment is available. Its ROI is 16 percent, which is above its cost of capital of 15 percent; thus taking this project would increase firm value. But if this project is accepted, the division's ROI falls to 18.7 percent (.90 × 19%

+ .10 × 16%). If the division is evaluated based on increasing ROI, management will reject the project, even though it has a return in excess of its cost of capital.

Finally, a manager with a short time horizon who is evaluated based on ROI would prefer projects that boost ROI in immediate years (the horizon problem) even if they are unprofitable projects. Maximizing ROI leads managers to ignore risk differences which account for various among projects' ROIs.

Accounting Residual Income.   To overcome some of the incentive deficiencies of ROI, such as divesting of projects with ROIs above their cost of capital but below the division's average ROI, some firms use *residual income* to evaluate performance. Residual income measures divisional performance by subtracting a stated return on investment from division profits. For example, suppose a division has profits of $20 million and investment (total assets) of $100 million. Furthermore, this division has a required cost of capital of 15 percent. Its ROI is 20 percent, which is in excess of its cost of capital (15 percent). Residual income is $5 million ($20M − 15 percent × 100M). Under the residual-income approach, divesting a project with an ROI of less than 20 percent but above 15 percent lowers residual income, although it raises average ROI.

Nevertheless, residual income has problems. Residual income is an absolute number, and thus larger divisions typically have larger residual incomes than smaller divisions; this makes relative performance evaluation comparisons across investment centers of different sizes difficult. To implement residual-income measures requires senior managers to estimate the cost of capital for each division. If the divisions differ in terms of riskiness, then each will have a different cost of capital. These risk adjustments allow more precise performance evaluations to be produced by controlling for risk differences across divisions. However, the risk adjustments also potentially lead to greater influence costs as divisional managers seek to have lower cost of capital estimates imposed on them.

At the beginning of this chapter, CSX's use of EVA® (economic value added) was described as a performance measurement scheme that is being widely heralded and adopted by such companies as AT&T, Coca-Cola, Quaker Oats, and Briggs & Stratton.[6] EVA® is a variant of residual income. The formula for EVA® is:

EVA® = Adjusted accounting earnings −
[weighted average cost of capital × total capital].

This is the same formula as residual income. The only difference is that the terms on the right-hand-side are more carefully measured than usually was done in the past.[7] The following discussion gives some examples of how the right-hand-side variables are adjusted to give a supposedly more accurate performance measure.

_____

[6]S. Tully, "The Real Key to Creating Wealth," *Fortune* (September 20, 1993), pp. 38–50.

[7]For a more complete description of EVA® see B. Stewart *The Quest for Value* (Harper Business, 1991). Also see D. Solomons, *Divisional Performance: Measurement and Control* (Homewood, Ill.: Richard D. Irwin, Inc. 1968) for a discussion of residual income.

Instead of using the same accounting procedures that are used in reporting to shareholders, different accounting procedures are used. Standard U.S. accounting rules require that the entire amount spent on research and development each year be deducted from earnings. This creates incentives for managers with a short horizon to cut R&D spending. One adjustment to accounting earnings is to add back R&D spending and treat it as an asset to be depreciated, usually over five years. Total capital, in the above formula, consists of all the firm's assets including the amount invested in R&D and other adjustments made to earnings.

Another right-hand-side variable in EVA® is the weighted average cost of capital which includes the cost of equity and cost of debt. The cost of equity is the price appreciation and dividends the shareholders could have earned in a portfolio of companies of similar risk. This is the opportunity cost the shareholders bear by buying the company's stock. The cost of debt is the current market yield on debt of similar risk. The costs of debt and equity are weighted by the relative amounts of debt and equity. Suppose the cost of equity is 18 percent, the cost of debt is 10 percent, and the firm's capital structure is 40 percent debt and 60 percent equity. Then, the weighted average cost of capital is 14.8 percent (0.60 × 18% + 0.40 × 10%).

EVA®, like residual income, measures the total return after deducting the cost of all capital employed by the firm. It estimates the *true* profitability of the firm in the period (usually a year). Many of the firms adopting EVA® to measure divisional performance did so as part of a corporate reorganization. AT&T was organized as a huge corporate monolith only providing balance sheets for a few huge groups such as long distance services. In 1992, AT&T reorganized into investment centers, each resembling an independent company. The long distance service function now has 40 units selling 800 service, telemarketing, and public telephones. Each is measured using EVA®. Besides decentralizing decision rights and adopting EVA® as the performance measure, firms also change the third leg of the three-legged stool, the reward system. Manager bonuses are based on their EVA®.

EVA® Is Often Linked to a Change in the Compensation Scheme

Besides introducing EVA® in 1988, CSX also changed its management compensation plan. In 1991 CSX introduced a stock incentive program whereby 160 managers accepted a plan to purchase CSX stock at the market price of $48. They paid 5 percent in cash and CSX lent them the balance at 7.9 percent interest. If the stock price is above $69 per share in July 1994, CSX will forgive the loan's interest and 25 percent of the principal. If the stock is below $69, the managers must pay all the interest and principal. With the stock selling at about $75 at the end of April 1994, the managers stand to make a substantial profit, but so do the shareholders.

Notice that besides linking pay to the performance measure, EVA®, in CSX's case, also changed the part of the performance reward system.

Suggested by S. Tully, "The Real Key to Creating Wealth," *Fortune* (September 20, 1993), pp. 38–50.

Transfer Pricing

As discussed above, firms organize into business units. Whenever business units transfer goods or services among themselves, measuring their performance requires that a ''transfer price'' be established for the goods and services exchanged. The purchasing division pays the transfer price and the producing division receives the transfer price. For example, suppose a large chemical company is organized into profit centers. These profit centers produce and sell to external customers. But they also sell to other profit centers in the chemical company. Each of these internal transactions requires a transfer price.

Transfer prices are much more prevalent in organizations than most managers realize. Firms often have extensive recharge or chargeback schemes for internal service departments. Consider the charges that the advertising department receives from the maintenance department for janitorial service, or the monthly charge for telephones, security services, data processing, and legal and personnel services. Most firms charge inside users for these internally provided services. These chargeback schemes are internal transfer prices. Chargebacks also exist in hospitals, universities, and other nonprofit organizations.

Because transfer pricing (including chargeback systems) is widespread in many firms and because transfer pricing affects performance evaluation and hence the rewards managers receive, fighting over the transfer price between divisions is inevitable. Transfer pricing is a constant source of tension within firms. It is not uncommon for managers in most multidivisional firms to be involved in a succession of transfer pricing disputes over the course of their careers.

The topic of transfer pricing is very complicated. One additional complicating factor is taxes. When a company transfers a product from the manufacturing division to a distribution division which sells the product, and these divisions are in different countries with different tax rates, then taxes affect the opportunity cost of the product and thus the transfer price chosen. The manufacturing division pays income taxes on the difference between the transfer price and its costs. The distribution division pays taxes on the difference between what it sells each unit for and its costs, which include the transfer price. In general, to minimize the sum of the two taxes, the firm wants to set the transfer price to allocate as much of the profits to the division in the country with the lower tax rate. International tax treaties and local legislation regulate the transfer-pricing methods firms can use for tax purposes.* This section describes the economics of transfer pricing and some common transfer-pricing methods.

Economics of Transfer Pricing

Sometimes senior managers do not view the transfer-pricing problem as important from the firm's overall perspective. Rather many managers think that changing

---

*See M. Scholes and M. Wolfson *Taxes and Business Strategy* (Englewood Cliffs, NJ: Prentice Hall, 1992).

transfer-pricing methods merely shifts income among divisions, and except for relative performance evaluation little else is affected. Transfer price is mistakenly viewed as simply determining how the firm's profit is split among the internal divisions with no effect on the total level of firm profit. But transfer prices do affect the overall level of firm profits. The important point to remember is: *The choice of transfer-pricing method does not merely reallocate total company profits among the profit centers; rather it also affects the firm's total profits.* Think of the firm's total profit as a pie. Choice among transfer-pricing methods not only changes how the pie is divided among the business units but also the size of the pie to be divided.

The optimal transfer-pricing rule is really quite simple to state. Unfortunately, as we will see, it is often difficult to implement in practice. The optimal transfer price is the product's opportunity cost: the resources foregone from using the unit transferred in its next best alternative use. Suppose the firm has two profit centers, Manufacturing and Distribution, and is considering transferring one unit of the product. Also assume that manufacturing's marginal cost is $3 and it has excess capacity. It produces a product that it sells to end users, and it can transfer the product to Distribution. Distribution can sell it and receive $5, net of its marginal cost. Consider two alternatives: (1) don't manufacture and transfer and (2) manufacture and transfer. If the unit is not manufactured, the firm foregoes $5 but saves $3, a net loss of $2. If the unit is manufactured and transferred, the firm foregoes $3 (marginal cost to produce) and receives $5 for a net receipt of $2. The better alternative is to make the transfer. The resources foregone (opportunity cost) from transferring are $3, Manufacturing's marginal cost of production.

As in the above example, often the marginal cost of producing the unit is the opportunity cost. Sometimes, however, the opportunity cost is the market price of selling the intermediate good externally. Suppose Manufacturing can produce one unit for $3. But if it transfers it to Distribution, the firm foregoes selling the intermediate good in the market. Suppose Manufacturing can sell the unit now for $4. The opportunity cost of making the transfer is $4. Even though the marginal cost of producing the unit is $3, the firm foregoes $4 if it is transferred to Distribution instead of sold immediately. If Manufacturing has enough capacity to both supply the external market at $4 and transfer it to Distribution, then the opportunity cost of the transfer is $3, the marginal cost of production. Thus, if the firm has market power in the external market for the internal goods, then the external market price exceeds the internal transfer price.

When opportunity cost is used to set the transfer price, Manufacturing will produce units to the point that the marginal cost of the last unit equals the transfer price. Likewise, Distribution will buy units from Manufacturing as long as Distribution's net receipts just cover the transfer price. When both A and B are maximizing their respective profits, assuming there are no interdependencies between the business units (a case we consider later), total firm profits are maximized. Thus, in this simple example, the transfer price represents the marginal cost to distribution. If the transfer price is too high or too low relative to opportunity cost, distribution purchases too few or too many units and firm profits are not maximized.

In summary, the correct transfer price is opportunity cost. To maximize the value of the firm, all internal transfers should be charged at what the firm foregoes in making the transfer: the next best alternative use of the resources consumed in making and transferring the goods/services from one business unit to the other. Usually marginal cost is the optimal transfer price unless the firm has limited capacity and foregoes selling the intermediate good outside and transfers the unit internally.

The preceding discussion assumes that everyone knows Manufacturing's marginal production cost is $3, the intermediate product has an external price of $4, Distribution's marginal revenue is $5, and whether Manufacturing has excess capacity or not. If all this knowledge is readily available, there would be no reason to decentralize decision making down the organization. Central management has the knowledge to make the decision and would retain the decision rights. In reality, much of the information is not readily available to central management. The knowledge resides at lower levels of the firm where it is private knowledge, costly to either transfer or verify by senior management. In some circumstances, lower-level managers have incentives to distort the information they pass up to senior managers. To illustrate these incentives, we consider a firm with market power. (See Chapter 6.)

Consider the situation where the manager of Manufacturing is the only person with knowledge of his division's marginal costs. This profit-center manager seeks to maximize the profits of his division. If Manufacturing has market power in setting the price, and information regarding the division's costs is costly to transfer, inefficiencies can result. Manufacturing, with monopoly rights to set the transfer price, will set price above marginal cost to increase the division's profits. Unfortunately, the owners bear a cost. In particular, additional units can be produced at a lower marginal cost than the marginal value placed on them by Distribution. But the monopolist does not produce them. This is analogous to the social loss from monopoly described in Chapter 6.

This problem can be illustrated by example. For simplicity, consider a firm that produces one product with the following demand:

$$P = 110 - 5Q.$$

Assume the product is produced at a constant marginal cost of $10. Profit maximization occurs by setting marginal revenue = marginal cost. At this condition $Q^* = 10$ and $P^* = 60$. Firm profits are $500 ($60 \times 10 - 10×10). Figure 14.1 depicts this situation.

Assume Manufacturing produces the good at a $MC = 10$ and transfers it to Distribution at a transfer price, P_t. Suppose the only cost to the distribution division is the transfer price. (For simplicity additional distribution costs are equal to zero.)

Distribution's demand curve for the product is the firm's demand curve. How many units of the good will the manager of this unit want to buy at each possible transfer price? Note that Distribution's marginal cost is the transfer price $MC_d = P_t$. Distribution maximizes profit (for the unit) by setting $MC_d = MR_d$. Hence in this case, the firm's marginal revenue curve represents Distribution's demand for the

FIGURE 14.1   Profit Maximizing Price

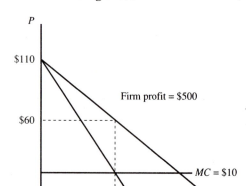

good and is, therefore, the demand curve facing Manufacturing: $P_t = 110 - 10Q$ (the marginal revenue curve in the above graph).

Next assume that Manufacturing sets the transfer price; it has monopoly power and because of costly information, senior management cannot monitor the decision. What price will Manufacturing set and what quantity of the good will be produced? The manager of Manufacturing sets marginal cost equal to marginal revenue: $MC_m = MR_m$. The marginal cost $= 10$. As discussed above, Manufacturing faces a *demand curve* equal to the marginal revenue curve for the firm: $P_t = 110 - 10Q$. The marginal revenue for the manufacturing division is, therefore, $P_t = 110 - 20Q$. Profit maximization for Manufacturing will involve setting the transfer price at $60 and selling five units of the good. (See the left-hand graph in Figure 14.2.) Facing a transfer price of $60, Distribution will in turn sell the five units to the external market at a price of $85 (right-hand-side graph in Figure 14.2). Total firm profits are $375 (5 × $85 − 5 × $10), which are lower than at the profit maximizing output of 10 units ($500). Manufacturing has profits of $250, while Distribution has profits of $125. Both divisions are making profits, but total firm profits are lower in Figure 14.2 than in Figure 14.1.

The basic problem is that Distribution, facing a transfer price of $60, is not considering the *true* marginal cost to the firm of producing extra units of the good ($10). Hence, from the firm's standpoint, Distribution stops short of the optimal quantity to be sold to the external market. The transfer price that assures firm profit maximization in this example is the true marginal cost of the unit. Note, however, that Manufacturing does not want to transfer at that price because it makes a lower profit ($0 in this example).

The above simple example illustrates the basic incentive problems of internal transfers when information is privately held by divisional managers. Opportunity

FIGURE 14.2   Decentralized Firm

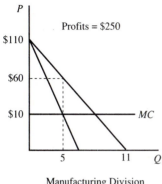
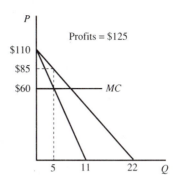

Manufacturing Division   Distribution Division

cost is the transfer price that maximizes firm value. But knowledge of opportunity costs is held by the profit-center manager who has incentives to distort the information if given the decision rights to set the transfer price. Senior management doesn't have the specialized knowledge of the opportunities facing the profit-center managers. Calculating opportunity costs is difficult because opportunity costs depend on the firm's *next best* alternative use of the good/service. But the next best alternative changes as the firm's opportunity set changes. Sometimes the firm has excess capacity and Manufacturing can sell the good both internally and externally. At other times, the firm only has enough short-run capacity to produce for either the inside or outside user. The specialized knowledge of the alternatives is only known by the business-unit managers. This is why the firm organized into business units, to link the specialized knowledge and decision rights. If transfer prices are used only to coordinate exchanges between business units and not in setting managerial rewards, business-unit managers are more likely to honestly disclose the next best alternative. But once transfer prices are used for performance evaluation, which is the major reason for calculating them, business unit-managers have incentives to begin distorting their reported opportunity costs to improve their performance ratings.

Problems arise if either the buying or selling division has the decision rights to set the price of the goods or services transferred, and the other division cannot purchase or sell outside. The selling division will set a price above true opportunity cost to capture some monopoly profits, and the buying division will purchase fewer units than if the correct (lower) transfer price is set. The buyer, if given the decision rights to determine the price, will set a transfer price below the true opportunity cost, and the selling division will supply too few units. Again, the number of units transferred is below the profit-maximizing level. If central management knows the true opportunity cost, it doesn't have to decentralize decision making to the profit centers and can dictate both price and quantity decisions.

Several solutions have been proposed to induce both divisions to reveal their private, specialized knowledge and to arrive at a transfer price that maximizes firm profits. In a dual-transfer-pricing scheme, both divisions state a transfer price. The buying division then pays the price stated by the selling division, and the selling division receives the price quoted by the buying division. Neither division benefits from misstating their price. However, this scheme is rarely used in practice. One explanation why firms infrequently use this practice is that dual prices create incentives for the two managers to collude to jointly misstate their prices to benefit each other through increased bonus compensation. Also, dual pricing can lead to the two divisions showing positive profits, even though the firm shows a loss.

Another possible solution is to allow the buying and selling divisions to negotiate both the transfer price and the number of units to be transferred. In this case, the two divisions have the incentive to set the number of units to maximize the combined profits of the two divisions. Once the value-maximizing number of units is determined, the transfer price set just determines how the total profits are divided between the two divisions. In terms of Figure 14.1, if the two divisions negotiate over both price and quantity, they have the joint incentive to set $Q = 10$ because this maximizes the total profit pie to be split, $500. If the two divisions just negotiate over price, there is no guarantee they will arrive at the transfer price that maximizes firm value.

The economics of transfer pricing is best summarized by the following:

> The economist's first instinct is to set the transfer price equal to marginal cost. But it may be difficult to find out marginal cost. As a practical matter, marginal cost information is rarely known to anybody in the firm, because it depends on opportunity costs that vary with capacity use. And even if marginal cost information were available, there is no guarantee that it would be revealed in a truthful fashion for the purpose of determining an optimal transfer price.[8]

Common Transfer-Pricing Methods

The correct transfer price is opportunity cost. But determining opportunity costs is expensive. Special studies by experts who examine the opportunities available are costly and become outdated whenever the firm's business opportunities change. Alternatively, if the decision rights to set the transfer price are vested with either the buying or selling division, too few units are transferred and again the firm bears a cost. Because determining opportunity costs is expensive, managers resort to various lower-cost approximations. There are a variety of ways that firms can approximate the opportunity cost of the units transferred: market price, marginal cost, full cost, and negotiated price. As discussed below, one method is better than the others in one situation, but not in others; none of these measures strictly dominates the others in all situations in terms of reducing agency problems and maximizing the

---

[8]B. Holmstrom and J. Tirole, "Transfer Pricing and Organizational Form," *Journal of Law, Economics, & Organizations* 7 (1991), pp. 201–228.

value of the firm. For example, if the divisions operate in different countries with different tax rates, then the choice of method will be driven, in part, by tax considerations. For instance, if Manufacturing faces lower tax rates than Distribution, full-cost prices will allocate more of the profit to the lower-taxed unit than would marginal-cost prices. Our goal is to describe the advantages and disadvantages of each so as to allow managers to select the best transfer-pricing method for their particular situation.

Market-Based Transfer Prices.   The standard rule offered by most textbooks is: Given a competitive external market for the good, the product should be transferred at the external market price. If the selling division cannot make a long-run profit at the external price, then the company is better off not producing internally and should purchase instead in the external market. If the purchasing division cannot make a long-run profit at the external price, then the company is better off not processing the transferred units and should instead sell it in the external market. The external market price allows the decisions of the purchasing and producing divisions to be independent of each other. Market price *presumably* allows the correct make/buy decision to be made. However, market price is not necessarily the opportunity cost in all situations.

If both the *firm* and the *market* are making the transferred units, the question arises, "Can both survive in the long run?" If one can produce the good cheaper than the other, the other should not be producing the transferred units. Recall that transactions take place inside the firm because the cost of internal repetitive contracting is cheaper than contracting across markets. Production occurs inside the firm if there are interdependencies among cost, profit, or investment centers such as lower contracting costs or other synergies. Advantages to internal transactions include the elimination of credit risk, lower marketing costs, and learning from production.[9] As these interdependencies become more important, they reinforce the internal production and, at the same time, reduce the ability of the external market price to accurately reflect the opportunity cost of producing inside.

It is often the case that the good is not being produced by other firms or that the good produced externally is not identical to the good produced internally. These situations reduce the ability of market prices to approximate opportunity cost. Producing internally (even though "cheaper" external markets exist) makes sense if timeliness of supply is important for internal sourcing, to ensure quality control, and because of proprietary information. When these factors are included in the analysis, the external market is no longer "cheaper," nor is the market price the

---

[9]P. Milgrom and J. Roberts, *Economics, Organizations & Management* (Englewood Cliffs, NJ: Prentice-Hall, 1992), Ch. 3. R. Coase, "The Nature of the Firm," *Economica* 4 (1937), pp. 386–405. Also, see R. Watts, "Accounting Choice Theory and Market-Based Research in Accounting," *British Accounting Journal* 24 (1992), p. 242–246 for a summary of the arguments for the types of costs that are lowered by firms. These arguments include economies of scale in contracting, team production and monitoring, post-contractual opportunism, and knowledge costs.

"right" transfer price.[10] For example, suppose a transferred product can be purchased externally for $3 per unit, but synergies exist that make it beneficial to produce the item internally. These synergies are difficult to estimate, but can arise for a number of reasons. By producing the transferred product internally, the firm maintains lower cost access to a skilled work force that can apply the same production technology to other manufactured products. Suppose there are $0.14 of synergies, so that the "correct" transfer price is $2.86 in the sense that $2.86 is the opportunity cost to the firm. If the market price of $3 is used as the transfer price, the buying division will purchase fewer units than if $2.86 was used, and the value of the firm will not be maximized.[11]

Marginal-Cost Transfer Prices.   If no external market for the intermediate good exists or if large interdependencies across business units cause the market price to be an inaccurate measure of opportunity cost, then marginal cost is an alternative transfer price. Marginal cost represents the value of the resources forgone to produce the last unit. However, as with other transfer-pricing methods, there are problems with marginal cost as a measure of opportunity cost.

One problem with marginal-cost transfers is that the producing business unit does not necessarily recover its fixed costs. If *all* the selling division's output is transferred internally and marginal cost is below its average total cost, the selling division's fixed costs are not recovered. Thus, sellers show losses and appear to be losing money. If central management knows the magnitude of the fixed costs, they can budget for this loss. However, if central management knows the magnitude of the fixed costs, then they know marginal cost, and there is no reason to have a decentralized division and transfer pricing.

Another problem with marginal-cost transfer pricing occurs if the marginal cost per unit is not constant as volume changes. If the marginal cost per unit increases as volume expands (a night shift at higher wages per hour is added), then which buyer bears the higher marginal cost? Disputes will occur within the firm debating the appropriate measure of marginal cost. A related issue arises as the selling division approaches capacity and is considering adding more capacity, for say $2.5 million. These additional capacity costs of $2.5 million are variable in the long run but become short-run fixed costs (depreciation and higher utilities and maintenance). Conflicts arise between the buying and selling divisions as to whether these additional capacity costs should be included in the transfer price or not.

---

[10] "Observed market prices cannot directly guide the owner of the input to perform in the same manner as if every activity he performs were measured and priced." S. Cheung, "The Contractual Nature of the Firm," *Journal of Law & Economics* 26 (April 1983), p. 5. See also R. Ball, "The Firm as a Specialist Contracting Intermediary: Applications to Accounting and Auditing," unpublished working paper, William E. Simon Graduate School of Business Administration, University of Rochester (1989).

[11] Interdependencies/synergies that cause production to occur inside the firm are classic economic *externalities*. If interdependencies in production or demand functions exist, the market price does not capture these interdependencies. The same occurs inside the firm and causes the external price to mis-measure the opportunity cost of one more unit being transferred.

Marginal cost has to be estimated, usually from accounting records. Marginal costs are not published in *The Wall Street Journal*. While most of the components of marginal cost are easily observed such as the cost of direct labor and direct material, some components are less easily observed. For example, it is not straightforward to estimate marginal costs the purchasing department bears as Manufacturing expands output. Marginal-cost transfer pricing creates incentives for selling-division managers to classify costs as marginal. Since these classifications are to some extent arbitrary, resources are dissipated as managers in the selling and buying divisions and senior managers arbitrating such disputes debate various cost terms and their applications. Moreover, the selling-division manager has incentives to convert a dollar of fixed costs into more than a dollar of marginal costs even though this reduces the value of the firm (outsourcing parts instead of internal manufacturing). The buying division pays the extra cost, not the selling division, and the selling division is relieved of the burden of the fixed cost.

A variation of marginal-cost transfer pricing is to price all transfers at marginal cost, but charge the purchasing division a fixed fee for these services. The purchasing division pays incremental cost for the additional units and buys the number of units that maximize firm profits. The selling division covers full cost and earns a profit. The fixed fee represents the rights by the buyer to acquire the product at marginal cost and is set to cover the seller's fixed cost plus a return on equity. However, the selling division again has incentives to inflate the reported marginal-cost figures.

Full-Cost Transfer Prices.   Simple, objective, hard-to-change transfer-price rules can lead to higher firm value than transfer-price rules which give one manager discretion over the transfer price. To avoid wasteful disputes over measuring marginal costs, objective transfer-pricing rules such as full accounting cost are often adopted. Since full cost is the sum of fixed and marginal cost, full cost cannot be changed by simply reclassifying a "fixed" cost as "marginal" cost. But full-cost transfer pricing causes the buying division to purchase too few units when full cost is above marginal cost.

Full cost does not represent the opportunity cost to the firm of producing and transferring one more unit internally. The buying division buys too few units internally when full cost is above marginal cost. Full cost also allows the producing division to transfer all of its inefficiencies to the purchasing division. Under a full-cost transfer-price rule, the selling division has little incentive to be efficient. (Note: Marginal-cost transfer prices allow the selling division to export some of its inefficiencies to the purchasing division.) The problem of exporting inefficiencies to the buying division via cost-based transfer prices is reduced if the purchasing division can purchase externally as well as from the selling division. This forces the selling division to remain competitive.

Despite all these problems, full-cost transfer pricing is very common. In various surveys of corporate practice, full-cost transfer prices are used 40 to 50 percent of the time.[12] Full cost includes both direct materials and labor as well as a charge

---

[12]J. Zimmerman, *Accounting for Decision Making and Control* (Burr Ridge, IL: Richard D. Irwin, 1995), chapter 4.

for overhead. Applying the survival-of-the-fittest principle from Chapter 8, we must search for unrecognized benefits to full-cost transfer pricing that outweigh its costs. As a plant begins to reach capacity, marginal costs are likely to rise because of congestion and opportunity costs of using finite capacity. Hence marginal cost is likely to be higher than direct materials and labor costs. In this case, full cost might be a closer approximation to opportunity cost than just the cost of materials and labor. Another benefit of full-cost transfer pricing is its simplicity and low cost of implementation. Full-cost transfer pricing reduces influence costs. Senior management does not have to arbitrate disputes over what costs are to be included in calculating the transfer price. Nevertheless, firms should consider carefully whether full cost pricing is optimal for their particular situation. If the opportunity cost is substantially different than full cost, the firm's loss in profits can be significant.

Negotiated Transfer Prices.   Transfer prices can be set by the purchasing and selling divisions negotiating a price. The two managers agree on a transfer price. This method can result in transfer prices that approximate opportunity cost because the selling division will not agree to a price that is below its opportunity cost, and the buying division will not pay a price that is above what it can buy the product for elsewhere. While negotiation is a fairly common method, it too has drawbacks. It is time consuming and leads to conflicts among divisions. Divisional performance measurement becomes sensitive to the relative negotiating skills of the two division managers.

No matter what transfer-pricing method is used, it is important to allow both the buying and selling divisions to use the external market. In this case, the external market usually acts as a check on the managers behaving opportunistically. But again, if an external market exists, one must examine whether the firm should be producing the intermediate product at all.

To summarize the discussion on transfer pricing, firms decentralize and form profit and investment centers to take advantage of the divisional manager's specialized knowledge of local conditions. Decentralization requires that business unit managers be allowed to make local decisions and be held responsible for their division's performance. Transfer-price systems offer desirable mechanisms for permitting local managers to exploit specialized information which they possess about local opportunities.[13] A change of transfer-pricing methods does more than shift income among divisions, because transfer pricing does more than change the relative performance evaluation of the profit centers. The level of the firm's output changes, as does firm-wide profitability. The transfer price not only changes how the total profits pie is divided among responsibility centers, it also affects the size of pie. If

[13]For an expanded discussion of transfer pricing, strategy implications, and organizational issues, see R. Eccles, "Analyzing Your Company's Transfer Pricing Practices," *Journal of Cost Management* (Summer, 1987) pp. 21–33 and R. Eccles, *The Transfer Pricing Problem: A Theory for Practice* (Lexington MA: Lexington Books, 1985). A more mathematical discussion is provided by B. Holmstrom and J. Tirole, "Transfer Pricing and Organizational Form," *Journal of Law, Economics, & Organizations* 7 (1991), pp. 201–28.

the knowledge necessary to determine opportunity costs is costless, then opportunity cost is the correct transfer price. However, since information is costly (this is the reason for decentralizing), calculating opportunity costs can become very expensive, especially in rapidly changing environments. Therefore, managers must rely on approximations, such as market values, marginal costs, full costs, and negotiated prices. Each of these approximations works better than others in certain circumstances.

Reorganization and Other Methods to Reduce Transfer-Pricing Problems

In some cases the transfer-pricing conflicts among divisional managers can become so great and so filled with animosity that large influence costs are incurred by the firm. Heated transfer-pricing disputes usually occur when the relative volume of transactions among business units is large. Whenever the relative volume of internal transfers is large, a small change in the transfer price can have a large effect on the unit's profits. Whenever the quantity of transactions among internal divisions becomes large, the potential for opportunistic transfer-pricing actions among managers grows, and the amount of influence costs grows. One solution is to reorganize the firm. Take two units with large bilateral transfers and combine them into one division. Combining units, however, can increase the incentives of managers to free-ride on the efforts of other managers who are also responsible for the new unit's profits (since more managers will be important in determining the new unit's profits). Alternatively, the firm might not want to organize as two profit centers. In some cases, Manufacturing can be converted to a cost center rather than a profit center with the manager compensated based on the efficiency of production. The firm might organize both business units as cost centers and keep the pricing and quantity decisions at the central office.

A final possibility is to give the buying division the right to produce the input. That is change the decision rights allocation and allow both Manufacturing and Distribution the rights to make the transferred good. However, this alternative can be expensive (due to duplication of effort).

Internal Accounting System and Performance Evaluation

This chapter describes how the firm's internal accounting systems are used to measure performance. Accounting costs, revenues, profits, return on investment, and residual income are used as performance measures of cost, discretionary expense, revenue, profit, and investment centers. Accounting costs are frequently used as transfer prices. The accounting system is an important component of the firm's performance-evaluation system and thus is an integral part of the firm's control system (performance-evaluation and reward systems). This section elaborates on accounting's role within the firm.

Uses of the Accounting System

We usually think of the firm's accounting system as its external financial reports (balance sheets and income statements) to the shareholders, taxing authorities, regulators, and lenders. The external financial reports (both quarterly and annual) are a vastly-aggregated view of the enormous amount of data provided internally. Internally, managers rely on detailed operating reports of expenses, product costs, and customer account balances, from the accounting system. Much of this information is now computer-accessible on demand with reports produced daily, weekly, or monthly.

The internal reports are used by management for two general purposes: decision management and decision control. As discussed in Chapter 9, the decision-making process is divided into decision management (initiation and implementation) and decision control (ratification and monitoring). Managers have both decision-management and control rights, but not for the same decisions. Managers higher in the hierarchy tend to hold more decision-control rights while the decision-management rights tend to be delegated to managers below them in the hierarchy. To exercise both decision management and decision-control rights managers require knowledge. Some of that knowledge is provided by the accounting system. Therefore, the accounting system is used for both decision management and decision control, but (as described below) its primary function in most firms is decision control.

Decision management requires estimates of future costs and benefits. Initiating an investment decision to build a new plant requires the manager to forecast future alternative uses of this plant. Designing a marketing campaign requires judgments of likely future sales and competitors' responses. Accounting systems are based on historical costs and revenues. They record what the firm paid for its current resource base. Accounting systems are not designed to measure the costs of future resource flows or of likely customer reactions. Accounting systems do a good job of tracking historical costs and revenues. Therefore, when it comes to providing managers with information for decision management, accounting systems are often found wanting.

One area where accounting systems are useful for decision management is where they encourage coordination and the sharing of specialized knowledge. Most firms have accounting-based budget systems. Managers forecast costs and revenues for the next year in preparing their budgets. This process forces managers to be forward-looking, to coordinate their operations with those managers most directly affected by their decisions, and to share specialized knowledge of their markets and production technologies. Accounting-based budgets provide the framework for coordination and knowledge sharing.

While helpful as budgets, accounting systems are most useful for decision control. In fact, this is the primary reason they evolved. Internal accounting systems protect against theft of company assets, fraud, embezzlement. They also provide a scorecard for how a business unit did historically by measuring profits or residual income. Budgets thus provide a benchmark against which performance can be appraised. Decision control consists of ratification and monitoring. Monitoring is by definition an historical function, one well served by accounting data. Therefore, accounting systems are primarily used for decision control (to prevent theft and to measure historical performance).

Tension between Decision Management and Control

Considering how the accounting system is used for both decision management and decision control leads to a number of important insights. First, accounting measures, to the extent they are used for monitoring purposes, are not under the complete control of the people being monitored (the operating managers). Second, non-accounting measures are more timely than accounting measures. Not every decision requires ratification or monitoring. Decision monitoring can be based on aggregate data to average out random fluctuations. Instead of monitoring every machine set-up, it is usually cost-efficient to aggregate all set-ups occurring over the week or month together and make sure the average set-up cost is within acceptable levels. Third, managers with decision-management rights tend to be dissatisfied with financial measures for making operating decisions. The accounting numbers will not be particularly timely for operating decisions. The data often are at too aggregate a level and do not provide sufficient detail for the decision. In response, operating managers develop their own, often non-financial, information systems to provide some of the knowledge required for decision management. But at the same time, they rely on accounting-system output to monitor the managers who report to them. One survey reports that managers rely on non-financial data (labor counts, units of output, units in inventory, units scrapped) to run their day-to-day operations. But when asked about their "most valuable report in general," they said it was the monthly income or expense statement because this was one of the measures used to judge their performance.[14]

In choosing among alternative accounting systems, managers must trade-off the net benefits of decision management for the net benefits from decision control. Consider the transfer-pricing decision. The transfer-pricing method that most accurately measures the opportunity cost to the firm of transferring one more unit inside the firm might not be the transfer-pricing method that gives internal managers incentive to maximize firm value. For example, if the transfer-pricing method that most accurately measures the opportunity cost of units transferred (decision management) also requires managers producing the units to reveal privately-held and hard-to-verify knowledge of their costs, then these managers have much discretion over the transfer prices. If these prices are important in rewarding managers

---

[14]S. McKinnon and W. Bruns, *The Information Mosaic* (Boston: Harvard Business School Press, 1992).

(decision control), the producing managers can distort the system to their benefit. A transfer-pricing scheme that is less subject to managerial discretion might in the end be a more accurate measure of opportunity costs than one that requires managers to disclose private, hard-to-verify knowledge.

Activity Based Costing

In the later 1980s and early 1990s discussions of a new accounting system, Activity-Based Costing or ABC, appeared in every popular professional magazine. *Fortune* magazine declared, "Trim waste! Improve service! Increase productivity! But it does all that—and more." Under traditional accounting systems, overhead costs are allocated to products or lines of business using very simple formulas such as percent of direct labor or percent of total revenue. The old system mis-costs complex products requiring more specialized overhead resources. Managers claimed to be misled and underpriced products they thought were profitable, when they were not.

Under ABC, different categories of overhead (purchasing, engineering, inspection) are assigned to products based on the underlying cost-drivers of that overhead department. Purchasing department costs are allocated based on the quantity of purchase orders issued or the number of different parts purchased. ABC is claimed to give a more accurate estimate of a product's true costs.

ABC proponents argue their product costs are more useful for decision making than the traditional numbers. While numerous firms have investigated ABC systems and have conducted pilot studies, few firms have dismantled their old, simpler cost-allocation schemes. These firms use the ABC-based numbers for special studies, but still base performance evaluation on their traditional accounting systems. Why?

The ABC systems are designed by the operating managers. These are the people with the specialized knowledge of the overhead cost-drivers. Yet these are the people whose performance is being judged. One reason ABC is not replacing traditional accounting systems is the dictum of not giving control of the accounting system to the people being monitored by the accounting system.

There is a second reason why ABC is not replacing traditional systems. The accounting measures are used for performance evaluation as well as decision making (product pricing decisions). Altering the way the purchasing department costs are allocated to products causes some product costs to increase and others to decrease, causing some product managers to appear less profitable and other product managers to appear more profitable. Changes in the accounting system are changes in the performance-evaluation systems. And without corresponding modifications in the compensation schemes, accounting system changes create windfall gains for some managers and windfall losses for others. Altering accounting cost allocations creates "winners" and "losers" who impose influence costs on the organization.

Suggested by T. P. Paré, "A New Tool for Managing Costs," *Fortune* (June 14, 1993), pp. 124–129.

All accounting (and non-accounting) performance measures are prone to managerial opportunism in the form of accounting manipulations and dysfunctional decisions. Managers can choose depreciation methods that reduce expenses and increase reported earnings (straight-line depreciation). These accounting choices artificially raise ROI. Investment-center managers can increase ROI by rejecting (or divesting) profitable projects with ROIs below the average ROI of the division. Most accounting measures are short-term measures of performance. They all suffer from the "horizon problem," whereby managers emphasize short-term performance at the expense of long-term returns. Therefore, each accounting-based performance measurement scheme requires careful monitoring by senior managers to reduce non-optimal subordinate behavior from the viewpoint of the owners.

All performance-measurement schemes, including accounting-based methods, if used mechanically and in isolation from other measures, are likely to produce misleading results and induce dysfunctional behavior. For example, at one time Moscow cab drivers were evaluated on miles driven. This scheme caused cab drivers to circle the city on the uncongested outer highways while most of the demand for cabs remained in the congested center of Moscow, where there were no cabs.

Finally, no performance-measurement and reward system works perfectly. There always remains some managerial decisions that enhance the manager's welfare at the expense of the shareholders. The key question is: Does the system outperform the next best alternative after all the costs and benefits are included? One should avoid the "nirvana fallacy" which advocates discarding a system because it allows some remaining managerial opportunism. The nirvana fallacy occurs when one compares a real system to an assumed, but not achievable, "perfect" system.[15]

Summary

The last chapter described individual performance-evaluation systems: subjective versus objective, explicit schemes, absolute versus relative-performance evaluations, and evaluating individuals in teams. This chapter extended the discussion to evaluating divisional performance.

Decision rights are allocated to smaller subunits of the organization (e.g., cost, expense, revenue, investment, and profit centers). These centers often are then evaluated and rewarded based on accounting-based performance measures. Cost centers are delegated decision rights over how to produce the product or part but not over price or quantity. Cost centers are evaluated based on meeting cost, delivery schedules, and quality. Expense centers such as personnel departments are like cost centers except that their output is not easily quantifiable. The lack of quantifiable output means users often are not charged for the expense center's output, and hence the demand for expense center services tends to grow faster than the firm's output.

---

[15]H. Demsetz, "Information and Efficiency: Another Viewpoint," *Journal of Law and Economics* XII (1969), pp. 1–22.

Revenue centers also are similar to cost centers with the difference that they are responsible for selling and distributing the products. They have decision rights over how to sell or distribute the product, but not over the price/quantity decision. Revenue centers are evaluated on maximizing revenue given price/quantity and a fixed budget for their operating expenses.

Profit centers have all the decision rights of cost centers plus the pricing decision. They do not have decision rights over the level of investment in their profit center. Profit centers are evaluated based on total profits. Finally, investment centers are like profit centers except they have decision rights over the amount of capital invested in their division. Evaluating performance of investment centers involves adjusting profits for the amount of capital invested. Two commonly used investment center measures are return on investment (ROI) and residual income (now called economic value added, EVA®). Both measures create incentives for managers to eliminate assets that are not covering their opportunity cost of capital. However, ROI gives incentives to eliminate profitable projects with returns below the average ROI for the division. Residual income does not have this incentive problem but as a performance measure makes comparing divisions of different sizes difficult.

Measuring costs, profits, and investments at the divisional level requires interdivisional transfers of goods and services to be recorded. Transfer pricing is very prevalent in firms and involves not just the transfer of intermediate products but also cost allocations and chargeback systems for internal services. It is important to remember that choice of transfer pricing method does not merely reallocate total company profits among business units; rather, it also affects the firm's total profits. The reason is that different transfer-pricing methods face decision makers with different prices. They will choose different amounts to buy, thereby affecting the scale of operations and total profits.

The correct transfer price to account for the interdivisional exchanges is opportunity cost. But opportunity cost is usually private specialized knowledge of the local divisional managers. If either the buying or selling division can set the transfer price unilaterally and the other division must accept this price, each division will behave monopolistically. The selling division will set too high a price to capture monopoly profits, and too few units will be transferred. If the buying division is allowed to set the transfer price, a price below the true opportunity cost will be chosen and again too few units will be transferred.

If central headquarters knows the opportunity costs of the divisions, there is little reason to decentralize into profit centers. There are a variety of alternative transfer pricing methods to proxy for opportunity cost (market price, marginal cost, full cost). All methods are flawed in the sense that they approximate opportunity cost with errors. Some methods are more costly to estimate and administer than others in certain cases. Market-based transfer prices are useful when external markets exist. But if an external market exists, why is the firm producing the goods or services? If there are synergies favoring internal production, the external market price probably does not capture these synergies. Marginal-cost transfer pricing is another popular transfer-pricing method. But marginal cost is costly to estimate and can lead to influence costs as managers debate whether certain expenditures are marginal or not.

Full-cost transfer prices are objective, simple-to-compute transfer prices. They are also widely used in practice. However, full-cost transfer prices likely suffer from setting the transfer price on the last unit above marginal cost. Another transfer-pricing alternative is negotiated prices. Negotiated transfer prices are time-consuming. On the other hand, if the parties are negotiating both the price and quantity to transfer, they jointly have the incentive to negotiate the quantity that maximizes the size of the pie (firm profits) and then negotiate over the transfer price about how the pie will be divided.

Finally, most divisional-performance evaluation systems rely on internally-generated accounting-based numbers. These accounting-based performance metrics are for decision control (decision ratification and decision monitoring). Besides exercising decision-control rights, workers also exercise decision-management rights (decision initiation and implementation). Exercising decision-management rights also requires knowledge; and often managers again turn to their accounting systems for the information. But the accounting systems of most firms are designed for decision control, not necessarily for decision management. This leads to a trade-off between these two uses and to the general conclusion that most managers find their accounting systems somewhat wanting when it comes to providing information for decision management.

CHAPTER 15 Leadership

In 1982, David Kearns was appointed CEO of Xerox Corporation, the major producer of copy machines in the world.[1] At that time, the company was in significant trouble. Between 1976 and 1982, Xerox's share of installations of copiers in the United States dropped from about 80 percent to 13 percent. Japanese companies such as Canon, Minolta, Ricoh and Sharp had become major players in this market. These companies were then selling copiers at prices that were lower than Xerox's costs for producing competing machines.

A primary reason for Xerox's decline in market share was poor product quality. As Kearns put it:

> Our customer cancellations were rapidly on the rise, our response to the problem was to try to outrun them by pushing hard to get enough new orders to offset the customers we had lost. Customers were fed up with our copiers breaking down and our service response.

Kearn's reasoned that if something was not done "Xerox was destined to have a fire sale and close down by 1990." The "only hope for survival was to urgently commit the company to vastly improving the quality of its products and services."

According to Kearns, however, most Xerox employees understood neither how bad the problem was nor the importance of enhancing product quality. He realized that even as CEO he could not implement his vision of improving product quality by simply ordering 100,000 employees to focus on quality. First, the workers were not trained to produce quality products. Second, unless employees were convinced that it was in their interests to focus on quality, the agency problem of motivating them to alter their behavior would be enormous. Certainly, Kearns did not have the time to monitor each employee to see if his vision was carried out. Third, Kearns feared that painting too dismal a picture would induce some key people to leave the company.

---

[1]The information about David Kearns and Xerox is based on David T. Kearns and David A. Nadler, *Prophets in the Dark*, Harper Business Press, New York, 1992.

In response to these concerns, Kearns (with the help of outside consultants) initiated a strategy to shift corporate direction. He began by convincing a select group of key executives that focusing on quality was essential. These people in turn helped to refine the quality vision and to convince other employees of the potential benefits of this change in focus. Employees throughout the company received substantial training in quality techniques and the importance of quality was stressed at every opportunity (media releases, management speeches, signs on bulletin boards and so forth). The potential crisis posed by the Japanese successes was emphasized.

After much training and promotion, however, the desired change in culture simply was not occurring. It was then that Kearns came to the recognition that to affect employee behavior, top management had to do more than just cajole and plead—the performance-evaluation and incentive systems also had to change. As Kearns says:

> Unless people get rewarded and punished for how they behave, no one will really believe that this is anything more than lip service. A widespread problem [with implementing culture change] that was singled out was that people said we were still promoting and rewarding employees who weren't true believers and users of the quality process. This was creating noise in the system and sending mixed signals. It had to stop.

Kearns accordingly initiated changes in the criteria for promotions and salary decisions, placing major emphasis on customer satisfaction and quality. Eventually, the culture at Xerox did change. In 1989, Xerox won the Malcolm Baldridge National Quality Award.

Kearns displayed important leadership skills in his tenure as Xerox CEO. His example, however, suggests that effective leadership is more than developing an appropriate vision for the company. It is also critical to be effective in motivating people to follow the vision. As this example illustrates, changes in the firm's organizational architecture (the assignment of decision rights, reward, and performance-evaluation systems) can play an important role in motivating significant organizational change.

In this chapter, we use the framework developed in this book to provide insights for more effective leadership. The analysis presents an important example of how this framework can be used to provide a structured discussion of a popular, but poorly understood, topic.[2] Subsequent chapters on outsourcing, total quality management/reengineering, and ethics present additional examples. The insights in this chapter are useful not only for people at the top of the organization, but also for employees throughout the firm who have the opportunity to perform various leadership roles. Indeed, the analysis is helpful for all employees who want to have their ideas implemented within an organization.

The chapter is organized as follows. We begin by discussing the concept of leadership and how it relates to organizational architecture. We then consider an example of a middle manager who has conceived an idea for improving quality and productivity within her division. Leadership in this context involves working *within the firm's architecture* to get the *initiated* decision *ratified* and *implemented*.

---

[2]Numerous books have been written on the subject of leadership, and the topic is often featured in business publications.

We argue that the ratification process involves more than just a careful analysis of the relevant alternatives. Rather the typical process is characterized by a set of agency problems and in many ways resembles a political process within government. Based on this perspective, we present strategies for getting proposed decisions ratified and implemented within a firm. These strategies require careful analysis, including an understanding of the firm's architecture. We begin with the easiest case, where the proposed decision benefits some of the people in the organization and is expected to harm no one. Even in this case, getting a decision adopted can be difficult. We then consider decisions that have important distributional consequences—some employees benefit, while others are harmed. Towards the end of the chapter, we briefly discuss whether organizational power is ''bad'' as well as the use of symbols (role modeling, formal creeds, stories, and legends) in leadership.

Leadership

Webster's dictionary defines *leadership* as ''leading others along a way, guiding.'' This definition suggests that there are at least two important characteristics of good leadership. First, the leader must play a key role in helping the organization to choose the right path (vision, goal, or plan). Second, the leader must help motivate people to follow it. Much of the popular literature on leadership stresses these two characteristics. To quote John Gardner, ''The two tasks at the heart of the popular notion of leadership are goal setting and motivating.''[3] Since these tasks are performed by people throughout the organization, leadership is in no sense the exclusive domain of top management. Rather, many employees in the firm play important leadership roles.

Vision Setting

By vision we simply mean a proposed strategy, plan, or course of action for the firm. Sometimes leaders conceive of corporate visions by themselves. For example, according to Kearns, he was among the first people to envision Xerox as a quality-based organization. Top management, however, usually does not have all the relevant specific knowledge and cannot be expected to conceive important visions entirely by themselves. Indeed, in many cases visions emanate from lower-level employees or even from people outside the firm (for example, consultants). Often the information for formulating a vision has to be assembled by combining the knowledge of numerous individuals. For instance, firms typically involve many employees in developing a mission statement. One aspect of effective leadership involves structuring the organization in a manner that motivates employees with the relevant specific knowledge to initiate value-enhancing proposals and take part in

---

[3]John W. Gardner, *On Leadership,* The Free Press, New York, 1990, p. 11.

vision setting. It is this view that has motivated much of the current literature on the role of managers in empowering workers to "unleash their untapped creativity."

Motivation

While an appropriate vision is important, it cannot create firm value unless it is implemented. Thus, the task of motivation is at least as important as the task of goal-setting. Indeed, it is often better to implement a "second-best" plan than to identify the best plan but fail to implement it. Based on this argument, the literature on leadership often emphasizes motivation skills:[4]

- "Leadership is the *process of persuasion* or example by which an individual induces a group to pursue objectives held by the leader or his or her followers."
- "I define leadership as leaders *inducing* followers to act for certain goals that represent the values and the motivations—the wants and needs, the aspirations and expectations—of both leaders and followers."
- "The task of leadership is not only to make policy, but *to build* it into the organization's social structure."
- "The one who knows the right thing but cannot achieve it fails because he is ineffectual. The great leader *needs . . . the capacity to achieve.*"

Some authors argue that leaders motivate people to follow visions through personal charisma, style, and inspiration.[5] Under this view, the bonds between leader and follower are more emotional than rational. Strong emotional ties motivate individuals to follow the leader's call to action. Leaders who are cited as charismatic include Gandhi, John F. Kennedy, and Martin Luther King. Charisma probably explains much of the behavior of individuals in some settings (for example, individuals in certain religious cults). Unfortunately, charisma is difficult to teach.

The economic framework, however, suggests other factors that also determine effective leadership that can be taught. Economics takes the view that people make choices that are in their own self-interest. In this context, the problem of motivating employees to follow a vision is the standard agency problem. If a leader wants to increase the likelihood that others take certain actions, the leader can design an incentive system that makes it in an employee's self-interest to follow the leader. As we discussed, David Kearns came to realize this principle at Xerox.

---

[4]Italics are ours. The four quotes are taken, respectively, from: (1) John W. Gardner, *On Leadership,* The Free Press, New York, 1990, p. 1; (2) James MacGregor Burns, *Leadership,* New York, 1978, p. 19; (3) Philip Selznick, *Leadership in Administration,* New York, 1957, p. 62, (4) Richard M. Nixon, *Leaders,* Warner Books, New York, 1982, p. 5.

[5]See, for example, Robert J. House, William D. Spangler, and James Woycke, "Personality and Charisma in the U. S. Presidency: A Psychological Theory of Leadership," Unpublished manuscript, Wharton School, University of Pennsylvania, 1989.

Leadership and Organizational Architecture

Our discussion indicates that effective leadership entails at least two basic tasks—helping to develop an appropriate vision and direction for the firm and motivating employees to implement this vision. To accomplish these objectives, it is useful to consider the firm's architecture. In particular, management can design decision-right, reward, and performance-evaluation systems that effectively link the relevant specific knowledge with decision-making authority (including vision-setting) and provide the appropriate incentives for decision makers to act on their information. In this sense, much of this book already has focused on key components of leadership. As we will discuss below, however, effective leadership also involves understanding how to get things done *within the existing architecture.*

The Decision-Making Process

David Kearns wanted to make dramatic changes in the culture at Xerox. To motivate these changes, he altered the firm's performance-evaluation and reward systems. Most employees must exercise leadership within the existing architecture, since they do not have the authority to make changes in either the performance-evaluation or reward systems. Indeed, in most cases, even leaders must work within the existing organizational architecture to motivate change in the firm because changing architecture can be expensive. (For example, frequent changes in the evaluation and reward systems can discourage employees from making long-run investments, developing relationships with co-workers—see Chapter 8.)

In this context, assume that a middle-level manager, Maria Hernandez, conceives an idea for enhancing quality and productivity within her division. In particular, Maria wants to decentralize decision rights for employee scheduling, training, and work procedures to workgroups. Maria must work within the existing architecture to motivate the adoption of her vision.

In Chapter 9, recall that we divided decision rights into four categories: *initiation, ratification, implementation,* and *monitoring.* In these terms, Maria has initiated a decision; her problem is to get the decision ratified and implemented. We begin by considering the problem of ratification.

Ratification

Academic discussions often treat the ratification of decisions as a purely intellectual exercise. In the standard treatment, the relevant alternatives are identified. Analysis is conducted and the best alternative is chosen. In this context, good leadership is equivalent to careful analysis—Maria will get her proposal ratified if her analysis is convincing. In most firms, however, the ratification process is much more complicated than this simple characterization. While good analysis is important, it is far from sufficient for effective leadership.

There are at least three factors that complicate the ratification process in most firms. First, most decisions have distributional consequences for employees within the firm. (Some win, while others lose.) For instance, Maria's plan to form self-empowered workgroups might result in the layoffs of some supervisors and middle managers. Second, much of the analysis is qualitative. For example, Maria's analysis will include forecasts about what other companies are going to do in the industry. Such forecasts and other assumptions in the analysis are subject to debate and alternative speculation. Third, decision-making authority is often not clear cut. Decisions frequently require approval from several individuals, and it is not always well specified who has actual decision-making authority. Correspondingly, individuals can argue that they should have an input in the decision process even if they do not have formal authority. In Maria's case, the divisional vice presidents in charge of manufacturing, finance, marketing, and sales will play major roles in the decision process. The middle managers who will be affected by the plan are also likely to claim that they should be consulted in the decision process.

These three factors imply that decision processes often entail significant agency problems. The groups that are harmed by decisions are likely to oppose them, while those that gain are likely to be supportive. For example, certain middle-level managers are likely to oppose the plan, while certain lower-level workers are likely to support it. Neither side will necessarily be acting to maximize firm value. When it is not obvious whether a decision is value-increasing, both sides can marshall arguments to defend their positions. In addition, numerous individuals are likely to assert that they should have a role in making important decisions—the more directly affected by the decision are the individuals, the more strenuously they will lobby for such a role. Key managers, in turn, often rely on people for advice and "consensus decision making" because the managers do not have all the relevant specific knowledge to make good decisions.

This discussion suggests that decision making in firms often resembles decision making in *political settings,* such as government. To quote Jeffrey Pfeffer:

> Organizations, particularly large ones, are like governments in that they are fundamentally political entities. To understand them, one needs to understand organizational politics, just as to understand governments, one needs to understand government politics.[6]

Implementation

Getting a decision ratified is a critical first step towards the realization of a vision or plan. However, ratified plans often fail because of implementation problems. Again, a primary concern is the standard agency problem—those charged with implementing a plan might not have incentives to carry it out. For example, Maria might be successful in getting the company to ratify her plan for quality improvements. However, unless the workers in her division are motivated to implement the plan, it will be ineffective.

---

[6]Jeffrey Pfeffer, *Managing with Power,* Harvard Business School Press, Boston, 1992, p. 8.

Henry Kissinger on Decision Making

Former Secretary of State Henry Kissinger made the following observation about decision making:

> "Before I served as a consultant to Kennedy, I had believed, like most academics, that the process of decision-making was largely intellectual and all one had to do was to walk into the President's office and convince him of the correctness of one's view. This perspective I soon realized is as dangerously immature as it is widely held."

Suggested by Henry Kissinger, *The White House Years*, Little, Brown, Boston, 1979, p. 39.

Organizational Architecture and Decision Making

Maria will increase the likelihood of achieving ratification and implementation of her proposal if she carefully analyzes her firm's architecture. It is important to recognize who will be involved in the decision-making process. (The relevant individuals include not only actual decision makers, but their advisors, as well.) In addition, it is important to appreciate the distributional consequences of the decision—who benefits from the decision and who is harmed. A major determinant of these distributional consequences is the organization's incentive system. For example, workers paid on a piece-rate basis might oppose Maria's program with its emphasis on quality because they anticipate lower output and compensation. Thus, they might try to block the proposal by arguing against it. If the proposal is ratified, they might ignore the decision and continue to emphasize output at the expense of quality.

A detailed understanding of the firm's architecture will help Maria to develop a strategy for seeking ratification. If her analysis suggests that the proposal has little chance of succeeding, she can either modify the proposal so ratification is more likely (for example, by reducing the negative effects on the opponents of the plan) or abandon the idea without wasting valuable resources and reputation by backing a losing cause. The knowledge is also important in devising a strategy to maximize the likelihood that the proposal will be successfully implemented. In the next two sections, we discuss the use of organizational knowledge in developing a strategy for gaining support to ratify the proposed decision. We then consider strategies for implementation.

Ratification of Plans with Limited Distributional Effects

The easiest decisions to get ratified are those that are expected to make some people in the organization better off without making others worse off. For example, suppose that Maria's proposal increases the expected profits of her division and thus the likely payouts to employees through the profit-sharing plan. In addition, assume that the plan is not expected to cause any layoffs. (Middle-level managers and supervisors will be reassigned to other comparable positions.) Since everyone expects to benefit by this proposal, it would seem that Maria would have an easy time in "leading" the organization to ratify her quality program. As we will see, however, even in these simple cases it is not always easy to obtain ratification—*there is a predisposition for decision makers to say no.*

Mismanaging Organizational Politics at Xerox

Xerox's Palo Alto Research Center (PARC) invented the first personal computer, the first graphics-oriented monitor, one of the first hand-held computer mouses, the first word-processing program for nonexpert users, the first local area communications network, the first object-oriented programming language, and the first laser printer. Xerox, however, failed to capitalize commercially on this inventive technology. One reason was that PARC was physically removed from the rest of Xerox and did not understand the importance of motivating other units in the firm (such as marketing) to support their technological visions. Employees at PARC were characterized as being arrogant and suffering from a "we/they attitude toward the rest of Xerox." In the words of Jeffrey Pfeffer:

> "By not appreciating the interdependence involved in a new product launch and the skills required to manage that interdependence, PARC researchers lost out on their ambition to change the world of computing, and Xerox missed some important economic opportunities."

Suggested by Jeffrey Pfeffer, *Managing with Power*, Harvard Business School Press, Boston, 1992, pp. 38–39.

Risk Aversion and the Tendency to Say No

Individuals are likely to be uncertain about the consequences of even relatively straight-forward decisions. For instance, even though employees expect to benefit from the proposal, they will be concerned that the program will lead to less desirable jobs or layoffs. Similarly, divisional managers will worry about potential cost overruns. Thus, even if the proposed change appears better, people are likely to worry about outcomes that reduce their welfare. In contrast, decision makers are more certain about the consequences of the status quo.

Given the increased uncertainty, *risk-averse* decision makers are likely to oppose new proposals even if it is unlikely that the proposal will affect them. For illustration, suppose that when initially confronted with Maria's proposal decision makers think that it will entail a small but equal chance of increasing or decreasing their personal wealth by $10,000. (There is some chance that the proposal might have a significant effect on profits and thus executive bonuses.) In this case, the expected wealth of the decision makers remains the same, but it is less certain under the new proposal. As discussed in Chapter 12, a risk-averse individual prefers a certain income flow to an uncertain income flow with the same expected value. Thus the decision makers will oppose the proposal, even though they expect that on average they will be unaffected. Decision makers will support the proposal only if the gain in expected wealth is enough to offset the costs from increased risk-bearing, or they are confident that the proposal does not increase risk.

Strategies for Sponsoring Proposals

Careful Analysis and Groundwork.   Our analysis suggests that Maria can anticipate opposition to her proposal because people are risk-averse—individuals who are unfamiliar with her analysis will be unsure of the personal consequences of the action and are likely to oppose it. This argument suggests that Maria should take the time to explain the analysis to decision makers (as well as their key advisors) and to convince them that the analysis is correct. For instance, she might want to meet with key decision makers to discuss the proposal and answer questions about the analysis. This action can reduce uncertainty and make it more likely that decision makers will agree to the proposal. It is generally unwise to introduce important proposals at meetings and request on-the-spot decisions. Without laying the proper groundwork, such proposals are likely to be tabled for further study or simply rejected.

Emphasizing a Crisis.   A complementary strategy to overcome the normal preference for the status quo is to argue that the current situation is worse than people think. The popular literature, for instance, frequently argues that employees are most likely to favor change when an organization is in a *crisis*. (If change doesn't occur, the organization is going to fail.) Individuals, in turn, can promote a willingness to change if they can convince employees that the firm faces a crisis. For example, David Kearns gained support for his program by continually pointing out the threat to Xerox from Japanese competition. This strategy is likely to work in the long run only if the firm faces an actual crisis. Individuals understand the incentives that proponents of proposals have to state that the organization faces a crisis and correspondingly are unlikely to accept this argument unless it is credible. In the case of Xerox, it was easy to document that business had been lost to the Japanese. Also, it was easy to point to other industries, such as steel and automobiles, which were having similar experiences.

Maintaining Flexibility.   Another way to convince people that the risk of a proposal is low is to design proposals that can be modified easily once they are underway. In our example, Maria might suggest starting with a limited pilot program, involving only one region or a single product. If the test is successful, the program could be expanded. If not, it could be discontinued at low cost. Tests of this type provide more precise estimates of the costs and benefits of proposed actions while only committing limited resources. A small-scale test does not commit the firm to adopt the program throughout the company, but provides an ''option'' to do so.

Tying the Proposal to a Popular Program or Initiative.   Maria might increase the support for her proposal by casting it up as part of a popular on-going program or initiative. For example, perhaps the CEO has stressed the importance of product quality to the media and to customers through a program entitled ''Quality 2000.'' Maria can claim that her proposal is an integral part of the CEO's vision for the company and fits nicely within the Quality 2000 program. Casting up the proposal in this manner makes it less likely that other employees will raise objections because they will not want to argue against an important initiative sponsored by the CEO.

Developing a Good Reputation for Decision Making.   People have reasons to listen to a person with an established reputation for offering sound proposals. First, past success is an indicator of skills and the likelihood of future success. Second, a successful person has strong incentives to conduct a careful analysis to avoid damaging that reputation. The importance of reputations in an organization suggests that people, such as Maria, should conduct careful analyses and consider well what they recommend. Also it is important not to fight too many losing battles—to avoid a reputation of always being on the wrong side of issues.

Reputation and Influence

Decision makers often rely on the advice of people with established reputations. This tendency is emphasized by H. Mintzberg:

> ''I found that chief executives faced complex choices. They had to consider the impact of each decision on other decisions and on the organization's strategy. They had to ensure that the decision would be acceptable to those who influence the organization as well as ensuring that resources would not be overextended. They had to understand the various costs and benefits as well as the feasibility of the proposal. They also had to consider questions of timing. All this was necessary for the simple approval of someone else's proposal. At the same time, however, delay could cost time, while quick approval could be ill considered and quick rejection might discourage the subordinate who had spend months developing a pet project.
>
> One common solution to approving projects is to pick the man instead of the proposal. That is, the manager authorizes those projects presented to him by people whose judgment he trusts.''

Suggested by H. Mintzberg, ''The Manager's Job: Folklore and Fact,'' *Harvard Business Review*, July–August 1975, pp. 49–61.

Ratification of Plans with Distributional Effects

Sponsoring Plans with Distributional Effects

Many proposals have significant distributional consequences for employees within the firm. For example, Maria's proposal might result in lost jobs for some middle managers and promotions for other lower-level workers. In this case, careful analysis and communication are not enough. Some people will oppose the proposal even if they are confident that the project is value-increasing for the firm as a whole. For example, certain middle managers will have strong incentives to develop arguments against the proposal and correspondingly to lobby key decisions makers not to approve the plan.

If the influence of these middle managers is strong enough the proposal will be blocked, even though it is good for the company. Maria, therefore, must have more *power* than the opponents of the proposal. (Being more powerful means that she can garner enough support among decision makers for the proposal to be ratified.) While Maria can increase her support among decision makers by following the principles outlined in the last section—such as being careful in her analysis—often these activities will not be enough. Rather, she must have additional power or influence to gain sufficient support for her proposal.

Sources of Power

Where does power in organizations come from? There are no laws that require people to obey or support the wishes of others within the firm. Thus, corporate power does not come from the ability to force others to follow commands. Rather power ultimately comes from other people who *voluntarily agree* to comply with a leader's wishes or proposals. For this voluntary action to occur, it must be in the perceived interests of these people to cooperate with the leader. Below we discuss potential sources of power and influence.[7]

Formal Authority.   Some power comes from the formal position within the organization. For instance, if a boss has the right to fire, promote and compensate a subordinate, the subordinate obviously has an economic incentive to comply with the boss's wishes. Maria, therefore, probably can count on some support from her subordinates (assuming she makes it clear that this issue is important to her). These employees are likely to speak in favor of the proposal at meetings. In addition, Maria's formal authority gives her the right to make certain decisions without consulting others. For example, she might already have the authority to form work-groups within her own unit. The power that is attached to a formal position, however, is not without limits. First, there is the usual agency problem that subordinates might ignore their boss's wishes. Second, subordinates can take actions to get the boss replaced (a "palace revolt"). For instance, Maria's subordinates might form a coalition to complain to her boss that she is incompetent. Third, some companies conduct 360-degree performance reviews, where subordinates provide formal input into the performance evaluations of the managers.

---

[7]For a more extensive discussion of some of these sources of power, see Jeffrey Pfeffer, *Managing with Power,* Harvard Business School Press, Boston, 1992.

Control of Physical and Monetary Resources.   People are granted rights to control resources within organizations. For instance, some individuals have budget authority, while others decide on the allocation of office space or the priority for using copy machines. Control over these resources is a source of power. Individuals are reluctant to challenge a person who controls an important resource because they fear that it will affect their access to the resource. For example, people in other departments might support Maria if she controls a budget from which they receive funds.

Power and Resource Control—Voting on Anti-takeover Amendments

Economic theory suggests that the control of important resources provides a person with power. Other people are afraid not to support the person's proposals because they fear that they will lose access to the important resource.

An illustration of the importance of this argument is provided by studies of corporate voting on anti-takeover amendments. These amendments make it more difficult for outsiders to take control of a company through a corporate takeover. The existing evidence suggests that some of these amendments reduce the wealth of shareholders but benefit incumbent managers who become more secure in their jobs. The decision on whether or not to adopt these management-sponsored amendments is held by the shareholders, who would appear to have the incentives to vote against the amendments. Management, however, has power over certain institutional investors, such as banks, insurance companies, and nonbank trusts, because they derive business from the firm that is under management control—if they don't vote in favor of management-sponsored amendments they risk losing important business. Indeed, empirical evidence indicates that these types of institutional investors are more likely to support management-sponsored anti-takeover amendments than other, more independent, investors. The evidence also suggests that management groups who do not have enough power to get amendments passed tend not to propose amendments because they do not want to bear the reputation costs of proposing an amendment that fails.

Suggested by James A. Brickley, Ronald C. Lease, and Clifford W. Smith, "Corporate Voting: Evidence from Charter Amendment Proposals," *Journal of Corporate Finance* 1, 1994, pp. 5–31.

This discussion suggests that individuals can increase their organizational power by gaining control over key resources. This concept can be important in deciding whether to apply for a particular job or task within the firm—jobs and tasks are more attractive if they contain decision rights over resources others value. Also, a person can sometimes create power by developing a service or product that is important to other people in the organization. For example, the data-processing manager in a company might increase his power by offering a repair service for computers within the organization. This action will be more successful in creating power if the firm requires employees to use this internal service for computer repair.

Ford Motor Company and the $5 Dollar Day

In 1914, Ford Motor Company paid a wage rate of $2.20/day to factory workers. This rate was very close to the prevailing market rate in the Detroit area. Annual turnover at Ford was over 300 percent, as workers would take jobs at different companies for slightly higher wages. Management had little power over its workers. If a supervisor was too demanding or difficult, employees would simply quit and go to work for a different firm. To combat this problem, Henry Ford increased the daily wage to $5.00 per day. This wage rate gave Ford tremendous power over his employees since they did not want to lose their jobs and work for someone else at $2.20 per day. To quote Henry Ford,

> "I have a thousand men who if I say 'Be at the northeast corner of the building at four a.m.' will be there at four a.m. That is what we want: obedience."

Suggested by David Halberstam, *The Reckoning*, Avon Books, New York, 1986, and Stephen Meyer, III, *The Five Dollar Day: Labor, Management, and Social Control in the Ford Motor Company, 1908–1921,* State University of New York Press, Albany NY, 1981.

Control of Information.   A particularly important resource in most organizations is information. The information held by any particular employee depends on such things as the employee's position, office location, social network, and special skills. Not all employees have equal access to information. Since most employees require various types of information to be effective in their jobs, people with information have power—they can trade information for support. For instance, some people might support Maria because they depend on her to keep them informed about what is going on in the division. Individuals can try to increase their access to information (and power) by lobbying for centrally located office space (for example, at the corporate headquarters), developing a social network within the organization, applying for jobs that are "in the information loop," or volunteering for key committee assignments.

One way of thinking about the control of information in a firm is provided by the *nexus-of-contracts* view of the firm (see Chapter 7). Under this view, the firm is characterized as a network of contracts between the firm and other parties, such as suppliers, customers, and employees. Many of these contracts are informal, and important information is held by people at the contracting nodes. Controlling access to this information can vest a person with substantial power. For instance, it would be quite difficult for a firm to fire an employee who has been the primary contact with a key customer for 20 years. The employee possesses specific information on items from company promises to customer requirements, and turnover in this position would be costly for the firm. Along these lines, Shleifer and Vishny (1989) argue that managers sometimes choose investment projects that give them an informational advantage and thus make it more costly for shareholders to replace them.[8]

---

[8]See Andrei Shleifer, and Robert W. Vishny, 1989, "Management Entrenchment: The Case of Manager-Specific Investments, *Journal of Financial Economics* 25, 123–139.

The Power of Information
Evidence from a French Tobacco Factory

An interesting example of the power of information comes from a French cigarette plant in the 1960s. The equipment in this plant was highly automated and subject to mechanical failures. The manuals that explained how to repair this equipment had been destroyed in a fire, and the only people with the knowledge to fix the machines were the maintenance engineers at the factory. This monopolistic access to important information gave the engineers enormous power. Without them, the plant could not run, and it was impossible to replace them. Indeed the engineers had sufficient power to have a managing director of the company removed from his job. When new engineers were trained in the plant, they were instructed verbally and asked to destroy any notes once they mastered the material. These actions helped the engineers to maintain their power over time.

Suggested by Michel Crozier, *The Bureaucratic Phenomenon,* University of Chicago Press, Chicago, 1964.

Friends and Allies.   Close personal ties with decision makers increase the likelihood that they will act on your behalf. For instance, managers sometimes hire or promote their friends to key positions over more-qualified candidates. One potential reason for this action is that the managers believe that they can trust their friends for support. Some employees make a point of doing favors for other individuals in the firm (for example, providing assistance on difficult projects or filling in for a person when they are on vacation) to increase the likelihood that these individuals will help or support them in the future.[9] Thus, Maria is more likely to obtain ratification for her proposal if she has developed allies within the company.

Coalitions and Logrolling

Maria's personal power will induce some people to support her proposal (through her formal authority or control over resources, for example). In addition, Maria can count on the backing of people who think that they will gain from her proposal. Her level of support from these sources, however, might be insufficient for proposal ratification. In this case, Maria will have to recruit additional individuals to join her *coalition* of supporters. One effective technique she can use is *logrolling.*[10]

---

[9]For an economic analysis of gift giving and exchange, see George Akerlof, 1982, "Labor Contracts as Partial Gift Exchange," *Quarterly Journal of Economics* 97, 543–69. Also, see Julio Rotemberg, 1994, "Human Relations in the Workplace," *Journal of Political Economy* 102, 684–718.

[10]See William Riker, *The Theory of Political Coalitions,* Yale University Press, New Haven, 1962.

A logroll consists of a coalition of individuals who are largely indifferent to each other's demands, but agree to support each other's requests so that each can get what he wants. A classic example of a logroll is the coalition that forms each year in the United States Congress to pass the Rivers and Harbors Act. This act contains many local projects that individually would not receive support from more than a few legislators. The act, however, passes by a majority vote because certain legislators ban together to provide mutual support for each other's proposals. Maria might form a logroll with plant managers in her division. For instance, she could agree to support the proposals of these managers to expand their plants if they back her quality proposal.[11] In business firms (as in many other settings), these types of agreements almost always take the form of implicit promises or understandings, rather than formal contracts.

Logrolling in Government and Business

Many of the classic examples of logrolling come from government. For example, one stylized example involves big business, unions, and farmers, where a winning coalition consists of any of the two groups. Farmers have an advantage in this setting because their demands are more likely to be consistent with the demands of unions and big business than are the demands of big business and unions likely to be consistent with the demands of farmers. Indeed, farmers often want things that are relatively unimportant to the other two groups. Farmers, in turn, often don't care much about the demands of the other groups. This mutual indifference makes farmers good partners in a coalition. In contrast, big business and labor unions are likely to make a poor coalition. This helps explain why farmers have been unusually successful in getting favorable regulation established by the government.

While many of the examples of logrolling come from government, it is also prevalent in most types of organizations. For example, a marketing executive and a manufacturing manager might form a logroll to provide mutual support for each other's funding requests. In contrast, two manufacturing executives who are interested in mutually exclusive projects would not enter into a coalition. To quote Professor James March:

> "Logrolls are found not only in the United States Congress, but also in business firms, military organizations and Universities."

Suggested by James G. March, *A Primer on Decision Making*, The Free Press, New York, 1994, pp. 157–159.

In trying to form a logroll, Maria should anticipate at least three potential problems. First, identifying potential candidates for the logroll is not always easy. The people Maria knows best are her co-workers, who are unlikely to be indifferent

---

[11]Implicit in this discussion is the assumption that the plant managers either have some decision-making authority with respect to Maria's proposal or that decision makers rely on the plant managers for advice.

about the proposal (since they are directly affected). Second, there is the issue of trust. Decisions in firms do not all occur at the same time. For instance, Maria might need immediate support from the plant managers, while proposals for plant expansions might not be considered until next year. The plant managers might be reluctant to support Maria, because they do not trust that she will follow through on her part of the bargain. Third, there is likely to be asymmetric information about how the proposal affects other people's welfare. In particular, Maria will not know for certain who is indifferent about her proposal. Individuals who are truly indifferent might claim that they would be harmed by the proposal, but are willing to support her if she makes many concessions to their wishes. As discussed in Chapter 7, this type of strategic misrepresentation can result in bargaining failures—in this case the logroll might fail to materialize. Despite these problems, however, Maria may well be able to develop an effective coalition. Indeed, this type of deal making or ''horse trading'' is common in organizations.

Implementation Strategies

Getting a proposal ratified does not assure that the proposal will be implemented. One concern again is the standard agency problem. For instance, Maria might get her proposal ratified, yet employees might not act in accord with the plan. Maria can anticipate some of these problems by carefully analyzing employee incentives. Through this analysis, she can identify the employees who are most likely to resist implementation. For example, middle managers might claim that they tried to implement the policy, but it did not work. Based on this analysis, Maria might structure her proposal to reduce the anticipated problems. For example, she might include provisions for certain groups of employees to be *monitored* closely in the implementation phase (recall that monitoring is the fourth step in the decision-making process). She also might recommend changes in the performance-evaluation and reward systems. For example, she might suggest that middle managers be rewarded (for example, through promotions) for successfully implementing the workgroup concept.

Maria also can reduce this agency problem by being very specific about the details that must be followed in implementing the plan. This action, however, comes at the cost of not allowing employees to act on their specific knowledge in the implementation phase. In this sense, Maria faces the basic tension in project design that we have emphasized throughout this book—the tension between the optimal use of specific information and agency problems. Being overly specific in the ratification phase might also make it more difficult for Maria to assemble an effective coalition. Logrolling often requires that the terms of the proposal be somewhat unclear in order to limit potential conflicts.[12]

---

[12]See James G. March, *A Primer on Decision Making,* The Free Press, New York, 1994, pp. 170–171.

Is Organizational Power Bad?

We have argued that effective leadership often requires personal power and skills for dealing within an organizational system characterized by self-interest and agency problems (*political skills*). Yet words like power and politics frequently connote negative images to many people. It is easy to conjure up images of Machiavelli offering insidious advice to the prince on how to increase his power. Similarly, one can envision managers getting overly-absorbed in office politics and favoritism.

Obviously, attempts to gain power involve costs. For instance, having key employees spend time on logrolling can be expensive. In Chapter 9, we discussed how these *influence costs* can affect the optimal architecture of the organization. Indeed, firms that survive in the marketplace are likely to be those firms that limit the unproductive uses of employee time. It is also important to recognize, however, that power and political skills can have important benefits. Organizations involve people working together. Without political skills and power, leaders often would fail to implement value-increasing plans and the organization would suffer immensely. Jeffrey Pfeffer summarizes the point well:[13]

> "The development and exercise of power in organizations is about getting things accomplished. The very nature of organizations—interdependent, complex systems with many actors and many points of view—means that taking actions is often problematic. Failures in implementations are almost invariably failures to build successful coalitions. Although networks of allies can obviously be misused, they are nevertheless essential in order to get things done."

Thus, power and political skills are, in and of themselves, neither good nor bad. Rather, they are important attributes which can be used either for productive or unproductive purposes. Managers are simply naive if they think that they can be effective without them.

The Use of Symbols

The popular literature often stresses that effective leadership requires clever use of symbols, such as role modeling, formal creeds, stories, and legends. For example, an executive interested in increasing customer service might take the time to talk to customers directly and ensure that these actions are visible to other employees through media releases and company filmstrips. Similarly, the executive might tell stories about employees who have gone out of their way to serve customers. The company also might adopt formal creeds and statements to emphasize the basic vision of the company.

We view these types of symbols as an aspect of corporate culture which performs a potentially important communication function; they inform employees about what is valued in the company (see Chapters 8 and 18). But again, symbols

---

[13]Jeffrey Pfeffer, *Managing with Power*, Harvard Business School Press, Boston, 1992, p. 108.

are unlikely to be effective in motivating employees to take particular actions unless reinforced by the firm's performance-evaluation and reward systems. David Kearns came to realize this and ultimately had to change the reward system at Xerox before he could successfully implement his quality program.

The Use of Symbols at Nordstrom's

Nordstrom's is a department store chain that is famous for stressing customer service and satisfaction. The vision of the Nordstrom family (who manage the firm) is to offer the customer the best in service, selection, quality, and value.

The importance of customer service is stressed to employees by the frequent telling of stories about sales clerks who performed such heroics as changing a customer's flat tire in a store parking lot, paying a customer's parking ticket, and lending money to a customer who was short on cash to make a purchase. One particularly interesting story is the one about the sales clerk who refunded money to a customer irate about some newly-purchased tires. The clerk cheerfully refunded the money even though the customer did not have a receipt. The interesting part of the story is that Nordstrom's does not sell tires!

Nordstrom's, however, does not rely on these types of stories alone to motivate employees to provide customer service. Rather they have an extensive incentive system that stresses sales and customer service.

Suggested by Hillary Weston, *Nordstrom: Dissension in the Ranks,* Harvard Business School Case, N9–191–002, 2/19/91.

Summary

This chapter uses the framework developed in this book to provide insights into more effective *leadership*. The analysis presents an important example of how this framework can be used to provide a structured discussion of a popular, but poorly understood, topic. Subsequent chapters on outsourcing, TQM/reengineering, and ethics provide additional examples.

The leadership literature stresses two important tasks that all leaders must perform, goal setting and motivating. To accomplish these tasks, management must design decision-right, performance-evaluation, and reward systems that effectively link relevant specific knowledge with decision-making authority and provide appropriate incentives for decision makers to act on their information. In this sense, most of this book has focused on key components of leadership.

Sometimes, change requires significant alterations in the firm's organizational architecture (decision-right, performance-evaluation and reward systems). Often, however, leaders must work *within the firm's architecture* to motivate change. Using the vocabulary from Chapter 9, a leader who has *initiated* an idea must work within the architecture to get the proposal *ratified* and *implemented*.

Academic discussions often treat the process of decision ratification as a purely intellectual exercise. In most firms, however, the ratification process involves significant agency problems. The groups that are harmed by decisions are likely to oppose them, while those that gain are likely to be supportive. Since it usually is not obvious whether a decision is value-increasing, both sides can marshall arguments to defend their positions. In addition, numerous individuals are likely to assert that they should have a role in making important decisions. Even if a decision is ratified, employees might not have the correct incentives for implementation.

Effective leadership is facilitated by a detailed knowledge of the organization's decision and incentive systems. By carefully diagnosing the firm's architecture using the framework in this book, a sponsor of a proposal can forecast which of the decision makers will be for and which against the proposal. The sponsor can then design a strategy that maximizes the likelihood that the proposal will be ratified and implemented.

Some decisions are expected to make certain groups within the organization better off without making others worse off. Even these decisions are not always easily ratified. There is a *predisposition for decision makers to say no,* due to risk aversion. The status quo is usually more certain than a proposal for change, and thus decision makers tend to favor the status quo. Decision makers will support proposals only if either they expect to gain enough to offset any increased risk-bearing, or they are confident that, from their standpoint, the proposal imposes no risk. Strategies for sponsoring a proposal include conducting a careful analysis and groundwork, convincing decision makers that the firm faces a crisis, designing more flexible proposals, casting the proposal up as being part of a popular program or initiative, and developing a good reputation for sound decision making.

Many proposals have significant distributional consequences for employees within the firm. To get such a proposal ratified, the sponsor must have more *power* than the opponents of the proposal. Being more powerful means that the sponsor can garner enough support among decision makers to ratify the proposal. Power in organizations generally does not come from the ability to force others to follow commands. Rather power comes from other people who *voluntarily agree* to comply with a leader's proposals. For this voluntary action to occur, it must be in the interests of these other people to cooperate with the leader. Sources of power include formal authority derived from the position in the firm, control over important physical or monetary resources, control over information, and friends/allies. Employees can also gain support for proposals by forming *coalitions* and *logrolls.* A logroll consists of a coalition of individuals who are largely indifferent to each other's demands, but agree to support each other's requests so that each can get what she wants.

Implementation problems can be anticipated by carefully analyzing the incentives of employees who will be responsible for carrying out the plan. These potential problems can be controlled by recommending appropriate *monitoring* and/or changes in the performance-evaluation and reward systems. Agency problems can also be reduced by being very specific about the details in implementation. However, this action can come at the expense of not allowing employees to act on specific knowledge during the implementation phase.

Words like power and politics often conjure up negative images. Our view is that power and political skills are neither universally good or bad. Rather they are important attributes that can be used for either productive or unproductive purposes. Managers are naive if they think that they can be effective without them.

Symbols such as role modeling, formal creeds, stories, and legends can play an important role in communicating the leader's vision to employees. However, they are unlikely to be effective in motivating employees to take particular actions, unless they are reinforced by the firm's performance-evaluation and reward systems.

CHAPTER 16 Outsourcing

In 1989, Eastman Kodak sold its mainframe computers to IBM and contracted with IBM to do much of Kodak's data processing for the next ten years.[1] This *outsourcing* of computer services made big news because no company of Kodak's size or prominence had ever turned over its computers to outsiders. Other large companies began considering similar moves. In 1990, U.S. businesses spent $7.2 billion on outsourcing computer operations. According to some estimates, these expenditures were expected to double by 1995.

Under the contract with Kodak, IBM is responsible for operating Kodak's data center. IBM provides the operating software and hardware and is responsible for back-ups and file-protection. Kodak, in turn, has its own staff for developing applications software and is responsible for most of the data entry. For example, Kodak provides IBM with the basic data for running its sales-forecasting models and has developed much of the specific software for this application. IBM is responsible for running the programs on its operating system.

Outsourcing has not been limited to information systems. For instance, Chrysler Motors now buys about 70 percent of its parts from external suppliers. Reebok, while it is one of the leading athletic shoe companies in the world, owns no plants. Rather, it contracts out all footwear production to suppliers in various Asian countries. Among the services most often outsourced are trucking, catering, data processing, copying, and accounting. For instance, in 1992, DuPont sold its copy machines to Lanier and contracted with the company to provide copying services. Kodak used to operate its own kitchens to provide meals for the 40,000 employees at its headquarters in Rochester, New York. In 1992, Kodak sold this operation to the Marriott Corporation.

Outsourcing involves a fundamental change in organizational architecture. First, it reassigns many of the decision rights regarding certain assets and employees

---

[1] See David Kirkpatrick, "Why Not Farm Out Your Computing," *Fortune,* September 23, 1991, 103–112 and Shawn Tully, "The Modular Corporation," *Fortune,* February 8, 1993, 106–114.

from one firm to another. For instance, IBM hired about 300 people who had formerly worked for Kodak to work in its new data center. Correspondingly, the decision rights for compensating, promoting, and firing these workers were transferred from Kodak to IBM. Similarly, IBM now owns the mainframes that serve Kodak and has the decision rights on the utilization, maintenance, and replacement of these machines. Second, incentive systems also change with outsourcing. For example, Kodak previously had evaluated its data processing units as cost centers. In contrast, the senior managers at the IBM-run data center are evaluated on business growth, operational efficiency, and the satisfaction of Kodak users. Overall, the IBM unit more closely resembles a profit center than a cost center. Third, Kodak pays scheduled fees for computer services. Thus, IBM directly benefits from higher profits if it can improve the efficiency of the operation and cut costs. Formerly, Kodak was the *residual claimant* for this operation.

This discussion of outsourcing raises a number of important questions:

- What are the costs and benefits in choosing among the alternate architectures that are implied by the outsourcing decision?

- What activities make the most sense to outsource? For instance, why are data processing, catering, copying, and trucking among the most frequently outsourced services? Correspondingly, why did Kodak outsource the operation of its data center to IBM, but maintain the responsibility for developing applications software?

- When a company outsources, what are the determinants of the specific contract provisions? For instance, why did Kodak and IBM negotiate a ten-year contract instead of one-year contract? Why do some firms grant distributors exclusive rights to particular territories?

- What has motivated the recent trend in increased outsourcing?

The purpose of this chapter is to use this book's framework to provide answers to these and other related questions. We begin by defining various terms. Next, we present the benefits of purchasing in competitive markets. Third, we discuss several factors that can motivate firms to acquire goods and services through nonmarket transactions. Fourth, we consider the trade-offs in choosing between internal production and long-term contracting. Fifth, we discuss the optimal length of a contract. Sixth, we analyze issues that arise in dealing with independent distributors and how specific contract provisions can address these concerns. Finally, we present some reasons for the recent increase in outsourcing.

Definitions

When a firm participates in more than one successive stage of the production or distribution of a product or service it is said to be *vertically-integrated*. Firms vary significantly in their degree of vertical-integration. For example, Dell Computers, which sells IBM-compatible PCs, owns no plants and manufacturers almost none

FIGURE 16.1   **Input Production—Choosing Along a Continuum.**

It is often useful to think of the outsourcing decision as choosing along a continuum of possibilities. At one extreme, a product or service can be purchased from any one of a large number of potential suppliers in the spot market. At the other extreme, the company can produce the product or service internally within a division of the firm through vertical integration. Between these extremes are long-term contracts. Contracts take a variety of forms including standard supply and distribution contracts, joint ventures, lease contracts, franchise contracts and strategic alliances.

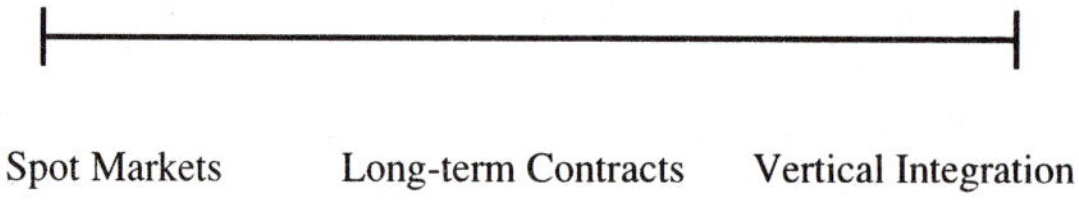

|---|

Spot Markets   Long-term Contracts   Vertical Integration

of its component parts. Similarly, it does not make or even stock the over 650 software products that it sells. Dell simply leases two small factories to assemble computers from parts acquired from other companies and orders software products from Merisel, a large distribution company. In contrast, IBM is much more vertically integrated, producing many of its component parts and software in house. IBM also maintains its own sales force for mainframe computers.

Firms change their degree of integration over time. An organization that begins to produce its own inputs is engaging in *backward* or *upstream* integration, while an organization that begins to market its own goods or to conduct additional finishing work is engaging in *forward* or *downstream* integration. For example, Lincoln Electric integrated backward recently, when it began manufacturing certain inputs for its welding machines that previously were supplied by outside companies. Pepsico, on the other hand, integrated forward when it acquired Pizza Hut and Taco Bell, which sell Pepsico's soft drinks.

The term *outsourcing* is frequently used to describe a movement away from vertical integration — moving an activity outside the firm that was formerly done within the firm. An example of this usage is "Kodak recently outsourced its computer operations to IBM." The term outsourcing, however, is also used to describe an on-going arrangement, where a firm obtains a part or service from an external firm. An example of this usage is "Reebok has always outsourced much of its footwear production to foreign companies."

It is often useful to think of the outsourcing decision as choosing along a continuum of possibilities. As pictured in Figure 16.1, at one extreme the part or service can be purchased from any one of a large number of potential suppliers in the *spot*

FIGURE 16.2   Competitive Equilibrium.

This figure illustrates that competitive markets result in efficient production. Production occurs at the lowest possible long-run average cost (LAC). Buyers acquire the product at cost (P* = LAC = LMC, where LMC = long-run marginal cost). The analysis suggests that when competitive outside markets are available for inputs, firms should use them. In most cases, the firm cannot produce the product more cheaply itself, and in many cases it will cost more.

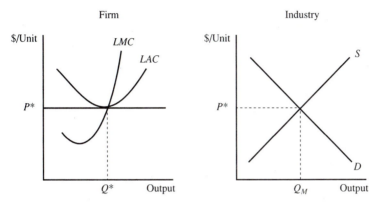

market (where the exchange is made immediately at the current market price with no long-term committment between the buyer and the seller). At the other extreme, a company can vertically integrate and produce the part or service internally. In the middle are long-term contracts between independent or quasi-independent firms. Long-term contracts take many forms, including long-term supply and distribution contracts, franchise contracts, leasing contracts, joint ventures, and strategic alliances. Many of the recent outsourcing decisions move the firm from vertical integration to long-term contracting (for example, Kodak and IBM for computer services, Kodak and Marriot for food service, Du Pont and Lanier for copying services).

We begin our analysis of outsourcing by considering the advantages of acquiring parts and services in spot markets. Subsequently, we analyze why firms do not always use spot markets and, correspondingly, how firms choose between long-term contracting and vertical integration. We then examine specific issues in long-term contracting, such as the optimal contract length. We use the term *market transactions* to refer to sales and purchases in the spot market. We use the term *nonmarket transactions* to refer to either vertical integration or long-term contracts.

The Benefits of Buying in Competitive Markets

Figure 16.2 presents the standard diagram of a competitive equilibrium (as discussed in Chapter 6). The figure illustrates that competitive markets result in efficient production—production occurs at the lowest possible average cost per unit. Also price is equal to average cost, implying that buyers acquire the product at cost (which includes a normal rate of return on investment).[2] Over time, suppliers adopt technological advances that lower the costs of production and/or enhance the quality of the product. Lower costs, in turn, are passed along to buyers in the form of lower prices. This analysis suggests that when competitive outside markets are available to purchase goods and services, firms should use them. In most cases, a firm cannot acquire the product more cheaply through a non-market transaction, and in many cases it will cost more.

One concern with internal production is producing a high enough volume to take advantage of scale economies in production. In Figure 16.2, the minimum point on the average cost curve is at Q^* units. Individual firms in the market place produce this volume. If a firm requires less than Q^* units and produces the amount internally, it will have a higher average cost. The firm could produce Q^* and sell the surplus in the open market. However, this choice requires the firm to enter a new market that is not its primary line of business.

Another concern with non-market procurement is the cost of motivating efficient production. Divisions within large firms can be inefficient yet continue to survive if they are subsidized by more profitable units in the firm. Thus, the firm must adopt costly incentive and control systems to motivate internal managers to engage in efficient production. Similarly, parties to a long-term supply contract must be motivated to carry out their parts of the agreement. Independent firms, on the other hand, tend to face more direct market pressures. If they are inefficient in their main line of business, they lose money and eventually are forced to liquidate.

Due to these concerns, most firms use markets to acquire many, if not most, of their inputs. For example, few companies produce their own automobiles, trucks, fuel, copy machines, pencils, staples, telephones, office furniture, or bathroom fixtures. Many of these products, in turn, are acquired through simple market transactions. Similarly, firms often rely on external markets for many of their downstream activities, such as product distribution. For instance, Procter and Gamble sells many of its products (soap and toothpaste, for instance) through independent grocery stores and drugstores. The punchline is that well-functioning markets provide powerful incentives for efficient production and low prices. Thus, it is value-maximizing to acquire many goods and services through market transactions.

Reasons for Non-market Transactions

Our analysis appears to argue against non-market transactions—firms should concentrate on a particular stage of the production/distribution process and acquire other inputs and services through market transactions with outside suppliers and

---

[2]Recall that if price is above long-run average cost firms are making abnormal profits and new firms enter the industry. The increase in supply drives down the price. Alternatively, if price is below long-run average cost firms are losing money and exit occurs.

distributors. There are, however, at least three primary reasons why firms often use nonmarket transactions to acquire inputs and downstream services: transaction costs, taxes/regulation, and monopoly power.

Made in the USA

Companies sometimes label their products "Made in the USA." This statement is made to appeal to the sentiment among some consumers that Americans should purchase only American-made products to protect domestic jobs. The claim also helps companies gain contracts from the U.S. government. The common practice of acquiring many inputs from outside suppliers, however, makes it difficult to define what really is made in the USA. For instance, in early September 1994, the FTC charged two small athletic shoe companies, New Balance and Hyde Athletic Industries Inc., with deceptive advertising for saying that their products were "Made in the USA." While the companies sew and glue the bulk of their shoes in the U.S., they import many of the component parts, such as soles and uppers, from Asia. Hyde Athletic agreed to change their label to "Made in the USA from domestic and imported components." New Balance disputed the claim. This issue could affect many companies, ranging from Dell Computers to General Motors, who emphasize domestic production, but rely on foreign companies for various inputs and services.

Suggested by Michael Oneal, "Does New Balance have an American Soul?" *Business Week,* December 12, 1994, 86–90.

Transaction Costs

In Chapter 3, we discussed the architecture of markets. We argued that markets effectively link specific knowledge and decision rights; moreover, they provide incentives for decision makers to make effective use of this information. We posed the question: Why aren't all economic transactions conducted through markets? We noted that Ronald Coase proposed an answer to this question based on the concept of *transaction costs.* According to his argument, market transactions are not costless. For instance, they involve the costs of searching for trading partners and negotiating the relevant prices. Parties to a transaction have incentives to use other mechanisms, such as internal production, when the transaction can be completed at a lower cost. There are at least four factors that can make the costs of non-market transactions lower than the costs of market exchanges. These factors include firm-specific assets, costs of measuring quality, coordination problems, and externalities.

Firm-Specific Assets.   Production typically requires investment in assets. For example, IBM has to have mainframe computers to provide computer services to Kodak and suppliers need machines to make parts. Sometimes these assets can be transferred easily among alternative uses. For example, particular mainframe computers could be used to serve either Kodak or other companies. These are general-purpose computers designed to be used by a variety of customers. In contrast, other assets are significantly more valuable in their current use than in their next best alternative. For example, the Alaskan Pipeline is significantly more valuable for hauling oil than for any other conceivable use. Similarly, if IBM writes a specialized computer program to run Kodak's payroll, the program is more valuable for Kodak's payroll than for some other firm's payroll (which has different fringe-benefits, for instance). The program could be adapted for use by other firms. However, changing the program is costly. Assets that are significantly more valuable in their current use than in their next best alternative use are referred to as *firm-specific assets.* Oliver Williamson suggests four particular instances in which asset specificity is most likely to occur[3]:

- *Site specificity:* the asset is located in a particular area that makes it useful only to a small number of buyers or suppliers, and it cannot be moved easily. An example is the Alaskan Pipeline which can be used only by oil producers in Alaska.

- *Physical-asset specificity:* the product design makes it especially useful to a small number of buyers. An example is a specialized machine tool that is used to make parts for one particular type of automobile.

- *Human-asset specificity:* the transaction requires specialized knowledge on the part of the parties to the transaction. An example is the knowledge that IBM employees must acquire about Kodak's unique processes in order to provide computer services to the company.

- *Dedicated assets:* the expansion in facilities is necessitated only by the requirements of one or several buyers. An example is a chip producer who adds extra capacity to serve one particular computer company.

If a supplier invests in a specific asset to serve a particular customer, the supplier places itself in a tenuous position for future negotiations. For example, consider a supplier who invests $50,000 for a machine tool (such as a metal punch-press die) to produce a particular part. The part is used only by one manufacturer, and the machine tool has no other uses or salvage value. (It is very specific.) The variable cost of production is $1 per unit and the useful life of the machine tool is 50,000 units. Here, the supplier must be able to sell the parts for at least $2 per unit to break even. The buyer, however, is in a strong position to argue for a price concession after the investment is made. At this point, the investment is a *sunk cost,* and the supplier will continue to operate as long as he can cover his variable costs of $1 per unit. Thus, the buyer can potentially force the supplier to accept a price as low as $1, even though the supplier loses on his initial investment. Anticipating this *hold-up problem,* the supplier will not invest in the machine tool in the first place, unless he receives a guarantee that the buyer will continue to pay $2 per unit in the future.

---

[3]See Oliver E. Williamson, *The Economic Institutions of Capitalism,* The Free Press, New York, 1985.

Thus, the buyer cannot expect to obtain the part from outside suppliers through a simple spot-market transaction.

Buyers also face potential hold-up problems if they purchase key inputs from a single supplier, who has invested in the relevant firm-specific assets. For example, a supplier might force a firm to pay higher prices for its inputs during periods when the firm's demand for the inputs is especially high. For instance, a chip supplier might demand a large price increase when it knows that a computer company has a large backlog of orders and that there are no alternative sources of supply.

These potential hold-up problems can be controlled by vertical integration. If the buyer invests in the machine and produces the part internally, she does not have to worry about subsequently arguing with another firm over prices. An alternative to integration is for the buyer and supplier to enter into a long-term supply contract. For example, the buyer might agree to purchase 50,000 units from the supplier over the next five years at a cost of $2 per unit. Contracts, however, are not costless to write or to enforce, and so the preferred alternative depends on the relative costs of vertical integration versus contracting. This trade-off is considered in greater detail below.

Measuring Quality.   It is difficult to monitor the quality of some inputs and services. For example, the firm might not learn that a particular part is defective until long after purchase. In this case, the seller can have the incentive to cheat the buying firm—once a price is agreed upon, the supplier can increase her profits by supplying a lower cost/quality product. Buyers can sometimes avoid these problems by transacting with companies that have established reputations for quality and/or who can offer credible warranties of their products. Otherwise, it can be best to produce the products in-house or to negotiate a long-term supply contract that provides appropriate incentives for quality production, especially when maintaining quality of the part is critical for the overall success of the product. (We discuss this issue further in Chapter 18.)

Extensive Coordination.   Some activities require extensive coordination. For example, railroads rely on extensive feeder traffic for their routes. In principle, it would be possible to use the price system for each link in the network. For instance, rail companies could pay each other to use their lines, with prices adjusting to changes in supply and demand. However, such a system would be complicated and expensive to operate. An alternative is for the railroad companies in the network to merge and to address the various coordination problems internally. Railroad companies were among the first large firms in the United States. These large firms were motivated at least in part by the benefits of using internal managers to coordinate rail activity.[4]

Reducing Externalities.   Firms often invest in developing reputations and customer loyalty. This investment can increase the demand for a company's products.

---

[4]See Alfred D. Chandler, *The Visible Hand—The Managerial Revolution in American Business,* Belknap Press, Cambridge, Mass., 1977.

Firms, however, can have problems motivating independently-owned distributors to invest sufficient resources to maintain a brand name—there is a freerider problem. For instance, independent retailers in a distribution system have incentives to shirk on advertising and depend on the efforts of other units in the system to attract customers. These retailers also might want to cut costs by hiring lower-priced, but less-skilled labor. A given owner of a retail unit receives all the benefits from reducing his unit's labor costs, but bears only part of the costs from providing poor service to customers—any decline in future sales is likely to be shared with other units. The incentives to freeride are particularly large when the retailer deals with customers who are not likely to make repeat purchases at his particular unit.

The freerider problem can be reduced through vertical integration, where managers of stores are compensated in ways that do not promote freeriding, or through long-term contracts with terms that motivate increased sales efforts. Below, we discuss the tradeoffs between these two solutions to the freerider problem.

A related reason for vertical integration is to coordinate pricing among retail units. The pricing decisions of individual retailers can have effects on other units in the system. For instance, it might be optimal from a companywide standpoint to set prices where some units sustain losses. (When stores stay open, customers do not try other brands.) Independent retailers, however, cannot always be expected to set optimal system-wide prices since they care only about the profits from their own units. Conceptually, the central company could set the retail prices; however, antitrust law does not allow it. Prices can be coordinated if the company owns its own retail outlets.

Taxes and Regulation

Taxes and regulation can also motivate vertical integration. For example, if one stage of production is heavily taxed while another is not, taxes might be reduced by shifting profits to the low-tax activity. A firm can potentially capture these gains by integrating vertically and having the low-tax unit charge inflated transfer prices to the high-tax unit. Tax authorities, however, are aware of this incentive and limit this type of activity. Similarly, a regulated company might want to integrate vertically to shift profits from a regulated segment of the business, where profits are restricted, to an unregulated segment of the business.

Monopoly Power

There are several ways that a firm might use vertical integration to increase monopoly power and profits. The following example illustrates one of these methods—using vertical integration to price-discriminate.[5] Consider a firm, Drugs Inc., that has a patent on a particular drug used as an input in the production of two different

---

[5]For additional methods, see Dennis W. Carlton and Jeffrey M. Perloff, *Modern Industrial Organization,* Harper Collins, USA, chapter 16.

pharmaceutical products. One of the products is a pain reliever that competes with many other products. The other helps to relieve the symptoms of AIDS, and there is no good substitute. The marginal cost to Drugs Inc. for producing the base drug is $10 per unit. For simplicity, assume that a retail drug manufacturer can take the base drug and transform it into one unit of either product at zero marginal cost and that there are no additional distribution or marketing costs. The industry demand for the two products is given by:

$$\text{Pain Relief: } P = 100 - 5Q$$
$$\text{AIDS Relief: } P = 200 - 10Q.$$

Finally, suppose that each of the product markets is characterized by pure competition. (That is, there are many manufacturers that can produce and distribute the retail drugs.)

To maximize total profits, Drug Inc. would like to set marginal revenue equal to marginal cost in each market. As shown in Figure 16.3, the optimal price to charge retail drug manufacturers who produce the pain reliever is $55. The optimal price for those who produce the AIDS drug is $105.[6] Since both markets are competitive and there are no other costs, the price to consumers in the two markets would be $55 and $105. However, if Drug Inc. tries to sell to some manufacturers at $55 and other manufacturers at $105, potential arbitrage is available. The manufacturers who buy at $55 can sell the drug to other manufacturers at less than $105 and make a profit. Thus, they will undercut any attempt by Drug Inc. to sell to some people at $105.

Price Discrimination and Antitrust Law

Firms that integrate vertically to engage in price discrimination can sometimes be held accountable under antitrust law. For example, Alcoa had monopoly power in the production of virgin-aluminum ingots, an intermediate good. It integrated into the lower-priced markets (for example, rolled sheet) and "squeezed" competitors in these markets. The judge who wrote the opinion in the antitrust case proposed a "transfer-price test" to assess whether a firm is engaged in a price-squeeze. The test considers whether the integrated firm could sell the final output profitably at prevailing prices, assuming it had to pay the same price for the input as it charges downstream competitors. The court determined Alcoa could not. Note in our example in the text, Drugs Inc. would operate at a loss if it paid $105 for the input and sold the pain reliever to consumers at $55.

Suggested by *United States v. Aluminum Company of America*, 148 F. 2d 416 (1945).

One way that Drug Inc. can avoid this problem is to integrate forward and manufacture the pain reliever. The company would price the pain reliever at $55

---

[6]Recall from Chapter 6 that these prices are easily found by setting the marginal cost of $10 equal to the marginal revenue in each market (implied by the two demand curves).

FIGURE 16.3   Using Vertical Integration to Price-Discriminate.

Drugs Inc. has a patent on a drug that is used as an input in the production of two different pharmaceutical products. One of the products is a pain reliever that competes with many other products. The other helps to relieve the symptoms of AIDS, and there is no good substitute. The marginal cost to Drugs Inc. for producing the base drug is $10 per unit. For simplicity, we assume that a manufacturer can take the base drug and transform it into one unit of either product at zero marginal cost and that there are no additional distribution or marketing costs. Both retail product markets are perfectly competitive. (There are many companies that can produce and distribute the two drugs.) Given these assumptions, the industry-level demand curves for the two products are the same demand curves facing Drugs Inc. for the base drug. To maximize total profits, Drug Inc. would like to set marginal revenue equal to marginal cost in each market. The optimal price to charge manufacturers who produce the pain reliever is $55. The optimal price for those who produce the AIDS drug is $105. However, if Drug Inc. tries to sell to some companies at $55 and other companies at $105, potential arbitrage is available. One way to effectively price-discriminate is for Drugs Inc. to integrate forward into the pain-reliever market. It would sell the pain reliever to consumers at $55 and the base drug to the manufacturers of the AIDS drug at $105.

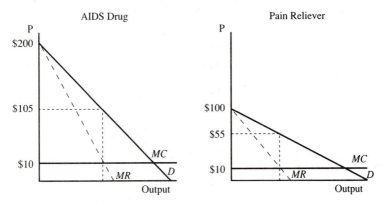

and sell the base drug at $105 in the open market. Arbitrage is no longer possible (assuming that the pain reliever cannot be transformed back into the basic drug at low cost). Note that manufacturing only the AIDS drug will not solve the problem. If Drug Inc. tried to price the AIDS drug at $105 and sell the base drug at $55, other manufacturers would begin to produce and market the AIDS drug (after buying the base drug at $55). Therefore, Drug Inc. would not be able to maintain a price of $105. It must integrate forward into the lower-priced (more *elastic*) pain-reliever market.

Other Reasons

Another potential reason for non-market procurement is to assure the supply of an important input. In contrast to the standard economic model, shortages sometimes occur in actual markets. For example, toy stores do not always raise their prices for "hot selling" toys around Christmas time. Rather, such toys are allocated on a first-come, first-serve basis. Similarly, companies sometimes face rationing or short supply of particular inputs. In this case, companies might integrate vertically to increase the likelihood of receiving an input in a timely fashion.

Firms also use non-market procurement to avoid sharing proprietary information with other firms. For instance, a firm might be reluctant to provide an independent supplier with detailed information about its production processes because it feared that the supplier will share the information with other firms. It is potentially easier to control the leakage of sensitive information when dealing with internal employees or long-term suppliers.

Faulty Arguments for Non-market Transactions

Other common explanations for non-market transactions rely on technological factors. For example, some people explain the common ownership of steel milling and steel production by the close technological links of the two processes. This argument, however, is flawed. While it is true that there are benefits from having these operations in one location, technology does not dictate ownership. Conceptually, steel mills could buy hot steel ingots from other companies located in the same building. The reasons they don't are not due to technological factors, but rather result from contracting problems—independent companies do not want to expose themselves to the hold-up problems that arise from this type of firm-specific investment.

Vertical Integration versus Long-Term Contracts

We have discussed several reasons why a firm might choose to acquire a good or service through a non-market transaction. Non-market transactions include both vertical integration, where the firm produces the part or service in-house, and long-term contracting, where the firm acquires the part or service from another firm on a contractual basis. This section considers the trade-offs between vertical integration and long-term contracts. We begin with a brief discussion of the various types of long-term contracts.

Long-Term Contracts.   Long-term contracts can take a variety of forms. First, there are *standard supply and distribution contracts* between independent firms. For instance, IBM and Kodak have a 10-year supply contract where IBM agrees to provide specific computer services to Kodak for a given price. The contract contains many provisions specifying the nature of the service and the duties and obligations of each of the contracting parties. Second, there are *joint ventures.* In the typical joint venture a new firm is formed that is jointly owned by two or more independent firms. The new firm might be responsible for conducting research, supplying inputs for a subset of the firms, or for downstream activities such as marketing or distributing a product. For instance, drug companies form research joint ventures to conduct basic research on new drugs. The output of this research is shared by the partners in the venture. Similarly, an American company and European company might form a joint venture to market the American company's products in Europe. Third are *lease contracts* where a firm acquires an asset, such as a machine or building, through a lease agreement with another firm. Fourth are *franchise agreements*. In its most basic form, franchising grants the rights to a specific market area to an independent business person, along with the rights to use the parent's proven name, reputation, and business format. Much of the central company's retail distribution is conducted through these franchised outlets. Fifth are *strategic alliances.* This term is used to describe a variety of agreements between independent firms to cooperate in the development and/or marketing of products. For instance, an airline company and a car rental company might agree to promote each others' products and to participate in joint promotional schemes.

This discussion suggests that contracts take many forms. In the following analysis, we group these forms together and consider the more general problem of choosing between vertical integration and long-term contracts. We focus on four especially important factors: firm-specific assets, uncertainty, economies from specialization, and labor unions. Subsequently, we consider some of the specific provisions that might be included in a contract.

Firm-Specific Assets and the Costs of Contracting.   There are two mechanisms for enforcing contracts, *legal enforcement* and *market-based enforcement.* Legal enforcement relies on the court system, while market-based enforcement relies on private incentives not to renege on contracts due to the costs of lost future business (see Chapter 7). The costs of both enforcement mechanisms are likely to increase with the level of specificity of the assets involved.[7] In particular, firms will spend much more time negotiating a contract over a specific asset than a general asset. In the case of a general asset (such as a standard truck), simple contracts can be negotiated. If the payment is not made the asset can be repossessed and redeployed. With specific assets a more detailed contract is called for since repossession is not a viable option. (The asset has a limited secondary market.) These contracts in turn are more expensive to litigate since complex clauses are often subject to alternative interpretations. Market enforcement becomes less effective as the gains from not complying with the contract increase. These gains increase as the asset becomes more specific—prices can be changed substantially without driving the other party out of business or to another contracting partner.

Vertical integration also involves costs, such as increased internal management costs and lost economies of scale. However, these costs are largely independent of

---

[7]See Benjamin Klein, Robert A. Crawford and Armen Alchian, 1978, "Vertical Integration, Appropriable Rents, and the Competitive Contracting Process," *Journal of Law and Economics* 24, 297–326, and Oliver E. Williamson, *The Economic Institutions of Capitalism,* The Free Press, New York, 1985.

the degree of specificity of the asset. Thus, as pictured in Figure 16.4, as an asset becomes more specific the costs of contracting are likely to rise at a faster rate than the costs of vertical integration.[8] This cost structure implies that *assets that are relatively firm-specific are more likely to be owned by the firm (since the costs of ownership are less than the costs of contracting), while less firm-specific assets are more likely to be owned by an independent firm that supplies products or services to the firm on a contractual basis.*

Contracting Problems with Firm-Specific Assets: Evidence from China

The early 1990s witnessed a substantial growth in American investment in China. American financial institutions loaned substantial amounts of money to Chinese businesses, while other American companies invested in a variety of Chinese business ventures. By 1995, however, many of these American companies experienced problems in collecting debts from Chinese businesses. One problem in enforcing contracts with Chinese businesses is that the legal system in China is "primitive." In addition, "China's corporate managers are accustomed to the old socialist system, where they could simply ignore their debts"—there is little market-based enforcement of contracts.

Leasing companies that have financed specific assets have been "particularly vulnerable because the collateral—usually heavy equipment or production lines—is difficult to seize once installed. And even if it can be repossessed, China lacks a good secondary market for equipment." On the other hand, lenders have experienced few problems in financing less specific assets, such as aircraft. For instance, GE Capital alone has some $1 billion worth of aircraft on lease in China. Aircraft is considered a "solid risk," in part because "many leased aircraft are flown overseas and are relatively easy to repossess."

Suggested by Pete Engardio, "Why Sweet Deals are Going Sour in China," *Business Week,* December 19, 1994, 50–51.

Uncertainty.   A second factor that is important in choosing between owning versus contracting is *uncertainty* in the environment. If the economic environment (for example, prices, costs, and other factors) is more stable and predicable, it is easier to negotiate contracts that detail future performance requirements. These contracts, in turn, are easier to enforce through threat of litigation. In contrast, it is difficult to plan for all contingencies when the economic environment is uncertain, and more actions must be left for future negotiation. For example, if technology is rapidly

---

[8]Disputes over firm-specific assets can also exist within firms. For example, divisions might argue over transfer prices. Thus, the costs of organizing assets within firms might also rise as the assets become more firm-specific. However, in contrast to the case of contracting between independent firms, these disputes can be resolved by higher-level managers within the firm, rather than by a court of law.

FIGURE 16.4   Vertical Integration versus Long-term Contracting.

As an asset becomes more specific, the transaction costs of contracting are likely to rise at a faster rate than the transaction costs of vertical integration. This cost structure implies that assets that are relatively firm-specific are more likely to be owned by the firm, while less firm-specific assets are more likely to be owned by an independent firm that supplies products or services to the firm on a contractual basis. In this figure, assets with specificity below S* are acquired through contract, while assets with specificity above S* are owned by the firm.

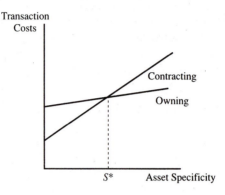

changing the parties will want to leave open the possibility of shifting to new production methods. Specifying the appropriate cost sharing, prices, and other terms in advance, however, would be infeasible given the difficulty in forecasting the exact technological change. This type of *contractual incompleteness* increases the likelihood of future opportunistic actions and thus the benefits from vertical integration (especially when assets are specific).

Lease versus Buy

Firms frequently decide between leasing and buying an asset. Economic theory suggests that firms are most likely to own assets that are highly firm-specific. For example, Le Roy Industries leases some of its forklifts and other vehicles, but buys outright the very specialized machinery it needs to make suspension parts for Ford, General Motors, and Chrysler cars. To quote Charles Teets, vice president and chief financial officer of the company:

> "It takes about a year to make the machinery we need. It would be very hard to find a lessor interested in our type of equipment because of the long lead-time. After the lease expired, no lessor would want the equipment back."

Suggested by "The New Attraction in Leasing," *Nation's Business*, March 1987.

Economies from Specialization.   As we previously discussed, sometimes firms must produce products in high volume to take advantage of economies of scale. In this case, it is often better for a firm to contract with a firm that specializes in producing a product, rather than engaging in low volume internal production. For instance, one of the advantages of having IBM provide computer services to Kodak is that IBM provides similar services to other companies. This higher volume can lower the cost for Kodak. For example, the costs of training technical specialists can be spread across more users; software can be written that is used by more than one company. Also, IBM is able to attract higher-quality computer specialists than Kodak, since IBM's scale of operation provides a much richer set of career opportunities. Conceptually, Kodak could capture some of these gains by purchasing IBM and operating the two companies as one large enterprise. However, the costs of managing such a large enterprise would be likely to outweigh the benefits.

Vertical Integration in the Aerospace Industry

Scott Masten studied the make-versus-buy policies of a major aerospace contractor. The firm made many products for the U. S. government. In each case, the company had to choose between making the product or subcontracting it to another firm for production. Economic theory suggests that internal production is more likely when the asset is specific and the uncertainties in contracting are large.

Masten used two measures of asset-specificity for each product. The first measured design (physical-asset) specificity, while the second measured site-specificity. He also measured the complexity of the product design, which was intended to proxy for uncertainties in contracting. Consistent with the theory, he found that products that were highly design-specific and highly complex were more likely to be produced internally. When the product was both design-specific and complex there was a 92 percent probability of internal production. If the product was design-specific, but not complex, the probability of internal production was 31 percent. The probability of internal production was only 2 percent when the product was neither design-specific nor complex. For this particular company, site-specificity was unimportant.

Suggested by Scott Masten, 1984, "The Organization of Production: Evidence form the Aerospace Industry," *Journal of Law and Economics* 27, 403–17.

Our analysis of firm-specific assets, uncertainty, and economies from specialization helps to explain why catering, trucking, copying, and mainframe computing are among the most frequently outsourced services. These activities involve assets that are not highly firm-specific. For example, copy machines and trucks can be used for many different purposes. In addition, for activities like copying, it is easy to write a relatively complete contract. These factors imply that the costs of contracting for these services are relatively low. At the same time, there are potential benefits from using independent firms that specialize in large volume production.

Labor Unions.   Unions are another factor that can affect the choice between vertical integration and contracting. For instance, some of the major airlines have threatened labor unions that they will contract their kitchen operations to other companies to avoid paying high union wages. The major automobile companies have made similar statements with respect to the manufacturing of component parts.

Faulty Arguments for Long-term Contracts.   The financial press often argues obtaining inputs through contracts with other firms "frees companies to use scarce capital for other purposes." This claim, however, is questionable given the existence of well-developed capital markets. Having some other firm produce a product does not reduce investment, it simply shifts the capital expenditures to another firm. Buyers still pay for this investment through the price of the product. The important question is whether more value is created by producing the product internally or externally. If internal production is more valuable, the firm can raise money in the capital market for financing the relevant assets. (Capital is not "scarce" for good projects.) If external production is more valuable, funds can be raised by the supplier.

Continuum of Choice.   While we have discussed long-term contracting versus vertical integration as a choice between two policies, it is important to keep in mind that the outsourcing decision actually falls on a continuum. For instance, sometimes it is desirable for a firm to maintain ownership of a firm-specific asset and contract with another firm to operate it. This ownership pattern reduces potential hold-up problems because if there is a contract dispute the owner can simply take the asset and contract with another firm to provide the service (neither side faces large losses). This ownership pattern is most viable if the asset can be moved at low cost. Also, the owner must be able to provide the service operator with sufficient incentives to maintain and not to abuse the asset.

A related example is Kodak's decision to contract with IBM for providing operating software and hardware, but to maintain responsibility for applications software. Development of applications software is likely to be more specific to Kodak than development of operating software that can be used for many different applications and firms. IBM, therefore, has greater incentives to focus on the development of the operating software, while Kodak has greater incentives to focus on the applications software. In addition, the location of specific knowledge reinforces these incentives—Kodak knows more about its specific applications, while IBM knows more about general computing. The observed organizational arrangement reflects these incentive and information effects.

Contract Length

A major advantage of long-term contracts over short-term contracts is that they increase the incentives of the contracting parties to make firm-specific investments. For example, IBM would have limited incentives to invest in learning Kodak's special computing demands if they anticipated a short-term relationship between the two companies. At the same time, it is costly to write and litigate long-term contracts in uncertain environments, where it is difficult to plan for potential changes in technology, input prices, product demands, and the like. Thus, firms might be expected to enter long-term contracts when the desired investment is relatively firm-specific and where the environment is relatively stable and predictable. Alternatively, if the firm faces a highly uncertain environment and large investments in firm-specific assets, vertical integration is likely to be the preferred alternative. Finally, if the investment in firm-specific assets is relatively low or the lives of the assets relatively short, the firm can either enter into short-term contracts with suppliers or, simply rely on spot-market transactions.

The "Marriage and Divorce" of Outsourcing Partners

Not all outsourcing ventures work—some end in divorce. For instance, Hibernia National Bank and Capital Bank used to outsource their computer operations to IBM. To cuts its costs, IBM pooled the software support staff for the two banks. Both banks used software from Hogan Systems, a business partner with IBM from 1987. In 1993, Hibernia estimated it could save $40 million over eight years by switching to a new outsourcing partner, Systematics Financial Services Inc. Capital followed Hibernia and also shifted to Systematics. Subsequently, Hogan and IBM parted ways. This example and others like it suggest that prospective outsourcing partners should anticipate the possibility that the venture will not work out and plan accordingly (for example, by negotiating the equivalent of a prenuptial agreement—what to do with assets, severance payments and so on).

Suggested by "ISSC: A Tale of Marriage and Divorce," *Information Week,* July 18, 1994, page 13.

Contracting with Distributors

Freerider Problems

We have discussed the incentives of independent distributors to freeride on the reputation of a brand name, and how these incentives can motivate sub-optimal sales efforts (for example, insufficient expenditures on advertising and other inputs). One method to reduce this problem is vertical integration. The other method is to use contracts with specific provisions that reduce the freerider problem. Two types of contract terms that specifically address this concern are advertising provisions and exclusive territories.

Advertising Provisions.   There are several related methods that firms use to increase advertising at the local level. First, the company can charge its retail subcontractors an advertising fee and have the central company be responsible for advertising. For instance, most franchise contracts require that, in addition to the base royalty payment, individual units pay a percent of sales to the central company to provide advertising. One potential problem with this approach is that the local unit, not the central company, can have the specific knowledge relevant for effective local advertising. An alternative that addresses this concern is for the central company to share in the local advertising costs. (For example, it might pay half of any advertising expenditures.) The decisions on local advertising, however, are made by the local managers. A third alternative is to require distributors to pay funds into regional advertising funds. The distributors, in turn, have the primary decision rights to decide how to spend the monies in the funds.

Exclusive Territories.   One of the most common methods for reducing freeriding is to grant individual distributors the exclusive rights to operate in a given market area. For example, a Toyota dealership might have a contract that prevents Toyota from opening another dealership within 30 miles. By giving distributors monopoly rights for specific market areas, there are fewer incentives to freeride, since the distributors internalize most of the benefits from their sales efforts. (Fewer benefits go to other units not owned by the given distributor).

Company Ownership versus Franchising

We have discussed how a central company can reduce the incentives of an independent distributor to freeride on the brand name through contracts with terms that motivate increased sales efforts. When the freerider problem is severe, however, it might be less expensive to simply own the distribution units centrally. A manager of a company-owned unit has fewer incentives than an independent distributor to freeride on the reputation, since he does not get to keep the profits from the unit—the reduction in costs (for example, from decreased advertising) flow through to the central company, not the manager.

Indeed, most franchise companies do not franchise all their retail outlets. The typical company franchises about 80 percent of the units and owns the other 20 percent. Our argument suggests that central companies are most likely to own the units that receive a significant amount of business from customers who are unlikely to make repeat purchases at the particular units (the incentives to freeride in this case are large). On average, fast-food restaurants are more likely to serve transient customers than auto-service companies. (Customers tend to use the same unit repeatedly for oil changes and tune-ups) Consistent with the theory, the typical restaurant franchise company owns about 30 percent of its units, while the typical auto-service franchise company owns about 13 percent of its units.

Suggested by IFA Educational Foundation and Horwath International, *Franchising in the Economy 1991*.

FIGURE 16.5   Optimal Output in an Example of the Double Mark-up Problem.

In this hypothetical example, Toyota Motor Company faces the above demand curve for its automobiles in the Medford, Oregon, market area. We assume that Toyota can produce the automobiles at a constant marginal cost of $5,000. To maximize profits Toyota must select the quantity and price where marginal revenue equals marginal cost. The optimal quantity and price are Q* = 250 and P* = $30,000. Firm profits are $6.25 million.

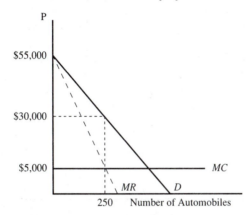

Double Mark-ups

Giving distributors monopoly power over specific market areas reduces freerider problems. However, it can create another problem—*double mark-ups*. Since both the manufacturer and the distributor face downward sloping demand curves, each has the incentive to mark-up the product above its marginal cost. The result is that the customer faces two mark-ups rather than one. Correspondingly, the quantity demanded of the product is lower than optimal, and the combined profits for the manufacturer and distributor are not maximized. We give a numerical example of this problem, and then discuss the contract terms that might be used to reduce it.

Example. Assume that the Toyota Motor Company faces the following demand for its automobiles in the Medford, Oregon, market area:

$$P = 55,000 - 100Q. \tag{1}$$

Assume that Toyota can produce the automobiles at a constant marginal cost of $5,000. To maximize profits, Toyota must select the quantity and price, where marginal revenue equals marginal cost. As pictured in Figure 16.5, the optimal quantity and price are $Q^* = 250$ and $P^* = \$30,000$. Firm profits are $6.25 million.

Now suppose that Toyota sells its vehicles through Medford Motors, an independent distributor which has the exclusive right to sell Toyotas in the Medford market area. Under the hypothetical contract, Toyota sets the wholesale price, while

Medford Motors selects the quantity to purchase and the retail price. For simplicity, assume that the only marginal cost facing Medford Motors for automobiles is the price charged by Toyota. (There are no variable distribution costs.) The owners of Medford Motors care only about their own profits, while the managers of Toyota care only about Toyota's profits. The problem facing Toyota is to choose the wholesale price, P_w, that maximizes its profits.

To solve this problem, Toyota's management would like to know the quantity that Medford Motors would purchase at each possible wholesale price. Toyota can infer this demand curve by analyzing the problem from the perspective of Medford Motors. Medford Motors faces the retail demand curve for autos, given in equation (1). Medford Motors maximizes its profits by setting its marginal revenue, implied by this retail demand curve, equal to P_w, its marginal cost. Thus, Medford Motors' marginal revenue curve is the demand curve facing Toyota. As pictured in Figure 16.5, this curve is:

$$P_w = 55,000 - 200Q. \tag{2}$$

Given Medford Motors' demand for automobiles, what wholesale price will Toyota choose? Toyota maximizes its profits by setting its marginal revenue equal to its marginal cost of $5,000. Since Toyota faces a demand curve of $P_w = 55,000 - 200Q$, its marginal revenue is $MR = 55,000 - 400Q$. Therefore, Toyota's profits are maximized by selecting a wholesale price of $P_w = \$30,000$. At this price, Medford Motors will buy 125 automobiles and set a retail price of $42,500. Toyota will have profits of $3.125 million, and Medford Motors will have profits of $1.563 million, for combined profits of $4.688 million.

This outcome, which is pictured in Figure 16.6, is particularly inefficient. Toyota and Medford Motors fail to maximize their joint profits. Conceptually, both parties could be made better-off by coordinating their prices and volume choices—we have already shown that they could earn up to $6.25 million (versus $4.688 million). In addition, with the double mark-ups, consumers pay $42,500 for Toyota automobiles rather than $30,000.

Note that this problem does not automatically disappear if Toyota merges with Medford Motors. Indeed, we saw in Chapter 14 that exactly the same problem can arise within firms, when products are sold between two profits centers through internal transfer prices. As we discussed, the transfer-pricing problem can be reduced by proper organizational design. Our current focus, however, is on how this problem can be reduced between two independent firms through specific contractual terms.

Two-Part Pricing.   Medford Motors will purchase 250 automobiles if Toyota sets a wholesale price of $5,000. This quantity maximizes the joint profits of the two firms and results in a retail price of $30,000. The entire profits, however, go to Medford Motors, since Toyota is selling the automobiles at cost. One solution is for Toyota to charge Medford Motors an up-front franchise fee to obtain a share of the profits, and then to sell automobiles to Medford Motors at $5,000 each. Since Medford Motors' purchasing decision is based on marginal cost, not total cost, it will still purchase 250 automobiles and set a retail price of $30,000. For instance, if

---

FIGURE 16.6   Example of Double Mark-ups.

In this hypothetical example, Toyota sets the wholesale price for its automobiles, while Medford Motors selects the quantity to purchase and the retail price. Medford Motors maximizes profit by setting the wholesale price equal to its marginal revenue. Thus, Medford Motors' marginal revenue curve is Toyota's demand curve. Toyota maximizes profit by setting its marginal cost of $5000 equal to its marginal revenue. Toyota selects a wholesale price of $30,000, a $25,000 mark-up above its marginal cost, while Medford Motors selects a retail price of $42,500, a $12,500 mark-up above its marginal cost. Medford Motors sells 125 cars at this price. The combined profits are $4.688 million. Conceptually, the two companies could earn combined profits of $6.25 million if they cooperate and sell 250 automobiles to consumers at a price of $30,000.

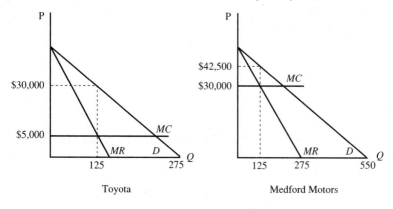

Toyota charges Medford Motors an up-front fee of $3.125 million for the exclusive rights to the Medford market area; the combined profits of $6.25 million are split evenly between the two companies. Once the fee is collected, however, Toyota might try to increase the wholesale price of the automobiles to increase its profits. Thus, for this solution to work, Toyota must be able to commit credibly to selling automobiles to Medford Motors at marginal cost.

Quotas.   An alternative method for maximizing the combined profits is for the two companies to agree on a minimum purchase requirement. For example, Medford Motors might agree to purchase at least 250 automobiles at some pre-specified wholesale price above $5,000. Given the details in this example, Medford Motors will purchase exactly 250 automobiles and sell them at $30,000 to retail customers. The wholesale price determines the split of the profits between the two companies. For instance, a wholesale price of $7,500 splits the profits evenly. Once again, Toyota must be able to commit credibly to the wholesale price.

Regulatory Issues

Some regulators and scholars are suspicious of contract terms such as exclusive territories that potentially limit competition. Nevertheless, most non-price contract terms are not *per se* illegal (always illegal) under federal antitrust law. Rather, they are judged on a *rule of reason,* where the court attempts to consider the benefits of the terms (such as increased sales efforts) against any anti-competitive effects. In some states, automobile dealers and franchisees have successfully lobbied their legislators to limit the control that central companies have over them (for example, in setting quotas and terminating contracts). In addition, federal law restricts central companies from directly controlling the pricing of distributors at the retail level. A detailed treatment of these regulatory issues is beyond the scope of this book. Suffice it to say that it usually is important for firms to engage expert legal counsel in designing supply and distribution contracts.

Recent Trends in Outsourcing

The 1990s have witnessed an increase in outsourcing by major companies. At least four factors have contributed to this trend. First, there has been a dramatic increase in world-wide competition. This competition has placed pressure on firms to reduce costs and become more efficient. Some scholars argue that many American firms were "flush with cash" in the 1960s and 1970s and tended to waste this cash through such actions as overly integrating.[9] In this context, the outsourcing trend might be viewed as correcting poor investment decisions of the past. Second, new flexible production technologies allow suppliers to adapt more easily to customer demands. Thus, in some cases assets are becoming less firm-specific, which favors contracting over vertical integration. Third, improvements in information and communications technology make it easier to identify potential partners and to communicate with them after an agreement is reached. For instance, electronic data interchange (EDI) allows different companies to connect their computers. These computers can automatically order inventory directly from a supplier with little human intervention. Fourth, during the first part of the 1990s there was a world-wide recession. This recession meant that there was excess capacity in many industries. Thus, firms could often obtain large discounts from external vendors. This last effect is potentially more cyclical than permanent.

It is important to note that many of the recent outsourcing decisions do not move firms from internal production to the other end of the spectrum, spot-market transactions. Rather, the movement has been to an intermediate arrangement, long-term contracting. Indeed, many firms have also moved away from acquiring inputs in the spot-market. For instance, firms such as Xerox and General Motors have dramatically cut their number of suppliers and correspondingly have increased the

---

[9] See Michael C. Jensen, 1986, "Agency Costs of Free Cash Flow, Corporate Finance and Takeovers," *American Economic Review* 76 323–329.

number of long-term partnerships with independent firms. Thus, the current trend can be viewed as a movement from both ends of the spectrum toward the middle. Recent technological changes, such as just-in-time production methods, electronic data interchanges, and total-quality manufacturing, require close links between manufacturers, suppliers, and distributors. While the various activities in the manufacturing/distribution process can be conducted by different firms, it is important that these firms remain closely-linked. These factors can make spot-market transactions undesirable in many cases.

Summary

When a firm participates in more than one successive stage of the production or distribution of a product or service, it is said to be *vertically integrated*. Firms change their degree of integration over time. An organization that begins to produce its own inputs is engaging in *backward* or *upstream* integration, while an organization that begins to market its own goods or to conduct additional finishing work is engaging in *forward* or *downstream* integration. The term *outsourcing* is frequently used to describe a movement away from vertical integration—moving an activity outside the firm that was formerly done within the firm. The term outsourcing also is used to describe an on-going arrangement, where a firm obtains a part or service from an external firm. It is often useful to think of the outsourcing decision as choosing along a continuum of possibilities, ranging from spot-market transactions to vertical integration, with long-term contracting being in the middle.

Well-functioning markets provide powerful incentives for efficient production and low prices. Thus, it is value-maximizing for firms to acquire many goods and services through market transactions. Economists, however, have identified at least three primary reasons why a firm might want to engage in non-market procurement: transaction costs, taxes/regulation, and monopoly power. At least four factors can make the transactions costs of non-market procurement lower than the costs of market exchange. These factors include firm-specific assets, costs of measuring quality, coordination problems, and externalities.

Firm-specific assets are assets that are significantly more valuable in their current use than in their next best alternative use. Investment in firm-specific assets can cause significant problems between suppliers and buyers and is a primary reason for non-market transactions. Once the investment in firm-specific assets is made, there is a *sunk cost*—the supplier has incentives to continue the relationship as long as he covers his variable cost (even if he does not cover his total costs). This incentive subjects the supplier to a potential *hold-up problem*. The buyer can also be held up by the supplier. One way to reduce these problems is to integrate vertically. The other method is to negotiate a detailed contract that spells out what is expected of each party. *Legal enforcement* and/or *market-based enforcement* can motivate the parties to comply with the contract.

A primary prediction of the economics literature is that as an asset becomes more firm-specific, the firm is more likely to choose vertical integration over long-term contracting. A second factor that is important in choosing between owning rather than contracting is *uncertainty* in the environment. *Contractual incompleteness,* arising from uncertainty, increases the likelihood of future opportunistic actions and thus the benefits from vertical integration. Finally, economies from specialization and the existence of labor unions can favor long-term contracting over vertical integration.

Our analysis suggests that firms will tend to enter long-term contracts when the desired investment is relatively firm-specific and where the environment is relatively stable and predictable. Alternatively, if the firm faces a highly uncertain environment and large investments in firm-specific assets, vertical integration is likely to be the preferred alternative. Finally, if the investment in firm-specific assets is relatively low or the lives of the assets relatively short, the firm can either enter into short-term contracts with suppliers or, in the limit, rely on spot-market transactions.

Independent distributors can have incentives to *freeride* on a brand name. One method to reduce this problem is vertical integration. The other method is to use contracts with specific provisions that reduce the freerider problem. Two types of contract terms that specifically address this concern are *advertising provisions* and *exclusive territories*. While exclusive territories help to reduce freerider problems, they create another problem—*double mark-ups*. This problem, which is analogous to the transfer-pricing problem studied in Chapter 14, can be reduced through either *two-part pricing* or *quotas*.

There are at least four factors that have contributed to the recent trend in increased outsourcing: increased world-wide competition, the development of less-firm-specific production technologies, improvements in information and communication technologies, and excess capacity from a world-wide recession. The recent trend, however, is not from vertical integration to spot-market transactions. Rather, it is a movement from both ends of the spectrum toward the intermediate arrangement of long-term contracting. Recent technological changes, such as just-in-time production methods, electronic data interchanges, and total-quality manufacturing, require close links between manufacturers, suppliers, and distributors. These changes have made spot-market transactions undesirable in many cases.

CHAPTER

17 Total Quality Management and Reengineering

Total quality management (TQM) and reengineering are two of the most popular management topics of the 1990s. One survey of 500 U.S. managers from large companies reports that 76 percent have used TQM and 69 percent have employed reengineering.[1] There is a coveted national award for the most successful company applying TQM principles. Consultants argue that restructuring via TQM and/or reengineering is critical and that firms must employ these techniques to survive.

While many consultants and managers endorse the importance of such restructuring, a significant number of these efforts have not met expectations. A 1991 survey of 300 large companies found executive satisfaction levels with TQM was 40 percent.[2] A Gallup poll of 1,237 corporate employees reports that over half say that quality is top priority; but only one-third say their companies' programs are effective.[3] Some firms—including McDonnell Douglas aircraft and Florida Power & Light—abandoned their TQM programs. Wallace Co. won the Baldrige National Quality Award in 1990, yet filed for bankruptcy in 1992.[4] Finally, a study of 584 U.S., Canadian, German, and Japanese firms in 1991 concluded that "many businesses may waste millions of dollars a year on quality-improvement strategies that don't improve their performance and may even hamper it."[5]

The popularity, despite lack of wide spread success of TQM and reengineering, raises a number of important questions, including:

• What explains the popularity of these types of restructurings?

---

[1] "Missions Possible," *The Globe and Mail*, (September 13, 1994), p. B22.
[2] *The Wall Street Journal*, July 6, 1993, p. A1.
[3] *The Wall Street Journal* (October 4, 1990), p. B1.
[4] *Newsweek* (September 7, 1992), pp. 48–49.
[5] *The Wall Street Journal* (October 10, 1992), p. B7.

• Why do they often fail to produce the desired benefits?

• Should all firms adopt TQM and/or reengineering? If not, which firms should adopt which technique: TQM or reengineering? Should any firm adopt these techniques?

• What can managers do to increase the likelihood that a particular restructuring will be successful?

The purpose of this chapter is to use this book's framework to answer these questions. We illustrate how this framework can be applied to provide insights into current management innovations, thereby providing a set of skills to analyze future organizational proposals. New organizational innovations undoubtedly will be forthcoming. This book's analytic framework provides a powerful tool to help understand the costs and benefits of these future innovations. Since most such organizational innovations focus on a specific aspect of solving business problems, the framework helps identify other facets of the organization that also require attention and complementary adjustment.

We begin by describing some alternative meanings of the term ''quality.'' We then provide a more detailed discussion of TQM and re-engineering. In each case, we give a concrete example, discuss specific details of the technique, relate it to organizational architecture, and address why the technique has become popular now, and not say ten years ago. Next we compare TQM and re-engineering and explore their similarities and differences. We address leadership issues which arise in managing these restructurings.

The final section addresses the question of why firms using these approaches often fail to achieve the desired benefits. In implementing these techniques, managers often ignore at least one leg of the three-legged stool. They usually focus on changing one or two of the legs but fail to make complementary adjustments in all three. Also, TQM programs often fail because—despite what consultants say—quality is not free; improving quality is costly. At some point, customers are not willing to pay the extra cost for additional quality improvement. Finally, not all firms can benefit from restructuring. TQM and re-engineering are investment decisions that should be adopted only when the benefits exceed the costs. Some firms adopt these techniques, only later to discover that the costs are greater or benefits smaller than anticipated. This discussion provides insights into whether a particular firm should adopt one of these techniques and how managers might better maximize the likelihood of success should they choose to restructure.

Total Quality Management

There is considerable debate surrounding what constitutes total quality management and how to define ''quality.'' Nonetheless, to most experts, TQM encompasses both improving the tangible aspects of product quality (performance, reliability, conformance to specification, durability, serviceability, aesthetics, and perceived quality) and enhancing the efficiency of the organization (lowering costs and enhancing productivity). Therefore, TQM seeks to improve all aspects of the company—its products, processes, and services. To apply TQM, managers must have a definition and a common understanding of what "quality" means.

What Is "Quality"?

Chapter 7 discussed implicit contracts and reputational concerns. While there are explicit warranties covering some products, most transactions occurring in markets are covered by implicit promises of product quality. If the customer expects a given level of quality and the firm shirks on that quality, the customer will switch to another supplier. Thus, the threat of losing future business creates incentives for firms to maintain promised levels of quality. The expression *caveat emptor* ("buyer beware") reflects a long-standing recognition that customers protect themselves from poor quality. The buyer's option to switch suppliers thus provides important incentives not to shirk. Economists use the term "brand-name capital" to refer to the value the market attaches to the firm's reputation for delivering a product of a promised quality.

Quality affects the market's demand for goods and services; thus quality is important in both the profit and nonprofit sectors of the economy. In attempting to improve quality, managers must grapple with what quality means and how to improve it. As we will see, the term "quality" is a catch-all for several different concepts, and the different meanings can conflict with each other. Quality can refer to "high mean," "low variance," "more options," or "meeting customer expectations." These alternative definitions are discussed in turn.

High Mean.   For any good or service, consumers value particular attributes. For example, in automobiles one attribute consumers value is acceleration. Cars of the same model and year have slightly different acceleration; testing a large sample of the same model generates a distribution of accelerations. The average (mean) acceleration of the sample is one measure of the model's quality. Chevrolet Corvettes have higher average acceleration than Toyota Corollas and hence are viewed as being of higher quality. Business schools with higher average starting salaries of their graduates are thought to be higher quality programs than those with lower average starting salaries.

Low Variance.   Besides calculating the automobile's average acceleration from the sample, the distribution's variance also can be computed and is another measure of quality. While Corvettes have higher mean acceleration, they might also have a greater variance than Corollas if the Corollas are subjected to tighter manufacturing tolerances. McDonald's hamburgers are higher quality than the local diner's because they taste the same wherever you buy them. The local diner's hamburgers vary from purchase to purchase depending on when and where the meat was purchased, how it was prepared and by whom, and what was cooked on the grill before your hamburger.

When faced with choosing between two products, one of which has a higher mean as well as a higher variance, it is not clear which is the higher quality product. It depends on whether the purchaser values a higher mean more than a lower variance. For example, consider a fax machine. Quality can be defined in terms of how precisely the average copy reflects the original. If 1,000 pages are transmitted and each one is compared to the original, how accurately does the average copy compare to the original? This is a measure of the average quality. A measure of quality related to variance is how badly the worst copy compares.

Toyotas are more reliable (have lower variance) than MGs because the Toyota has fewer component failures than an MG (or than MGs used to have). Reliability is often used as a synonym for quality. Conformance to standards or requirements is another measure of quality related to variance. Quality is often measured in terms of defects. For example, a component part must be within 0.001 millimeters of standard or else it is termed ''defective.'' If changing the machine producing the part reduces the defect rate from five per thousand to three per thousand, then quality is said to have increased.

More Options.   A VCR that can be programmed for five programs is said to be of higher quality than one with only two programs. Similarly, Burger King suggests their hamburgers are of higher quality than McDonald's because at Burger King the customer ''can have it your way'' (that is, more options). To some customers, product flexibility, the ability of a product to be used in a number of different ways, is an important attribute and one that is often associated with the term ''quality.'' For example, a video camera that can be used in low-light settings is more flexible and thus of higher quality than one that requires auxiliary lights in low-light situations.

Meeting Customer Expectations.   Customers have expectations with respect to all of the product's attributes, including delivery schedules, down time, operating characteristics, and service. These expectations include means, variances, *and* options. For example, a customer might expect one machine failure every three months, and when a breakdown occurs a service technician is expected to arrive on average within two hours after the call for service. If breakdowns occur monthly, but the service technician arrives within 1.5 hours on average, the firm has met one customer expectation (mean time for arrival) but has not met another expectation (one failure every quarter).

If quality is defined as meeting customer expectations, then measuring quality requires knowledge of the entire set of customer expectations, the actual realized values, and how much importance the customer attaches to that particular expectation. Each customer views deviations from expectations in some dimensions to be more important than deviations from expectations in others. For example, missed delivery schedules might be more important than missed service times for some customers. Moreover, preferences over various product attributes vary from customer to customer. In order to maximize the value of the firm, understanding customer preferences for various product attributes is important specialized knowledge to acquire. Different products can be offered to particular customer segments. For example, Federal Express offers both overnight and second day service at different prices.

When defining quality as meeting customer expectations, the term *total quality management* (TQM) includes those management processes and organizational changes necessary to meet customer expectations and to achieve continual improvement. Customers include external customers for the firm's products and services as well as internal customers. For example, the accounting department does not have any external customers, but its internal customers consist of all the users of the accounting reports. TQM programs seek to increase customer satisfaction by enhancing product and service quality and increase efficiency (lower costs). Lower (marginal) costs allow price reductions which further enhance customer satisfaction. The appendix to this chapter describes the Malcolm Baldrige quality award and how quality is measured for purposes of granting the award.

Computer Manufacturer's Quality Management Program

A large computer manufacturer redefined its business strategy as Market-Driven Quality. The goal is "total customer satisfaction," guided by the following four market-driven principles:

- Understand our markets.
- Commit to leadership in the markets we choose to serve.
- Execute with excellence across our enterprise.
- Make customer satisfaction the final arbiter.

To implement these principles, the following initiatives have been undertaken:

- Research, understand, and segment total potential market needs; commit to market leadership and deliver the right solutions at the right time.
- Remove defects in everything we do to achieve market-driven quality.
- Reduce the total time to fulfill customer's wants/needs.
- Give employees the authority and information they need to make timely decisions and carry out the activities necessary to ensure total customer satisfaction.
- Establish achievable business targets with a particular focus on quality and customer satisfaction.

Costs of Quality.   Improving product quality usually lowers the cost of reworking defects along with inspection costs, warranty costs, and customer complaints. The firm's brand-name capital is higher when product quality is increased. However, improving quality (lowering the number of defects and providing products with attributes customers value) is not free.[6] It is costly to discover the source of defects

---

[6]Some quality experts argue that quality is free—that the benefits of increasing quality always exceed the costs of quality improvements. See Philip Crosby, *Quality is Free* (New York: Mentor 1980). For a more balanced economic views, see Phillip J Lederer and Sevng-Kyu Rhee "Economics of Total Quality Management" *Journal of Operations Management* (1995) Vol 12 pp 353–367.

FIGURE 17.1   The Relation Between Quality and Firm Value.

Firm value increases as quality increases because consumer demand increases and manufacturing costs decline. Beyond some point, the cost of increasing quality is greater than the manufacturing cost savings and the increased consumer demand. Maximizing quality does not maximize firm value. Too much quality lowers value.

and to correct them. Figure 17.1 illustrates the relation between quality and firm value. Firm value increases as product quality improves. This is due to two factors: lower production costs and increased consumer demand. Profit-maximizing managers will want to undertake all quality improvements where the benefits from enhanced quality exceed the costs of improving quality. Ultimately, the product's customers must pay for the cost of the enhanced quality. At some point, the costs of making an additional improvement in quality will exceed what the customer is willing to pay and the reduced manufacturing costs. Consumers are presented with a wide variety of quality choices in most product lines. The wine lists at many restaurants contain a wide selection with a range of prices. Presumably, higher-priced wines are higher quality. Yet, we observe few customers ordering the most expensive wines. Few diners value the additional quality of the $275 bottle over the $20 house wine.

TQM: An Example

Sterling Chemicals, Inc., produces commodity chemicals with 1993 sales of about half a billion dollars.[7] In the late 1980s, Sterling initiated its Quality and Productivity Improvement (QPI) program. Once the CEO, the board of directors, and the top management team were committed to the plan, an intensive four-day training

---

[7]The following description of Sterling Chemicals' quality program is based on Scott Keating and Karen Wruck, Sterling Chemicals, Inc. (A), Harvard Business School case, 9–493–026, revised 9/8/94.

program by outside consultants was held for their top 20 managers. Within the first two years, each of Sterling's 950 employees had received a minimum of 16 hours of TQM training.

The training process involved teaching a sequence of problem-solving steps (Juran, 1989):

1. Analyze the symptoms of the problem.
2. Hypothesize as to causes.
3. Test hypotheses.
4. Establish the causes.
5. Simulate a remedy.
6. Test the remedy.
7. Institutionalize the remedy.

It emphasized how to brainstorm possible hypotheses, how to collect data to test the hypotheses, and how to apply simple statistical tests to reject hypotheses.

Once each employee was trained in problem-solving techniques, quality teams were formed. Any group could initiate a proposal to form a team to work on solving a particular problem. But before a team began working on a project, they had to recruit a management sponsor and write a one-page team charter describing the problem, the scope of the project, and performance targets. The charter had to be ratified by a Sterling quality committee. A project involving a single department could be approved by that department's quality committee; a project involving two departments in the same division required approval by the division's quality committee. Besides screening out vague or poorly-conceived initiatives, the various quality committees assured that each project team contained individuals with the likely requisite specialized knowledge to solve the problem. Sterling created three quality facilitator positions. These people were experts in applying TQM and worked with the project teams. Although Sterling's program focused on both quality and productivity improvements, the majority of the project teams worked on improving productivity and cutting costs.

Sterling employees' compensation is composed of a base salary, company stock, and profit sharing. Team performance is judged subjectively and rewarded indirectly through wage adjustments and promotions. Teams that enhance profits also share rewards through higher profit-sharing payouts and stock-price appreciation. (However, free-rider problems limit these incentives.) Another aspect of Sterling's TQM program is its no-layoff policy. Management announced that no layoffs would result from quality-team suggestions. Any head-count reductions would be implemental through attrition, not layoffs.

Sterling's pump-failure team illustrates how the process worked. About 15 pump failures per year occurred in one of their chemical processes. Each failure had a direct cost of $10,000. A group of engineers working for one year could not solve the problem. The maintenance engineers blamed the production people for not knowing how to operate the pumps; the production supervisors blamed poor repair work. Then a quality-improvement team was formed consisting of one mechanical engineer, three operators, four machinists, and a technical service engineer. They gathered data on pump failures and generated 57 potential reasons for the failures. Using the data they reduced the possible causes to four. They then experimented with actual pumps and discovered that excessive vibration and pump seal installation were the causes. New procedures were developed and over the next two years, no pumps failed.

TQM and Organizational Architecture

Sterling Chemical illustrates one company's use of total quality management (TQM) to try to increase firm value.[8] TQM programs can be viewed as a way to organize the firm. TQM programs seek to offer products that customers want and to lower operating costs. If knowledge of consumer preferences and operating cost savings resides lower down in the organization, then the analysis in Chapter 9 suggests one solution is to place the decision rights with those employees. After training their employees in problem-solving skills, the workers are better able to use their specific knowledge. Forming teams and assigning them decision rights is a way to assemble the specialized knowledge.

Most TQM programs argue for empowering employees to improve product and process quality. (Empowerment is another way of saying that decision rights are transferred to the person with the specialized knowledge.) But we have learned that if decision rights are repartitioned, then performance-evaluation and reward systems must also be modified to motivate the workers to use their new decision rights to maximize firm value. This section analyzes TQM in terms of how decision rights are repartitioned and how the reward and performance-evaluation systems are changed under TQM programs.[9]

Decision Rights Assignment.   As competition increases, firms face one or both of these alternatives. First, they can lower prices by reducing costs. Workers usually know how to improve the efficiency of their jobs. Second, they can compete in nonprice dimensions by satisfying more customer desires. A firm's customer base is usually heterogeneous, some valuing high means, others low variance, and others more options. TQM proponents advise "getting close to the customer," which means constructing an architecture that assigns decision rights to employees with specialized knowledge of the marketplace.

---

[8]In fact, Sterling's earnings and stock price fell from 1988 through 1993; operating profits in 1993 were about 25 percent lower than in 1988, and the average annual stock price was about 70 percent smaller. While this evidence does not allow one to argue that TQM increased Sterling's firm value, it is possible that Sterling's value could have been lower had they not adopted the TQM process.

[9]Much of this section is based in Karen Wruck and Michael Jensen, "Science, Specific Knowledge and Total Quality Management," *Journal of Accounting & Economics* (November 1994), pp. 247–287.

If the potential pool of customers is changing or if technology is causing product capabilities to change, the firm's architecture also must be able to adapt the products and services it supplies to different segments of the market. No single employee is likely to see all the customers or suppliers, so firms must devise mechanisms whereby knowledge can be assembled across a number of individuals, each with only a limited component of the relevant knowledge. Teams can do this.

If teams of workers with the relevant knowledge are empowered to solve problems and make decisions effectively, they must have appropriate training. As we saw with Sterling Chemicals, TQM programs generally train workers in problem-solving techniques. These training techniques apply the scientific method whereby hypotheses are first generated, data is used to test the hypotheses, proposed remedies are field-tested, and finally the accepted remedy is institutionalized. Although TQM is relatively new, it builds on the scientific method which has evolved over centuries.

Notice that training is costly. There is no guarantee that training costs will be recovered from the earnings by teams lowering production costs or increasing customer demand as we discuss further below, quality is not free. It would be foolish to believe that the benefits always exceed the costs.

Chapter 9 offered three general conditions when team decision making will be most productive: There are potential synergies from working as a team; there is the ability to assemble relevant specific knowledge; and freerider problems can be controlled. For TQM teams to be most effective, these conditions must hold. In particular, to elicit relevant specific knowledge from workers, not only must they be trained to use their knowledge, they must have incentives to recommend efficiency-enhancing staff reductions. One method of achieving this is by adopting a "no layoff" policy; in fact, this frequently accompanies TQM programs. Also, the freerider problems must be controlled, normally by limiting the size of the team.

Wruck and Jensen (1995) argue against indiscriminate decentralization of decision rights to TQM teams—they caution against "team mania." At one point, Sterling Chemicals had 77 quality teams each with six to ten people. It was difficult to provide technical support to so many teams, let alone to implement their recommendations successfully. To control team mania, Sterling Chemicals established quality committees to approve each quality project. By creating a hierarchy of quality committees with the decision rights to ratify and monitor quality teams, Sterling separated decision management from decision control (recall Chapter 9). Any individual or group of individuals has the decision rights to initiate a quality project. Once a quality project is ratified by the overseeing quality committee, the team must produce an action plan—which is again ratified by the quality committee. Once the action plan is approved, the quality team is responsible for its implementation. After finding and implementing a remedy, the quality team is disbanded.

Evaluating and Rewarding Performance of TQM Teams.   To lower costs and meet customer expectations, specialized knowledge is assembled by forming quality teams. Creating and monitoring the teams requires the allocation of decision rights to the teams. To control the agency problems of the teams, performance-evaluation and reward systems must be changed. In Sterling Chemical's case, each team's performance is measured by comparing the team's action plan and their stated goals (submitted to and approved by the quality committees) with the actual outcomes.

Rewarding quality-team performance is often based on both non-monetary and monetary rewards. By solving workplace problems, teams can improve their working conditions. Public recognition of quality-team achievements via plaques, jackets, and award ceremonies provides additional motivation. Participation on suc-cessful teams increases promotion opportunities. But the most controversial issue among quality experts involves the role of monetary incentives. Some argue to tie pay to team performance while others argue against such incentive schemes. One quality consultant says:

> People really don't work for money. They go to work for it, but once the salary has been established, their concern is appreciation. Recognize their contribution publicly and noisily, but don't demean them by applying a price tag to everything.[10]

As summarized in Chapter 12, critics of incentive compensation such as Crosby argue that pay-for-performance does not work because poorly-designed systems reward people for doing the wrong things. But this does not allow you to conclude that incentive pay should be discarded. Monetary and non-monetary incentives are not mutually exclusive. Both types of rewards are valued by workers. Excluding one type of incentive reduces management flexibility.[11]

Another important motivator in TQM is the presence of a management sponsor for each quality team. Lower-level workers on the quality team may for the first time in their careers have direct access to a senior manager. Team members often perceive this association will improve their future promotion possibilities or increase their appointment to another quality team with access to even more senior managers. The presence of the management sponsor probably increases the performance of the individual team members.

Why Quality Now?

The traditional approach to ensuring product quality was to ''inspect-it-in.'' In-spection stations and quality assurance inspectors were added along the production line to weed out inferior products. Statistical sampling methods were used to draw random samples from a batch and reject the entire batch if an unacceptable number of bad units were detected in the sample. (Notice that this process implicitly defines quality as low variance—meeting a certain set of specifications which might or might not be of interest to the consumer.) Sections of the factory stored defects waiting to be reworked or scrapped. In some cases, if market demand exceeded

---

[10]Crosby (1980), p. 218.

[11]George Baker, Michael Jensen, and Kevin Murphy, ''Compensation and Incentives: Practice and Theory: *Journal of Finance* (1988), pp. 593–616.

production in a period, marginally defective products were released. Defective products reaching the market were corrected by the field service organization under warranty arrangements.

TQM in Government

The Office of Quality Management at the U.S. Department of Energy spent in 1994 $3.5 annually and had a 12-person "culture team." This culture team oversees a variety of training programs for the Department's 20,000 federal employee workforce. Some of the training procedures include "customer focus advocates," "customer focus coordinators," and "habits facilitators."

The Office of Quality Management also produces training videos. One, dealing with creativity and innovation, touts one innovation, an employee newsletter posted in bathroom stalls at a Department's weapons plant. The newsletter is called the "Porcelain Press." The TQM training video describing the "Porcelain Press" even includes the sound of a flushing toilet and describes "this too, is the sound of communication . . . in the sanctuary of contemplation." The head of the Office of Quality Management describes the graffiti workers write on the newsletters as a "feedback feature."

A less enthusiastic Energy Department employee suggested that TQM stands for "time to quit and move."

Suggested by *The Wall Street Journal* (December 15, 1994), pp. A1 and A8.

By the 1980s, two factors combined to change the optimum approach to quality in many industries. First, the cost of detecting problems and monitoring production via computer instrumentation fell relative to the cost of maintaining quality via direct labor inspectors. The cost of labor (including fringe benefits) made the cost of manually detecting and correcting errors more expensive relative to performing these tasks electronically. Instead of manually detecting defects after production, improved instrumentation allowed earlier detection of problems, often while the product was in a production process. Second, world-wide competition expanded to such non-price forms of competition as quality. Customers had access to more reliable products. Once the Japanese automobile companies gained price competitiveness against the American auto makers, they turned their attention to achieving quality advantages. Both the lower cost of detecting defects and increased global competition fostered quality improvements.

To reduce defects, companies redesigned their products to require fewer different parts, making it easier to maintain tighter controls on the quality of their suppliers. Product designers redesigned parts that failed. Production processes were redesigned to reduce defects. Robots and more instrumentation were built into manufacturing to ensure more uniform production. Firms adopted Total Quality Management programs. While in many firms TQM programs were initially started to improve the tangible aspects of product and service quality, TQM programs have evolved to enhance products, processes, and services for both internal and external customers.

Reengineering

Reengineering—like TQM—is a popular management technique whose proponents promise will revolutionize business. It too involves organizational changes that can be analyzed using the tools of this book. Michael Hammer, a leading proponent of reengineering defines it as "the fundamental rethinking and radical redesign of business processes to achieve dramatic improvements in critical, contemporary measures of performance, such as cost, quality, service, and speed."[12] "Processes, not organizations, are the object of reengineering. Companies don't reengineer their sales or manufacturing departments; they reengineer the work the people in those departments do."[13] This section discusses reengineering, but first we provide an example of reengineering from the health care industry called "patient-focused care" to illustrate the technique.

Re-Engineering: An Example

Humana Hospital, a 555-bed hospital in Dallas, Texas, restructured its organization along a "patient-focused care" model; it began this restructuring process in 1990 to enhance patient care and reduce costs. Hospital costs in the 1980s and early 1990s increased faster than inflation, thereby contributing to the "health-care crisis." Insurance companies, private individuals, and employers that provided health-care benefits for their workers bore the higher expenses. To stem the rising health-care costs, large employers and insurance companies began pressuring their local health-care providers by threatening to require their workers be treated only at those hospitals and by those physicians that better controlled their costs. Hospitals thus began to worry more about competing for patients and cost containment.

Traditional Hospital Structure.   Prior to restructuring, Humana had the traditional organization whereby patient care was provided primarily by functionally organized individuals: physicians, nurses, and a score of specialists drawing blood samples, taking X-rays, and EKGs. A typical 650-bed hospital had the following breakdown of its health care dollar:[14]

Medical care (direct patient care and costs)	$0.16
Scheduling	0.14
Documentation (writing patient charts)	0.29
Idle labor time (waiting for patients to arrive)	0.20
Patient services (occupancy costs)	0.08
Transportation (wheelchair aides)	0.06
Management and supervision	0.07
Total	$1.00

[12]Michael Hammer and James Champy, *Reengineering the Corporation: A Manifesto for Business Revolution* (New York: Harper Business, 1993) p. 32.

[13]Hammer and Champy (1993), p. 117.

[14]J. Philip Lathrop, "The Patient-Focused Hospital," *Healthcare Forum Journal* (July/August 1991), pp. 17–20.

Only $0.16 of each dollar spent in the hospital went to direct patient care.

Most large hospitals are organized around numerous, small, clinically-focused nursing units with dedicated staffs and large centrally-dispatched services (IV teams, phlebotomists, transporters, and so on). They have 60 to 100 department heads, 150 responsibility centers, and seven to nine layers of management between the CEO and the bedside caregiver. Units are generally designed with excess capacity enabling them to handle the sickest patient with the most complex needs. Yet 60 to 80 percent of all medical procedures are for routine services (chest X-rays, basic lab tests, EKGs). Therefore, infrastructure costs and idle time account for up to 75 percent of the personnel costs for simple procedures.

Patient-Focused Care.   To better control costs and attract patients, the "patient-focused care" movement arose. Nursing roles were re-evaluated and tasks re-assigned. After the reorganization, patient care is delivered through a team approach where two-person caregiver teams of nurses and technicians are responsible for almost all the procedures performed on each patient. Patient-focused care re-engineers the hospital's basic functions by applying the following principles:[15]

Cross-train caregivers. Each caregiver learns to provide basic bedside nursing, basic X-ray films, respiratory care, EKGs, and the like. Routine care is provided by nurses, med-techs, lab-techs, phlebotomists, and other staff. working in two-person teams assigned to patients. The team "owns" the patient; they admit the patient, document the care, serve the meals, change linen, and even clean the room after discharge. Instead of interacting with an average of 55 employees during a three day stay, patients interact with 15. Instead of being transported throughout the hospital for routine tests and waiting for them to be performed, most tests are done in the patient's room.

Reaggregate patients to units. Most hospitals are arranged by level of acuity and broad medical category. For example, cardiac intensive-care units and orthopedic intensive-care units are two separate acute-care units specializing by medical category. But wireless technology is allowing more flexibility in how patients are grouped. Patient-focused care locates patients by the type of tests, therapies, and health-care resources needed. Instead of a 15 to 20 bed dedicated unit, 50 to 100 bed patient centers allow service lines to be developed.

Decentralize central-service functions. Each patient service center has satellite lab, radiology, and pharmacy units. The caregivers are cross-trained to perform many of the functions of the old centralized function. Large centralized service bureaucracies are dismantled and disbursed and under the control of the patient centers. However, the extent to which decentralized satellites are efficient depends on the costs of the equipment. Basic X-rays are decentralized, but CAT scans are not because small inexpensive, simple-to-operate X-ray machines are available whereas CAT scan equipment is still very expensive and requires more specialized training to operate.

---

[15]See Carl Schartner, "Principles of Patient-Focused Care," *Journal of the Healthcare Information and Management Systems Society* Vol. 7, No. 2, pp. 11–15.

Simplify processes. At admission, each patient is assigned to a unit and given a standard protocol (sometimes called a "care map") that details the standard set of tests and procedures to be followed by the caregivers. Instead of documenting every procedure and test performed, the staff only documents exceptions to the standard protocols. Exception-based charting has reduced documentation by as much as 50 percent.

Change the organization's culture. Unless the old hierarchy of specialized departments is eliminated and replaced with a new structure with new reporting mechanisms and incentives, most of the benefits of patient-focused care will not be realized.

Advocates of patient-focused care emphasize that all of the above changes are necessary if the benefits are to be achieved. That is, all the elements of reorganization are compliments, not substitutes.

> The kind of improvement our health care system requires cannot be obtained by isolating a redesign initiative to any one of the patient-focused care principles. We need a more comprehensive effort that understands the complex interrelationships between the principles.[16]

Hammer also recognizes the importance of the complementary nature of the decision-right assignments and the performance-evaluation and performance-reward systems in reengineering. "Companies that unfurl the banner (of re-engineering) and march into battle without collapsing job titles, changing compensation policy, and instilling new attitudes and values get lost in the swamp."[17]

The Reengineering Process

This section describes the process of reengineering in more detail. To reengineer, Hammer lists the following guiding principles:[18]

Organize Around Outcomes, Not Tasks.   One person should perform all the steps in the process. In the patient-focused care model, patients are organized around the treatments they will receive, and a two-person caregiving team provides all the basic services from nursing to X-rays.

Have Those Who Use the Output of the Process Perform the Process.   If the accounting department needs pencils, instead of requesting purchasing buy the pencils, accounting buys the pencils from pre-approved vendors. This reduces the overhead associated with managing the interfaces between processes since the same person performs sequential processes.

---

[16]Carl Schartner, "Principles of Patient-Focused Care," *Journal of the Healthcare Information and Management Systems Society* Vol. 7 No. 2, p. 15. See also Paul Milgrom and John Roberts, "Complementarities and Fit: Strategy, Structure, and Organizational Change in Manufacturing," forthcoming *Journal of Accounting & Economics* (1995).

[17]*Wall Street Journal* (July 6, 1993), p. A1.

[18]Michael Hammer, "Reengineering Work: Don't Automate, Obliterate," *Harvard Business Review* (July–August 1990), pp. 104–112.

Productivity Job Losses Large in Service Industries

In 1987 Capital Holding Corp., a financial services company, acquired two small insurance companies to add to its group of insurance companies. They had a combined administrative staff of 1,900. After reengineering in 1993, the insurance group employs 1,100 with plans to reduce the number to 800, even though its insurance business is up 25 percent.

Suggested by *The Wall Street Journal* (March 16, 1993), pp. A1.

Subsume Information-Processing into the Work Producing the Information. Scanners in supermarkets are linked to computers that maintain perpetual inventory levels. When a particular item drops below a reorder point, an electronic data interchange (EDI) sends an order to the supplier's computer to replenish the stock. As the check-out clerk scans the customers' purchases, this automatically updates the inventory records and reorders the merchandise. Likewise, in patient-focused care, the caregiver, by doing many of the tests, generates information and acts on it directly. A centralized lab technician does not have to produce the information and pass it to the caregiver for action.

Put the Decision Point Where the Work is Performed. Caregivers have the decision rights to follow the procedures specified in the protocols. The protocols (care maps) control the processes. Policies guide handling exceptions to the standards which are documented and monitored.

Capture Information Once and at the Source. Before a lab test could be performed, a physician had to order the test by hand-writing an order which was then copied into the patient's chart. After the test was performed, accounting received a copy of the original order which then entered the data into the patient's account for billing purposes. With standard protocols, orders do not have to be written, charted, and re-entered by accounting.

The preceding five points in effect say, marry knowledge and decision rights. Look at how tasks are assigned, how knowledge is generated, and repackage jobs to more efficiently use the way knowledge is generated. Caregivers in the patient-focused-care hospital perform the basic functions of admitting patients, drawing blood, performing lab tests and X-rays. They, therefore, spend less time informing the next person in the sequence of what they found. In a patient-focused care hospital, tasks are reassigned to better join knowledge and decision rights. The caregiver knows that blood was last drawn out of the patient's sore left arm, and so will now use the right arm.

Treat Geographically-Dispersed Resources as Though They Were Centralized. Each decentralized pharmacy on the patient centers can be linked to a centralized pharmacy data base that contains preapproved drugs and vendors. This allows the benefits of scale economies via large purchases while maintaining the benefits of flexibility and service.

Reengineering and Organizational Architecture

Decision Rights Assignment.   Chapter 9 proposed the general concept of trying to link decision rights with specialized knowledge. With rapid advances in information technology, old decision-right assignments become obsolete and must be changed. Some decision rights will have to become centralized and others decentralized—there is no general prediction that information technology necessarily causes decision rights to move either up or down the hierarchy. However, new information technology tends to make the status quo obsolete. Reengineering is a process whereby the organization begins to search for an improved organizational architecture by redesigning how tasks are bundled into jobs.

Reengineering is a procedure for changing task assignments from a functional organization to a process organization. In Chapter 10, we described functional versus process organizations. IBM Credit Corporation was cited as an example. When IBM Credit Corp. was organized functionally, workers were assigned narrow job tasks: credit checking, contract preparation, pricing, and document preparation. After re-engineering, workers at IBM Credit had broader task assignments. They were case workers and each was responsible for all the tasks necessary to process a credit application. Similarly, caregivers under patient-focused care have broader task assignments.

Functional organizations are more likely to be cost-beneficial than process organizations in environments with stable technology, where frequent communication among functional departments is relatively important and interactions can be handled through rules and procedures. This is especially true where higher-level management is likely to have the relevant specific knowledge to coordinate the various functions that make up the overall process, and economies of specialization can be exploited. But in less stable environments, direct communication across functional areas can be very important and situations more frequently arise that challenge established coordination procedures. In turn, higher-level managers are less likely to have all the relevant specific knowledge to address these challenges. The specific knowledge is likely held by workers throughout the firm. For example, the frequent introduction of new products increases the benefits of communication between salespeople and design engineers about customer preferences. Similarly, it is important for development and manufacturing personnel to share information when production techniques and technologies are frequently changing. Thus, in more dynamic environments, a process-oriented organization is more likely to be desirable.

Most of the contemporary writers on reengineering spend a considerable amount of time describing not only what reengineering is but also how to accomplish it. They emphasize the difficulty of the task and the importance of senior management backing the effort. Hammer and Champy (1993, pp. 103–116) have observed the following assignment of decision rights in companies reengineering:

Leader: A senior executive who authorizes and motivates the reengineering process. Consistent with our discussion of leadership in Chapter 15, the leader must set the vision and then motivate others to follow it.

Process owner: The manager responsible for the specific process being reengineered. This person's reputation and career are tied closely to the success of the reengineering effort.

Reengineering team: Five to 10 people with the specialized knowledge of the process (or its parts) who analyze the existing process, redesign it, and oversee its implementation. Individuals from both inside and outside the process working, usually full time for up to a year, form the self-directed team. Individual performance evaluation while serving on the team is based on the team's achievement. Most of the team should expect to become part of the newly reengineered process.

Steering committee: The policy making board of senior managers that establishes policies, ratifies particular reengineering proposals, and monitors each team. The leader chairs this committee. The reengineering steering committee performs the same function as the quality committees in TQM. They control team mania.

Reengineering czar: The person with the specialized knowledge of reengineering methods to act as a resource to the reengineering teams. The czar also helps to coordinate across the various teams.

As in the TQM process, there is separation of decision management from decision control. Both reengineering and TQM teams have decision rights to initiate and implement changes, but only after ratification by the policy making/monitoring board, the steering committee.

Evaluating and Rewarding Performance of Reengineering Teams. Chapter 13 described the general issues of evaluating team performance. Both the team's total output and the individual member's evaluation must be evaluated. The reengineering czar often has first-hand knowledge of individual members' contributions because this person has been working closely with the team. As with TQM, the steering committee that ratifies the reengineering teams plans also monitors the team's output, including the team's proposed reengineering plan.

Re-engineering efforts seek to make drastic changes in the way work is done. Often this results in large reductions in the work force. Those members of the reengineering team overseeing and implementing the plan usually have more job security than those not on the team. This can be a powerful motivator for the team to get their analysis right and to see their plan implemented.

Why Reengineering Now?

Prior to 1970, firms faced less world-wide competition and lower rates of technological innovation than they do now. Functional organization was more likely optimal and typically was adopted. But in the 1990s these firms face more dynamic environments, and their senior managers realize that the old functional organization is no longer optimal. Besides increased competition, technology has reduced the cost of transferring information both up and down the organization, thereby causing the old architecture to become increasingly inefficient.

New technology makes obsolete the old ways that tasks were bundled into jobs and jobs assembled to form processes: Sophisticated data bases can easily track basic information about customers and retailers thereby opening up new market opportunities; bar coding and scanners now provide enormous amounts of information about consumer purchases; and electronic data interchange (EDI) connects customers with supplier computers which automatically re-order inventory as the customer sales occur. Thus, as in the case of TQM, both increased competition and technological change cause managers to search for new organizational architecture.

TQM vs. Reengineering

TQM and reengineering are mechanisms for effecting organizational changes. Both involve changes in the three-legged stool. To be successful, both require coordinated and consistent changes in all three legs. Neither TQM nor reengineering is a substitute for the other. While both might be used simultaneously, such use would probably lead to more confusion and disruption among the workforce than the two were sequenced. This section compares and contrasts the two approaches.[19]

Continuous vs. Discontinuous

Cost savings from either TQM or reengineering often come from reducing labor content. Capital and materials can be used more efficiently, but Ford Motors' accounts payable re-engineering produced a drastic reduction in head-count (375 out of 500 clerks eliminated).

A principle some TQM consultants stress is job-security assurances. They argue that in order to motivate workers to be forthcoming with quality improvements, TQM programs must promise workers their jobs will not be eliminated. Not all TQM programs offer such assurances. Nevertheless, successful programs must offer employees incentives to be forthcoming with their specialized knowledge. Job security is one way to provide such assurance. On the other hand, not all employees need to have job security; in the limit, it might be offered only to those on TQM teams. But in companies having announced the need to down-size, a policy of job security only for TQM team members could produce team mania by creating incentives for employees to suggest numerous TQM projects to protect themselves from layoffs. Such a policy could also create strong incentives for other employees to generate large influence costs.

---

[19]A process related to both TQM and reengineering is Value Added Analysis. This technique dates back to when Lawrence Miles, an engineer at General Electric, sought to identify those unnecessary costs that do not add value nor customer features to the product's quality. Examples include product rework, scrap, ordering errors, and schedule changes. (*Financial Times*, January 16, 1995).

If firm-wide job security assurances are made, TQM productivity improvements are constrained by the rate of job attrition. If one out of 10 employees quits or retires each year, then only 10 percent of the jobs can be eliminated through attrition. And this attrition rate puts an upper bound on the productivity savings a TQM program can produce in any given year. If TQM is working properly, big problems are eventually solved and only small improvements are available.

Quality programs seek to improve existing processes. Reengineering does not focus on enhancing existing processes but seeks to replace them with entirely new ones. Reengineering seeks large improvements in productivity; cost reductions of successful reengineering programs exceed the attrition rate. Technological or market changes can cause an existing architecture to become obsolete quickly. Drastic job redesign is necessary and layoffs in excess of the attrition rate are necessary. In this situation, TQM coupled with job security guarantees will not produce the desired results. One way to achieve large savings is through reengineering—which only guarantees job security to members of the reengineering team.

Besides job guarantees, two other factors affect the willingness of employees to participate in organizational redesign programs: the firm's growth rate and the extent of job-specific human capital. Growing firms can absorb jobs eliminated from labor productivity improvements into other parts of the firm that are growing. However, the ability to transfer these employees to the growing parts of the firm depends on the extent they have job-specific human capital. If manufacturing jobs are being eliminated and software engineering jobs are being added, high re-training costs are incurred to transfer manufacturing workers into programming positions. However, when there is lower job-specific human capital, implicit job security exists. Sales people selling one set of products can be re-trained at fairly low cost to resell a new set of products if their customer base remains similar. Thus, high-growth firms with low job-specific human capital tasks are able to offer implicit employment guarantees and will have more employee participation in organizational redesign efforts than low-growth, high job-specific human capital firms.

Distributional Consequences in Effecting Organizational Change

It is easier to implement organizational changes when some individuals are made better off and no one is made worse off than in situations where some parties gain at the expense of others (see Chapter 15). In this latter situation, there are distributional consequences of the change, and thus more opposition to the change is expected. To the extent TQM projects include fewer layoffs, they tend to have fewer distributional consequences and hence generate less resistance than reengineering programs. Reengineering programs (which by definition is the ''radical redesign of business processes to achieve dramatic improvements'') usually involve large changes in task assignment and hence either the destruction of job-specific human capital or outright job cuts.

In Chapter 15, we described that parties likely to be harmed by restructurings, via reduced corporate resources under their control or by job loss, will try to block the organizational change. Agents with ratification rights harmed by the re-organization will lobby against it. Reengineering efforts when announced are likely to create great apprehension among the work force who have incentives to sabotage the project. Hammer and Champy recognize this and suggest establishing a reengineering team that is completely separate from the existing hierarchy. This team is guaranteed job security and positions in the reengineered organization. Working full time on the project removes the team from the social pressures of their former colleagues.

Making organizational changes with distributional consequences requires the use power. Power is derived from formal authority (senior managers with the decision rights to ratify and implement the change), control of physical and monetary resources, control of information, and friends and allies. Hammer and Champy's suggested use of the leader, process owner, team, and steering committee marshals all these elements of power. The leader, if the chief executive officer, and the steering committee, if composed of senior managers, have the formal authority to ratify and implement the change. Selecting team members with the specialized knowledge of the various parts of the process and of how the process interacts with other processes is critical to gaining control of the necessary information.

Reasons TQM and Reengineering Fail

The preceding sections have described the mechanics of TQM and reengineering and have analyzed these popular management techniques using this book's framework. TQM and reengineering are different ways of reorganizing work within firms. While most large firms have tried these methods, the evidence, casual as it is, seems to suggest that most adopters of these methods are less than completely satisfied with the results they achieve. This section suggests three reasons TQM and reengineering efforts can fall short of their anticipated outcomes.

Ignoring One or More Legs of the Stool

To successfully restructure the organization and push decision rights down to the people with the knowledge about processes and customer preferences, the performance-evaluation and performance-reward systems must also be changed. Empowering workers with decision rights requires systems to evaluate and reward their performance. Firms trying to implement TQM or reengineering without modifying their performance-measurement and reward systems to support the changes in decision rights are unlikely to garner the hoped-for benefits.

Much of the reengineering and patient-focused care literature focuses on how to design a process for re-assigning decision rights.[20] It focuses on a single leg of the three-legged stool: repartitioning decision rights via task reassignment. Most of the writers mention the importance of the performance-evaluation and reward

---

[20]For example, see Hammer and Champy (1993) and Hammer (1990).

systems, but offer little guidance or occasionally inappropriate advice for how the evaluation and reward systems must change. For example, Hammer and Champy (1993, p. 73) make the blanket assertion: Pay bonuses for outstanding performance, don't pay raises. Clearly, the compensation decision we describe in Chapters 11 and 12 is far more complex than is reflected in the Hammer and Champy suggestion.

An important part of the performance-reward system is promotions. But most reengineering articles are silent about how to create new career paths and promotion systems to motivate workers in a process-oriented organization. Within smaller, flatter organizations, advancement opportunities are more limited. If TQM and re-engineering are to work, significant effort must be expended on "reengineering" the performance-evaluation and reward systems—all three legs of the stool must be coordinated.

Linking TQM to Financial Returns and Compensation

A 1992 study by the American Quality Foundation and Ernst & Young found that in 80 percent of the firms surveyed, quality performance measures aren't important in senior manager's compensation. This suggests one reason why most TQM programs fail.

Suggested by "TQM: More than a Dying Fad?" *Fortune* (October 18, 1993), p. 68.

Quality Is Not Free

One noted quality expert argues, "Quality is free. It's not a gift, but it is free. What costs money are the unquality things—all the actions that involve not doing jobs right the first time."[21] "The cost of quality is the cost of doing things wrong."[22] The costs of not doing things right the first time include prevention (design reviews, supplier evaluations, tool control, preventive maintenance), appraisal (prototype tests, receiving inspection and test, packaging inspection), and failure (redesign, engineering change order, rework, scrap, product warranty, product liability). It is certainly the case that if managers can at zero cost cause prevention, appraisal, or failure costs to go down, quality goes up and profits improve. In this sense, "quality is free." And if we could get oil to jump out of the ground and into our cars as gasoline, "oil is free." However, reducing scrap, inspections, engineering change orders (that is, improving a product's quality) requires management time and other resources. Defects must be discovered, their cause investigated and corrected. Employees must be trained in quality methods. In this sense, improving quality is costly. Figure 17.1 illustrated the tradeoff between quality and firm value.

---

[21]Philip Crosby, *Quality is Free* (New York: Mentor 1980), p. 1.
[22]Crosby (1979), p. 15.

Managers might systematically underestimate the total costs of poor quality. Given the wide range of costs of providing quality, ranging from scrap, rework, inspection, to lost customer goodwill, top management might systematically underestimate the benefits of reducing defects. While manufacturing might optimize its production process with respect to quality, it does not take into account in its calculations the costs marketing and distribution incur having to fix problems in the field. If some managers underestimate all the benefits from improving quality, they might underinvest in programs to improve quality. They might not fully appreciate the costs of reduced consumer confidence in their products. If managers are about to retire, they may be reluctant to spend money today on quality programs that yield benefits after they retire. But this is just the standard horizon problem that occurs with all decisions where outlays occur now and the benefits span several periods; in this sense quality programs are no different from capital investment, R&D, and advertising. Successful firms must control these horizon problems.

If managers are not aware of all the possible benefits of improved quality, educational programs are required. However, quality is still not free. Quality decisions, like all decisions, require accurate estimates of all the expected costs and benefits. It is just as dangerous to underestimate the benefits of quality programs as it is to underestimate the costs by arguing "quality is free." In both cases, non-firm-value-maximizing decisions are likely to result.

While Crosby recognizes that improving quality is costly, he unambiguously believes that the benefits of improving quality exceeds the costs. "If you concentrate on making quality certain, you can probably increase your profit by an amount equal to 5 to 10 percent of your sales. That is a lot of money for free."[23] In this sense, Crosby asserts that the benefits unambiguously exceed the costs for all firms. Without offering any systematic evidence, other than a few anecdotal stories, he asserts that all firms (including those currently following his advice) are systematically foregoing profitable projects.

Restructurings Are Investment Decisions

Any restructuring is costly. Senior managers must devote their limited time to designing the new architecture and then implementing it. Implementation often entails confrontations with those managers in the firm made worse off by the reorganization (influence costs). When down-sizings are required because of reengineering, managers bear additional costs of having to fire employees.

How much a firm should invest in quality is an investment decision. So too is the amount to invest in restructuring via TQM and reengineering. Not all firms face the same expected benefits from restructuring. Decentralizing decision rights, even to employees with specialized knowledge, still might not be firm-value maximizing if agency costs increase. As discussed earlier, these restructurings occur because of changes in the firm's markets or technology. If firms are in stable markets and

---

[23]Crosby (1979), p. 1.

technological advances have not been rapid, the benefits of restructuring are likely low, and for these firms, the expected costs of restructuring are more likely to exceed the benefits. TQM and reengineering are more likely to be profitable investments where the firm's markets and technology are changing. Since firms in the same industry face similar markets and technology, you would expect firms in the same industry to restructure at approximately the same time.

The Costs of Reorganizing

Many managers face psychological stress from having to fire people because of reorganizations. One IBM manager remarked, "I came home every night worried how this one or that one was going to support himself. I snapped at my husband, I had trouble sleeping." After accepting the next early retirement package offered by IBM, she said, "Reorganization had been five years out of my life, and when I quit, I felt the biggest load in the world had been lifted from my shoulders."

One manager who had gone through several rounds of firing subordinates was described as: "He was smoking, had lost weight, had trouble looking me in the eye, was extremely nervous. It seemed to me that a few months of telling people they were out the door had gone a long way in destroying his personality."

Nolan Brohaugh of the Menninger Clinic, a noted psychiatric hospital, has been conducting weeklong seminars for 15 years for Professionals in Crisis. He says, "In my experience, they (managers) have a lot of trouble firing people who deserve to get canned."

Suggested by "Burned Out Bosses," *Fortune* (July 25, 1994), pp. 44–52.

Summary

TQM and re-engineering are popular management techniques promising to add value to the firm. Yet, these approaches have failed to achieve many of their claimed benefits. This chapter illustrates how the analytic framework of this book can be applied to emerging management trends, in particular to total quality management and reengineering. TQM is the process whereby employees are trained in the scientific method and then use these skills to improve product quality and production efficiency by forming multi-disciplinary teams. TQM involves repartitioning decision rights by empowering teams who have the knowledge to increase firm value. This is accomplished only if the quality teams have the incentives to discover value-increasing changes because the performance-evaluation and reward systems (the other two legs of our three-legged stool) support the quality program. One important assurance quality teams often receive is the guarantee of job security if they discover a way to improve a process that requires layoffs. TQM is a procedure that seeks continuous, small improvements in processes. To control the quality program, a hierarchy of quality committees are created to ratify and then monitor the behavior of each quality team.

Reengineering, like TQM, is a mechanism for changing the organization's architecture. But unlike TQM, reengineering seeks drastic, radical changes in processes. Advances in information technology change where knowledge is captured in the firm and how it can be transmitted. The old architecture which attempted to link decision rights and knowledge is obsolete. Garnering the benefits of the new information technology often requires entirely new bundling of tasks into jobs. Instead of having several employees specializing by task and handing off work from one to another to complete a process, one employee now performs the entire process for routine transactions. Networked, on-line data bases, or expert computer systems provide the necessary support for the newly-created multifunctional job.

Like TQM, reengineering requires a team of people knowledgeable about the old process being redesigned. This team has the decision rights to initiate and implement the design change. This team also requires incentives to do this, thus necessitating changes in the performance-evaluation and reward systems. But since reengineering usually results in large layoffs, only those individuals on the re-engineering team are normally given job-security guarantees.

One of the key questions posed at the beginning of this chapter is why restructurings fail to produce the desired benefits. While both TQM and reengineering involve empowering teams of employees to discover substantive improvements in the organization, managers implementing both TQM and reengineering often fail to emphasize changing the other two legs of the three-legged stool; the performance-evaluation and reward systems. Processes can be improved or radically redesigned, but changing the performance-evaluation and reward systems for the new task assignments is usually not emphasized as much as the reassignment of decision rights. Also, TQM programs will fail to maximize firm value if management over-invests in quality. Since improving quality is costly, only those quality enhancements valued by customers at more than their cost should be undertaken. Maximizing quality (or minimizing the number of defects) does not necessarily lead to maximizing firm value. Finally, managers must realize that since TQM and re-engineering are costly, only firms facing substantial opportunities to benefit should invest in these restructurings. Typically, the benefits of restructuring will be large in firms facing rapid changes in technology or in market competition.

APPENDIX: THE BALDRIGE NATIONAL QUALITY AWARD

In 1987 the Federal government established the Malcolm Baldrige National Quality Award to recognize quality achievement of U.S. companies. The annual awards are administered by the National Bureau of Standards of the U.S. Department of Commerce. After paying an application fee, companies wishing to apply for the award file a written report describing their company and information on 24 examination items that will be scored by an examining team from the government. These 24 items form seven categories listed in Table 17.1. For example, under leadership, one of the specific items is "Senior Executive Leadership." The applicant is asked to describe "how the company's senior executives set strategic directions and build and maintain a leadership system conducive to high performance, individual development, and organizational learning." The examiners then assign point scores using specific scoring criteria.

It is interesting to compare the contents of Table 17.1 with the analytic framework developed in this book. Most of the key elements to insure that the organizational architecture is designed to increase quality are present in the Baldrige criteria. The firm must demonstrate that it gathers knowledge of the customer and competitors, that decision rights are partitioned to promote participation, and that employees have incentives to increase customer satisfaction.

Table 17.2 lists the firms that have won the Baldrige award. Up to two awards in each of three categories are presented annually to companies or subsidiaries. A 1991 U.S. Government Accounting Office report studied 20 of the top-scoring companies in the 1988 and 1989 Baldrige competitions. These companies had quality programs in place for an average of two and a half years. The surveyed companies reported an increase in reliability and on-time delivery. Product defects and development time for new products dropped. Market share increased 13.7 percent a year, and profits rose 0.4 percent. Customer complaints dropped 12 percent.

Partly due to the public relations and advertising value of winning the Baldrige award, the number of applications has risen from 203 for the first three years to over 180,000 requests for applications in 1990. Since 1991, the number of applicants has fallen sharply.[25] The government hires hundreds of examiners (who are paid out of the application fees) to assign the point values. Companies hire former examiners as consultants to advise them on filing applications. Once a company reaches the semi-finalist stage, which includes an on-site visit, additional consulting teams, coach managers, and employees who might be chosen randomly are interviewed by the Baldrige examiners. *The Wall Street Journal* (12/90) reports that the Baldrige award creates consulting engagements lasting up to six months and costing as much as $175,000, and has become "the full employment act for quality consultants."

TABLE 17.1   **1995 Malcolm Baldrige National Quality Award Examination Categories (and Point Values)[24]**

1. Leadership (90 pts.)

The *Leadership* Category examines senior executives' personal leadership and involvement in creating and sustaining a customer focus, clear values and expectations, and a leadership system that promotes performance excellence. Also examined is how the values and expectations are integrated into the company's management system, including how the company addresses its public responsibilities and corporate citizenship.

2. Information and Analysis (75 pts.)

The *Information and Analysis* Category examines the management and effectiveness of the use of data and information to support customer-driven performance excellence and marketplace success.

3. Strategic Quality Planning (55 pts.)

The *Strategic Quality Planning* Category examines how the company sets strategic directions, and how it determines key plan requirements. Also examined are how the plan requirements are translated into an effective performance management system.

4. Human Resource Development and Management (140 pts.)

The *Human Resource Development and Management* Category examines how the work force is enabled to develop and utilize its full potential, aligned with the company's performance objectives. Also examined are the company's efforts to build and maintain an environment conducive to performance excellence, full participation, and personal and organizational growth.

5. Process Management (140 pts.)

The *Process Management* Category examines the key aspects of process management, including customer-focused design, product and service delivery processes, support services and supply management involving all work units, including research and development. The Category examines how key processes are designed, effectively managed, and improved to achieve higher performance.

6. Business Results (250 pts.)

The *Business Results* Category examines the company's performance and improvement in key business areas—product and service quality, productivity and operational effectiveness, supply quality, and financial performance indicators linked to these areas. Also examined are performance levels relative to competitors.

7. Customer Focus and Satisfaction (250 pts.)

The *Customer Focus and Satisfaction* Category examines the company's systems for customer learning and for building and maintaining customer relationships. Also examined are levels and trends in key measures of business success—customer satisfaction and retention, market share, and satisfaction relative to competitors.

TABLE 17.2   Malcolm Baldrige National Quality Award Winners

Manufacturing Category
   Motorola (1988)
   Westinghouse Electric Commercial Nuclear Fuel Division (1988)
   Commercial Nuclear Fuel Division (1989)
   Milliken & Co. (1989)
   Xerox Business Products and Systems (1989)
   Cadillac (1990)
   IBM Rochester, MN (1990)
   Solectron Corp. (1991)
   Zytec Corp. (1991)
   AT&T Network Systems Group Transmission Systems (1992)
   Texas Instruments Defense Systems & Electronics Group (1992)
Service Category
   Federal Express (1990)
   AT&T Universal Card Services (1992)
   Ritz-Carlton Hotel Co. (1992)
Small Business Category
   Globe Metallurgical Inc. (1988)
   Wallace Co. (1990)
   Marlow Industries (1991)
   Granite Rock Co. (1992)

CHAPTER

18

Ethics and Organizational Architecture

In December 1990, the head of Salomon Brother's government-bond trading desk, Paul W. Mozer, submitted bids for 35 percent of a four-year Treasury note auction. He also submitted another $1 billion bid under the name of Warburg Asset Management, a Salomon Brothers' customer, but without the customer's authorization. The two bids, which represented 46 percent of the issue, violated the Treasury's auction rules.[1] Mr. Mozer repeated this tactic in February and April at auctions for five-year notes.

In April, Mr. Mozer apparently became concerned that the Treasury was about to uncover his bidding tactics. He informed Salomon Chairman John Gutfreund, President Thomas Strauss, Vice Chairman John Meriwether, and General Counsel Donald Feuerstein of his illegal bid in the February auction. No immediate action was taken. In May, he again employed this tactic in an auction of two-year notes. In June, the Securities and Exchange Commission and Justice Department issued subpoenas to Salomon and some of its clients for records involving bond auctions. Salomon then initiated a review of its government-bond operations and in August disclosed its illegal bids in the period between December and May.

By May 1992, the government had imposed a number of penalties on Salomon Brothers. Treasury barred Salomon from bidding in government securities auctions for customer accounts. The Federal Reserve Bank of New York, while allowing Salomon to retain its designation as a primary dealer, suspended its authority to trade with the Bank for two months. The firm agreed to pay $122 million to the Treasury for violating securities laws and $68 million for claims made by the Justice Department. It established

---

[1] In auctioning Treasury Bonds, the U.S. Treasury awarded bonds first to the highest bidder at their quoted prices, then they moved to the next highest bidder. This process continued until the issue was exhausted. If the Treasury received multiple bids at the price that exhausted the issue, it allocated bonds in proportion to the bid size. But Treasury auction rules limited the amount of an issue sold to a single bidder to no more than 35 percent of the issue.

380

a $100 million restitution fund for payments of private damage claims that might result from approximately fifty civil lawsuits stemming from the scandal that the firm still faced. (Unclaimed amounts in this fund revert to the Treasury, not Salomon.) While these legal/regulatory penalties were substantial, they represent only a fraction of the total costs imposed on the firm. In the week that the information about the illegal bids was released, Salomon Brothers' stock price dropped by one third. This $1.5 billion fall in market value suggests that the market expected Salomon to bear significant costs as a result of these actions and seems too large to simply reflect fines and other expected legal/regulatory sanctions. In addition to the penalties and decline in the market value of Salomon's stock, all of the senior officers who knew of the illegal bids but did not act swiftly were forced to leave the firm, and none of these individuals have worked in a major securities firm again. The case of Solomon Brothers illustrates that market forces can impose material sanctions on parties to unethical behavior.[2]

Over the past decade, much public attention has been devoted to the issues of business ethics and corporate social responsibility. Politicians and social critics have deplored the materialism of the 80s; the media have treated the public to sensational accounts of corporate scandal; and business schools across the country have begun offering courses in ethics.

In recent years, many U.S. corporations have responded by issuing formal codes of conduct, appointing ethics officers, and offering employee-training programs in ethics. Such codes and programs cover a wide range of behavior, but most emphasize the following:

- Compliance with laws and statutory regulations.
- Honesty and integrity in dealings with customers and other employees.
- The avoidance of conflicts of interest with the company.

While few would quarrel with such aims, equally few proponents of such corporate initiatives have bothered to ask questions like the following: Are such codes and programs likely to be effective in deterring unethical behavior by corporate managers and employees? And, more pointedly, is the behavior enjoined by such codes consistent with the normal incentives of employees or managers, *given the current organizational architecture* of the firm?

Although it is rarely recognized in most public discussions of the subject, corporate ethics and organizational architecture are closely related. To increase the likelihood that business people are to behave ethically in their roles as managers and employees, corporate performance-evaluation systems, reward systems, and systems that partition decision rights can be designed to encourage such behavior.

In this chapter, we make five basic arguments:

1. The term "ethics" is elusive. It has many different meanings, and these meanings change across cultures and over time. The term "business

---

[2]For a more complete account of the Solomon Brothers case see Clifford W. Smith, "Economics and Ethics: The Case of Salomon Brothers," *Journal of Applied Corporate Finance,* Vol. 5, No. 2 (Summer 1992).

ethics'' can mean everything from corporate social responsibility to maximizing shareholder value.

2. If the corporation is to survive in a competitive environment, it must maximize its value to its owners (primarily the stockholders). Taking care of other corporate ''stakeholders'' such as employees and local communities is important, but such care can be taken too far. If the firm reaches the point where it reduces the owners' value, this care can endanger corporate survival.

3. A company's reputation for ethical behavior, including its integrity in dealing with non-investor stakeholders, is part of its brand-name capital; as such, it is reflected in the value of its securities. By the same token, individuals' human capital—that which determines their future earnings prospects—is based in large part on their reputation for ethical behavior. In this sense, private markets provide strong incentives for ethical behavior by imposing substantial costs on institutions and individuals that depart from accepted social standards. The Salomon Brothers trading scandal illustrates that the magnitude of these costs can be large.

4. Considerable emphasis in corporate ethics programs is put on misplaced efforts to change employees' preferences by attempting to persuade them to put the interests of the organization or its customers ahead of their own. Our approach, instead, accepts people's preferences as given and assumes they will follow their perceived self-interest. We focus on structuring the organization in ways that better align the incentives of managers and employees with the corporate aim of maximizing value.

5. Even if ethical guidelines and training programs are unlikely to alter fundamental preferences, they have the potential to add value by more explicitly communicating the firm's expectations to its employees. To be effective, however, such guidelines must be reinforced by the firm's performance-evaluation and reward systems.

Ethics and Choices

A fundamental cornerstone of this book is that individuals make choices to maximize their utility. Individuals have preferences over just about everything and choose how much to spend on food, transportation, housing, charities, and other purchases. People choose how to spend their time between work and leisure and how to allocate their time among alternate leisure activities, for example watching T.V., attending church, or raising money for a local charity. People make choices. Economics is the study of how people make choices and is basically a descriptive study seeking to understand and explain people's observed decisions. In this book, our analysis has been positive, not normative. We have not argued what decisions people should make; we have not argued that people should spend more time fundraising for their local charities and less time watching T.V. We have argued

(Chapter 2) that given people's preferences, they will tend to select those activities that maximize their well-being.

This chapter is also about choices, in particular, ethical decisions. But much of the study of "ethics" specifically focuses on how people should make choices; it is the study of those behaviors people should pursue. In large, ethics is normative. When philosophers speak of ethics, they are dealing with the 3,000 year-old discipline that seeks to identify those behaviors that are right or wrong, good or bad, virtue or vice.[3] Moral philosophers have been debating ethics since ancient times and all religions involve statements of which behaviors are ethical and which are unethical. All major religions—Buddhism, Christianity, Confucianism, Hinduism, Islam, and Judaism—espouse the Golden Rule: "Do unto others as you would have them do unto you."[4] Western religions are based on the Ten Commandments, a code of ethical behavior.

Behaviors such as lying, cheating, stealing, and killing are almost universally viewed as wrong except under mitigating circumstances. (Murder in self-defense is usually acceptable.) However, certain behaviors are viewed as wrong by some, while others view them as right. For example, some view abortion as wrong, while others view denying women the right to choose as wrong. Similar conflicts exist regarding birth control and a person's right to die. In these cases there is no universally accepted code of ethics one can rely on to assess right and wrong.

Business ethics seek to proscribe those behaviors in which businesses should not engage. Such actions range from the giving or taking of gifts, bribing government officials, misrepresentation of data, discrimination in hiring, and third-party boycotts. For example, some deem it unethical for a company to do business in South Africa while that country practiced apartheid.

Business ethics and organizational architecture are interdependent. Organizational architecture, we have argued throughout this book, affects the incentives and thus the decisions managers undertake. If it is important for business people to behave ethically in their roles as managers and employees, it is important that the organization be structured to elicit ethical behavior.

Corporate Mission

What is the mission of the corporation and does it involve ethics? Most people have a pretty good idea what they mean when they describe an individual as "ethical." Most of us feel an emotional allegiance to the "golden rule" that urges us to treat others as we would have them treat us, and we value qualities such as honesty, integrity, fairness, and commitment to the task at hand. But what does it mean for a corporation to behave "ethically"? First, we have to understand what the term "ethical" means and then how it relates to the firm's mission.

---

[3]Dagobert D. Runes, *Dictionary of Philosophy* 15th ed. (New York: Philosophical Library, 1960), p. 98.2

[4]William H. Shaw, *Business Ethics*, (Belmont, Calif.: Wadsworth Publishing Co., 1991), p. 12.

Ethics

Ethics is a branch of philosophy. Western ethical philosophy can be traced back at least twenty-five hundred years to Socrates, Plato, and Aristotle. These ancient Greeks searched for a generally understood set of principles of human conduct. Their treatises revolve around the terms "happiness" and "virtue." Writing in the 13th century, St. Thomas Aquinas "argues that the first principle of thought about conduct is that good is to be done and pursued and evil avoided."[5]

There are numerous ethical theories. Ranging from egoism (an act is correct if and only if it promotes the individual's long-term interests)[6] to utilitarianism (behaviors should "produce the greatest possible balance of good over bad for everyone affected by our action"[7]). Kantian ethics judges the nature of the act, not the outcome. Kant argued that only good deeds matter.[8] Adam Smith argued that through the invisible hand of market competition driven by self-interest resources are directed to their most productive use and societal wealth maximized. Finally, ethical relativism holds "that moral principles cannot be valid for everybody; and . . . that people ought to follow the conventions of their own group."[9]

Even a cursory review of the major ethical philosophies yields two immediate observations. First, ethics is an enormous subject area that has engaged some of history's best minds. Second, despite considerable human endeavor, there is no generally accepted philosophical consensus across time and societies as to which behavior is ethical and which is not.

When it comes to defining the ethics of organizations like public corporations that encompass large groups of people, there is bound to be confusion. A corporation, after all, is simply a collection of individuals—or, more precisely, a set of contracts that bind together individuals with different, often conflicting, interests. In this sense, corporations themselves do not behave ethically or unethically—only individuals do. And if corporate managers and employees are not pursuing their own interests, then whose interests are they serving? Their bosses'? The shareholders'? The board's? And what if there are major conflicts among these various interests?

Value Maximization

Maximizing firm value is the mission most economists ascribe to managers. By maximizing the size of the pie, more can be distributed to each party contracting with the firm including the shareholders, bondholders, managers, employees, customers, and

---

[5]John Haldane, "Medieval and Renaissance Ethics," in *A Companion to Ethics,* edited by Peter Singer (Oxford: Basil Blackwell, 1991) p. 135.

[6]Kurt Bair, "Egoism," in, *A Companion to Ethics,* edited by Peter Singer (Oxford: Basil Blackwell, 1991), p. 197.

[7]Shaw (1991), p. 49.

[8]Shaw (1991), p. 74.

[9]Richard Brandt, "Ethical Relativism," in *Ethical Issues in Business: A Philosophical Approach* edited by Thomas Donaldson and Patricia Werhane (Englewood Cliffs: Prentice-Hall, Inc. 1979), p. 78.

suppliers. As described in Chapter 6, if the firm faces competition for both inputs and outputs, the prices the firm pays for its inputs and receives for its outputs will be driven to the competitive levels, and the firm will not receive any abnormal profits. Long-run survival in a competitive environment dictates that firms seek to produce products at the lowest possible cost. Absent barriers to entry, firms that survive in the long run are the ones that deliver products consumers want at the lowest cost. This means that managers must adopt policies that maximize the value of the firm—or, what amounts to the same thing, the net present value of future cash flows distributable to the firm's investors. If managers follow other policies that raise their costs, value-maximizing competitors enter, manufacture products at lower costs, and sell them at lower prices. Eventually, the non-value-maximizing firm will be shut out of the market.

Maximizing firm value requires managers to assess all costs and benefits of proposed actions accurately. Suppose a firm is considering entering the business of disposing of hazardous wastes. Workers exposed to such hazards usually demand a compensating wage differential to offset the higher risks of illness from such work (Chapter 11). Therefore, when evaluating whether to enter this business, value-maximizing managers must factor in the compensating differentials. Likewise, when considering businesses with ethical dimensions such as producing birth control products, some employees of the firm have personal beliefs that conflict with the new business. Some of these employees will leave the firm. Some will seek transfers to another division. Others may require compensating differentials to stay. Workers with strong moral beliefs opposed to the company's position may sabotage the project or misreport data to dissuade senior managers from accepting the project. In all cases, the costs of business decisions that some view as unethical are higher because of the compensating differentials, labor turnover, agency problems, and adverse publicity associated with the decisions.

Corporate Social Responsibility

One source of confusion is the concept of ''corporate social responsibility,'' which is often used interchangeably with corporate ethics. In 1969, Ralph Nader and several other lawyers launched their Project on Corporate Responsibility with the following statement:

> Today we announce an effort to develop a new kind of citizenship around an old kind of private government—the large corporation. It is an effort which rises from the shared concern of many citizens over the role of the corporation in American society and the uses of its complex powers. It is an effort which is dedicated toward developing a new constituency for the corporation that will harness these powers for the fulfillment of a broader spectrum of democratic values.[10]

---

[10]John Collins, ''Case Study—Campaign to Make General Motors Responsible,'' reprinted in *Ethical Issues in Business,* ed. Thomas Donaldson and Patricia Werhane (Englewood Cliffs: Prentice-Hall, 1979), p. 90.

As Nader's statement suggests, the aim of advocates of corporate social responsibility is nothing less than to change the objective function of the corporation. In his view, the corporation is to be transformed from a means of maximizing investor wealth into a vehicle for using private wealth to redress social ills. The corporate social responsibility movement seeks to make management responsible for upholding "a broader spectrum of democratic values." Corporate support for such values could take the form of philanthropic activities, the provision of subsidized goods and services to certain segments of the community, or the use of corporate resources on public projects such as education, environmental improvement, and crime prevention. If all firms in the world face the same social requirements, then the survival of any given firm is less of an issue. However, if some firms are exempted from redressing social ills, others' survival in a competitive environment requires that they maximize their market value.

Phone Companies Charged with Electronic "Redlining"

A coalition of public-interest groups recently charged that four leading telephone companies are engaging in "electronic redlining" by by-passing low-income and minority communities as they begin to build advanced communication networks. These groups asked the Federal Communications Commission to clarify its rules and issue a policy statement opposing discrimination in the building of such networks. By raising charges of redlining, these groups seek to persuade the firms to provide early, subsidized service to less profitable markets. A spokesman for one firm pointed out that to achieve its plan of "wiring" half of the state of California by 2000 "without raising rates," the company "must [first] bring the network to areas where it will generate some new business and revenues, so ultimately we can bring it to everyone in the state."

Suggested by *The Wall Street Journal*, May 24, 1994.

Economists' View of Social Responsibility

The conflict between Nader's and economists' views of the corporation is not quite as pronounced as it might appear. Corporations intent on maximizing firm value often find it in their interest to devote resources to non-investor stakeholders such as employees, customers, suppliers, and local communities. For example, a company with a large plant in an inner city might decide that investing corporate resources and personnel to improve area schools leads to better trained workers and eventually lower-cost products. Giving money to the local university might benefit the firm by improving its R & D and increasing its access to top graduates. Improving the environment lowers the company's legal exposure to damage claims and might also lower its wage bill to the extent a cleaner local environment makes it easier to attract skilled workers.

Milton Friedman's View of Corporate Social Responsibility

"What does it mean to say that the corporate executive has a "social responsibility" in his capacity as businessman? If this statement is not pure rhetoric, it must mean that he is to act in some way that is not in the interest of his employers. For example . . . that he is to make expenditures on reducing pollution beyond the amount that is in the best interests of the corporation or that is required by law in order to contribute to the social objective of improving the environment. . . .

[The problem in this case is that] the corporate executive would be spending someone else's money for a general social interest . . . [when] the stockholders or the customers or the employees could separately spend their own money on the particular action if they wished to do so."

Milton Friedman, "The Social Responsibility of Business Is to Increase Its Profits," *New York Times Magazine* (September 13, 1970).

Maximizing firm value means devoting resources to members of each important corporate constituency to improve the terms on which they contract with the company, to maintain the firm's reputation, and to reduce the threat of restrictive regulation. More precisely, it means allocating corporate resources to all groups or interests that affect firm value—but only to the point where the incremental benefits from such expenditures at least equal the additional costs.

One potential benefit to the owners of a firm from having the corporation donate to charities is a reduction in taxes paid to the government. Assume that both the corporate and personal tax rate is 50 percent. Suppose a corporation has profits of $5,000 before taxes and distributes all its after-tax profits to the shareholders. The firm has four equal shareholders who collectively want to give $1,000 to a particular charity. If the firm makes the contribution, it is deductible from corporate income before taxes. Thus, the corporation has $4,000 of taxable income ($5,000 − $1,000) of which $2,000 is paid in taxes and $2,000 is paid to the owners who pay personal taxes. After personal taxes, each shareholder has $250 ($2,000 ÷ 4 × 50%).

If the shareholders donate $250 each to the charity and the corporation makes no contribution, the firm pays taxes of $2,500 (50% of $5,000) and distributes $2,500. Each shareholder receives $625 ($2,500 ÷ 4) before personal taxes, makes her contribution ($250) and has taxable income of $375 ($625 − $250). Each pays taxes of $187.50 and has after taxes $187.50 ($625 − $250 − $187.50). By having the firm make the charitable contribution, each shareholder has $62.50 ($250 − $187.50) more than when she makes it. When the firm makes the contribution, the gift shields $1,000 from corporate taxation.

These tax-reduction gains for corporate philanthropy are most compelling when all the shareholders agree on the amount and nature of the donations. Gifts to charities not valued by some shareholders reduce these owners' welfare. Unfortunately, there is unlikely to be agreement among corporate stakeholders about which charities should receive corporate donations. Customers, employees, or independent sales agents objecting to the firm's choice of charities may take their business or services elsewhere. Moreover, corporate managers do not obviously have a comparative advantage in choosing which charities to support. If it is time-consuming for managers to sort through charitable requests and make the selections, this is time that could have been spent on other activities which more predictably increase firm value.

Corporate Philanthropy Comes under Fire

Pioneer Hi-bred International, the world's largest seed company, provided financial support for Planned Parenthood of Greater Iowa. But when right-to-life groups voiced strong objections in the farming communities where the firm does business, the company was forced to withdraw its sponsorship. As *The Wall Street Journal* reported,

" 'We were blackmailed,' declares Pioneer chairman and president Thomas Urban. 'But,' he says, 'you can't put the core business at risk,' even though the company concedes that canceling funding probably upset as many farmers as it appeased and the boycott didn't end."

Suggested by *The Wall Street Journal*, June 10, 1992, p B1.

Absent tax benefits, it is usually more efficient for the corporation to focus on creating wealth and to let its shareholders, employees, and customers choose the beneficiaries of their charitable contributions. By maximizing their shareholders' (or owners') wealth, corporations effectively maximize the size of the pie available for distribution; in so doing, they enlarge the pool of individual (non-corporate) resources available for charity.[11]

The experience of the 1980s, incidentally, is consistent with this argument: During this decade of large shareholder gains, total charitable giving—by individuals, corporations and foundations—expanded in real dollars at a compound annual growth rate of over 5 percent, a growth rate over 50 percent higher than in the previous 25 years. Moreover, private donations rose from an historic low of 2.1 percent of national income in 1979 to 2.7 percent in 1989.[12]

People who advocate ever larger corporate contributions to charities and social causes such as retraining displaced workers and environmental clean-up (without consideration of their own long-run profitability) are effectively calling for higher implicit taxes on corporations. If all companies are so taxed, the taxes are ultimately

---

[11]James Brickley, "Managerial Goals and the Court System: Some Economic Insights," *Canada-United States Law Journal*, Vol. 13 (1988), p. 79.

[12]See Richard B. McKenzie, "Decade of Greed: Far From It," *The Wall Street Journal*, July 24, 1991, p. A10.

borne not only by shareholders in the form of lower returns to capital, but also by workers in the form of lower wages and by customers in the form of higher prices. Thus, ironically, the likely social consequences of such an increase in corporate social responsibility are lower rates of economic growth, lower corporate values, higher unemployment, and overall reductions in charitable donations—that is, reductions in donations by individuals that more than offset the increases in corporate giving.

New York Times Standard

The above example of Pioneer Hi-bred International illustrates the often important interaction among ethics, public relations, and the media. Ethics consultants regularly counsel corporate managers to apply the *New York Times* standard to help determine which behaviors are ethical. This criteria suggests that to judge whether an action is ethical, ask if you would be comfortable reading about what you did on the front page of the *New York Times*.

Using publication of your behavior in the *Times* as an ethical benchmark for judging a decision highlights the linkage between ethical behavior and reputation (brand-name capital). Later, we discuss market forces that create incentives for people and firms to behave ethically. The argument is that unethical behavior adversely affects reputation and one way to assess a decision's reputational effects is to ask how it would read in the *New York Times*.

Agency Costs and Ethics

Many managers are inclined to endorse Milton Friedman's prescription that the social mission of the corporation is "to make as much money for its owners as possible while conforming to the basic rules of society." As we noted, some companies will find it in their shareholders' interest to "invest" in social causes of various kinds, but corporate investments that systematically fail to provide adequate long-term returns to private investors are wealth transfers that end up reducing social as well as private wealth.

Besides corporate social responsibility, another issue often linked to ethics involves the agency problem between owners and workers. Chapter 7 described the general agency problem as the difficulty in making corporate managers and employees perform in ways consistent with the aims of owners. This section makes two key points: first, the agency problem of shirking or opportunistic actions by the agent is often labeled an ethical lapse; and second, if all agents reduced their opportunistic actions (behaved more ethically), agency costs would be lower.

To review the agency problems that can arise with performance evaluation and monitoring, take the case of hiring someone to paint your house. Especially in performing tasks that are hard to monitor such as surface preparation (sanding and priming), the painter has incentives to shirk—or, at least, to do a job that may not be as thorough as you might like. Of course, this same painter will also be prompted by other considerations to do a good job. It may be a matter of private conscience; that is, the painter's sense of self-worth might be tied up with the quality of the workmanship, and violating such a self-imposed standard would impose major "costs" in the form of a tarnished self-image. Or the painter is constrained by the desire to maintain his commercial reputation (and, though it might take some time for a poor job of surface preparation to show its effects, the quality will eventually reveal itself). As we noted earlier in this chapter and discussed in Chapter 7, reputation is an important contributor to one's "human capital," or the capitalized value of one's expected future earnings.

But because the promptings of conscience and the desire to maintain a reputation are neither universal nor constant, it's impossible for you to know the extent to which your painter is bound by such considerations. You face an information problem: You do not know when hiring the painter the kind of surface preparation you will get, nor will you be capable of ascertaining that until well after the job is done and the bill is paid.

To reduce your vulnerability in such circumstances of informational asymmetry, you will likely ask for a list of references (if the painter has not already provided one). Such references should give you some basis for assessing the painter's time horizon and the importance he attaches to reputation. The painter might also offer, or you might insist upon, a one-or-more-year warranty on the job. (As we discuss later, such common practices as the use of warranties, third-party references, and credit checks play an important role in reducing agency costs in the business world.)

But despite such assurances, some uncertainties about the painter's level of performance remain. For example, will he be around to make good on the warranty if the paint peels in a year? Perhaps the painter has heavy debts and is about to declare personal bankruptcy. Or perhaps yours will be the painter's last job before he embarks on a new career painting still-lifes and family portraits.

As a consequence of the possibility of shirking and your own remaining uncertainty, you as the principal effectively reduce the price you are willing to pay. Or, to state the converse of this proposition, if there were some means for the painter to provide you with complete assurance about his level of commitment, you would offer to pay a higher price for the job.

Three points emerge from this simple example. First, let's assume you were able to design a perfect contract; for the sake of argument, let's say you had a camera that enabled you to observe the painter's activity at random intervals (and the painter knew you had it), and that you were able to structure a pay schedule based on the observed effort. Even if you were able to devise such a monitoring and reward scheme, it would clearly not pay you to do so. The cost to you of writing, administering, and, most important, monitoring compliance with such a contract would be substantial—perhaps greater than the value of the painting job itself.

Thus, as this simple illustration is meant to point out, in most cases it does not pay to attempt to eliminate all possible shirking; because of the costs of writing and monitoring compliance with contracts, it is efficient to leave some slack in the system. As explained in Chapter 7, the *optimal* amount of shirking or opportunistic behavior by the agent is not zero.

Second, the *expected* level of opportunism or shirking—which, again, is greater than zero—is priced in the contract. Thus, the principals do not bear the full costs of opportunistic actions by their agents. Typically, at least some of these costs are shifted back to agents in the form of lower prices for their services or products.

Third, higher ethical standards among agents, whether corporate employees or participants in market exchanges, would lead (over time) to a reduction in the level of *expected* opportunistic behavior and hence a reduction in agency costs. As a result, there would be more transactions (including more jobs created) and higher prices paid to agents by principals (including higher corporate wages). This would occur not only because of a reduction in the amount of shirking, but also because the costs of writing and monitoring contracts would fall. Both principals and agents would be better off. As economist Jack Hirshleifer makes this last point, "Altruism economizes on the costs of policing and enforcing contracts."[13] In discussing economic development, one writer lists low business ethics as an important factor impeding growth. During the late 19th century, such practices as confidence men selling shares, bankruptcy with concealed assets, and squandering capital increased the difficulty of raising capital to finance new ventures such as the construction of the railroads.[14]

A Retired CEO's View of Verbal Contracts

"Most of our products were custom-made. Customers called in their orders over the phone. The orders, ranging in value from a few hundred dollars to tens of thousands of dollars, generally required delivery of goods within one or two days. It meant we would usually begin production before receiving a confirming purchase order. (This was before faxes.) The customer's word alone was enough. In my 20-year stint as CEO, not once did a customer go back on it. Unusual? Not at all. Without such trust, business couldn't be conducted. Similar transactions happen every day. . . . (W)e learned there are two ways to go: An eye for an eye, or do unto others what you would have them do unto you. In business, the latter philosophy is far more common, simply because it makes things work better."

Suggested by Hugh Aaron, "The Myth of the Heartless Businessman," *Wall Street Journal* (February 7, 1994), p. A14.

The retired CEO's story makes an important point about the economic consequences of ethics: If we as a society could get everyone voluntarily to reduce opportunistic behavior such as withholding important information about product

---

[13]Jack Hirshleifer, "Economics from a Biological Viewpoint," *Journal of Law and Economics* (April 1977), p. 28.

[14]Thomas Cochran, *The Inner Revolution,* (New York: Harper and Row, 1964).

quality, then the resources devoted to monitoring and enforcing exchanges could be used in more productive pursuits.[15]

Codes of Ethics

We view important aspects of the corporate ethics problem primarily as problems of reducing agency costs. And, generalizing from the above discussion, there are several potential ways that they can be reduced. One is to use contracts that better align the interests of managers and the employees they supervise with those of shareholders. Examples of such contracts in corporations are executive or employee stock options, bonus plans, and profit-sharing arrangements (see Chapter 12).

A second way to reduce agency costs is to get corporate managers and employees to voluntarily accept higher, more stringent ethical standards. (Even in cases where such costs are self-imposed, sanctions will also act as a reinforcing deterrent.) Both more cost-effective incentive contracts and higher ethical standards can be expected to lead to lower agency costs, greater corporate efficiency, higher corporate values, and greater social welfare.

As mentioned earlier, many companies and most professions have written codes of conduct, and some companies also have educational programs dealing with ethics for their employees. Most codes and programs emphasize the following:[16]

- Employees must obey the laws and observe statutory regulations.
- Customer relations in terms of the reputation and integrity of the company are of great importance.
- Employees must support the company's policies to customers.
- Conflicts of interest between the company and the employee must be avoided.
- Confidential information gained in the course of business must not be used improperly.
- It is improper to conceal dishonesty and protect others in their dishonesty.
- Advice to customers should be restricted to facts about which the employee is confident.

Why have corporations adopted such codes? The most cynical view is that a corporate code of ethics is nothing more than a document that helps the firm defend itself against charges of illegality. The new sentencing guidelines issued by the United States Sentencing Commission in November 1991 strongly encourage corporations to establish and communicate compliance standards and procedures for

---

[15]Eric Noreen, "The Economics of Ethics: A New Perspective on Agency Theory," *Accounting, Organizations and Society,* Vol. 13 no. 4 (1988), pp. 359–369.

[16]Note that these codes are not unique to the United States. For example, similar codes are observed in Australian firms. See Bruce Kaye, "Codes of Ethics in Australian Business," *Journal of Business Ethics,* Vol. 11 (1992).

employees and other agents through training programs and publications. For example, a company found guilty of wrongdoing in fulfilling a government contract can reduce its penalties by more than 50 percent simply by demonstrating that it has a compliance program that meets the Sentencing Commission's standards.[17]

But corporate ethical codes, as we have just argued, also have the potential to perform the economically-valuable function of reducing the costs of monitoring and enforcing contracts. To the extent they reduce managerial and employee opportunism, better ethical standards can increase corporate brand-name capital and hence shareholder wealth.

The critical questions, however, are these: *Are ethical codes effective in deterring unethical behavior? And if they are, how or why are they effective?*

Alter Preferences

There are two basic ways to view the function of corporate codes of conduct in reducing opportunistic behavior. One way is by appealing directly to employees' consciences and so attempting to instill in them loyalty to the organization and its goals. Economists describe this as an attempt to alter people's "preferences."

Now, there is undoubtedly some value to this approach. As we noted earlier, personal codes of conduct and the guilt one suffers in violating such codes are undeniably constraints on many people's behavior. As described in Chapter 2, individuals' utility functions contain many non-pecuniary factors, including conscience and guilt. As the following statement by Nobel Laureate Kenneth Arrow suggests, even subjective concepts like ethics and morality are consistent with the economist's notion of rational self-interest:

> Certainly one way of looking at ethics and morality . . . is that these principles are agreements, conscious or, in many cases, unconscious, to supply mutual benefits. . . . Societies in their evolution have developed implicit agreements to certain kinds of regard for others, agreements which are essential to the survival of the society or at least contribute greatly to the efficiency of its working. . . . [T]he fact we cannot mediate all our responsibilities to others through prices . . . makes it essential in the running of society that we have what might be called "conscience," a feeling of responsibility for the effects of one's actions on others.[18]

The problem in applying this logic to corporate management, however, is that such "agreements to supply mutual benefits to others" are likely to be too amorphous to serve as a practicable guide to individual behavior in large public companies with diffuse stock ownership. If corporate factory workers are understandably unmoved by serving an anonymous group of "wealthy" shareholders, then who precisely are "the others" whose interests their morality is intended to serve? And what should employees do in those cases, noted earlier, where there appear to be (at least short-run) conflicts between the interests of the corporation and those of its

---

[17]See Nick Gilbert, "1–800–22ETHIC," *Financial World*, August 16, 1994, pp. 20–25.

[18]Kenneth Arrow, *Limits of Organization* (New York: W. W. Norton, 1974), pp. 26–27.

non-investor constituencies? After all, as we have seen earlier, the effective management of scarce resources often means saying no to the requests or desires of some employees, customers, and local communities. Moreover, the entire situation is complicated by the fact that the fundamental goal of the corporation—making money for its owners—is viewed as "immoral" or "unethical" by many advocates of corporate ethics.

Given this confusion about, and even conflict between, some professed ethical objectives and the goal of the corporation, we are skeptical about corporate attempts to instill conscience or a sense of guilt in their employees—that is, to alter employees' preferences. To the extent these corporate ethics programs are aimed at trying to change employees' preferences, they are likely to fail.

Consider the transfer-pricing problem faced by corporations with multiple divisions that buy and sell to one another. In Chapter 14 the firm value-maximizing solution to this problem was described as setting the transfer price to the buyer at the seller's opportunity cost of producing one more unit. But let's assume, as tends to be the case, that the selling or manufacturing division has better information about its costs than the purchasing division.

In such a situation, to the extent the manager's compensation is based on divisional profits, the selling division's manager has the incentive to set the transfer price substantially above opportunity cost. In such a case, the manufacturing division's pursuit of its own profits will come at the expense of total firm-wide profits (because the buying division will purchase less than the optimal number of units).

Now, if adoption of a code of ethics somehow succeeded in inducing divisional managers to reveal their information about costs, units within the firm would be transferred at opportunity cost, and firm profits would be increased. But as long as division managers are being *paid* based on the profits of their own divisions, they are unlikely to reveal their actual opportunity costs.

Most economists generally assume that individuals' preferences are given and for the most part difficult to alter. We thus believe that managers, instead of attempting to alter preferences, should redesign the firm's architecture to change their employees' incentives to take certain actions. For example, in the above case, top management should attempt to find a means of giving the divisional manager some stake in the profitability of the division to which he "sells" his product. A common, though only partly effective, solution to this problem is to give divisional managers stock options with payoffs tied to overall company value as well as bonuses for divisional performance.

Education

Even if corporate codes of ethics are unlikely to change preferences or eradicate self-interest, such codes can still play a potentially important role in modifying behavior. Up to this point, we have assumed that corporate managers and employees know what is the "right thing" to do to promote the interests of the organization. But it is unlikely that this assumption always holds. In many cases, managers' and employees' uncertainty about ethical standards—or how to live up to them in practice—may well be a greater corporate problem than their failure to work hard or to act in accordance with standards that are well established and clearly defined.

We earlier described the confusion about the corporate mission stemming from the aims and actions of the social responsibility movement. Another potential source of confusion resides in the variability of ethical standards. What may have been acceptable behavior ten or twenty years ago may not be so today. Social changes such as those brought about by movements as different as civil rights and women's rights, on the one hand, and corporate restructuring, on the other, have clearly altered conceptions of socially-accepted behavior. Moreover, the progressive globalization of corporations is increasingly forcing corporate employees to recognize and adapt to differences in national or regional cultural expectations.

Given this large and, in some ways, growing uncertainty about what constitutes ethical behavior in large organizations, corporate codes of ethics and training programs can play an important educational role by effectively communicating corporate expectations to employees and by demonstrating to them how certain kinds of behavior reduce the value of the firm. For example, misrepresentations of products and services to customers for short-term gain can be shown to reduce the value of the firm by hurting its reputation and thus lowering its brand-name capital. Moreover, in the process of globalizing and thus dealing with customers worldwide, companies may be forced to respond to the increasing cultural differences—or absence of shared expectations—among their managers and employees by providing more explicit communication of standards and expectations.

The Appearance of Impropriety at Citibank, Argentina

A newspaper article reported that H. Richard Handley, the president of Citibank Argentina, had sold portions of Citibank's Argentine assets to some of his friends at "what now look like bargain prices." Citicorp spokesmen dismissed that talk as "Monday morning quarterbacking," pointing out that, at the time of the first sales, there was an equal chance that the value of Argentine investments would rise or fall thereafter.

For our purposes, it is not important whether the terms of this particular set of transactions were appropriate or not; they may well have been deals that furthered important business interests of Citicorp in Argentina. What this case highlights, however, are the costs associated with the *potential* for self-dealing by corporate managers, and the importance of stating and enforcing policies for business dealings on less than an arms-length basis. The structure of this deal has forced Citibank to defend its actions to employees, investors, and regulators.

Suggested by *Miami Herald*, April 24, 1994.

Besides issuing a clear set of rules governing employee relations with consumers, corporations are also likely to benefit from communicating guidelines for dealings among managers and employees within the firm. For example, many companies develop their executives by rotating them through a series of jobs. The resulting management turnover can undermine the "implicit" agreements among managers and employees. The explicit, corporate-wide communication of expectations to employees can reduce uncertainty about the enforcement of informal agreements and thereby increase internal efficiency.

Virtually all professions such as doctors, lawyers, and accountants have professional ethics codes. Prospective candidates must pass entry exams that test their understanding of these codes. Most professional codes contain detailed descriptions of behaviors that reduce the value of the profession's services. For example, professional accountants are prohibited by their code of ethics from serving on the board of directors of their client firms. Such memberships reduce the appearance of independence of the auditor when rendering an opinion on the client's financial statements. If one accountant is caught not disclosing a known financial fraud, this reduces the value of other accountants' audit opinions. Thus, professions, like firms, have incentives to monitor their members for ethical breaches.

Corporate Culture

More generally, codes of conduct and training programs in ethics have the potential to contribute to the building and maintaining of a "value-based" corporate "culture." Like corporate ethics, *corporate culture* is an ill-defined term, but as discussed in Chapter 8 it generally encompasses things such as the ways work and authority are organized within a company as well as organizational features such as customs, taboos, company slogans, heroes, and social rituals. For example, slogans like that of Federal Express,' "When it absolutely positively has to be there overnight" help communicate the message that employees are expected to focus on meeting delivery schedules and that this focus will be recognized and rewarded by the organization. Singling out role models or heroes for special awards is another way of communicating the values of the company. Similarly, "social rituals" such as training sessions and company parties can help disseminate information by increasing interaction among workers and encouraging discussion of ethical standards. Indeed, the *process* by which a code of ethics is produced and the training programs through which these standards are communicated are potentially more important than the code itself in developing and maintaining the desired corporate culture.

Nevertheless, to create the "value-based" or "consumer-focused" organization that many companies seek to become, these less tangible aspects of corporate culture must be reinforced by more tangible actions. That is, the more formal corporate systems that partition decision rights and evaluate and reward performance, as well as sanctions for unethical behavior must all be internally consistent and designed to encourage firm value-increasing behavior.

Mechanisms for Encouraging Ethical Behavior

As stated earlier, ethical lapses are a manifestation of a conflict of interest, or agency problem, and, in most market exchanges, parties to the contracts have incentives to devise mechanisms to reduce agency costs, thereby raising the prices they receive for their products or services. For example, when taking their firms public for the first time, founders of companies typically continue to hold large portions of the stock and voluntarily impose restrictions on their own selling to help ensure that their interests are consistent with those of their IPO investors. Such arrangements effectively raise the price investors are willing to pay.

Likewise, external public auditors voluntarily prohibit themselves from owning stock in the companies they audit. By not owning any stock, auditors do not reap any gain by withholding unfavorable financial information. This increases their independence from their clients and increases the value and hence price of the audit.

As we also noted earlier, because reputational capital is an important determinant of future earnings, market forces provide incentives for firms and individuals to behave ethically. But the effectiveness of market forces in reducing conflicts of interest and enforcing contracts varies among different kinds of transactions. Among the most important characteristics of such transactions are the difficulty of ascertaining product quality prior to purchase and the likelihood that the transaction will be repeated.

Take the case of a buyer purchasing a product. For products whose quality can be determined at low cost prior to purchase, markets readily solve this problem. If buyers can cheaply monitor quality, they have strong incentives to do so. For example, a buyer negotiating a purchase of silver for Kodak can confidently and cheaply ascertain its quality by assay.

For some products such as the earlier house-painting example, quality is virtually impossible to determine prior to purchase. For example, the quality of an airplane ticket can be known only after the plane has landed, parked at the gate, and the passengers have retrieved their luggage. Although sellers have incentives to cheat on quality when quality is expensive to measure, rational sellers will provide products of lower than promised quality only if the expected gains exceed the expected costs.

Repeat Sales

One important constraint on such cheating is the potential for future sales.[19] Moreover, corporations with established market positions and substantial franchise values face higher costs of cheating and hence are less likely to cheat than start-up firms. The costs of cheating on quality are also higher if the information about such activities is more rapidly and widely distributed to potential future customers. For example, in markets like the diamond trade in New York, which is dominated by a close-knit community of Hasidic Jews, cheating on quality is extremely rare.

---

[19]L. G. Telser, "A Theory of Self-enforcing Agreements," *Journal of Business,* Vol. 53 (January 1980), pp. 27–44.

Adam Smith on Merchant Reputation

''Of all the nations in Europe, the Dutch, the most commercial, are the most faithful to their word. The English are more so than the Scotch, but much inferior to the Dutch, and in the remote parts of this country they [are] far less so than in the commercial parts of it. This is not at all to be imputed to national character, as some pretend; there is no natural reason why an Englishman or a Scotchman should not be as punctual in performing agreements as a Dutchman. It is far more reducible to self-interest, that general principle which regulates the actions of every man, and which leads men to act in a certain manner from view of advantage, and is as deeply implanted in an Englishman as a Dutchman. A dealer is afraid of losing his character, and is scrupulous in observing every engagement. When a person makes perhaps 20 contracts a day, he cannot gain so much by endeavoring to impose on his neighbors, as the very appearance of a cheat would make him lose. When people seldom deal with on another, we find that they are somewhat disposed to cheat, because they can gain more by a smart trick than they can lose by the injury which it does to the character.''

Adam Smith, *Lectures on Justice, Police, Revenue, and Arms,* Edwin Cannan, ed. (New York: Augustus M. Kelley, 1964). Suggested by Paul Milgrom and John Roberts, *Economics, Organizations & Management* (Englewood Cliffs, NJ: Prentice-Hall, 1992), p. 257.

Warranties

Seller-provided product warranties are another mechanism to reduce the likelihood of cheating. Seller warranties will be most prevalent when product failures result from factors that are under the firm's control (such as manufacturing tolerances). In this case, warranties directly impose the cost of failure on the parties who have the most input into their control. However when failures are due primarily to factors that are under the customers' control, the moral-hazard problem will be greater and warranties are less useful as a quality-assurance mechanism.

Third-Party Monitors

In some markets, specialized information services monitor the market, certify quality, and help to ensure contract performance. For example, *Consumer Reports* evaluates products from toasters to automobiles, the *Investment Dealer Digest* reports on activities of investment bankers, and A.M. Best Company rates insurance companies' financial conditions. These third-party information sources lower the costs for potential customers to determine quality and so increase the expected costs of cheating.

Signaling Quality by External Monitoring: Rice Aircraft

In 1991, Rice Aircraft Company became the first company in its industry to earn ISO 9002 accreditation, the highly regarded international standard for quality management. This was a significant, highly visible signal of change within the firm. For in August 1989, Bruce J. Rice, CEO of Rice Aircraft, had pled guilty to fraud and was sentenced to four years in prison. The Defense Department forbade its contractors to do business with the company for five years, and annual sales fell from $15 million to $5 million. At this point, Paula DeLong Rice, Rice's wife, took over and set out to save the company by visibly and radically transforming it. She implemented a total quality initiative and provided classes in statistical process control, time management, and communications for all the company's employees.

Ms. Rice's strategy appears to have been quite effective. Profit margins increased from 12 percent in 1992 to 27 percent in 1993 without benefit of price increases; order cycle time was reduced by 50 percent; and on-time deliveries increased 98 percent. Ms. Rice, moreover, is now in great demand as a speaker on managing for quality.

Suggested by Tarence Pare, "Rebuilding a Lost Reputation," *Fortune*, May 20, 1994, P. 176.

In credit markets, specialized credit-information services like Moody's and Dun and Bradstreet perform both a monitoring and an information dissemination function. The existence of such intermediaries provides an opportunity for the firm to guarantee quality. For this reason, corporate issuers pay Moody's to have their debt rated over the life of the bond issue. By issuing rated public debt, a firm lowers the cost to other potential corporate claimholders (including potential customers) of ascertaining the firm's financial condition.[20]

Capital Structure

Companies in financial distress are more likely to cheat on quality than financially healthy firms because repeat sales are less likely. Some firms can help "bond" product quality by adopting conservative financial policies. Since financial distress is more costly for firms that market products where quality is difficult to ascertain, such firms have incentives to adopt financing policies—including lower leverage, fewer leases, and more hedging—that lead to a lower probability of financial distress.

---

[20]L. Macdonald Wakeman, "The Real Function of Bond Rating Agencies," in *Issues in Corporate Finance* (New York: Stern Stewart Putnam & Macklis, Ltd., 1983), pp. 24–28.

Disclosure

The required level of disclosure in markets can also be important in determining quality. For example, a study of two wholesale used car markets with different levels of required disclosure found that prices in the market with more required disclosure are higher.[21] The ability to ''precommit'' to disclose information reduces the potential information disparity between buyer and seller and so reduces that discount buyers apply to their demand prices.

Organizational Architecture

Incentives to provide high-quality products vary across ownership structures. Take the case of franchise companies such as fast-food and lawn-care firms. Such companies typically franchise some units instead of owning all their stores in order to take advantage of the incentive benefits of decentralized ownership while retaining scale economies in advertising and brand-name promotion.

Outlets that have little repeat business create a special problem. The franchise owners of these stores have an incentive to cheat on quality because they can benefit from a steady stream of one-time sales while hurting the reputation of the entire organization. At these locations the central company is more likely to own the unit than to franchise it, in part because a salaried manager has less incentive to cheat on quality.[22]

Summary

Business ethics is the study of those behaviors that business people should or should not follow. This book is also about business behaviors, in particular, how firms are organized to motivate and control the behavior of self-interested workers to maximize firm value. The focus of this book has been primarily descriptive. Assuming people are motivated by self-interest, how are they expected to behave under alternative organizational architectures? Ethics is primarily normative—how should people behave. Managers often endorse the ethical philosophy espoused by Adam Smith. In Smith's view, through private ownership of property, self-interest, and competition, a society's resources are put to the best use and produce the highest quantity and quality of goods and services at the lowest prices (value maximization).

Value maximization requires that all costs and benefits be considered. If a particular business decision conflicts with a worker's or customer's own personal

---

[21]Helen Grieve, ''Quality Certification in a 'Lemons' Market: An Empirical Test of Certification in Wholesale Leased-Car Auctions,'' Working paper, University of Rochester, 1984.

[22]One study finds that franchise companies in lines of business with more repeat sales at individual units (e.g., lawn-care and beauty shops) are likely to franchise a higher percentage of total units than franchise lines with less repeat business (such as motels, car rental agencies, and restaurants). See James Brickley and Frederick Dark, ''The Choice of Organizational Form: The Case of Franchising,'' *Journal of Financial Economics* (1987).

belief, that person is worse off. If enough people are affected, costs are imposed on the firm through compensating wage differentials, higher turnover, and lost sales.

Moral philosophers and all religions have debated ethics since the beginning of man, and yet we still do not have a generally-accepted, universal code of ethics. Witness the current debates over abortion and birth control. There is considerable confusion about the meaning of "corporate ethics." It is highly unlikely that a universally-accepted code of business conduct will emerge. The corporate social responsibility movement has focused less on raising corporate ethical standards than on transferring shareholder wealth to other parties such as customers, employees, and local communities. While these corporate stakeholders are important, if the corporation is to survive, it must maximize its value to its owners—a goal which in turn promotes efficient use of scarce social resources.

Many of the issues raised in this chapter are recurring themes in the popular press and will continue to be so over your career as a manager. You may be called upon to resolve a sexual harassment case, an environmental issue, or a product quality recall. There is no doubt that at least once during your career you will be faced with a key decision that some will label a major ethical dilemma. This chapter seeks to demonstrate that the economic framework presented in the earlier chapters can provide guidance for understanding future issues involving ethics.

There are a number of important managerial implications raised by the discussion in this chapter:

• Behaviors that others classify as "unethical" impose real costs on the firm by lowering the firm's brand-name capital, especially when reported in the media. These costs from reduced reputation include lost sales or higher costs because parties outside the firms are less willing to contract with the firm. Many "ethical" problems are similar to agency problems discussed throughout the text, and much of the same apparatus used to analyze agency problems can be used to analyze ethical problems.

• "Ethics" has many different meanings ranging from making firms socially responsible (transferring wealth from the firm to other parties) to trying to make workers not self-interested. Another use of "ethics" means informing employees that certain behaviors impose large reputational costs on the firm, and hence the firm will impose sanctions on employees engaging in such actions.

• Mechanisms arise to constrain unethical behavior. Like agency costs, costs of unethical behavior create incentives to minimize these costs. Managers should understand these mechanisms to ascertain under what conditions ethical behavior is most likely. For example, extra care should be exerted when structuring deals with firms in financial distress.

• When "ethics" programs are evoked to get employees to work hard on the job instead of taking on-the-job leisure, these programs try to alter people's preferences. Senior managers concerned about the ethical conduct of their employees would do better to spend less time searching, like Diogenes, for "an honest man." They should instead pay more attention to the incentives created by its organizational architecture (that is, the three-legged stool). As discussed in Chapter 2, it is unlikely Sears would have faced the widely-reported consumer indignation and legal sanctions from unnecessary auto repairs had it anticipated the (quite predictable) effect of its compensation plan on its managers and its employees to overcharge customers. Incentives work. If the compensation plan pays employees for unethical behavior, then unethical behavior is exactly what the company will get.

The approach in this book is to redesign organizational architecture, not people's preferences. Managers must structure their subordinates' incentives to insure they do not reduce total firm value.

• Ethical guidelines can provide effective communication of behaviors that reduce firm value. Codes of conduct, rather than trying to change workers' preferences, can inform workers of firm-value-reducing actions that will not be tolerated and that can lead to sanctions imposed on the worker.

• Decisions that have major ethical dimensions almost invariably involve potential adverse publicity and a decline in the firm's brand-name capital. How the firm responds to the press affects how the public perceives the issue. In dealing with the media the following application of this book's framework is usually helpful:

News reporters are pursuing their own self interest, not yours. They are trying to maximize their value which usually means increasing their audience in order to sell more newspapers and TV and radio advertising. Reporters know more about their job than you do.

Having access to the media is valuable. Developing brand-name capital is very costly to do through advertising. Use your access to the media to present the firm's position in a credible, honest way. Lying or misrepresenting the facts to the media is likely to backfire because reporters have the incentive and skills to uncover these misrepresentations, again, because such discovered lies make juicy stories.

Index